AH

Presented To

Anthony AIKEN

For

'Highly Commended' Citation
Junior Verse-Speaking

Date: *30. 11. 91*

ARNOLD HOUSE SCHOOL

Detective Stories from The Strand

Detective Stories
from
The Strand

Selected and introduced by
Jack Adrian

Foreword by Julian Symons

Oxford   New York
OXFORD UNIVERSITY PRESS
1991

Oxford University Press, Walton Street, Oxford OX2 6DP

Oxford New York Toronto
Delhi Bombay Calcutta Madras Karachi
Petaling Jaya Singapore Hong Kong Tokyo
Nairobi Dar es Salaam Cape Town
Melbourne Auckland

and associated companies in
Berlin Ibadan

Oxford is a trade mark of Oxford University Press

British Library Cataloguing in Publication Data
Data available

Library of Congress Cataloging in Publication Data
Detective stories from the Strand / selected and introduced by Jack
Adrian; foreword by Julian Symons
p. cm.
Includes bibliographical references.
1. Detective and mystery stories, English. 2. English
fiction—20th century. I. Adrian, Jack. II. Strand magazine.
PR1309.D4D4 1991 823'.087208—dc20 91–21476 CIP
ISBN 0–19–212306–8

Typeset by Cambridge Composing (UK) Ltd
Printed in Great Britain by
Biddles Ltd, Guildford and King's Lynn

Dedicated to the Editors
of the
Strand Magazine

H. Greenhough Smith (1891–1930)
Reeves Shaw (1930–1941)
R. J. Minney (1941–1942)
Reginald Pound (1942–1946)
Macdonald Hastings (1946–1950)

Foreword

WHAT people remember about the *Strand Magazine* a hundred years after its birth, sometimes all they remember, is that in the seventh issue appeared the very first Sherlock Holmes story, 'A Scandal in Bohemia'. That was a marvellous coup for the publisher George Newnes, but the fame of Sherlock has tended to obscure the multiplicity of pleasures to be found in other *Strand* stories. Newnes, who said he knew what the average man wanted because he *was* the average man, called for exciting stories that would hold the reader's attention on the railway journey to and from the office. In its first twenty years the magazine was in particular demand on railway bookstalls.

When the car began to replace the railway train after the First World War the flavour of the stories in the magazine changed too, along with the settings. They became more sophisticated and more ingenious, although no less exciting, reflections of a period when as Auden wrote:

> We make ourselves cosy when the weather is wet
> With a shocker, a spaniel and a crystal set.

Jack Adrian's selection does not forget the railway journey. In Marguerite Steen's story a traveller mistakenly bound for dismal Coalford instead of Crewe finds himself in the company of an uncomfortable little man who insists on telling the story of an unsolved murder, and even leading him to the place where it happened. In 'The Inquest' by Loel Yeo (surely a pseudonym?) a chance meeting on the Stanton express with a man last seen two years earlier brings revelations about an inquest and its aftermath. More numerous, though, are stories set in the world of the shocker (or as it is called in one place, the 'seven and sixpenny thriller') and the crystal set, or at least the 'wireless', which in A. J. Alan's story the narrator helps his friend Henry to install.

The *Strand* successfully survived the First World War, but not the Second. Reading habits had changed, the audience had changed,

and although the magazine lingered on until 1950 the demand for
its particular kind of popular fiction had temporarily faded. But that
left Jack Adrian sixty years to choose from in making this selection,
and his dredging has brought up real treasure trove, forgotten or
almost unknown tales of remarkable ingenuity. The famous names
are here of course, often not represented by their best-known
stories, so that one reads them with a pleasant shock of surprise. I
thought I knew Aldous Huxley's work well, but hadn't encountered
'A Deal in Old Masters' before, nor did I know the Somerset
Maugham story. And it was particularly felicitous to put beside the
three Holmes stories Ronald Knox's brilliant pastiche. Writing bad
imitation Holmes is not difficult, and many of us have done it, but
'The Adventure of the First Class Carriage' (another railway story)
can almost stand beside the master.

But I come back to ingenuity, the quality possessed in full
measure by the best of the other stories. I should have thought I
could never be really gripped or baffled nowadays by one more
variation on the perfect crime or the unbreakable alibi, but the
stories by 'Seamark', Hylton Cleaver, and Richard Keverne prove
me wrong. They show that there is always another way of turning
an old trick, so that it comes up shining brightly. W. W. Jacobs and
Marguerite Steen produce very effective chillers, and Julian
Maclaren-Ross perhaps the only genuinely comic story here, one
marked by his characteristic easy skill in writing dialogue.

Finally, the collection offers a little puzzle of its own. There is
not a single story between 'Charles Augustus Milverton' (1904) and
'The Idol's Eye' (1919). Are we to believe that nothing in those
fifteen years made the grade, along with a similarly fallow period in
the last decade of the nineteenth century? Or has Mr Adrian a
second selection in mind? If it is half as good as this one, I hope so.

Julian Symons

Acknowledgements

I should like to express my gratitude to the staff of the Bodleian Library, Oxford—to the staff in the Old Library Reading Rooms, the Copying Department, and the Stack, and in particular R. J. Roberts, Deputy Librarian and Keeper of Printed Books—for all their varied and crucial assistance in the preparation of this volume. I should also like to acknowledge warmly the patience and persistence of my editor, Michael Cox (who sparked the whole thing off), as well as the very generous help given to me, at one time or another, by Bob Adey, the late Derek Adley, Bill Lofts, Tony Medawar, James Miller, Barry Pike, and Joke and the late Joe Whitt.

The full history of the *Strand* was vividly set down by Reginald Pound (the magazine's fourth editor) in *The Strand Magazine: 1891–1950* (1966), a fascinating slice of social and literary history. John Sutherland's *Companion to Victorian Fiction* (1988), too, has been of inestimable value as a source-book.

Contents

xii   *Contents*

Introduction

THE immediate, enormous, and for the time unparalleled success of the *Strand Magazine*—the lavishly illustrated monthly launched in 1891 and which ran for nearly sixty years—was due to a great extent to the abundant energy and shrewd promotional abilities of its founder and proprietor, George Newnes. Newnes was the very epitome, almost to the point of caricature, of the late nineteenth-century entrepreneur and man of action, who had a sudden idea, saw immense moral possibilities or financial benefits in it, and then pursued it relentlessly, even ruthlessly, until it was 'made flesh'. In the case of George Newnes this was true in a very real sense.

Ten years earlier, in the late summer of 1881, Newnes spotted in his evening paper a paragraph about a runaway train. There were no fatalities, though at the climax of their headlong journey the carriages smashed through buffers, then a brick wall, and into a printing shop, partially demolishing it. The story mentioned the remarkable escape of some children on the train who were shaken but otherwise unharmed, and was buried in a page of similarly brief news items. In his unpublished memoirs he recalled thinking, 'Why shouldn't there be a paper filled with tit-bits like that?'

At the time Newnes was in haberdashery, with no experience of printing or anything remotely connected with the publishing industry. He had no capital and could not get credit. Yet two days short of two months later—on 22 October 1881 (the news item he'd read had appeared in the Manchester *Evening News* for 24 August)—the first issue of *Tit-Bits from All the Most Interesting Books, Periodicals and Newspapers in the World* was published. In the end the problem of his lack of capital had proved easily surmountable: he had simply opened a vegetarian restaurant which, within a few weeks, he sold at the useful net profit of £400.

Tit-Bits was wildly successful. It was clearly what a vast public had been waiting for and was eager to read. Newnes filled it with all kinds of trivia—news items, sensational murders, strange coincidences, curious facts—a good deal of which (copyright law being virtually non-existent) he simply lifted, often unacknowledged, from other sources. It was a scissors-and-paste enterprise on the grand scale. If he did make any acknowledgement—for an interesting chapter from a travel book, perhaps, or a précis of conclusions from a volume of popular science—and the injured author demanded a fee, Newnes testily pointed out that he was giving the book free publicity and that as the extract would be seen by tens of thousands of readers, really the author ought to be paying him.

This cavalier treatment soon ceased when circulation, and thus profits out of which such payments could be made, took off in a spectacular fashion. Half-way through its first year, selling only in the Manchester area, *Tit-Bits* reached a figure of 40,000 copies a week, and one of the businessmen from whom Newnes had originally tried to beg a mere £500 for a half-share in the paper, prior to launch, now offered £16,000. Newnes refused. When, still before the end of its maiden year, the paper's circulation soared to over 100,000 an offer of £30,000 was made. Newnes refused that too. As he remarked to his brother-in-law, in mildly awe-struck tones, 'I believe I'm going to be rich.'

He was. His bright idea launched a publishing empire, soon enabled him to turn philanthropist, and was in the long run responsible for the baronetcy bestowed on him in less than two decades. It was also responsible for the *Strand*.

In 1884 Newnes removed himself and his burgeoning publishing business to rooms and an accommodation address in London, a year later setting up shop in Burleigh Street, just off the Strand. In that same year, 1885, he became MP for Newmarket on the Liberal ticket. He enjoyed the fame of being proprietor of the biggest-selling weekly paper in the land, indeed in publishing history—he even enjoyed the later success of younger entrepreneurs whom he had groomed and nurtured and who had struck out on their own. Alfred Harmsworth (later Lord Northcliffe, founder of the *Daily Mail*) was employed by Newnes for a time, left, and in 1888 launched *Answers to Correspondents*, quickly shortened to *Answers*, in direct competition to *Tit-Bits*; then *Harmsworth's Magazine*, later retitled the *London*, as a rival to the *Strand*. Arthur Pearson, another bright young journalist, strode out along much the same road, starting *Pearson's Weekly* in 1890 and *Pearson's Magazine* in 1896. It had been the same in the first few years after *Tit-Bits* itself was launched: a multitude of imitations, some quite shameless—*Sketchy Bits*, *Rarebits*, *Bits and Pieces*, *Quick Bits*. None of this worried Newnes, whose confidence in himself and his publications was boundless. Whatever was thrown together by others, as far as he was concerned his product was, quite simply, better. In any case, as he pointed out, 'The world is wide.'

Even so, although he was gratified by the popularity of *Tit-Bits*—which, alone, was soon giving him a personal income of £30,000 a year, net—the paper in no sense bestowed on him the *gravitas*, certainly as an MP, he now sought. He had long since thrust into the very deepest recesses of his mind the genuine horror he had experienced on discovering, in the early months of the paper, that his clever title had indecent connotations. A naïve man, it had never occurred to him that the reason some retailers were anxious to take the paper while others resolutely refused to have anything to do with it was because in certain quarters a 'tit-bit' was a dirty joke. By the time this had been explained to him it was far too late to alter the title, or do anything other than ignore the sniggers and hope for the best.

Happily, the jokes were soon forgotten as *Tit-Bits* rapidly became a household name. Even so the outstanding success of the paper brought only a measure of dignity: it was too popular, too (as it would be termed today) downmarket. The obvious answer was to move 'upmarket', but instead of aping the shilling 'literary' monthlies such as the *Cornhill*, *Temple Bar*, or *Belgravia*, full as these were of columns of dreary type and little else, the magazine would have to be quite different, if possible unique.

Opinion is divided as to who actually devised the *Strand Magazine*. Newnes' name was on the masthead and whenever an anniversary occurred (the hundredth issue, say, or the tenth year) Newnes himself invariably provided a signed—though by no means swaggering—editorial; it was surely he who wanted something with 'pictures on every page' in it (the columns of *Tit-Bits* were full of cartoons and sketches), and no one but the canny Newnes would have decided on a price of sixpence instead of the shilling at which all the stodgy monthlies were priced. Nevertheless, it is more than likely that the man who came up with the overall package—a budget of fiction, illustrated articles, popular politics ('From Behind the Speaker's Chair' ran for years), art features, and interviews with the great and the good—was the journalist (ex-*Temple Bar*) H. Green-hough Smith, who was initially awarded the post of 'literary editor' but whose steadying hand directed the entire enterprise.

From the outset the *Strand* gave Newnes the respectability he craved. No snob, he was yet attracted to the highborn, and was certainly in awe of the monarchy. One of the reasons for the magazine's eventual success was that it was seen to have received the royal imprimatur at an early stage. In one number it published an etching of Queen Victoria's first child, executed half a century before by Her Majesty herself, and now printed with her blessing. This was a distinct coup. Others followed. Not too long afterwards there appeared an extended article on Victoria's childhood dolls, the proofs of which she read and to which she appended notes. She also revised an article dealing with her studies in Hindustani and 'graciously accorded permission' to a Strand journalist to write a nineteen-page piece on Buckingham Palace, interiors and all.

Though the magazine's première number was dated January 1891, Newnes had it on sale well before Christmas 1890, advertising it energetically in *Tit-Bits* and the trade, and billboarding it all over the country, especially in mainline railway stations. Astonishingly—even allowing for the extensive promotion and the magazine's innovatory aspect and approach—it not only sold out but had to be reprinted three times. In all, nearly 300,000 copies of that first issue were moved.

Still, while 300,000 copies of a magazine's first number is a colossal figure, in periodical publishing it is axiomatic (then as now) that a triumphant launch is no indication of future success; indeed, however excellent the product, however muscular the promotion, sales will inevitably fall off after 'the shock of the new' has been absorbed, more often than not after the first half-dozen issues. With the *Strand* the reverse was the case. Sales actually rose after the first half-dozen issues, and kept on rising, finally reaching a quite extraordinary peak of nearly half a million copies a month, a figure which held well into the 1930s (with a probable readership of between two and three million).

All this was due to a remarkable stroke of good fortune which neither Newnes nor Smith could have foreseen, and which had nothing to do with the look of the magazine, its revolutionary nature, or even its price. In the late spring of 1891 Smith received two short stories from a contributor who had already appeared once in the magazine with a neat and ingenious twist-ending tale. The contributor was a Dr A. C. Doyle; the two stories, which featured a detective called Sherlock Holmes, were entitled 'A Scandal in Bohemia' and 'The Red-Headed League'. When Doyle, now Sir Arthur Conan Doyle, died in 1930 Smith wrote in a tribute: 'I at once realized that here was the greatest short story writer since Edgar Allan Poe. I remember rushing into Mr Newnes's office and thrusting the stories before his eyes.'

This sounds like hyperbole, if not being wise after the event. Yet whatever Smith's real reactions on that spring day in 1891 they were surely something akin to those he recalled to mind, for the two stories were quite different from anything that had been published in the *Strand* thus far; indeed, quite different from any story published in any of the monthly magazines of the day.

The good fortune was that Doyle sent them to Smith in the first place, since at that time he could easily have tried them out on any one of half a dozen, perhaps more, periodicals to which he had successfully sold stories over the past two or three years—such as *London Society*, *Belgravia*, the *Cornhill*, or *Cassell's Saturday Journal*. He could have sent them to Tillotson's Fiction Bureau, which specialized in buying material from not quite front-line authors and syndicating it in provincial newspapers across the north of England. Fees were by no means regal (Doyle had sold a story to the chain in 1889, receiving four guineas for two placings in that year), but Tillotson was hungry for copy: he had a giant maw to feed and the more an author produced the more he was paid. He could certainly have offered them to *Lippincott's Magazine*, the prestigious American monthly whose editor had already commissioned *The Sign of Four* from him, had wined and dined him at the Langham Hotel (with Oscar Wilde as table-mate), and paid him the not inconsiderable sum of £100 for the rights to the 45,000-word novella.

That Doyle did none of these things, sending the two detective stories instead straight to the *Strand*, is almost certainly due to the enthusiastic reception Smith had given to the first (non-Holmes) story he had tried out on this new magazine, 'The Voice of Science', which had appeared anonymously in the *Strand*'s third issue (although Doyle was credited on the contents page). About that earlier story Smith was to write much later: 'Here, to an editor jaded with wading through reams of impossible stuff, [came] . . . a godsend in the shape of a story that brought a gleam of happiness into the despairing life of this weary editor—there was no mistaking the ingenuity of the plot, the limpid clearness of the style, the perfect art of telling a story.'

This is a penetrating judgement. Doyle is indeed an outstanding story-teller who effortlessly engages the reader's attention. His style is simple and straightforward, with none of the late-Victorian fustian to be found in the work of so many of his peers, indeed so many of his own followers; and even when he is mildly pedantic—'I find it recorded in my notebook that it was a bleak and windy day . . .'; 'In glancing over the somewhat incoherent series of memoirs . . .'—he charms. In any case, he was also capable of writing a sentence such as 'I clapped a pistol to his head', and could handle action sequences with rare mastery.

Doyle admired the *romans-policiers* of the French writer Gaboriau ('[he] had rather attracted me by the neat dove-tailing of his plots') and the ingenuity displayed by Poe in his Chevalier Dupin tales. Combining the sensational with the clever, the exciting with the cerebral, and serving it up in short-story form with a continuing character, he had struck a new and rich vein that was to revolution-ize popular fiction.

Ironically, he cared little for Holmes, tiring of him even while writing the first half-dozen stories. Indeed six, at £30 a time, were all he ever intended to write, and once he had finished them he refused to write more. This would have been perfectly acceptable to Greenhough Smith were it not for the undeniable fact that with the publication of the first three stories his readers had gone, so it seemed, Sherlock Holmes mad. Letters praising the series in intemperate terms were arriving by every post; retailers were reporting unprecedented enthusiasm and were re-ordering copies in massive quantities. He urged Doyle to reconsider his decision. Doyle thought he might, for another £20 a story, certain that George Newnes would never sanction such a high-handed demand. Smith wrote back by return of post, agreeing and urging him to send copy in as soon as possible (Doyle could have had no idea then that the final Holmes story—'Shoscombe Old Place', to be written thirty-six years in the future—would bring him, from both US and UK first sales, a sum approaching £2,400).

Doyle had created what every popular fiction writer dreams of creating and so seldom does: a cult hero. When, in the December 1893 issue of the *Strand*, he finally rid himself of the succubus that was draining (so he thought) his talent away from the great historical dramas he wanted to write, there were any number of his fellow-authors, both male and female, who were eager to fill the yawning breach left by Holmes' 'death'. In fact no one came anywhere near to emulating Doyle's immense popularity or success.

Arthur Morrison, who had previously been penning larky articles on zoos for the *Strand*, created Martin Hewitt, plump and genial where Holmes had been lean and hungry. The stories were attractive, but no more than that. After a single series Morrison took his hero off to the *Windsor Magazine*, one of Newnes' newer rivals. Of rather more interest were the various series by Mrs L. T. Meade (usually in tandem with a collaborator who supplied the technical detail), whose stories were an engaging blend of late-Victorian sensationalism and strange science, often with more than a hint of the weird. Something of a Stakhanovite (her canon ran to upwards of 250 books written over a forty-year period), Mrs Meade was responsible for two series of 'Stories from the Diary of a Doctor' as well as 'The Sorceress of the Strand', 'Stories from the Sanctuary Club', and 'The Brotherhood of the Seven Kings', amongst others. Grant Allen, the 'new woman' novelist and science popularizer, tried the oblique approach by writing a series around a confidence trickster, 'An African Millionaire', then (a feminist by inclination) the splendid 'Miss Cayley's Adventures' about a spirited bluestocking who turns sleuth; his final series, 'Hilda Wade', was completed after his death by Conan Doyle himself.

It has to be said that in many ways Doyle's success had a deleterious effect on the genre, his influence lying like a dead hand over the efforts of his fellow-authors, far too many of whom tried far too hard to write precisely in his style, and always failing (not a few—Sapper, for instance—simply plagiarized his plots). Despite those who complained that after Holmes returned from the dead in 1903 he was never quite the same, Doyle's Holmesian appearances—spasmodic after 1905—are distinctly refreshing when compared to those of the detectives of most of his rivals in the *Strand*.

The truth is, Doyle's real rivals—those who were indebted to Doyle's original breakthrough but whose approach to the genre now deviated from source—were not writing for the *Strand* at all. R. Austin Freeman, whose Dr Thorndyke was undeniably Holmes-inspired (even down to his faithful but slightly obtuse henchman/chronicler), was inventing an entirely fresh sub genre: the 'inverted' crime story, in which the reader is told who commits the crime and how it is done, and then follows Thorndyke on the criminal's trial. Thorndyke's exploits appeared mainly in *Pearson's Magazine*. Baroness Orczy's unusual 'Old Man in the Corner', the first 'armchair' detective who solves all his criminous problems in a Lyon's corner-shop, appeared in the *Royal Magazine*, whilst G. K. Chesterton's Father Brown stories were mostly published in *Cassell's Magazine* and *The Storyteller*. The inevitable conclusion is that while Conan Doyle was still alive there was simply no room in the *Strand* for experimentation.

During the 1920s, though pure detective fiction still surfaces, the mystery genre that featured most prominently in the *Strand* was the thriller, its principal exponent being Edgar Wallace, who, in 1921, contributed a profoundly influential series of murder stories set around his characters the Four Just Men. Wallace's work was clever and always absorbing but was not lit by any brilliant deductive shafts; his restless temperament was ill suited to the painstaking planting of clues within the body of a story. E. Phillips Oppenheim, who had cornered the market in Riviera make-believe and, like Wallace, was disinclined to grapple with the puzzle story, was the author who appeared most often on the *Strand*'s contents pages from 1920 to 1930. A hugely successful writer, whose thrillers sold in their hundreds of thousands, his stories have a surface glamour only; too much Oppenheim palls.

Conan Doyle died in 1930; Greenhough Smith, his most loyal champion (save in the matter of Spiritualism and fairy photographs), retired from active duties in the same year. Almost at once the Bright Young Hopes began crowding in. The 1930s, under the *Strand*'s second editor Reeves Shaw (erstwhile editor of *The Humorist*, who welcomed writers with the lighter touch), is the decade of Agatha Christie, Margery Allingham, Dorothy Sayers, E. C. Bentley (hardly young, to be sure, but suddenly reinvigorated after an absence from detective fiction of over twenty years), Richard Keverne, Frank King, and John Dickson Carr (who wrote under his own name and 'Carter Dickson' and whose speciality was that most appealing of sub-genres, the 'impossible' crime). This final decade before the Second World War, far more than the 1920s, may be considered a genuine 'Golden Age', rich in ingenious nuggets, psychological twists, fast cars, literary allusions, brain-wracking complexities, corpses in conservatories.

The 1940s, a starker decade altogether—the *Strand* was dying slowly, its half a million circulation now shrivelled to 95,000—is notable for the virtual absence of detective stories in the classic, or indeed any, tradition. Those that do appear gleam like beacons. Nicholas Blake's 'The Snow Line' is a puzzle story in which the reader is asked to join the investigation, spot the clues, name the guilty party—solution at the end of the issue. It is cleverly and entertainingly done. But perhaps the most striking story of all (in a way the most melancholy) is one that takes the reader back over half a century to a different world, another time, and the fountainhead and inspiration himself, Sherlock Holmes, in a dazzling pastiche by Mgr. Ronald Knox of which, surely, Arthur Conan Doyle himself would have approved.

In a sense, the *Strand Magazine* created the detective story, one of two distinct genres at which it excelled. The other, the weird tale, may be experienced in this anthology's companion volume, *Strange Tales from* The Strand. Here, however, are collected all manner of mysteries, devised by some of the best and most cunning writers of the past hundred years. Some are known; some, today, wholly unknown. All knew how to entertain.

Jack Adrian
April 1991

I

THE GREAT DETECTIVES

One of the most industrious journalists and magazine writers of his day (perhaps only Edgar Wallace was more prolific), *G. K. Chesterton* (1874–1936) wrote only one story and one article for the *Strand* (though he appeared briefly in a handful of its famous symposia). As he was such a towering figure, literally as well as metaphorically, in the literary world of the time, it seems possible his non-appearance was due to a dislike by Greenhough Smith, the *Strand*'s editor from 1891 to 1930, of his work. If this is the case it was one of Smith's more singular prejudices, for he delighted in detective fiction and Chesterton's own contribution to the roster of Great Detectives, the apologetic little priest with the 'harmless, human name of Brown', is a magnificent and enduring creation. Like Conan Doyle, however, Chesterton could cast a jaundiced eye over his character, in later life treating him as a milch-cow when funds were running low. Even so he rarely failed to produce an ingenious twist to his plots, in the matter of 'whodunit' and 'howdunit' again and again pulling the wool over his readers' eyes until the final revelation. Adept at the 'miracle problem', or 'impossible crime', he wrote stories—such as 'The Miracle of Moon Crescent', 'The Dagger With Wings', and 'The Invisible Man'—that are classics of the genre. There were five series of Father Brown tales collected in Chesterton's lifetime. 'The Vampire of the Village' was the penultimate Father Brown story, published posthumously (the manuscript of the last—actually the second in what was surely to be a sixth series—was only recently discovered and published).

Agatha Christie (1890–1976) was one of the most consistently dazzling detective fiction plotters of this century. In other respects—characterization, dialogue, scene-setting, atmosphere—she was neither as good as some, nor as bad as others; but her writing had vitality and high good humour and this served to conceal her defects. In the matter of plotting, however, she was peerless, time after time triumphantly originating a new and wickedly ingenious twist to an old convention. She was a devious puppeteer, the mistress of misdirection, effortlessly forcing not only her characters but the readers themselves to dance to her manipulations. She was particularly adept at slipping into a scene or a conversation information, innocuous enough in itself and thus ignored by the reader, crucial to the solution of the problem (in *The Murder of Roger Ackroyd* [1926] just three sentences, carefully ambiguous, hold the key to the mystery). 'The Dream' is a Poirot story which has, as an extra ingredient, that touch of the macabre Christie could deploy so well.

A. E. W. Mason (1865–1948) was a man of action as well as ideas. At one time or another he was an enthusiastic yachtsman, an actor (appearing in the 1894 première of Shaw's *Arms and the Man*), a devout cricketer, an MP (whose experiences in Parliament were put to good use in his excellent novel *The Turnstile* [1912]), and a spy who, unlike Somerset Maugham, on occasion steered dangerously close to the wind. A skilled and robust story-teller, he wrote nearly thirty novels in a variety of genres—adventure, romance, historical, crime—and was successful in all. *The Four Feathers* (1902) is the superb story of a coward's redemption and was a bestseller throughout his career; his handling of the difficult metempsychosis theme in *The Three Gentlemen* (1932) is masterly; his use of period detail—in novels such as *Musk And Amber* (1942, *castrati* in eighteenth-century Venice), *Fire Over England* (1936, the Armada), and *Königsmark* (1938, the story of the lover of the wife of George I)—is always lavish yet unforced. In the field of crime and detective fiction his reputation rests on *No Other Tiger* (1927), a riveting thriller with skilfully dabbed-in touches of the bizarre and a horrifying denouement, and his stories of Inspector Hanaud of the Sûreté. Hanaud, stout and comfortable with a dry wit, appeared in five books, including *At the Villa Rose* (1910)—only the second novel not by Conan Doyle to be serialized in the *Strand* (the first was Wells' *The First Men in the Moon*)—the flawlessly constructed *The House of the Arrow* (1924), and *The Prisoner in the Opal* (1928), in which Mason's fascination with the weird is well to the fore. Hanaud also appeared in the novella 'The Affair at the Semiramis Hotel'. 'The Ginger King' is the only Hanaud short story, its eponymous 'hero' Mason's real-life, and slightly deranged, companion in old age.

There is a satisfying irony in the fact that although *E. C. Bentley* (1875–1956) wrote his novel *Trent's Last Case* (1913) as a satire on detective fiction, it has come to be accepted as a classic of the genre (the critic Charles Shibuk is not alone in his judgement that it is 'one of the ten best mystery novels of all time'). Though called to the Bar in 1902, Bentley never practised but joined the *Daily News* as a reporter, transferring to the *Daily Telegraph* in 1912, on which paper he spent the rest of his working life, as a foreign leader-writer, retiring in 1934 then, on the departure of Harold Nicolson to the War Office, returning as chief literary critic from 1940 to 1947. In his early days he wrote political columns for the weeklies, reviews and light verse for *Punch*, often utilizing the 'clerihew' (his middle name), a formless quatrain which, with his friend G. K. Chesterton, he had invented in 1893 while at St Paul's School. Bentley was by no means prolific in his chosen genre, writing only a dozen or so short stories, a further Trent novel with H. Warner Allen, and a later thriller, *Elephant's Work* (1950). He edited a number of anthologies by Damon Runyon (of whom he was inordinately fond) for the British market as well as a collection of 'best' detective fiction, *The Second Century of Detective Stories* (1938), to which he contributed a short but perceptive Introduction. Though written in 1938, 'The Ministering Angel' appeared too late to be included in Bentley's only, but outstanding, short-story collection, *Trent Intervenes* (1938).

H. Warner Allen (*fl.* 1925–37) wrote less than a handful of crime novels, of which *The Uncounted Hour* (1936, featuring a triple murderer) is the best known. Allen was a close friend of E. C. Bentley, with whom he collaborated on *Trent's Own Case* (1938), in which Bentley's celebrated detective Philip Trent is himself the murder suspect. Allen wrote infrequently for the monthlies, a few of his short stories appearing in the *Strand*; only 'Tokay of the Comet Year', however, starred his wine-connoisseur detective (later to appear in a full-length novel) with the oddly familiar name.

The Vampire of the Village

G. K. Chesterton

AT the twist of a path in the hills, where two poplars stood up like pyramids dwarfing the tiny village of Potter's Pond, a mere huddle of houses, there once walked a man in a costume of a very conspicuous cut and colour, wearing a vivid magenta coat and a white hat tilted upon black ambrosial curls, which ended with a sort of Byronic flourish of whisker.

The riddle of why he was wearing clothes of such fantastic antiquity, yet wearing them with an air of fashion and even swagger, was but one of the many riddles that were eventually solved in solving the mystery of his fate. The point here is that when he had passed the poplars he seemed to have vanished; as if he had faded into the wan and widening dawn or been blown away upon the wind of morning.

It was only about a week afterwards that his body was found a quarter of a mile away, broken upon the steep rockeries of a terraced garden leading up to a gaunt and shuttered house called The Grange. Just before he had vanished, he had been accidentally overheard apparently quarrelling with some bystanders, and especially abusing their village as 'a wretched little hamlet'; and it was supposed that he had aroused some extreme passions of local patriotism and eventually been their victim. At least the local doctor testified that the skull had suffered a crushing blow that might have caused death, though probably only inflicted with some sort of club or cudgel. This fitted in well enough with the notion of an attack by rather savage yokels. But nobody ever found any means of tracing any particular yokel; and the inquest returned a verdict of murder by some persons unknown.

A year or two afterwards the question was reopened in a curious way; a series of events which led a certain Dr Mulborough, called by his intimates Mulberry in apt allusion to something rich and fruity about his dark rotundity and rather empurpled visage, travelling by train down to Potter's Pond, with a friend whom he had often consulted upon problems of the kind. In spite of the somewhat port-winy and ponderous exterior of the doctor, he had a shrewd eye and was really a man of very remarkable sense; which he considered that he showed in consulting a little priest named Brown, whose acquaintance he had made over a poisoning case long ago. The little priest was sitting opposite to him, with the air of a patient baby absorbing instruction; and the doctor was explaining at length the real reasons for the journey.

'I cannot agree with the gentleman in the magenta coat that Potter's Pond is only a wretched little hamlet. But it is certainly a very remote and secluded village; so that it seems quite outlandish, like a village of a hundred years ago. The spinsters are really spinsters—damn it, you could almost imagine you saw them spin. The ladies are not just ladies. They are gentlewomen; and their chemist is not a chemist, but an apothecary; pronounced potecary. They do just admit the existence of an ordinary doctor like myself to assist the apothecary. But I am considered rather a juvenile innovation, because I am only fifty-seven years old and have only been in the county for twenty-eight years. The solicitor looks as if he had known it for twenty-eight thousand years. Then there is the old Admiral, who is just like a Dickens illustration; with a house full of cutlasses and cuttle-fish and equipped with a telescope.'

'I suppose,' said Father Brown, 'there are always a certain number of Admirals washed up on the shore. But I never understood why they get stranded so far inland.'

'Certainly no dead-alive place in the depths of the country is complete without one of these little creatures,' said the doctor. 'And then, of course, there is the proper sort of clergyman; Tory and High Church in a dusty fashion dating from Archbishop Laud; more of an old woman than any of the old women. He's a white-haired studious old bird, more easily shocked than the spinsters. Indeed, the gentlewomen, though Puritan in their principles, are sometimes pretty plain in their speech; as the real Puritans were. Once or twice I have known old Miss Carstairs-Carew use expressions as lively as anything in the Bible. The dear old clergyman is assiduous in reading the Bible; but I almost fancy he shuts his eyes when he comes to those words. Well, you know I'm not particularly modern. I don't enjoy this jazzing and joy-riding of the Bright Young Things——'

'The Bright Young Things don't enjoy it,' said Father Brown. 'That is the real tragedy.'

'But I am naturally rather more in touch with the world than the people in this prehistoric village,' pursued the doctor. 'And I had reached a point when I almost welcomed the Great Scandal.'

'Don't say the Bright Young Things have found Potter's Pond after all,' observed the priest, smiling.

'Oh, even our scandal is on old-established melodramatic lines. Need I say that the clergyman's son promises to be our problem? It would be almost irregular, if the clergyman's son were quite regular. So far as I can see, he is very mildly and almost feebly irregular. He was first seen drinking ale outside the Blue Lion. Only it seems he is a poet, which in those parts is next door to being a poacher.'

'Surely,' said Father Brown, 'even in Potter's Pond that cannot be the Great Scandal.'

'No,' replied the doctor gravely. 'The Great Scandal began thus. In the house called The Grange, situated at the extreme end of The Grove, there lives a Lady. A Lonely Lady. She calls herself Mrs Maltravers (that is how we put it); but she only came a year or two ago and nobody knows anything about her. "I can't think why she wants to live here," said Miss Carstairs-Carew. "We do not visit her."'

'Perhaps that's why she wants to live there,' said Father Brown.

'Well, her seclusion is considered suspicious. She annoys them by being good-looking and even what is called good style. And all the young men are warned against her as a vamp.'

'People who lose all their charity generally lose all their logic,' remarked Father Brown. 'It's rather ridiculous to complain that she keeps herself to herself; and then accuse her of vamping the whole male population.'

'That is true,' said the doctor. 'And yet she is really rather a puzzling person. I saw her and found her intriguing; one of those brown women, long and elegant and beautifully ugly, if you know what I mean. She is rather witty, and though young enough certainly gives me an impression of what they call—well, experience. What the old ladies call a Past.'

'All the old ladies having been born this very minute,' observed Father Brown. 'I think I can assume she is supposed to have vamped the parson's son.'

'Yes, and it seems to be a very awful problem to the poor old parson. She is supposed to be a widow.'

Father Brown's face had a flash and spasm of his rare irritation. 'She is supposed to be a widow as the parson's son is supposed to be the parson's son, and the solicitor is supposed to be a solicitor and you are supposed to be a doctor. Why in thunder shouldn't she be a widow? Have they one speck of prima facie evidence for doubting that she is what she says she is?'

Dr Mulborough abruptly squared his broad shoulders and sat up. 'Of course you're right again,' he said. 'But we haven't come to the Scandal yet. . . . Well, the Scandal is that she is a widow.'

'Oh,' said Father Brown; and his face altered and he said something soft and faint, that might almost have been, 'My God!'

'First of all,' said the doctor, 'they have made one discovery about Mrs Maltravers. She is an actress.'

'I fancied so,' said Father Brown. 'Never mind why. I had another fancy about her, that would seem even more irrelevant.'

'Well, at that instant it was scandal enough that she was an actress. The dear old clergyman of course is heartbroken, to think that his white hairs should be brought in sorrow to the grave by an actress and adventuress. The spinsters shriek in chorus. The Admiral admits he has sometimes been to a theatre in town; but objects to such things in what he calls "our midst". Well, of course I've no particular objection of that kind. This actress is certainly a lady, if a bit of a Dark Lady, in the manner of the Sonnets; the young man is very much in love with her; and I am no doubt a sentimental old fool in having a sneaking sympathy with the misguided youth who is sneaking round the Moated Grange; and I was getting into quite a pastoral frame of mind about this idyll, when suddenly the thunderbolt fell. And I, who am the only person who ever had any sympathy with these people, am sent down to be the messenger of doom.'

'Yes,' said Father Brown, 'and why *were* you sent down?'

The doctor answered with a sort of groan:

'Mrs Maltravers is not only a widow, but she is the widow of Mr Maltravers.'

'It sounds a shocking revelation, as you state it,' acknowledged the priest seriously.

'And, Mr Maltravers,' continued his medical friend, 'was the man who was apparently murdered in this very village a year or two ago; supposed to have been bashed on the head by one of the simple villagers.'

'I remember you told me,' said Father Brown. 'The doctor, or some doctor, said he had probably died of being clubbed on the head with a cudgel.'

Dr Mulborough was silent for a moment in frowning embarrassment, and then said curtly, 'Dog doesn't eat dog, and doctors don't bite doctors, not even when they are mad doctors. I shouldn't care to cast any reflection on my eminent predecessor in Potter's Pond, if I could avoid it; but I know you are really safe for secrets. And, speaking in confidence, my eminent predecessor at Potter's Pond was a blasted fool; a drunken old humbug and absolutely incompetent. I was asked, originally by the Chief Constable of the County (for I've lived a long time in the County, though only recently in the village) to look into the whole business; the depositions and reports of the inquest and so on. And there simply isn't any question of it. Maltravers may have been hit on the head; he was a strolling actor passing through the place; and Potter's Pond probably thinks it is all in the natural order that such people should be hit on the head. But whoever hit him on the head did not kill him; it is simply impossible for the injury, as described, to do more than knock him out for a few hours. But just lately I have managed to turn up some other facts bearing on the matter; and the result of it is pretty grim.'

He sat louring at the landscape as it slid past the window, and then said more curtly:

'I am coming down here, and asking your help, because there's going to be an exhumation. There is very strong suspicion of poison.'

'And here we are at the station,' said Father Brown, cheerfully. 'I suppose your idea is that poisoning the poor man would naturally fall among the household duties of his wife.'

'Well, there never seems to have been anyone else here who had any particular connection with him,' replied Mulborough, as they alighted from the train. 'At least there is one queer old crony of his, a broken-down actor, hanging round; but the police and the local solicitor seem convinced he is an unbalanced busybody; with some *idée fixe* about a quarrel with an actor who was his enemy; but who certainly wasn't Maltravers. A wandering accident, I should say, and certainly nothing to do with the problem of the poison.'

Father Brown had heard the story. But he knew that he never knew a story until he knew the characters in the story. He spent the next two or three days in going the rounds, on one polite excuse or another, to visit the chief actors of the drama. His first interview with the mysterious widow was brief but bright. He brought away from it at least two facts; one that Mrs Maltravers sometimes talked in a way which that Victorian village would call cynical; and, second, that like not a few actresses, she happened to belong to his own religious communion.

He was not so illogical (nor so unorthodox) as to infer from this alone that she was innocent of the alleged crime. He was well aware that his old religious communion could boast of several distinguished poisoners. But he had no difficulty in understanding its connection, in this sort of case, with a certain intellectual liberty which these Puritans would call laxity; and which would certainly seem to this parochial patch of an older England to be almost cosmopolitan. Anyhow, he was sure she could count for a great deal, whether for good or evil. Her brown eyes were brave to the point of battle, and her enigmatic mouth, humorous and rather large, suggested that her purposes touching the parson's poetical son, whatever they might be, were planted pretty deep.

The parson's poetical son himself, interviewed amid vast village scandal on a bench outside the Blue Lion, gave an impression of pure sulks. Hurrel Horner, son of the Revd Samuel Horner, was a square-built young man in a pale grey suit with a touch of something arty in a pale green tie, otherwise mainly notable for a mane of auburn hair and a permanent scowl. But Father Brown had a way with him in getting people to explain at considerable length why they refused to say a single word. About the general scandalmongering in the village, the young man began to curse freely. He even added a little scandalmongering of his own. He referred bitterly to alleged past flirtations between the Puritan Miss Carstairs-Carew and Mr Carver the solicitor. He even accused that legal character of having attempted to force himself upon the acquaintance of Mrs Maltravers. But when he came to speak of his own father, whether out of an acid decency or piety, or because his anger was too deep for speech, he snapped out only a few words.

'Well, there it is. He denounces her day and night as a painted adventuress; sort of barmaid with gilt hair. I tell him she's not; you've met her yourself, and you know she's not. But he won't even meet her. He won't even see her in the street or look at her out of a window. An actress would pollute his house and even his holy presence. If he is called a Puritan he says he's proud to be a Puritan.'

'Your father,' said Father Brown, 'is entitled to have his views respected, whatever they are; they are not views I understand very well myself. But I agree he is not entitled to lay down the law about a lady he has never seen and then refuse even to look at her, to see if he is right. That is illogical.'

'That's his very stiffest point,' replied the youth. 'Not even one momentary meeting. Of course, he thunders against my other theatrical tastes as well.'

Father Brown swiftly followed up the new opening, and learnt much that he wanted to know. The alleged poetry, which was such a blot on the young man's character, was almost entirely dramatic poetry. He had written tragedies in verse which had been admired by good judges. He was no mere stage-struck fool; indeed he was no fool of any kind. He had some really original ideas about acting Shakespeare; it was easy to understand his having been dazzled and delighted by finding the brilliant lady at the Grange. And even the priest's intellectual sympathy so far mellowed the rebel of Potter's Pond that at their parting he actually smiled.

It was that smile which suddenly revealed to Father Brown that the young man was really miserable. So long as he frowned, it might well have been only sulks; but when he smiled it was somehow a more real revelation of sorrow.

Something continued to haunt the priest about that interview with the poet. An inner instinct certified that the sturdy young man was eaten from within, by some grief greater even than the conventional story of conventional parents being obstacles to the course of true love. It was all the more so, because there were not any obvious alternative causes. The boy was already rather a literary and dramatic success; his books might be said to be booming. Nor did he drink or dissipate his well-earned wealth. His notorious revels at the Blue Lion reduced themselves to one glass of light ale; and he seemed to be rather careful with his money. Father Brown thought of another possible complication in connection with Hurrel's large resources and small expenditure; and his brow darkened.

The conversation of Miss Carstairs-Carew, on whom he called next, was certainly calculated to paint the parson's son in the darkest colours. But as it was devoted to blasting him with all the special vices which Father Brown was quite certain the young man did not exhibit, he put it down to a common combination of Puritanism and gossip. The lady, though lofty, was quite gracious, however, and offered the visitor a small glass of port-wine and a slice of seed-cake, in the manner of everybody's most ancient great-aunts, before he managed to escape from a sermon on the general decay of morals and manners.

His next port of call was very much of a contrast; for he disappeared down a dark and dirty alley, where Miss Carstairs-Carew would have refused to follow him even in thought; and then into a narrow tenement made noisier by a high and declamatory voice in an attic. . . . From this he re-emerged, with a rather dazed expression, pursued on to the pavement by a very excited man with a blue chin and a black frock-coat faded to bottle-green, who was shouting argumentatively:

'He did not disappear! Maltravers never disappeared! He appeared; he appeared dead and I've appeared alive. But where's all the rest of the company? Where's that man, that monster, who deliberately stole my lines, crabbed my best scenes and ruined my career? I was the finest Tubal that ever trod the boards. He acted Shylock—he didn't need to act much for that! And so with the greatest opportunity of my whole career. I could show you press-cuttings on my rendering of Fortinbras——'

'I'm quite sure they were splendid and very well-deserved,' gasped the little priest. 'I understood the company had left the village before Maltravers died. But it's all right. It's quite all right.' And he began to hurry down the street again.

'He was to act Polonius,' continued the unquenchable orator behind him. Father Brown suddenly stopped dead.

'Oh,' he said very slowly, 'he was to act Polonius.'

'That villain Hankin!' shrieked the actor. 'Follow his trail. Follow him to the ends of the earth! Of course he'd left the village; trust him for that. Follow him—find him; and may the curses——' But the priest was again hurrying away down the street.

Two much more prosaic and perhaps more practical interviews followed this melodramatic scene. First the priest went into the bank, where he was closeted for ten minutes with the manager; and then paid a very proper call on the aged and amiable clergyman. Here again all seemed very much as described, unaltered and seemingly unalterable; a touch or two of devotion from more austere traditions, in the narrow crucifix on the wall, the big Bible on the bookstand and the old gentleman's opening lament over the increasing disregard of Sunday; but all with a flavour of gentility that was not without its little refinements and faded luxuries.

The clergyman also gave his guest a glass of port; but accompanied by an ancient British biscuit instead of seed-cake. The priest had again the weird feeling that everything was almost too perfect, and that he was living a century before his time. Only on one point the amiable old parson refused to melt into any further amiability; he meekly but firmly maintained that his conscience would not allow him to meet a stage-player. However, Father Brown put down his glass of port with expressions of appreciation and thanks; and went off to meet his friend the doctor by appointment at the corner of the street; whence they were to go together to the offices of Mr Carver, the solicitor.

'I suppose you've gone the dreary round,' began the doctor, 'and found it a very dull village.'

Father Brown's reply was sharp and almost shrill.

'Don't call your village dull. I assure you it's a very extraordinary village indeed.'

'I've been dealing with the only extraordinary thing that ever happened here, I should think,' observed Dr Mulborough. 'And even that happened to somebody from outside. I may tell you they managed the exhumation quietly last night; and I did the autopsy this morning. In plain words, we've been digging up a corpse that's simply stuffed with poison.'

'A corpse stuffed with poison,' repeated Father Brown rather absently. 'Believe me, your village contains something much more extraordinary than that.'

There was abrupt silence, followed by the equally abrupt pulling of the antiquated bell-pull in the porch of the solicitor's house; and they were soon brought into the presence of that legal gentleman, who presented them in turn to a white-haired, yellow-faced gentleman with a scar, who appeared to be the Admiral.

By this time the atmosphere of the village had sunk almost into the subconsciousness of the little priest; but he was conscious that the lawyer was indeed the sort of lawyer to be the adviser of people like Miss Carstairs-Carew. But though he was an archaic old bird, he seemed something more than a fossil. Perhaps it was the uniformity of the background; but the priest had again the curious feeling that he himself was transplanted back into the early nineteenth century, rather than that the solicitor had survived into the early twentieth. His collar and cravat contrived to look almost like a stock as he settled his long chin into them; but they were clean as well as clean-cut; and there was even something about him of a very dry old dandy. In short, he was what is called well-preserved, even if partly by being petrified.

The lawyer and the Admiral, and even the doctor, showed some surprise on finding that Father Brown was rather disposed to defend the parson's son against the local lamentations on behalf of the parson.

'I thought our young friend rather attractive, myself,' he said. 'He's a good talker and I should guess a good poet; and Mrs Maltravers, who is serious about that at least, says he's quite a good actor.'

'Indeed,' said the lawyer, 'Potter's Pond, outside Mrs Maltravers, is rather more inclined to ask if he is a good son.'

'He is a good son,' said Father Brown. 'That's the extraordinary thing.'

'Damn it all,' said the Admiral. 'Do you mean he's really fond of his father?'

The priest hesitated. Then he said, 'I'm not quite so sure about that. That's the other extraordinary thing.'

'What the devil do you mean?' demanded the sailor with nautical profanity.

'I mean,' said Father Brown, 'that the son still speaks of his father in a hard unforgiving way; but he seems after all to have done more than his duty by him. I had a talk with the bank manager, and as we were enquiring in confidence into a serious crime, under authority from the police, he told me the facts. The old clergyman has retired from parish work; indeed, this was never actually his parish. Such of the populace, which is pretty pagan, as goes to church at all, goes to Dutton-Abbot, not a mile away. The old man has no private means, but the son is earning good money; and the old man is well looked after. He gave me some port of absolutely first-class vintage; I saw rows of dusty old bottles of it; and I left him sitting down to a little lunch quite recherché in an old-fashioned style. It must be done on the young man's money.'

'Quite a model son,' said Carver, with a slight sneer.

Father Brown nodded, frowning, as if revolving a riddle of his own; and then said:

'A model son. But rather a mechanical model.'

At this moment a clerk brought in an unstamped letter for the lawyer; a letter which the lawyer tore impatiently across after a single glance. As it fell apart, the priest saw a spidery, crazy, crowded sort of handwriting and the signature of 'Phoenix Fitzgerald'; and made a guess which the other curtly confirmed.

'It's that mad melodramatic actor that's always pestering us,' he said. 'He's got some fixed idea of an old feud with some dead and gone fellow mummer of his, which can't have anything to do with the case. We all refuse to see him, except the doctor who did see him; and the doctor says he's mad.'

'Yes,' said Father Brown, pursing his lips thoughtfully. 'I should say he's mad. But of course there can't be any doubt that he's right.'

'Right?' cried Carver sharply. 'Right about what?'

'About this being connected with the old theatrical company,' said Father Brown. 'Do you know the first thing that stumped me about this story? It was that notion that Maltravers was killed by villagers because he insulted their village. It's extraordinary what coroners can get jurymen to believe; and journalists, of course, are quite incredibly credulous. They can't know much about English rustics. I'm an English rustic myself; at least I was grown, with other turnips, in Essex. Can you imagine an English agricultural labourer idealizing and personifying his village, like the citizen of an old Greek city state; drawing the sword for its sacred banner, like a man in the tiny mediaeval republic of an Italian town? Can you hear a jolly old gaffer saying, "Blood alone can wipe out one spot on the escutcheon of Potter's Pond." By St George and the Dragon, I only wish they would! But, as a matter of fact, I have a more practical argument for the other notion.'

He paused for a moment, as if collecting his thoughts, and then went on:

'They misunderstood the meaning of those few last words poor Maltravers was heard to say. He wasn't telling the villagers that the village was only a hamlet. He was talking to an actor; they were going to put on a performance in which Fitzgerald was to be Fortinbras, the unknown Hankin to be Polonius, and Maltravers, no doubt, the Prince of Denmark. Perhaps somebody else wanted the part or had views on the part; and Maltravers said angrily, "You'd be a miserable little Hamlet"; that's all.'

Dr Mulborough was staring; he seemed to be digesting the suggestion slowly but without difficulty. At last he said, before the others could speak:

'And what do you suggest that we should do now?'

Father Brown rose rather abruptly; but spoke civilly enough. 'If these gentlemen will excuse us for the moment, I propose that you and I, doctor, should go round at once to the Horners. I know the parson and his son will both be there just now. And what I want you to do, doctor, is this. Nobody in the village knows yet, I think, about your autopsy and its result. I want you simply to tell both the clergyman and his son, while they are there together, the exact fact of the case; that Maltravers died by poison and not by a blow.'

Dr Mulborough had reason to reconsider his incredulity when told that it was an extraordinary village. The scene which ensued, when he actually carried out the priest's programme, was certainly of the sort in which a man, as the saying is, can hardly believe his eyes.

The Revd Samuel Horner was standing in his black cassock, which threw up the silver of his venerable head; his hand rested at the moment on the lectern at which he often stood to study the Scriptures, now possibly by accident only; but it gave him a greater look of authority. And opposite to him his mutinous son was sitting asprawl in a chair, smoking a cheap cigarette with an exceptionally heavy scowl; a lively picture of youthful impiety.

The old man courteously waved Father Brown to a seat, which he took and sat there silent, staring blandly at the ceiling. But something made Mulborough feel that he could deliver his important news more impressively standing up.

'I feel,' he said, 'that you ought to be informed as in some sense the spiritual father of this community, that the one terrible tragedy in its record has taken on a new significance; possibly even more terrible. You will recall the sad business of the death of Maltravers; who was adjudged to have been killed with the blow of a stick, probably wielded by some rustic enemy.'

The clergyman made a gesture with a wavering hand. 'God forbid,' he said, 'that I should say anything that might seem to palliate murderous violence in any case. But when an actor brings his wickedness into this innocent village, he is challenging the judgement of God.'

'Perhaps,' said the doctor gravely. 'But anyhow it was not so that the judgement fell. I have just been commissioned to conduct a post-mortem on the body; and I can assure you, first, that the blow on the head could not conceivably have caused the death; and, second, that the body was full of poison, which undoubtedly caused death.'

Young Hurrel Horner sent his cigarette flying and was on his feet with the lightness and swiftness of a cat. His leap landed him within a yard or so of the reading-desk.

'Are you certain of this?' he gasped. 'Are you absolutely certain that that blow could not cause death?'

'Absolutely certain,' said the doctor.

'Well,' said Hurrel, 'I almost wish this one could.'

In a flash, before anyone could move a finger, he had struck the parson a stunning crack on the mouth, dashing him backwards like a disjointed black doll against the door.

'What are you doing?' cried Mulborough, shaken from head to foot with the shock and mere sound of the blow. 'Father Brown, what is this madman doing?'

But Father Brown had not stirred; he was still staring serenely at the ceiling.

'I was waiting for him to do that,' said the priest placidly. 'I rather wonder he hasn't done it before.'

'Good God,' cried the doctor. 'I know we thought he was wronged in some ways; but to strike his father; to strike a clergyman and a non-combatant——'

'He has not struck his father; and he has not struck a clergyman,' said Father Brown. 'He has struck a blackmailing blackguard of an actor dressed up as a clergyman, who has lived on him like a leech for years. Now he knows he is free of the blackmail, he lets fly; and I can't say I blame him much. More especially as I have very strong suspicions that the blackmailer is a poisoner as well. I think, Mulborough, you had better ring up the police.'

They passed out of the room uninterrupted by the two others, the one dazed and staggered, the other still blind and snorting and panting with passions of relief and rage. But as they passed, Father Brown once turned his face to the young man; and the young man was one of the very few human beings who have seen that face implacable.

'He was right there,' said Father Brown. 'When an actor brings his wickedness into this innocent village, he challenges the judgement of God.'

'Well,' said Father Brown, as he and the doctor again settled themselves in a railway carriage standing in the station of Potter's Pond. 'As you say, it's a strange story; but I don't think it's any longer a mystery story. Anyhow, the story seems to me to have been roughly this. Maltravers came here, with part of his touring company; some of them went straight to Dutton Abbot, where they were all presenting some melodrama about the early nineteenth century; he himself happened to be hanging about in his stage dress, the very distinctive dress of a dandy of that time. Another character was an old-fashioned parson, whose dark dress was less distinctive and might pass as being merely old-fashioned. This part was taken by a man who mostly acted old men; had acted Shylock and was afterwards going to act Polonius.

'A third figure in the drama was our dramatic poet, who was also a dramatic performer, and quarrelled with Maltravers about how to present Hamlet, but more about personal things, too. I think it likely that he was in love with Mrs Maltravers even then; I don't believe there was anything wrong with them; and I hope it may now be all right with them. But he may very well have resented Maltravers in his conjugal capacity; for Maltravers was a bully and likely to raise rows. In some such row they fought with sticks, and the poet hit Maltravers very hard on the head, and, in the light of the inquest, had every reason to suppose he had killed him.

'A third person was present or privy to the incident, the man acting the old parson; and he proceeded to blackmail the alleged murderer, forcing from him the cost of his upkeep in some luxury as a retired clergyman. It was the obvious masquerade for such a man in such a place, simply to go on wearing his stage clothes as a retired clergyman. But he had his own reason for being a very retired clergyman. For the true story of Maltravers' death was that he rolled into a deep undergrowth of bracken, gradually recovered, tried to walk towards a house, and was eventually overcome, not by the blow, but by the fact that the benevolent clergyman had given him poison an hour before, probably in a glass of port. I was beginning to think so, when I drank a glass of the parson's port. It made me a little nervous. The police are working on that theory now; but whether they will be able to prove that part of the story, I don't know. They will have to find the exact motive; but it's obvious that this bunch of actors was buzzing with quarrels and Maltravers was very much hated.'

'The police may prove something now they have got the suspicion,' said Dr Mulborough. 'What I don't understand is why you ever began to suspect. Why in the world should you suspect that very blameless black-coated gentleman?'

Father Brown smiled faintly. 'I suppose in one sense,' he said, 'it was a matter of special knowledge; almost a professional matter, but in a peculiar sense. You know our controversialists often complain that there is a great deal of ignorance about what our religion is really like. But it is really more curious than that. It is true, and it is not at all unnatural, that England does not know much about the Church of Rome. But England does not know much about the Church of England. Not even as much as I do. You would be astonished at how little the average public grasps about the Anglican controversies; lots of them don't really know what is meant by a High Churchman or a Low Churchman, even on the particular points of practice, let alone the two theories of history and philosophy behind them. You can see this ignorance in any newspaper; in any merely popular novel or play.

'Now the first thing that struck me was that this venerable cleric had got the whole thing incredibly mixed up. No Anglican parson could be so wrong about every Anglican problem. He was supposed to be an old Tory High Churchman; and then he boasted of being a Puritan. A man like that might personally be rather Puritanical; but he would never call it being a Puritan. He professed a horror of the stage; he didn't know that High Churchmen generally don't have that special horror, though Low Churchmen do. He talked like a Puritan about the Sabbath; and then he had a crucifix in his room. He evidently had no notion of what a very pious parson ought to be, except that he ought to be very solemn and venerable and frown upon the pleasures of the world.

'All this time there was a subconscious notion running in my head; something I couldn't fix in my memory; and then it came to me suddenly. This is Stage Parson. That is exactly the vague venerable old fool who would be the nearest notion a popular playwright or play-actor of the old school had of anything so odd as a religious man.'

'To say nothing of a physician of the old school,' said Mulborough good-humouredly, 'who does not set up to know much about being a religious man.'

'As a matter of fact,' went on Father Brown, 'there was a plainer and more glaring cause for suspicion. It concerned the Dark Lady of the Grange, who was supposed to be the Vampire of the Village. I very early formed the impression that this black blot was rather the bright spot of the village. She was treated as a mystery; but there was really nothing mysterious about her. She had come down here quite recently, quite openly, under her own name, to help the new enquiries to be made about her own husband. He hadn't treated her too well; but she had principles, suggesting that something was due to her married name and to common justice. For the same reason, she went to live in the house outside which her husband had been found dead. The other innocent and straightforward case, besides the Vampire of the Village, was the Scandal of the Village, the parson's profligate son. He also made no disguise of his profession or past connection with the acting world. That's why I didn't suspect him as I did the parson. But you'll already have guessed a real and relevant reason for suspecting the parson.'

'Yes, I think I see,' said the doctor, 'that's why you bring in the name of the actress.'

'Yes, I mean his fanatical fixity about not seeing the actress,' remarked the priest. 'But he didn't really object to seeing her. He objected to her seeing him.'

'Yes, I see that,' assented the other.

'If she had seen the Revd Samuel Horner, she would instantly have recognized the very unreverend actor Hankin, disguised as a sham parson with a pretty bad character behind the disguise. Well, that is the whole of this simple village idyll, I think. But you will admit I kept my promise; I have shown you something in the village considerably more creepy than a corpse; even a corpse stuffed with poison. The black coat of a parson stuffed with a blackmailer is at least worth noticing and my live man is much deadlier than your dead one.'

'Yes,' said the doctor, settling himself back comfortably in the cushions. 'If it comes to a little cosy company on a railway journey, I should prefer the corpse.'

The Dream

Agatha Christie

HERCULE POIROT gave the house a steady appraising glance. His eyes wandered a moment to its surroundings, the shops, the big factory building on the right, the blocks of cheap mansion flats opposite.

Then once more his eyes returned to Northway House, relic of an earlier age—an age of space and leisure, when green fields had surrounded its well-bred arrogance. Now it was an anachronism, submerged and forgotten in the hectic sea of modern London, and not one man in fifty could have told you where it stood.

Furthermore, very few people could have told you to whom it belonged, though its owner's name would have been recognized as one of the world's richest men. But money can quench publicity as well as flaunt it. Benedict Farley, that eccentric millionaire, chose not to advertise his choice of residence. He himself was rarely seen, seldom making a public appearance. From time to time he appeared at board meetings, his lean figure, beaked nose, and rasping voice easily dominating the assembled directors. Apart from that, he was just a well-known figure of legend. There were his strange meannesses, his incredible generosities, as well as more personal details—his famous patchwork dressing-gown, now reputed to be twenty-eight years old, his invariable diet of cabbage soup and caviare, his hatred of cats. All these things the public knew.

Hercule Poirot knew them also. It was all he did know of the man he was about to visit. The letter which was in his coat pocket told him little more.

After surveying this melancholy landmark of a past age for a minute or two in silence, he walked up the steps to the front door and pressed the bell, glancing as he did so at the neat wrist-watch which had at last replaced an earlier favourite—the large turnip-faced watch of earlier days. Yes, it was exactly nine-thirty. As ever, Hercule Poirot was exact to the minute.

The door opened after just the right interval. A perfect specimen of the genus butler stood outlined against the lighted hall.

'Mr Benedict Farley?' asked Hercule Poirot.

The impersonal glance surveyed him from head to foot, inoffensively but effectively.

'*En gros et en détail*,' thought Hercule Poirot to himself with appreciation.

'You have an appointment, sir?' asked the suave voice.

'Yes.'

'Your name, sir?'

'M. Hercule Poirot.'

The butler bowed and drew back. Hercule Poirot entered the house. The butler closed the door behind him.

But there was yet one more formality before the deft hands took hat and stick from the visitor.

'You will excuse me, sir. I was to ask for a letter.'

With deliberation Poirot took from his pocket the folded letter and handed it to the butler. The latter gave it a mere glance, then returned it with a bow. Hercule Poirot returned it to his pocket. Its contents were simple.

Northway House, W8

M. Hercule Poirot.

Dear sir,

Mr Benedict Farley would like to have the benefit of your advice. If convenient to yourself he would be glad if you would call upon him at the above address at 9.30 tomorrow (Thursday) evening.

Yours truly,
Hugo Cornworthy
(Secretary).

PS. Please bring this letter with you.

Deftly the butler relieved Poirot of hat, stick, and overcoat. He said:

'Will you please come up to Mr Cornworthy's room?'

He led the way up the broad staircase. Poirot followed him, looking with appreciation at such *objets d'art* as were of an opulent and florid nature! His taste in art was always somewhat bourgeois.

On the first floor the butler knocked on a door.

Hercule Poirot's eyebrows rose very slightly. It was the first jarring note. For the best butlers do not knock at doors—and yet indubitably this was a first-class butler!

It was, so to speak, the first intimation of contact with the eccentricity of a millionaire.

A voice from within called out something. The butler threw open the door. He announced (and again Poirot sensed the deliberate departure from orthodoxy):

'The gentleman you are expecting, sir.'

Poirot passed into the room. It was a fair-sized room, very plainly furnished in a workmanlike fashion. Filing cabinets, books of reference, a couple of easy chairs, and a large and imposing desk covered with neatly docketed papers. The corners of the room were dim, for the only light came from a big green-shaded reading-lamp which stood on a small table by the arm of one of the easy chairs. It was placed so as to cast its full light on anyone approaching from the door. Hercule Poirot blinked a little, realizing that the lamp bulb was at least 150 watts. In the armchair sat a thin figure in a patchwork dressing-gown—Benedict Farley. His head was stuck forward in a characteristic attitude, his beaked nose projecting like that of a bird. A crest of white hair like that of a cockatoo rose above his forehead. His eyes glittered behind thick lenses as he peered suspiciously at his visitor.

'Hey,' he said at last—and his voice was shrill and harsh, with a rasping note in it. 'So you're Hercule Poirot, hey?'

'At your service,' said Poirot politely and bowed, one hand on the back of the chair.

'Sit down—sit down,' said the old man testily.

Hercule Poirot sat down—in the full glare of the lamp. From behind it the old man seemed to be studying him attentively.

'How do I know you're Hercule Poirot—hey?' he demanded fretfully. 'Tell me that—hey?'

Once more Poirot drew the letter from his pocket and handed it to Farley.

'Yes,' admitted the millionaire grudgingly. 'That's it. That's what

I got Cornworthy to write.' He folded it up and tossed it back. 'So you're the fellow, are you?'

With a little wave of his hand Poirot said:

'I assure you there is no deception!'

Benedict Farley chuckled suddenly.

'That's what the conjuror says before he takes the goldfish out of the hat! Saying that is part of the trick, you know.'

Poirot did not reply. Farley said suddenly:

'Think I'm a suspicious old man, hey? So I am. Don't trust anybody! That's my motto. Can't trust anybody when you're rich. No, no, it doesn't do.'

'You wished,' Poirot hinted gently, 'to consult me?'

The old man nodded.

'That's right. Always buy the best. That's my motto. Go to the expert and don't count the cost. You'll notice, M. Poirot, I haven't asked you your fee. I'm not going to! Send me in the bill later—*I* shan't cut up rough over it. Damned fools at the dairy thought they could charge me two and nine for eggs when two and seven's the market price—lot of swindlers! I won't be swindled. But the man at the top's different. He's worth the money. I'm at the top myself—I know.'

Hercule Poirot made no reply. He listened attentively, his head poised a little on one side.

Behind his impassive exterior he was conscious of a feeling of disappointment. He could not exactly put his finger on it. So far Benedict Farley had run true to type—that is, he had conformed to the popular idea of himself; and yet—Poirot was disappointed.

'The man,' he said disgustedly to himself, 'is a mountebank— nothing but a mountebank!'

He had known other millionaires, eccentric men too, but in nearly every case he had been conscious of a certain force, an inner energy that had commanded his respect. If they had worn a patchwork dressing-gown, it would have been because they liked wearing such a dressing-gown. But the dressing-gown of Benedict Farley, or so it seemed to Poirot, was essentially a stage property. And the man himself was essentially stagey. Every word he spoke was uttered, so Poirot felt assured, sheerly for effect.

He repeated again unemotionally, 'You wished to consult me, Mr Farley?'

*

Abruptly the millionaire's manner changed. He leaned forward. His voice dropped to a croak.

'Yes. Yes . . . I want to hear what you've got to say—what you think. . . . Go to the top! That's my way! The best doctor—the best detective—it's between the two of them.'

'As yet, Monsieur, I do not understand.'

'Naturally,' snapped Farley. 'I haven't begun to tell you.'

He leaned forward once more and shot out an abrupt question.

'What do you know, M. Poirot, about dreams?'

The little man's eyebrows rose. Whatever he had expected, it was not this.

'For that, Monsieur Farley, I should recommend Napoleon's *Book of Dreams*—or the latest practising psychologist from Harley Street.'

Benedict Farley said soberly, 'I've tried both . . .'

There was a pause, then the millionaire spoke, at first almost in a whisper, then with a voice growing higher and higher.

'It's the same dream—night after night. And I'm afraid, I tell you—I'm afraid. . . . It's always the same. I'm sitting in my room next door to this. Sitting at my desk, writing. There's a clock there and I glance at it and see the time—exactly twenty-eight minutes past three. Always the same time, you understand.

'*And when I see the time, M. Poirot, I know I've got to do it.* I don't want to do it—I loathe doing it—but I've got to . . .'

His voice had risen shrilly.

Unperturbed, Poirot said, 'And what is it that you have to do?'

'At twenty-eight minutes past three,' Benedict Farley said hoarsely, 'I open the second drawer down on the right of my desk, take out the revolver that I keep there, load it and walk over to the window. And then—and then——'

'Yes?'

Benedict Farley said in a whisper:

'*Then I shoot myself . . .*'

There was silence.

Then Poirot said, 'That is your dream?'

'Yes.'

'The same every night?'

'Yes.'

'What happens after you shoot yourself?'

'I wake up.'

Poirot nodded his head slowly and thoughtfully. 'As a matter of interest, do you keep a revolver in that particular drawer?'

'Yes.'

'Why?'

'I have always done so. It is as well to be prepared.'

'Prepared for what?'

Farley said irritably, 'A man in my position has to be on his guard. All rich men have enemies.'

Poirot did not pursue the subject. He remained silent for a moment or two, then he said:

'Why exactly did you send for me?'

'I will tell you. First of all I consulted a doctor—three doctors to be exact.'

'Yes?'

'The first told me it was all a question of diet. He was an elderly man. The second was a young man of the modern school. He assured me that it all hinged on a certain event that took place in infancy at that particular time of day—three twenty-eight. I am so determined, he says, not to remember that event, that I symbolize it by destroying myself. That is his explanation.'

'And the third doctor?' asked Poirot.

Benedict Farley's voice rose in shrill anger.

'He's a young man too. He has a preposterous theory! He asserts that I, myself, am tired of life, that my life is so unbearable to me that I deliberately want to end it! But since to acknowledge that fact would be to acknowledge that essentially I am a failure, I refuse in my waking moments to face the truth. But when I am asleep, all inhibitions are removed, and I proceed to do that *which I really wish to do*. I put an end to myself.'

'His view is that you really wish, unknown to yourself, to commit suicide?' said Poirot.

Benedict Farley cried shrilly:

'And that's impossible—impossible! I'm perfectly happy! I've got everything I want—everything money can buy! It's fantastic—unbelievable even to suggest a thing like that!'

Poirot looked at him with interest. Perhaps something in the shaking hands, the trembling shrillness of the voice, warned him that the denial was *too* vehement, that its very insistence was in itself suspect. He contented himself with saying:

'And where do I come in, Monsieur?'

Benedict Farley calmed down suddenly. He tapped with an emphatic finger on the table beside him.

'There's another possibility. And if it's right, you're the man to know about it! You're famous, you've had hundreds of cases—fantastic, improbable cases! You'd know if anyone does.'

'Know what?'

Farley's voice dropped to a whisper:

'Supposing someone wants to kill me. . . . Could they do it this way? Could they make me dream that dream night after night?'

'Hypnotism, you mean?'

'Yes.'

Hercule Poirot considered the question.

'It would be possible, I suppose,' he said at last. 'It is more a question for a doctor.'

'You don't know of such a case in your experience?'

'Not precisely on those lines, no.'

'You see what I'm driving at? I'm made to dream the same dream, night after night, night after night—and then—one day the suggestion is too much for me—*and I act upon it*. I do what I've dreamed of so often—kill myself!'

Slowly Hercule Poirot shook his head.

'You don't think that is possible?' asked Farley.

'*Possible*?' Poirot shook his head. 'That is not a word I care to meddle with.'

'But you think it improbable?'

'Most improbable.'

Benedict Farley murmured, 'The doctor said so too. . . .' Then his voice rising shrilly again, he cried out, 'But why do I have this dream? Why? Why?'

Hercule Poirot shook his head. Benedict Farley said abruptly, 'You're sure you've never come across anything like this in your experience?'

'Never.'

'That's what I wanted to know.'

Delicately, Poirot cleared his throat.

'You permit,' he said, 'a question?'

'What is it? What is it? Say what you like.'

'Who is it you suspect of wanting to kill you?'

Farley snapped out, 'Nobody. Nobody at all.'

'But the idea presented itself to your mind?' Poirot persisted.

'I wanted to know—if it was a possibility.'

'Speaking from my own experience, I should say No. Have you ever been hypnotized, by the way?'

'Of course not. D'you think I'd lend myself to such tomfoolery?'

'Then I think one can say that your theory is definitely improbable.'

'But the dream, you fool, the dream.'

'The dream is certainly remarkable,' said Poirot thoughtfully. He paused and then went on. 'I should like to see the scene of this drama—the table, the clock, and the revolver.'

'Of course, I'll take you next door.'

Wrapping the folds of his dressing-gown round him, the old man half-rose from his chair. Then suddenly, as though a thought had struck him, he resumed his seat.

'No,' he said. 'There's nothing to see there. I've told you all there is to tell.'

'But I should like to see for myself——'

'There's no need,' Farley snapped. 'You've given me your opinion. That's the end.'

Poirot shrugged his shoulders. 'As you please.' He rose to his feet. 'I am sorry, Mr Farley, that I have not been able to be of assistance to you.'

Benedict Farley was staring straight ahead of him.

'Don't want a lot of hanky-pankying around,' he growled out. 'I've told you the facts—you can't make anything of them. That closes the matter. You can send me in a bill for a consultation fee.'

'I shall not fail to do so,' said the detective dryly. He walked towards the door.

'Stop a minute.' The millionaire called him back. 'That letter—I want it.'

'The letter from your secretary?'

'Yes.'

Poirot's eyebrows rose. He put his hand into his pocket, drew out a folded sheet, and handed it to the old man. The latter scrutinized it, then put it down on the table beside him with a nod.

*

Once more Hercule Poirot walked to the door. He was puzzled. His busy mind was going over and over the story he had been told. Yet in the midst of his mental preoccupation, a nagging sense of something wrong obtruded itself. And that something had to do with himself—not with Benedict Farley.

With his hand on the door knob, his mind cleared. He, Hercule Poirot, had been guilty of an error! He turned back into the room once more.

'A thousand pardons! In the interest of your problem I have committed a folly! That letter I handed to you—by mischance I put my hand into my right-hand pocket instead of the left——'

'What's all this? What's all this?'

'The letter that I handed you just now—an apology from my laundress concerning the treatment of my collars.' Poirot was smiling, apologetic. He dipped into his left-hand pocket. 'This is *your* letter.'

Benedict Farley snatched at it—grunted: 'Why the devil can't you mind what you're doing?'

Poirot retrieved his laundress's communication, apologized gracefully once more, and left the room.

He paused for a moment outside on the landing. It was a spacious one. Directly facing him was a big old oak settle with a refectory table in front of it. On the table were magazines. There were also two armchairs and a table with flowers. It reminded him a little of a dentist's waiting-room.

The butler was in the hall below waiting to let him out.

'Can I get you a taxi, sir?'

'No, I thank you. The night is fine. I will walk.'

Hercule Poirot paused a moment on the pavement waiting for a lull in the traffic before crossing the busy street.

A frown creased his forehead.

'No,' he said to himself. 'I do not understand at all. Nothing makes sense. Regrettable to have to admit it, but I, Hercule Poirot, am completely baffled.'

That was what might be termed the first act of the drama. The second act followed a week later. It opened with a telephone call from one John Stillingfleet, MD.

He said with a remarkable lack of medical decorum:

'That you, Poirot, old horse? Stillingfleet here.'

'Yes, my friend. What is it?'

'I'm speaking from Northway House—Benedict Farley's.'

'Ah, yes?' Poirot's voice quickened with interest. 'What of—Mr Farley?'

'Farley's dead. Shot himself this afternoon.'

There was a pause, then Poirot said:

'Yes . . .'

'I notice you're not overcome with surprise. Know something about it, old horse?'

'Why should you think that?'

'Well, it isn't brilliant deduction or telepathy or anything like that. We found a note from Farley to you making an appointment about a week ago.'

'I see.'

'We've got a tame police inspector here—got to be careful, you know, when one of these millionaire blokes bumps himself off. Wondered whether you could throw any light on the case. If so, perhaps you'd come round?'

'I will come immediately.'

'Good for you, old boy. Some dirty work at the crossroads—eh?'

Poirot merely repeated that he would set forth immediately.

'Don't want to spill the beans over the telephone? Quite right. So long.'

A quarter of an hour later Poirot was sitting in the library, a low long room at the back of Northway House on the ground floor. There were five other persons in the room. Inspector Barnett, Dr Stillingfleet, Mrs Farley, the widow of the millionaire, Joanna Farley, his only daughter, and Hugo Cornworthy, his private secretary.

Of these, Inspector Barnett was a discreet soldierly-looking man, Dr Stillingfleet, whose professional manner was entirely different from his telephonic style, was a tall, long-faced young man of thirty. Mrs Farley was obviously very much younger than her husband. She was a handsome dark-haired woman. Her mouth was hard and her black eyes gave absolutely no clue to her emotions. She appeared perfectly self-possessed. Joanna Farley had fair hair and a freckled face. The prominence of her nose and chin were clearly inherited from her father. Her eyes were intelligent and shrewd. Hugo Cornworthy was a somewhat colourless young man, very correctly dressed. He seemed intelligent and efficient.

After greetings and introductions, Poirot narrated simply and clearly the circumstances of his visit and the story told him by Benedict Farley. He could not complain of any lack of interest.

'Most extraordinary story I've ever heard!' said the inspector. 'A dream, eh? Did you know anything about this, Mrs Farley?'

She bowed her head.

'My husband mentioned it to me. It upset him very much. I—I told him it was indigestion—his diet, you know, was very peculiar—and suggested his calling in Dr Stillingfleet.'

That young man shook his head.

'He didn't consult me. From M. Poirot's story, I gather he went to Harley Street.'

'I would like your advice on that point, doctor,' said Poirot. 'Mr Farley told me that he consulted three specialists. What do you think of the theories they advanced?'

Stillingfleet frowned.

'It's difficult to say. You've got to take into account that what he passed on to you wasn't exactly what had been said to him. It was a layman's interpretation.'

'You mean he had got the phraseology wrong?'

'Not exactly. I mean they would put a thing to him in professional terms, he'd get the meaning a little distorted, and then recast it in his own language.'

'So that what he told me was not really what the doctors said.'

'That's what it amounts to. He's just got it all a little wrong, if you know what I mean.'

Poirot nodded thoughtfully. 'Is it known whom he consulted?' he asked.

Mrs Farley shook her head, and Joanna Farley remarked:

'None of us had any idea he had consulted anyone.'

'Did he speak to *you* about this dream?' asked Poirot.

The girl shook her head.

'And you, Mr Cornworthy?'

'No, he said nothing at all. I took down a letter to you at his dictation, but I had no idea why he wished to consult you. I thought it might possibly have something to do with some business irregularity.'

Poirot asked: 'And now as to the actual facts of Mr Farley's death?'

Inspector Barnett looked interrogatively at Mrs Farley and at Dr Stillingfleet, and then took upon himself the role of spokesman.

'Mr Farley was in the habit of working in his own room on the first floor every afternoon. I understand that there was a big amalgamation of businesses in prospect——'

He looked at Hugo Cornworthy who said, 'Consolidated Coachlines.'

'In connection with that,' continued Inspector Barnett, 'Mr Farley had agreed to give an interview to two members of the press. He very seldom did anything of the kind—only about once in five years, I understand. Accordingly two reporters, one from the Associated Newsgroups, and one from Amalgamated Press-sheets, arrived at a quarter past three by appointment. They waited on the first floor outside Mr Farley's door—which was the customary place for people to wait who had an appointment with Mr Farley. At twenty past three a messenger arrived from the office of Consolidated Coachlines with some urgent papers. He was shown into Mr Farley's room where he handed over the documents. Mr Farley accompanied him to the door of the room, and from there spoke to the two members of the Press. He said:

'I am sorry, gentlemen, to have to keep you waiting, but I have some urgent business to attend to. I will be as quick as I can.'

'The two gentlemen, Mr Adams and Mr Stoddart, assured Mr Farley that they would await his convenience. He went back into his room, shut the door—and was never seen alive again!'

'Continue,' said Poirot.

'At a little after four o'clock,' went on the inspector, 'Mr Cornworthy here came out of his room which is next door to Mr Farley's, and was surprised to see the two reporters still waiting. He wanted Mr Farley's signature to some letters and thought he had also better remind him that these two gentlemen were waiting. He accordingly went into Mr Farley's room. To his surprise he could not at first see Mr Farley and thought the room was empty. Then he caught sight of a boot sticking out behind the desk (which is placed in front of the window). He went quickly across and discovered Mr Farley lying there dead, with a revolver beside him.

'Mr Cornworthy hurried out of the room and directed the butler to ring up Dr Stillingfleet. By the latter's advice, Mr Cornworthy also informed the police.'

'Was the shot heard?' asked Poirot.

'No. The traffic is very noisy here, the landing window was open. What with lorries and motor horns it would be most unlikely if it had been noticed.'

Poirot nodded thoughtfully. 'What time is it supposed he died?' he asked.

Stillingfleet said:

'I examined the body as soon as I got here—that is, at thirty-two minutes past four. Mr Farley had been dead at least an hour.'

Poirot's face was very grave.

'So then, it seems possible that his death could have occurred at the time he mentioned to me—that is, at twenty-eight minutes past three.'

'Exactly,' said Stillingfleet.

'Any finger-marks on the revolver?'

'Yes, his own.'

'And the revolver itself?'

The inspector took up the tale.

'Was one which he kept in the second right-hand drawer of his desk, just as he told you. Mrs Farley has identified it positively. Moreover, you understand, there is only one entrance to the room, the door giving on to the landing. The two reporters were sitting exactly opposite that door and they swear that no one entered the room from the time Mr Farley spoke to them, until Mr Cornworthy entered it at a little after four o'clock.'

'So that there is every reason to suppose that Mr Farley committed suicide?'

Inspector Barnett smiled a little.

'There would have been no doubt at all but for one point.'

'And that?'

'The letter written to you.'

Poirot smiled too.

'I see! Where Hercule Poirot is concerned—immediately the suspicion of murder arises!'

'Precisely,' said the inspector dryly. 'However, after your clearing up of the situation——'

Poirot interrupted him. 'One little minute.' He turned to Mrs Farley. 'Had your husband ever been hynotized?'

'Never.'

'Had he studied the question of hypnotism? Was he interested in the subject?'

She shook her head. 'I don't think so.'

Suddenly her self-control seemed to break down. 'That horrible dream! It's uncanny! That he should have dreamed that—night after night—and then—and then—it's as though he were—*hounded* to death!'

Poirot remembered Benedict Farley saying—'*I proceed to do that which I really wish to do. I put an end to myself.*'

He said. 'Had it ever occurred to you that your husband might be tempted to do away with himself?'

'No—at least—sometimes he was very queer . . .'

Joanna Farley's voice broke in clear and scornful. 'Father would never have killed himself. He was far too careful of himself.'

Dr Stillingfleet said, 'It isn't the people who threaten to commit suicide who usually do it, you know, Miss Farley. That's why suicides sometimes seem unaccountable.'

Poirot rose to his feet. 'Is it permitted,' he asked, 'that I see the room where the tragedy occurred?'

'Certainly. Dr Stillingfleet——'

The doctor accompanied Poirot upstairs.

Benedict Farley's room was a much larger one than the secretary's next door. It was luxuriously furnished with deep leather-covered armchairs, a thick pile carpet, and a superb outsize writing-desk.

Poirot passed behind the latter to where a dark stain on the carpet showed just before the window. He remembered the millionaire saying '*At twenty-eight minutes past three I open the second drawer down on the right of my desk, take out the revolver that I keep there, load it, and walk over to the window. And then—and then I shoot myself.*'

He nodded slowly. Then he said:

'The window was open like this?'

'Yes. But nobody could have got in that way.'

Poirot put his head out. There was no sill or parapet and no pipes near. Not even a cat could have gained access that way. Opposite rose the blank wall of the factory, a dead wall with no windows in it.

Stillingfleet said, 'Funny room for a rich man to choose as his own sanctum with that outlook. It's like looking out on to a prison wall.'

'Yes,' said Poirot. He drew his head in and stared at the expanse of solid brick. 'I think,' he said, 'that that wall is important.'

Stillingfleet looked at him curiously. 'You mean—psychologically?'

Poirot had moved to the desk. Idly, or so it seemed, he picked up a pair of what are usually called lazytongs. He pressed the handles; the tongs shot out to their full length. Delicately, Poirot picked up a burnt match stump with them from beside a chair some feet away and conveyed it carefully to the waste-paper basket.

'When you've finished playing with those things,' said Stillingfleet irritably.

Hercule Poirot murmured, 'An ingenious invention,' and replaced the tongs neatly on the writing-table. Then he asked:

'Where were Mrs Farley and Miss Farley at the time of the—death?'

'Mrs Farley was resting in her room on the floor above this. Miss Farley was painting in her studio at the top of the house.'

Hercule Poirot drummed idly with his fingers on the table for a minute or two. Then he said:

'I should like to see Miss Farley. Do you think you could ask her to come here for a minute or two?'

'If you like.'

Stillingfleet glanced at him curiously, then left the room. In another minute or two the door opened and Joanna Farley came in.

'You do not mind, mademoiselle, if I ask you a few questions?'

She returned his glance coolly. 'Please ask anything you choose.'

'Did you know that your father kept a revolver in his desk?'

'No.'

'Where were you and your mother—that is to say your step-mother—that is right?'

'Yes, Louise is my father's second wife. She is only eight years older than I am. You were about to say——?'

'Where were you and she on Thursday of last week? That is to say, on Thursday night.'

She reflected for a minute or two.

'Thursday? Let me see. Oh, yes, we had gone to the theatre. To see *Little Dog Laughed*.'

'Your father did not suggest accompanying you?'

'He never went out to theatres.'

'What did he usually do in the evenings?'

'He sat in here and read.'

'He was not a very sociable man?'

The girl looked at him directly. 'My father,' she said 'had a singularly unpleasant personality. No one who lived in close association with him could possibly be fond of him.'

'That, mademoiselle, is a very candid statement.'

'I am saving you time, M. Poirot. I realize quite well what you are getting at. My stepmother married my father for his money. I live here because I have no money to live elsewhere. There is a man I wish to marry—a poor man; my father saw to it that he lost his job. He wanted me, you see, to marry well—an easy matter since I was to be his heiress!'

'Your father's fortune passes to you?'

'Yes. That is, he left Louise, my stepmother, a quarter of a million free of tax, and there are other legacies, but the residue goes to me.' She smiled suddenly. 'So you see, M. Poirot, I had every reason to desire my father's death!'

'I see, mademoiselle, that you have inherited your father's intelligence.'

She said thoughtfully, 'Father was clever. . . . One felt that with him—that he had force—driving power—but it had all turned sour—bitter—there was no humanity left . . .'

Hercule Poirot said softly, '*Grand Dieu*, but what an imbecile I am . . .'

Joanna Farley turned towards the door. 'Is there anything more?'

'Two little questions. These tongs here,' he picked up the lazytongs, 'were they always on the table?'

'Yes. Father used them for picking up things. He didn't like stooping.'

'One other question. Was your father's eyesight good?'

She stared at him.

'Oh no—he couldn't see at all—I mean he couldn't see without his glasses. His sight had always been bad from a boy.'

'But with his glasses?'

'Oh, he could see all right then, of course.'

'He could read newspapers and fine print?'

'Oh yes.'

'That is all, mademoiselle.'

She went out of the room.

Poirot murmured. 'I was stupid. It was there, all the time, under my nose. And because it was so near I could not see it.'

He leaned out of the window once more. Down below, in the narrow way between the house and the factory, he saw a small dark object.

Hercule Poirot nodded, satisfied, and went downstairs again.

The others were still in the library. Poirot addressed himself to the secretary.

'I want you, Mr Cornworthy, to recount to me in detail the exact circumstances of Mr Farley's summons to me. When, for instance, did Mr Farley dictate that letter?'

'On Wednesday afternoon—at five-thirty, as far as I can remember.'

'Were there any special directions about posting it?'

'He told me to post it myself.'

'And you did so?'

'Yes.'

'Did he give any special instructions to the butler about admitting me?'

'Yes. He told me to tell Holmes (Holmes is the butler) that a gentleman would be calling at 9.30. He was to ask the gentleman's name. He was also to ask to see the letter.'

'Rather peculiar precautions to take, don't you think?'

Cornworthy shrugged his shoulders.

'Mr Farley,' he said carefully, 'was rather a peculiar man.'

'Any other instructions?'

'Yes. He told me to take the evening off.'

'Did you do so?'

'Yes, immediately after dinner I went to the cinema.'

'When did you return.'

'I let myself in about a quarter past eleven.'

'Did you see Mr Farley again that evening?'

'No.'

'And he did not mention the matter the next morning?'

'No.'

Poirot paused a moment, then resumed, 'When I arrived I was not shown into Mr Farley's own room.'

'No. He told me that I was to tell Holmes to show you into my room.'

'Why was that? Do you know?'

Cornworthy shook his head. 'I never questioned any of Mr Farley's orders,' he said dryly. 'He would have resented it if I had.'

'Did he usually receive visitors in his own room?'

'Usually, but not always. Sometimes he saw them in my room.'

'Was there any reason for that?'

Hugo Cornworthy considered.

'No—I hardly think so—I've never really thought about it.'

Turning to Mrs Farley, Poirot asked:

'You permit that I ring for your butler?'

'Certainly, M. Poirot.'

Very correct, very urbane, Holmes answered the bell.

'You rang, madam?'

Mrs Farley indicated Poirot with a gesture. Holmes turned politely. 'Yes, sir?'

'What were your instructions, Holmes, on the Thursday night when I came here?'

Holmes cleared his throat, then said:

'After dinner Mr Cornworthy told me that Mr Farley expected a Mr Hercule Poirot at 9.30. I was to ascertain the gentleman's name, and I was to verify the information by glancing at a letter. Then I was to show him up to Mr Cornworthy's room.'

'Were you also told to knock on the door?'

An expression of distaste crossed the butler's countenance.

'That was one of Mr Farley's orders. I was always to knock when introducing visitors—business visitors, that is,' he added.

'Ah, that puzzled me! Were you given any other instructions concerning me?'

'No, sir. When Mr Cornworthy had told me what I have just repeated to you he went out.'

'What time was that?'

'Ten minutes to nine, sir.'

'Did you see Mr Farley after that?'

'Yes, sir, I took him up a glass of hot water as usual at nine o'clock.'

'Was he then in his own room or in Mr Cornworthy's?'

'He was in his own room, sir.'

'You noticed nothing unusual about that room?'

'Unusual? No, sir.'

'Where were Mrs Farley and Miss Farley?'

'They had gone to the theatre, sir.'

'Thank you, Holmes, that will do.'

Holmes bowed and left the room. Poirot turned to the million-aire's widow.

'One more question, Mrs Farley. Had your husband good sight?'

'No. Not without his glasses.'

'He was very short-sighted?'

'Oh, yes, he was quite helpless without his spectacles.'

'He had several pairs of glasses?'

'Yes.'

'Ah,' said Poirot. He leaned back. 'I think that that concludes the case . . .'

There was silence in the room. They were all looking at the little man who sat there complacently stroking his moustache. On the inspector's face was perplexity, Dr Stillingfleet was frowning, Cornworthy merely stared uncomprehendingly, Mrs Farley gazed in blank astonishment, Joanna Farley looked eager.

Mrs Farley broke the silence.

'I don't understand, M. Poirot.' Her voice was fretful. 'The dream——'

'Yes,' said Poirot. 'That dream was very important.'

Mrs Farley shivered. She said:

'I've never believed in anything supernatural before—but now—to dream it night after night beforehand——'

'It's extraordinary,' said Stillingfleet. 'Extraordinary! If we hadn't got your word for it, Poirot, and if you hadn't had it straight from the horse's mouth——' he coughed in embarrassment, and readopting his professional manner, 'I beg your pardon, Mrs Farley. If Mr Farley himself had not told that story——'

'Exactly,' said Poirot. His eyes, which had been half-closed, opened suddenly. They were very green. *'If Benedict Farley hadn't told me——'*

He paused a minute, looking round at a circle of blank faces.

'There are certain things, you comprehend, that happened that evening which I was quite at a loss to explain. First, why make such a point of my bringing that letter with me?'

'Identification,' suggested Cornworthy.

'No, no, my dear young man. Really that idea is too ridiculous. There must be some much more valid reason. For not only did Mr Farley require to see that letter produced, but he definitely demanded that I should leave it behind me. And moreover even then he did not destroy it! It was found among his papers this afternoon. *Why did he keep it?*'

Joanna Farley's voice broke in. 'He wanted, in case anything happened to him, that the facts of his strange dream should be made known.'

Poirot nodded approvingly.

'You are astute, mademoiselle. That must—that can only be— the point of the keeping of the letter. When Mr Farley was dead, the story of that strange dream was to be told! That dream was very important. That dream, mademoiselle, was *vital!*'

'I will come now,' he went on, 'to the second point. After hearing his story I ask Mr Farley to show me the desk and the revolver. He seems about to get up to do so, then suddenly refuses. Why did he refuse?'

This time no one advanced an answer.

'I will put that question differently. *What was there in that next room that Mr Farley did not want me to see?*'

There was still silence.

'Yes,' said Poirot, 'it is difficult, that. And yet there was some reason—some *urgent* reason why Mr Farley received me in his secretary's room and refused point blank to take me into his own room. *There was something in that room he could not afford to have me see.*'

'And now I come to the third inexplicable thing that happened on that evening. Mr Farley, just as I was leaving, requested me to hand him the letter I had received. By inadvertence I handed him a communication from my laundress. He glanced at it and laid it down beside him. Just before I left the room I discovered my error—and rectified it! After that I left the house and—I admit it— I was completely at sea! The whole affair and especially that last incident seemed to me quite inexplicable.'

He looked round from one to the other.

'You do not see?'

Stillingfleet said, 'I don't really see how your laundress comes into it, Poirot.'

'My laundress,' said Poirot, 'was very important. That miserable woman who ruins my collars, was, for the first time in her life, useful to somebody. Surely you see—it is so obvious. Mr Farley glanced at that communication—*one glance* would have told him that it was the wrong letter—and yet he knew nothing. Why? *Because he could not see it properly!*'

Inspector Barnett said sharply, 'Didn't he have his glasses on?'

Hercule Poirot smiled. 'Yes,' he said. 'He had his glasses on. That is what makes it so very interesting.'

He leaned forward.

'Mr Farley's dream was very important. He dreamed, you see, that he committed suicide. And a little later on, he did commit suicide. That is to say he was alone in a room and was found there with a revolver by him, and no one entered or left the room at the time that he was shot. What does that mean? It means, does it not, that it *must* be suicide!'

'Yes,' said Stillingfleet.

Hercule Poirot shook his head.

'On the contrary,' he said. 'It was murder. An unusual and a very cleverly planned murder.'

Again he leaned forward, tapping the table, his eyes green and shining.

'Why did Mr Farley not allow me to go into his own room that evening. What was there in there that I must not be allowed to see? I think, my friends, that there was—Benedict Farley himself!'

He smiled at the blank faces.

'Yes, yes, it is not nonsense what I say. Why could the Mr Farley to whom I had been talking not realize the difference between two totally dissimilar letters? Because, *mes amis*, he was a man of *normal sight* wearing a pair of very powerful glasses. Those glasses would render a man of normal eyesight practically blind. Isn't that so, doctor?'

Stillingfleet murmured, 'That's so—of course.'

'Why did I feel that in talking to Mr Farley I was talking to a *mountebank*, to an actor playing a part? Because he *was* playing a part! Consider the setting. The dim room, the green shaded light turned blindingly away from the figure in the chair. What did I see—the famous patchwork dressing-gown, the beaked nose (faked with that useful substance, nose putty) the white crest of hair, the powerful lenses concealing the eyes. What evidence is there that Mr Farley ever had a dream? Only the story I was told and the evidence of *Mrs Farley*. What evidence is there that Benedict Farley kept a revolver in his desk? Again only the story told me and the word of Mrs Farley. Two people carried this fraud through—Mrs Farley and Hugo Cornworthy. Cornworthy wrote the letter to me, gave instructions to the butler, went out ostensibly to the cinema, but let himself in again immediately with a key, went to his room, made himself up, and played the part of Benedict Farley.

'And so we come to this afternoon. The opportunity for which Mr Cornworthy has been waiting arrives. There are two witnesses on the landing to swear that no one goes in or out of Benedict Farley's room. Cornworthy waits until a particularly heavy batch of traffic is about to pass. Then he leans out of his window, and with the lazytongs which he has purloined from the desk next door he holds an object against the window of that room. Benedict Farley comes to the window. Cornworthy snatches back the tongs and as Farley leans out, and the lorries are passing outside, Cornworthy shoots him with the revolver that he has ready. There is a blank wall opposite, remember. There can be no witness of the crime. Cornworthy waits for over half an hour, then gathers up some papers, conceals the lazytongs and the revolver between them and goes out on to the landing and into the next room. He replaces the tongs on the desk, lays down the revolver after pressing the dead man's fingers on it, and hurries out with the news of Mr Farley's "suicide".

'He arranges that the letter to me shall be found and that I shall arrive with my story—the story I heard *from Mr Farley's own lips*— of his extraordinary "dream"—the strange compulsion he felt to kill himself! A few credulous people will discuss the hypnotism theory—but the main result will be to confirm without a doubt that the actual hand that held the revolver was Benedict Farley's own.'

Hercule Poirot's eyes went to the widow's face—the dismay— the ashy pallor—the blind fear.

'And in due course,' he finished gently, 'the happy ending would have been achieved. A quarter of a million and two hearts that beat as one . . .'

John Stillingfleet, MD, and Hercule Poirot walked along the side of Northway House. On their right was the towering wall of the factory. Above them, on their left, were the windows of Benedict Farley's and Hugo Cornworthy's rooms. Hercule Poirot stopped and picked up a small object—a black stuffed cat.

'*Voilà*,' he said. 'That is what Cornworthy held in the lazytongs against Farley's window. You remember, he hated cats? Naturally he rushed to the window.'

'Why on earth didn't Cornworthy come out and pick it up after he'd dropped it?'

'How could he? To do so would have been definitely suspicious. After all, if this object were found what would anyone think—that some child had wandered round here and dropped it.'

'Yes,' said Stillingfleet with a sigh. 'That's probably what the ordinary person *would* have thought. But not good old Hercule! D'you know, old horse, up to the very last minute I thought you were leading up to some subtle theory of high falutin' psychological "suggested" murder? I bet those two thought so too! Nasty bit of goods, the Farley. Goodness, how she cracked! Cornworthy might have got away with it if she hadn't had hysterics and tried to spoil your beauty by going for you with her nails. I only got her off you just in time.'

He paused a minute and then said:

'I rather like the girl. Grit, you know, and brains. I suppose I'd be thought to be a fortune hunter if I had a shot at her . . . ?'

'You are too late, my friend. There is already someone *sur le tapis*. Her father's death has opened the way to happiness.'

'Take it all round, *she* had a pretty good motive for bumping off the unpleasant parent.'

'Motive and opportunity are not enough,' said Poirot. 'There must also be the criminal temperament!'

'I wonder if you'll ever commit a crime, Poirot?' said Stillingfleet. 'I bet you could get away with it all right. As a matter of fact, it would be *too* easy for you—I mean the thing would be off as definitely too unsporting.'

'That,' said Poirot, 'is a typically English idea.'

The Ginger King

A. E. W. Mason

MONSIEUR HANAUD was smoking one of Mr Ricardo's special Havanas in the dining-room of Mr Ricardo's fine house in Grosvenor Square. The trial which had fetched him over from Paris had ended that morning. He had eaten a very good lunch with his friend; he had taken the napkin down from his collar; he was at his ease; and as he smoked, alas! he preached.

'Chance, my friend, is the detective's best confederate. A little unimportant word you use and it startles—a strange twist of character is provoked to reveal itself—an odd incident breaks in on the routine of your investigation. And the mind pounces. "Ping," you say, if you play the table-tennis. "Pong," you say, if you play the Mahjongh. And there you are! In at the brush.'

'I beg your pardon.'

For the moment Mr Ricardo was baffled.

'I said, "You are in at the brush,"' Hanaud repeated amicably.

Mr Ricardo smiled with indulgence. He too had eaten his share of an admirable saddle of lamb and drunk his half of a bottle of exquisite Haut Brion.

'You mean, of course, that you are in at the death,' he said.

'No, no,' Hanaud protested, starting forward. 'I do not speak of executions. Detectives are never present at executions and, for me, I find them disgusting. I say, you are in at the brush. It is an idiom from your hunting-field. It means that when all the mess is swept up, you are *there*, the Man who found the Lady under the thimble.'

Mr Ricardo was in no mood to pursue his large friend through the winding mazes of his metaphors.

'I am beginning to understand you,' he answered with resignation.

'Yes.' Hanaud nodded his head complacently. 'I speak the precision. It is known.'

With a gentle knock, Mr Ricardo's incomparable butler Thomson entered the room.

'A Mr Middleton has called,' he said, offering to Ricardo a visiting-card upon a salver.

Ricardo waved the salver away.

'I do not see visitors immediately after luncheon. It is an unforgivable time to call. Send him away!'

The butler, however, persisted.

'I took the liberty of pointing out that the hour was unseasonable,' he said, 'but Mr Middleton was in hopes that Monsieur Hanaud was staying with you. He seemed very anxious.'

Ricardo took up the card reluctantly. He read aloud.

'Mr John Middleton, Secretary of the Unicorn Fire Insurance Company. I am myself insured with that firm.' He turned towards his guest. 'No doubt he has some reason to excuse him. But it is as you wish.'

Monsieur Hanaud's strange ambition that afternoon was to climb the Monument and to see the Crown Jewels at the Tower, but his good nature won the day, and since he was to find more than one illustration of the text upon which he had been preaching, he never regretted it.

'I am on view,' he said simply.

'We will see Mr Middleton in the Library,' said Mr Ricardo; and into that spacious dormitory of deep armchairs and noble books Mr Middleton was introduced.

Hanaud was delighted with the look of him. Mr Middleton was a collector's piece of Victorian England. Middle-aged, with dangling whiskers like lappets at the sides of an otherwise clean-shaven face, very careful and a trifle old-maidish in his speech, he had a tittering laugh and wore the long black frock-coat and the striped trousers which once made the City what it was. He was wreathed in apologies for his intrusion.

'My good friend Superintendent Holloway, of Marlborough Street, whose little property is insured with us, thought that I might find you at Mr Ricardo's house. I am very fortunate.'

'I must return to Paris tomorrow,' Hanaud replied. 'For this afternoon I am at your service. You will smoke?'

From his pocket Hanaud tendered a bright blue packet of black stringy cigarettes, and Mr Middleton recoiled as if he suddenly saw a cobra on the carpet ready to strike.

'Oh no, no!' he cried in dismay. 'A small mild cigar when the day's work is done. You will forgive me? I have a little story to tell.'

'Proceed!' said Hanaud graciously.

'It is a Mr Enoch Swallow,' Mr Middleton began. 'I beg you not to be misled by his name. He is a Syrian gentleman by birth and an English gentleman by naturalization. But again I beg you not to be misled. There is nothing of the cunning of the Orient about him. He is a big, plain, simple creature, a peasant, one might say as honest as the day. And it may be so. I make no accusation.'

'He has a business, this honest man?' Hanaud asked.

'He is a furrier.'

'You begin to interest me,' said Hanaud.

'A year ago Enoch Swallow fitted up for his business a house in Berwick Street, towards the Oxford Street end of that long and narrow thoroughfare. The ground floor became his showrooms, he and his wife with a cook-general to wait on them occupied the first floor, and the two storeys above were elaborately arranged for his valuable stock. Then he came to us for an insurance policy.'

'Aha!' said Monsieur Hanaud.

'We hesitated,' continued Mr Middleton, stroking one of his side whiskers. 'Everything was as it should be—the lease of the house, compliance with the regulations of the County Council, the value of the stock—mink, silver fox, sables—all correct, and yet we hesitated.'

'Why?' asked Hanaud.

'Mind, I make no suggestion.' Mr Middleton was very insistent upon his complete detachment. 'It was held to be an accident. The Société Universelle paid the insurance money. But Mr Enoch Swallow did have a fire in a similar establishment on the Boulevard Haussmann in Paris three years before.'

'Enoch Swallow? The Boulevard Haussmann?' Hanaud dived deep amongst his memories but came to the surface with empty hands. 'No, I do not remember. There was no case.'

'Oh dear me, no,' Mr Middleton insisted. 'Oh none at all. Fires happen, else why does one insure? So in the end—it is our business and competition is severe and nothing could have been more straightforward than the conduct of our client—we insured him.'

'For a large sum?'

'For twenty-five thousand pounds.'

Hanaud whistled. He multiplied the amount into francs. It became milliards.

'For a Syrian gentleman, even if he is now an English gentleman, it is a killing.'

'And then last night it all happens again,' cried Mr Middleton, giving his whisker a twist and a slap. 'Would you believe it?'

'I certainly would,' replied Hanaud, 'and without bringing the least pressure upon my credulity.'

Mr Middleton raised a warning hand.

'But, remember please, there is no accusation. No. All is above board. No smell of petrol in the ruins. No little machine with an alarm-clock. Nothing.'

'And yet . . .' said Hanaud with a smile. 'You have your little thoughts.'

The secretary tittered.

'Monsieur Hanaud,' he said coyly, 'I have in my day been something of a dasher. I went once to the Moulin Rouge. I tried once to smoke a stringy black cigarette from a blue packet. But the strings got between my teeth and caused me extreme discomfort. Well, today I have Mr Enoch Swallow between my teeth.'

Mr Ricardo, who all this time had been sitting silent, thought it a happy moment to make a little jest that if the secretary swallowed Mr Swallow, he would suffer even more discomfort. But though Middleton tittered dutifully, Hanaud looked a thousand reproaches and Mr Ricardo subsided.

'I want to hear of last night,' said Hanaud.

It was the cook-general's night out. She had permission, moreover, to stay the night with friends at Balham. She had asked for that permission herself. No hint had been given to her that her absence would be welcome. Her friends had invited her and she had sought for this leave on her own initiative.

'Well, then,' continued Mr Middleton, 'at six o'clock she laid a cold supper for the Swallows in the dining-room and took an

A. E. W. Mason

omnibus to Balham. The employees had already gone. The show-rooms were closed and only Enoch Swallow and his wife were left in the house. At seven those two ate their supper, and after locking the front door behind them went to a cinema-house in Oxford Street where a French film was being shown. *Toto et Fils* was the name of the film.'

They arrived at the cinema-house a few minutes past eight. There was no doubt whatever about that. For they met the manager of the house, with whom they were acquainted, in the lobby, and talked with him whilst they waited for the earlier performance to end and its audience to disperse. They had seats in the Grand Circle, and there the manager found them just before eleven o'clock, when he brought them the news that their premises were on fire.

'Yes, the incontestable alibi,' said Hanaud. 'I was waiting for him.'

'They hurried home,' Middleton resumed, but Hanaud would not allow the word.

'Home? Have such people a home? A place full of little valueless treasures which you would ache to lose? The history of your small triumphs, your great griefs, your happy hours? No, no, we keep to facts. They had a store and a shop and a lodging, and they come back and it is all in flames. Good! We continue. When was this fire first noticed?'

'About half-past nine, a passer-by saw the smoke curling out from the door. He crossed the street and he saw a flame shoot up and spread behind a window—he thinks on the first floor. But he will not swear that it wasn't on the second. It took him a few minutes to find one of the red pillars where you give the alarm by breaking the glass. The summer has been dry, all those painted pitch-pine shelves in the upper storeys were like tinder. By the time the fire brigade arrived, the house was a bonfire. By the time the Swallows were discovered in the cinema and ran back to Berwick Street, the floors were crashing down. When the cook-general returned at six-thirty this morning, it was a ruin of debris and tottering walls.'

'And the Swallows?' Hanaud asked.

'They had lost everything. They had nothing but the clothes they were wearing. They were taken in for the night at a little hotel in Percy Street.'

'The poor people!' said Hanaud with a voice of commiseration and a face like a mask. 'And how do they explain the fire?'

'They do not,' said Middleton. 'The good wife she weeps, the man is distressed and puzzled. He was most careful, he says, and since the fire did not start until some time after he and his wife had left the house, he thinks some burglar is to blame. Ah yes!' and Mr Middleton pushed himself forward on his chair. 'There is a little something. He suggests—it is not very nice—that the burglar may have been a friend of the cook-general. He has no evidence. No. He used to think her a simple, honest, stupid woman and not a good cook, but now he is not sure. No, it is not a nice suggestion.'

'But we must remember that he was a Syrian gentleman before he became an English one, must we not?' said Hanaud. 'Yes, such suggestions were certainly to be expected. You have seen him?'

'Of course,' cried Mr Middleton, and he edged so much more forward in his chair that it seemed he must topple off. 'And I should esteem it a favour if you, Monsieur Hanaud, and your friend Mr Ricardo'—he gathered the derelict Ricardo gracefully into the council—'would see him too.'

Hanaud raised his hands in protest.

'It would be an irregularity of the most extreme kind. I have no place in this affair. I am the smelly outsider'; and by lighting one of his acrid cigarettes, he substantiated his position.

Mr Middleton waved the epithet and the argument away. He would never think of compromising Monsieur Hanaud. He meant 'see' and not examine, and here his friend Superintendent Holloway had come to his help. The superintendent had also wished to see Mr Enoch Swallow. He had no charge to bring against Enoch. To Superintendent Holloway, as Superintendent, Enoch Swallow was the victim of misfortune, insured of course, but still a victim. None the less the superintendent wanted to have a look at him. He had accordingly asked him to call at the Marlborough Street police station at five o'clock.

'You see, the superintendent has a kindly, pleasant reason for his invitation. Mr Swallow will be grateful and the superintendent will see him. Also you, Monsieur Hanaud, from the privacy of the superintendent's office can see him too and perhaps—who knows—a memory may be jogged?'

Mr Middleton stroked a whisker and smiled ingratiatingly.

'After all, twenty-five thousand pounds! It is a sum.'

'It is the whole multiplication table,' Hanaud agreed.

He hesitated for a moment. There was the Monument, there were the Crown Jewels. On the other hand, he liked Mr Middleton's polite, engaging ways, he liked his whiskers and his frock-coat. Also he, too, would like to see the Syrian gentleman. For . . .

'He is either a very honest unlucky man, or he has a formula for fireworks.' Hanaud looked at the clock. It was four.

'We have an hour. I make you a proposal. We will go to Berwick Street and see these ruins, though that beautiful frock-coat will suffer.'

Mr Middleton beamed. 'It would be worth many frock-coats to see Monsieur Hanaud at work,' he exclaimed, and thereupon Mr Ricardo made rather tartly—for undoubtedly he had been neglected—his one effective contribution to this story.

'But the frock-coat won't suffer, Mr Middleton. Ask Hanaud! It will be in at the brush.'

To north and south of the house, Berwick Street had been roped off against the danger of those tottering walls. The Salvage Company had been at work since the early morning clearing the space within, but there were still beams insecurely poised overhead, and a litter of broken furniture and burnt furrier's stock encumbered the ground. Middleton's pass gave them admittance into the shell of the building. Hanaud looked around with the pleased admiration of a connoisseur for an artist's masterpiece.

'Aha!' he said brightly. 'I fear that Misters the Unicorn pay twenty-five thousand pounds. It is of an admirable completeness, this fire. We say either "What a misfortune!" or "What a formula!"'

He advanced, very wary of the joists and beams balanced above his head, but shirking none of them. 'You will not follow me, please,' he said to Ricardo and Middleton. 'It is not for your safety. But, as my friend Ricardo knows, too many cooks and I'm down the drain.'

He went forward and about, mapping out from the fragments of inner walls the lie of the rooms. Once he stopped and came back to the two visitors.

'There was electric light of course,' he said rather than asked. 'I can see here and there plugs and pipes.'

'There was nothing but electric light and power,' Middleton

replied firmly. 'The cooking was done on an electric stove and the wires were all carried in steel tubes. Since the store and the stock were inflammable, we took particular care that these details were carried out.'

Hanaud returned to his pacing. At one place a heavy iron bath had crashed through the first-floor ceiling to the ground, its white paint burnt off and its pipes twisted by the heat. At this bath he stopped again, he raised his head into the air and sniffed, then he bent down towards the ground and sniffed again. He stood up with a look of perplexity upon his face, a man trying to remember and completely baffled.

He moved away from this centre in various directions as though he was walking outwards along the spokes of a wheel, but he always came back to it. Finally, he stooped and began to examine some broken lumps of glass which lay about and in the bath. It seemed to the watchers that he picked one of these pieces up, turned it over in his hands, held it beneath his nose and finally put it away in one of his pockets. He returned to his companions.

'We must be at Marlborough Street at five,' he said. 'Let us go!'

Mr Ricardo at the rope-barrier signalled to a taxi driver. They climbed into it, and sat in a row, both Middleton and Ricardo watching Hanaud expectantly, Hanaud sitting between them very upright with no more expression upon his face than has the image of an Egyptian king. At last he spoke.

'I tell you something.'

A sigh of relief broke from Mr Middleton. Mr Ricardo smiled and looked proud. His friend was certainly the Man who found the Lady under the thimble.

'Yes, I tell you. The Syrian gentleman has become an English gentleman. He owns a bath.'

Mr Middleton groaned. Ricardo shrugged his shoulders. It was a deplorable fact that Hanaud never knew when not to be funny.

'But you smelt something,' said Mr Middleton reproachfully.

'You definitely sniffed,' said Ricardo.

'Twice,' Mr Middleton insisted.

'Three times,' replied Hanaud.

'Ah!' cried Ricardo. 'I know. It was petrol.'

'Yes,' exclaimed Mr Middleton excitedly. 'Petrol stored secretly in the bath.'

Hanaud shook his head.

'Not 'arf,' he said. 'No, but perhaps I sniff,' and he laid a hand upon an arm of each of his companions, 'a formula. But here we are, are we not? I see a policeman at a door.'

They had indeed reached Marlborough Street police station. A constable raised the flap of a counter and they passed into a large room. An inner door opened and Superintendent Holloway appeared on the threshold, a large man with his hair speckled with grey, and a genial, intelligent face.

'Monsieur Hanaud!' he said, coming forward with an outstretched hand. 'This is a pleasant moment for me.'

'And the same to you,' said Hanaud in his best English.

'You had better perhaps come into my room,' the superintendent continued. 'Mr Swallow has not yet arrived.'

He led his visitors into a comfortable office and, shutting the door, invited them all to be seated. A large—everything about the Marlborough Street police station seemed to Hanaud to be large—a large beautiful ginger cat with amber-coloured lambent eyes lay with his paws doubled up under his chest on a fourth chair, and surveyed the party with a godlike indifference.

'You will understand, Monsieur Hanaud,' said the superintendent, 'that I have nothing against Mr Swallow at all. But I thought that I would like to see him, and I had an excellent excuse for asking him to call. I like to see people.'

'I too,' Hanaud answered politely. 'I am of the sociables.'

'You will have the advantage over me, of seeing without being seen,' said the superintendent, and he broke off with an exclamation.

The ginger cat had risen from the chair and jumped down on to the floor. There it stretched out one hind leg and then the other, deliberately, as though it had the whole day for that and nothing else. Next it stepped daintily across the floor to Hanaud, licked like a dog the hand which he dropped to stroke it, and then sprang on to his knee and settled down. Settled down, however, is not the word. It kept its head in the air and looked about in a curious excitement whilst its brown eyes shone like jewels.

'Well, upon my word,' said the superintendent. 'That's the first time that cat has recognized the existence of anyone in the station. But there it is. All cats are snobs.'

It was a pretty compliment, and doubtless Monsieur Hanaud

would have found a fitting reply had not the constable in the outer office raised his voice.

'If you'll come through and take a seat, sir, I'll tell the superintendent,' he was heard to say, and Holloway rose to his feet.

'I'll leave the door ajar,' he said in a low voice, and he went into the outer office.

Through the slit left open, Hanaud and Ricardo saw Enoch Swallow rise from his chair. He was a tall, broad man, almost as tall and broad as the superintendent himself, with black short hair and a flat, open, peasant face.

'You wished to see me?' he asked. He had a harsh metallic voice, but the question itself was ordinary and civil. The man was neither frightened, nor arrogant, nor indeed curious.

'Yes,' replied the superintendent. 'I must apologize for asking you to call at a time which must be very inconvenient to you. But we have something of yours.'

'Something of mine?' asked Mr Swallow, perhaps a little more slowly than was quite natural.

'Yes,' said the superintendent briskly, 'and I thought that you would probably like it returned to you at once.'

'Of course. I thank you very much. I thought we had lost everything. What is it?' asked Mr Swallow.

'A cat,' the superintendent answered, and Mr Swallow stood with his mouth open and the colour ebbing from his cheeks. The change in him was astonishing. A moment before he had been at his ease, confident, a trifle curious; now he was a man struck out of his wits; he watched the superintendent with dazed eyes, he swallowed, and his face was the colour of dirty parchment.

'Yes, a big ginger cat,' Holloway continued easily, 'with the disdain of an Emperor. But the poor beast wasn't disdainful last night, I can tell you. As soon as the door was broken in—you had a pretty good door, Mr Swallow, and a pretty strong lock—no burglars for you, Mr Swallow, eh?' and the superintendent laughed genially—'well, as soon as it was broken in, the cat scampered out and ran up one of my officer's legs under his cape and clung there, whimpering and shaking and terrified out of its senses. And I don't wonder. It had a near shave of a cruel death.'

'And you have it here, Superintendent?'

'Yes. I brought it here, gave it some milk, and it has owned my room ever since.'

Enoch Swallow sat down again in his chair, and rather suddenly, for his knees were shaking. He gave one rather furtive look round the room and the ceiling. Then he said:

'I am grateful.'

But he became aware with the mere speaking of the words that his exhibition of emotion required an ampler apology. 'I explain to you,' he said spreading out his hands. 'For me cats are not so important. But my poor wife—she loves them. All last night, all today, she has made great trouble for me over the loss of our cat. In her mind she saw it burnt, its fur first sparks then flames. Horrible!' and Enoch Swallow shut his eyes. 'Now that it is found unhurt, she will be happy. My store, my stock all gone, pouf! Of no consequence. But the Ginger King back again, all is well,' and with a broad smile, Enoch Swallow called the whole station to join him in a humorous appreciation of the eccentricities of women.

'Right!' the superintendent exclaimed. 'I'll fetch the Ginger King for you'; and at once all Enoch Swallow's muscles tightened and up went his hands in the air.

'Wait, please!' he cried. 'There is a shop in Regent Street where they sell everything. I will run there and buy a basket with a lid for the Ginger King. Then you shall strap him in and I will take him to my wife, and tonight there will be no unpleasantness. One little moment!'

Mr Enoch Swallow backed out of the entrance and was gone. Superintendent Holloway returned to his office with all the geniality gone from his face. He was frowning heavily.

'Did you ever see that man before, Monsieur Hanaud?' he asked.

'Never,' said Hanaud decisively.

The superintendent shook his head.

'Funny! That's what I call him. Yes, funny.'

Mr Ricardo laughed in a superior way. There was no problem for him.

'"Some that are mad if they behold a cat,"' he quoted. 'Really, really our William knew everything.'

Monsieur Hanaud caught him up quickly.

'Yes, this Enoch Swallow, he hates a cat. He has the cat complex. He grows green at the thought that he must carry a cat in a basket, yes. Yet he has a cat in the house, he submits to a cat which he cannot endure without being sick, because his wife loves it! Do you think it likely? Again I say "not arf".'

A rattle and creak of wickerwork against the raised flap of the counter in the outer office announced Enoch Swallow's return.

The superintendent picked up the Ginger King and walked with it into the outer office. Mr Ricardo, glancing through the open doorway, saw Mr Swallow's dark face turn actually green. The sergeant at the desk, indeed, thought that he was going to faint, and started forward. Enoch Swallow caught hold upon himself. He held out the basket to the superintendent.

'If you will put him into it and strap the lid down, it will be all right. I make myself ridiculous,' he said, with a feeble attempt at a smile. 'A big strong fellow whose stomach turns over at the sight of a cat. But it is so.'

The Ginger King resented the indignity of being imprisoned in a basket; it struggled and spat and bit as if it were the most communistic of cats, but the superintendent and the sergeant between them got it strapped down at last.

'I'll tell you what I'll do, sir,' said Holloway. 'I'll send the little brute by one of my men round to your hotel—Percy Street, wasn't it?—and then you won't be bothered with it at all.'

But Enoch wouldn't hear of putting the station to so much trouble.

'Oh no, no! You are kindness itself, Superintendent. But once he is in the basket, I shall not mind him. I shall take him home at once and my wife will keep him away from me. It is all right. See, I carry him.'

Enoch Swallow certainly did carry him, but very gingerly, and with the basket held well away from his side.

'It would be no trouble to send him along,' the superintendent urged, but again the Syrian refused, and with the same vehemence which he had shown before. The police had its work to do. It would humiliate him to interfere with it for so small a reason.

'I have after all not very far to go,' and with still more effusive protestations of his gratitude, he backed out of the police station.

The superintendent returned to his office.

'He wouldn't let me send it home for him,' he said. He was a very mystified man. 'Funny! That's what I call it. Yes, funny.' He looked up and broke off suddenly. 'Hallo! Where's Monsieur Hanaud gone to?'

Both Middleton and Ricardo had been watching through the crack in the door the scene in the outer office. Neither of them had seen or heard Hanaud go. There was a second door which opened on the passage to the street, and by that second door Hanaud had slipped away.

'I am sorry,' said the superintendent, a little stiffly. 'I should have liked to say goodbye to him.'

The superintendent was hurt, and Mr Ricardo hastened to reassure him.

'It wasn't discourtesy,' he said staunchly. 'Hanaud has manners. There is some reason.'

Middleton and Ricardo returned to the latter's house in Grosvenor Square, and there, a little more than an hour afterwards, Hanaud rejoined them. To their amazement he was carrying Enoch Swallow's basket, and from the basket he took out a contented, purring, gracious Ginger King.

'A little milk, perhaps?' Hanaud suggested. And having lapped up the milk, the Ginger King mounted a chair, turned in his paws under his chest and once more surveyed the world with indifferent eyes.

Hanaud explained his sudden departure.

'I could not understand why this man who could not abide a cat refused to let the superintendent send it home for him. No, however much he shivered and puked, he would carry it home himself. I had a little thought in my mind that he didn't mean to carry it home at all. So I slipped out into the street and waited for him and followed him. He had never seen me. It was as easy as the alphabet. He walked in a great hurry down to the Charing Cross Road and past the Trafalgar Square and along the Avenue of Northumberland. At the bottom of the Avenue of Northumberland there is—what? Yes, you have guessed him. The river Thames. "Aha," I say to myself "my friend Enoch, you are going to drown the Ginger King. But I, Hanaud, will not allow it. For if you are so anxious to drown him, the Ginger King has something to tell us."

'So I close up upon his heels. He crossed the road, he leaned over the parapet, swinging the basket carelessly in his hand as though he was thinking of some important matter and not of the Ginger King at all. He looked on this side and that, and then I slip my hand under the basket from behind, and I say in his ear:

'"Sir, you will drop that basket, if you don't look out."

'Enoch, he gave a great jump and he drop the basket, this time by accident. But my hand is under it. Then I take it by the handle, I make a bow, I hand it to him, I say "Dr Livingstone, I presume?" and lifting my hat, I walk away. But not so far. I see him black in the face with rage. But he dare not try the river again. He thinks for a little. Then he crosses the road and dashes through the Underground Station. I follow as before. But now he has seen me. He knows my dial,' and at Middleton's surprised expression, he added, 'my face. It is a little English idiom I use. So I keep further back, but I do not lose him. He runs up that steep street. Half-way up, he turns to the right.'

'John Street,' said Mr Ricardo.

'Half-way up John Street, there is a turning to the left under a building. It is a tunnel and dark. Enoch raced into the tunnel. I follow, and just as I come to the mouth of it, the Ginger King comes flashing out like a strip of yellow lightning. You see. He could not drown him, so in the dark tunnel he turns him loose with a kick no doubt to make him go. The Ginger King is no longer, if he ever was, the pet of the sad Mrs Swallow. He is just a stray cat. Dogs will set on him, no one will find him, all the time he must run and very soon he will die.

'But this time he does not need to run. He sees or smells a friend, Hanaud of the Sureté, that joke, that comic—eh, my friend?' and he dug a fist into Ricardo's ribs which made that fastidious gentleman bend like a sapling in a wind. 'Ah, you do not like the familiarities. But the Ginger King to the contrary. He stops, he mews, he arches his back and rubs his body against Hanaud's leg. So I pick him up and I go on into the tunnel. It winds, and at the point where it bends I find the basket with the lid. It is logical. Enoch has dismissed the Ginger King. Therefore he wants nothing to remind him of the Ginger King. He drops the basket. I insert the Ginger King once more. He has confidence, he does not struggle. I strap down the lid. I come out of the tunnel. I am in the Strand. I look right and left and everywhere. There is no Enoch. I call a taximan.'

'And you are here,' said Ricardo, who thought the story had been more than sufficiently prolonged. But Hanaud shook his head.

'No, I am not here yet. There are matters of importance in between.'

'Very well,' said Ricardo languidly. 'Proceed.'

And Hanaud proceeded.

'I put the basket on the seat and I say to the taximan, "I want"— guess what?—but you will not guess. "I want the top-dog chemist." The taximan wraps himself round and round with clothes and we arrive at the top-dog chemist. There I get just the information which I need and now, my friend Ricardo, here I am with the Ginger King who sits with a Chinese face and will tell us nothing of what he knows.'

But he was unjust. For later on that evening, in his own good time, the Ginger King told them plenty.

They were sitting at dinner at a small mahogany table bright with silver and fine glass: Mr Ricardo between Hanaud and Middleton, and opposite to Ricardo, with his head just showing above the mahogany, the Ginger King. Suddenly one of those little chancy things upon which Hanaud had preached his sermon, happened. The electric light went out.

They sat in the darkness, their voices silenced. Outside the windows the traffic rumbled by, suddenly important. An unreasonable suspense stole into the three men, and they sat very still and aware that each was breathing as lightly as he could. Perhaps for three minutes this odd tension lasted, and then the invaluable Thomson came into the room carrying a lighted lamp. It was an old-fashioned oil affair with a round of baize cloth under the base, a funnel and an opaque globe in the heart of which glowed a red flame.

'A fuse has blown, sir,' he said.

'At a most inconsiderate moment,' Mr Ricardo replied. He had been in the middle of a story and he was not pleased.

'I'll replace it at once, sir.'

'Do so, Thomson.'

Thomson set the glowing lamp in the middle of the table and withdrew. Mr Middleton leaned forward towards Ricardo.

'You had reached the point where you tiptoed down the stairs——'

'No, no,' Ricardo interrupted. 'The chain is broken. The savour of the story gone. It was a poor story, anyway.'

'You mustn't say that,' cried Hanaud. 'The story was of a thrill. The Miss Braddon at her best.'

'Oh well, well, if you really think so,' said Mr Ricardo, tittering modestly; and there were the three faces smiling contentedly in the light of the lamp, when suddenly Hanaud uttered a cry.

'Look! Look!'

It was a cry so sharp that the other two men were captured by it and must look where Hanaud was looking. The Ginger King was staring at the lamp, its amber eyes as red as the flame in the globe, its body trembling. They saw it rise on to its feet and leap on to the edge of the table, where it crouched again, and rose again, its eyes never changing from their direction. Very delicately it padded between the silver ornaments across the shining mahogany. Then it sat back upon its haunches and, raising its forepaws, struck once violently at the globe of the lamp. The blow was so swift, so savage that it shocked the three men who watched. The lamp crashed upon the table with a sound of broken glass and the burning oil was running this way and that and dropping in great gouts of fire on to the carpet.

Middleton and Ricardo sprang up, a chair was overturned.

'We'll have the whole house on fire,' cried Ricardo as he rang the bell in a panic; and Hanaud had just time to snatch up the cat as it dived at the green cloth on the base of the stand, before the flames caught it; and it screamed and fought and clawed like a mad thing. To get away? No, but to get back to the overturned lamp.

Already there was a smell of burning fabrics in the room. Some dried feathery grass in a vase caught a sprinkle of the burning oil and flamed up against the wallpaper. Thomson arrived with all the rugs he could hurriedly gather to smother the fire. Pails of water were brought, but a good many minutes had passed before the conflagration was extinguished, and the four men, with their clothes dishevelled, and their hands and faces begrimed could look round upon the ruin of the room.

'I should have guessed,' said Hanaud remorsefully. 'The Unicorn Company saves its twenty-five thousand pounds—yes, but Mr Ricardo's fine dining-room will need a good deal of restoration.'

*

Later on that night, in a smaller room, when the electric light was burning and the three men were washed and refreshed, Hanaud made his apology.

'I asked you, Mr Middleton, inside the burnt walls of the house in Berwick Street, whether it was lit with electric light. And you answered, "with that and with nothing else". But I had seen a broken oil lamp amongst the litter. I suspected that lamp, but the house was empty for an hour and a half before the fire broke out. I couldn't get over that fact. Then I smelt something, something acrid—just a whiff of it. It came from a broken bottle lying by the bath with other broken bottles and a broken glass shelf, such as a man has in his bathroom to hold his little medicines, his tooth paste, his shaving soap. I put the broken bottle in my pocket and a little of that pungent smell clung to my fingers.

'At the police station at once the cat made friends with me. Why? I did not guess. In fact I flattered myself a little. I say, "Hanaud, animals love you." But it was not so. The Ginger King loved my smelly fingers, that was all. Then came the strange behaviour of Enoch Swallow. Cats made him physically sick. Yet this one he must take away before it could betray him. He could not carry it under his coat—no, that was too much. But he could go out and buy a basket—and without any fear. Do you remember, how cunningly he looked around the office, and up at the ceiling, and how satisfied he was to leave the cat with us. Why? I noticed the look, but I could not understand it. It was because all the lights in the room were bulbs hanging from the ceiling. There was not a standing lamp anywhere. Afterwards I get the cat. I drive to the chemist, leaving the cat in its basket in the cab.

'I pull out my broken bottle and I ask the chemist. "What is it that was in this bottle?"

'He smells and he says at once, "Valerian".

'I say, "What is valerian?"

'He answers, "Valerian has a volatile oil which when exposed to the air develops a pungent and unpleasant smell. It is used for hysteria, insomnia and nervous ailments."

'That does not help me, but I draw a target at a venture. I ask, "Has it anything to do with cats?"

'The assistant, he looks at me as if I was off my rocker and he says, "It drives them mad, that's all," and at once I say:

'"Give me some!"' and Hanaud fetched out of his pocket a bottle of tincture of valerian.

'I have this—yes. But I am still a little stupid. I do not connect the broken lamp and the valerian and the Ginger King—no, not until I see him step up with his eyes all mad and on fire on to the mahogany table. And then it is too late.

'You see, the good Enoch practised a little first. He smears the valerian on the base of the lamp and he teaches the cat to knock it over to get at the valerian. Then one night he shuts the cat up in some thin linen bag through which in time it can claw its freedom. He smears the base of the lamp with the valerian, lights it and goes off to the cinema.

'The house is empty—yes. But the cat is there in the bag, and the lamp is lit and every minute the valerian at the bottom of the lamp smells more and more. And more and more the cat is maddened. Tonight there was no valerian on the lamp, but the Ginger King—he knows that that is where valerian is to be found. I shall find out when I get back to Paris whether there was any trace of a burnt cat at the fire on the Boulevard Haussmann.

'But,' and he turned towards Mr Middleton, 'you will keep the Ginger King that he may repeat his performance at the Courts of Law, and you will not pay one brass bean to that honest peasant from Syria.'

The Ministering Angel

E. C. Bentley

'WHATEVER the meaning of it may be, it's a devilish unpleasant business,' Arthur Selby said as he and Philip Trent established themselves on a sofa in the smoking-room of the Lansdowne Club. 'We see enough of that sort of business in the law—even firms like ours, that don't have much to do with crime, have plenty of unpleasantness to deal with, and I don't know that some of it isn't worse than the general run of crime. You know what I mean. Crazy spite, that's one thing. You wouldn't believe what some people— people of position and education and all that—you wouldn't believe what they are capable of when they want to do somebody a mischief. Usually it's a blood relation. And then there's constitutional viciousness. We had one client—he died soon after Snow took me into partnership—whose whole life had been one lascivious debauch.'

Trent laughed. 'That phrase doesn't sound like your own, Arthur. It belongs to an earlier generation.'

'Quite true,' Selby admitted. 'It was Snow told me that about old Sir William Never-mind-who, and it stuck in my memory. But come now—I'm wandering. A good lunch—by the way, I hope it *was* a good lunch.'

'One of the very best,' Trent said. 'You know it was too. Ordering lunches is one of the best things you do, and you're proud of it. That hock was a poem—a villanelle, for choice. What were you going to say about good lunches?'

'Why, I was going to say that a good lunch usually makes me inclined to prattle a bit; because, you see, all I allow myself most

days is a couple of apples and a glass of milk in the office. That's
the way to appreciate a thing: don't have it too often, and take a hell
of a lot of trouble about it when you do. But that isn't what I
wanted to talk to you about, Phil. I was saying just now that we get
a lot of unpleasantness in our job. We can usually understand it
when we get it, but the affair I want to tell you about is a puzzle to
me; and of course you are well known to be good at puzzles. If I tell
you the story, will you give me a spot of advice if you can?'

'Of course.'

'Well, it's about a client of ours who died a fortnight ago, named
Gregory Landell. You wouldn't have heard of him, I dare say; he
never did anything much outside his private hobbies, having always
had money and never any desire to distinguish himself. He could
have done, for he had plenty of brains—a brilliant scholar, always
reading Greek. He and my partner had been friends from boyhood;
at school and Cambridge together; had tastes in common; both rock-
garden enthusiasts, for one thing. Landell's was a famous rock-
garden. Other amateurs used to come from all parts to visit it, and
of course he loved that. Then they were both Lewis Carroll fans—
when they got together, bits from the *Alice* books and the *Snark*
were always coming into the conversation—both chess players,
both keen cricketers when they were young enough, and never tired
of watching first-class games. Snow used often to stay for weekends
at Landell's place at Cholsey Wood, in Berkshire.

'When Landell was over fifty, he married for the first time. The
lady was a Miss Mary Archer, daughter of a naval officer, and about
twenty years younger than Landell, at a guess. He was infatuated
with her, and she seemed to make a great fuss of him, though she
didn't strike me as being the warm-hearted type. She was a good-
looking wench with plenty of style, and gave you the idea of being
fond of her own way. We made his will for him, leaving everything
to her if there were no children. Snow and I were both appointed
executors. In his previous will he had left all his property to a
nephew; and we were sorry the nephew wasn't mentioned in this
later will, for he is a very useful citizen—some kind of medical
research worker—and he has barely enough to live on.'

'Why did he make both of you executors?' Trent wondered.

'Oh, in case anything happened to one of us. And it was just as
well, because early this year poor old Snow managed to fracture his

thigh, and he's been laid up ever since. But that's getting ahead of the story. After the marriage, Snow still went down to Landell's place from time to time, as before; but after a year or so he began to notice a great change in the couple. Landell seemed to get more and more under his wife's thumb. Couldn't call his soul his own.'

Trent nodded. 'After what you told me about the impression she made on you, that isn't surprising.'

'No: Snow and I had been expecting it to happen. But the worst of it was, Landell didn't take it easily, as some husbands in that position do. He was obviously very unhappy, though he never said anything about it to Snow. She had quite given up pretending to be affectionate or to consider him in any way, and Snow got the idea that Landell hated his wife like poison, though never daring to stand up to her. Yet he used to have plenty of character, too.'

'I have seen the sort of thing,' Trent said. 'Unless a man is a bit of a brute himself, he can't bear to see the woman making an exhibition of herself. He'll stand anything rather than have her make a scene.'

'Just so. Well, after a time Snow got no more invitations to go there; and as you may suppose, he didn't mind that. It had got to be too uncomfortable, and though he was devilish sorry for Landell, he didn't see that he could do anything for him. For one thing, she wouldn't ever leave them alone together if she could possibly help it. If they were pottering about with the rock-plants, or playing chess, or going for a walk, they always had her company.'

Trent made a grimace. 'Jolly for the visitor! And now, what was it you didn't understand?'

'I'll tell you. About a month ago a letter for Snow came to the office. I opened it—I was dealing with all his business correspondence. It was from Mrs Landell, saying that her husband was ill and confined to bed; that he wished to settle some business affairs, and would be most grateful if Snow could find time to come down on the following day.

'Well, Snow couldn't, of course. I got the idea from this letter, naturally, that the matter was more or less urgent. It read as if Landell was right at the end of his tether. So I rang up Mrs Landell, explained the situation, and said I would come myself that afternoon if it suited her. She said she would be delighted if I would; she was very anxious about her husband, whose heart was in a serious state.

I mentioned the train I would come by, and she said their car would meet it.

'When I got there, she took me up to Landell's bedroom at once. He was looking very bad, and seemed to have hardly strength enough to speak. There was a nurse in the room: Mrs Landell sent her out and stayed with us all the time I was there—which I had expected, after what I had heard from Snow. Then Landell began to talk, or whisper, about what he wanted done.

'It was a scheme for the rearrangement of his investments, and a shrewd one, too—he had a wonderful flair for that sort of thing, made a study of it. In fact'—Selby leant forward and tapped his friend's knee—'there was absolutely nothing for him to discuss with me. He knew exactly what he wanted done, and he needed no advice; he knew more about such matters than I did, or Snow either. Still, he made quite a show of asking my opinion of this detail and that, and all I could do was to look wise, and hum and haw, and then say that nothing could be better. Then he said that the exertion of writing a business letter was forbidden by his doctor, and would I oblige him by doing it for him? So I took down a letter of instructions to his brokers, which he signed; and his wife had the securities he was going to sell all ready in a long envelope; and that was that. The car took me to the station, and I got back in time for dinner, after an absolutely wasted half-day.'

Trent had listened to all this with eager attention. 'It was wasted, you say,' he observed. 'Do you mean he could have dictated such a letter to his wife, without troubling you at all?'

'To his wife, or to anybody who could write. And of course he knew that well enough. I tell you, all that business of consulting me was just camouflage. I knew it, and I could feel that he knew I knew it. But what the devil it was intended to hide is beyond me. I don't think his wife suspected anything queer; Snow always said she was a fool about business matters. She listened intently to everything that was said, and seemed quite satisfied. His instructions were acted upon, and he signed the transfers; I know that, because when I came to making an inventory of the estate, after his death, I found it had all been done. Now then, Phil: what do you make of all that?'

Trent caressed his chin for a few moments. 'You're quite sure that there *was* something unreal about the business? His wife, you say, saw nothing suspicious.'

'Of course I'm sure. His wife evidently didn't know that he was cleverer about investments than either Snow or me, and that anyhow it wasn't our job. If he *had* wanted advice, he could have had his broker down.'

Trent stretched his legs before him and carefully considered the end of his cigar. 'No doubt you are right,' he said at length. 'And it does sound as if there was something unpleasant below the surface. For that matter, the surface itself was not particularly agreeable, as you describe it. Mrs Landell, the ministering angel!' He rose to his feet. 'I'll turn the thing over in my mind, Arthur, and let you know if anything strikes me.'

Trent found the house in Cholsey Wood without much difficulty next morning. The place actually was a tract of woodland of large extent, cleared here and there for a few isolated modern houses and grounds, a row of cottages, an inn called the Magpie and Gate, and a Tudor manor-house standing in a well-tended park. The Grove, the house of which he was in search, lay half a mile beyond the inn on the road that bisected the neighbourhood. A short drive led up to it through the high hedge that bounded the property on this side, and Trent, turning his car into the opening, got out and walked to the house, admiring as he went the flower-bordered lawn on one side, the trim orchard on the other. The two-storied house, too, was a well-kept, well-built place, its porch overgrown by wistaria in full flower.

His ring was answered by a chubby maidservant, to whom he offered his card. He had been told, he said, that Mr Landell allowed visitors who were interested in gardening to see his rock-garden, of which Trent had heard so much. Would the maid take his card to Mr Landell, and ask if it would be convenient—here he paused, as a lady stepped from an open door at the end of the hall. Trent described her to himself as a handsome, brassy blonde with a hard blue eye.

'I am Mrs Landell,' she said, as she took the card from the girl and glanced at it. 'I heard what you were saying. I see, Mr Trent, you have not heard of my bereavement. My dear husband passed away a fortnight ago.' Trent began to murmur words of vague condolence and apology. 'Oh no,' she went on with a sad smile. 'You must not think you are disturbing me. You must certainly see the rock-garden now you are here. You have come a long way for the purpose, I dare say, and my husband would not have wished you to go away disappointed.'

'It is a famous garden,' Trent observed. 'I heard of it from some one I think you know—Arthur Selby, the lawyer.'

'Yes, he and his partner were my husband's solicitors,' the lady said. 'I will show you where the garden is, if you will come this way.' She turned and went before him through the house, until they came out through a glass-panelled door into a much larger extent of grounds. 'I cannot show it off to you myself,' she went on, 'I know absolutely nothing about that sort of gardening. My husband was very proud of it, and he was adding to the collection of plants up to the time he was taken ill last month. You see that grove of elms? The house is called after it. If you go along it you will come to a lily-pond, and the rock-garden is to the left of that. I fear I cannot entertain anyone just now, so I will leave you to yourself, and the parlour-maid will wait to let you out when you have seen enough.' She bowed her head in answer to his thanks, and retired into the house.

Trent passed down the avenue and found the object of his journey, a tall pile of roughly terraced grey rocks covered with a bewildering variety of plants rooted in the shallow soil provided for them. The lady of the house, he reflected, could hardly know less about rock-gardens than himself, and it was just as well that there was to be no dangerous comparing of ignorances. He did not even know what he was looking for. He believed that the garden had something to tell, and that was all. Pacing slowly up and down, with searching eye, before the stony rampart with its dress of delicate colours, he set himself to divine its secret.

Soon he noted a detail which, as he considered it, became more curious. Here and there among the multitude of plants there was one distinguished by a flat slip of white wood stuck in the soil among the stems, or just beside the growth. They were not many: searching about, he could find no more than seven. Written on each slip in a fair, round hand was a botanical name. Such names meant nothing to Trent; he could but wonder vaguely why they were there. Why were these plants thus distinguished? Possibly they were the latest acquisitions. Possibly Landell had so marked them to draw the attention of his old friend and fellow-enthusiast Snow.

Landell had been expecting Snow to come and see him, Trent remembered. Snow had been unable to come, and Arthur Selby had come instead. Another point: the business Landell had wanted done was trifling; anyone could have attended to it. Why had it been so important to Landell that Snow should come?

Had Landell been expecting to have a private talk with Snow about some business matter? No: because on previous occasions, as on this occasion, Mrs Landell had been present throughout the interview; it was evident, according to Selby, that she did not intend to leave her husband alone with his legal adviser at any time, and Landell must have realized that. Was this the main point: that the unfortunate Landell had been planning to communicate something to Snow by some means unknown to his wife?

Trent liked the look of this idea. It fitted into the picture, at least. More than that: it gave strong confirmation to the quite indefinite notion he had formed on hearing Selby's story; the notion that had brought him to Cholsey Wood that day. Snow was a keen amateur of rock-gardening. If Snow had come to visit Landell, one thing virtually certain was that Snow would not have gone away without having a look at his friend's collection of rock-plants, if only to see what additions might have been recently made. And such additions—so Mrs Landell had just been saying—had been made. Mrs Landell knew nothing about rock-gardening; even if she had wasted a glance on this garden, she would have noticed nothing. Snow would have noticed instantly anything out of the way. And what was there out of the way?

Trent began to whistle faintly.

The wooden slips had now a very interesting look. With notebook and pencil he began to write down the names traced upon them. *Armeria Hallerii*. And *Arcana Nieuwillia*. And *Saponaria Galspitosa*—good! And these delicate little blossoms, it appeared, rejoiced in the formidable name of *Acantholimon Glumaceum*. Then here was *Cartavacua Belmannii*. Trent's mind began to run on the nonsense botany of Edward Lear: *Nasticreechia Crawluppia* and the rest. This next one was *Veronica Incana*. And here was the last of the slips: *Ludovica Caroli*, quite a pretty name for a shapeless mass of grey-green vegetation that surely was commonly called, in the vulgar tongue——

At this point Trent flung his notebook violently to the ground, and followed it with his hat. What a fool he had been! What a triple ass, not to have jumped to the thing at once! He picked up the book and hurriedly scanned the list of names. . . . Yes: it was all there.

Three minutes later he was in his car on the way back to town.

In his room at the offices of Messrs Snow and Selby the junior partner welcomed Trent on the morning after his expedition to Cholsey Wood.

Selby pushed his cigarette box across the table. 'Can you tell it me in half an hour, do you think? I'd have been glad to come to lunch with you and hear it then, but this is a very full day, and I shan't get outside the office until seven, if then. What have you been doing?'

'Paying a visit to your late client's rock-garden,' Trent informed him. 'It made a deep impression on me. Mrs Landell was very kind about it.'

Selby stared at him. 'You always had the devil's own cheek,' he observed. 'How on earth did you manage that? And why?'

'I won't waste time over the how,' Trent said. 'As to the why, it was because it seemed to me, when I thought it over, that that garden might have a serious meaning underlying all its gaiety. And I thought so all the more when I found that Mary, Mary, quite contrary, hadn't a notion how her garden grew. You see, it was your partner whom Landell had wanted to consult about those investments of his; and it was hardly likely that your rock-gardening partner, once on the spot, would have missed the chance of feasting his eyes on his friend's collection of curiosities. So I went and feasted mine; and I found what I expected.'

'The deuce you did!' Selby exclaimed. 'And what was it?'

'Seven plants—only seven out of all the lot—marked with their botanical names, clearly written on slips of wood, *à la* Kew Gardens. I won't trouble you with four of the names—they were put there just to make it look more natural, I suppose; they were genuine names; I've looked them up. But you will find the other three interesting—choice Latin, picked phrase, if not exactly Tully's every word.'

Trent, as he said this, produced a card and handed it to his friend, who studied the words written upon it with a look of complete incomprehension.

'*Arcana Nieuwillia*,' he read aloud. 'I can't say that thrills me to the core, anyhow. What's an *Arcana*? Of course, I know no more about botany than a cow. It looks as if it was named after some Dutchman.'

'Well try the next,' Trent advised him.

'*Cartavacua Bellmannii*. No, that too fails to move me. Then what about the rest of the nosegay? *Ludovica Caroli*. No, it's no good, Phil. What *is* it all about?'

Trent pointed to the last name. 'That one was what gave it away to me. The slip with *Ludovica Caroli* on it was stuck into a clump of saxifrage. I know saxifrage when I see it; and I seemed to remember that the right scientific name for it was practically the same—*Saxifraga*. And then I suddenly remembered another thing: that Ludovicus is the Latin form of the name Louis, which some people choose to spell L-E-W-I-S.'

'What!' Selby jumped to his feet. 'Lewis—and Caroli! Lewis Carroll! Oh Lord! The man whose books Snow and Landell both knew by heart. Then it *is* a cryptogram.' He referred eagerly to the card. 'Well, then—*Cartavacua Bellmannii*. Hm! Would that be the Bellman in *The Hunting of the Snark*? And *Cartavacua*?'

'Translate it,' Trent suggested.

Selby frowned. 'Let's see. In law, *carta* used to be a charter. And *vacua* means empty. The Bellman's empty charter——'

'Or chart. Don't you remember?

He had bought a large map representing the sea,
    Without the least vestige of land:
And the crew were much pleased when they
        found it to be
    A map they could all understand.

And in the poem, one of the pages is devoted to the Bellman's empty map.'

'Oh! And that tells us——?'

'Why, I believe it tells us to refer to Landell's own copy of the book, and to that blank page.'

'Yes, but what for?'

'*Arcana Nieuwillia*, I expect.'

'I told you I don't know what *Arcana* means. It isn't law Latin, and I've forgotten most of the other kind.'

'This isn't law Latin, as you say. It's the real thing, and it means "hidden", Arthur, "hidden".'

'Hidden what?' Selby stared at the card again; then suddenly dropped into his chair and turned a pale face to his friend. 'My God, Phil! So that's it!'

'It can't be anything else, can it?'

Selby turned to his desk telephone and spoke into the receiver. 'I am not to be disturbed on any account till I ring.' He turned again to Trent . . .

'I asked Mr Trent to drive me down,' Selby explained, 'because I wanted his help in a matter concerning your husband's estate. He has met you before informally, he tells me.'

Mrs Landell smiled at Trent graciously. 'Only the other day he called to see the rock-garden. He mentioned that he was a friend of yours.'

She had received them in the morning-room at the Grove, and Trent, who on the occasion of his earlier visit had seen nothing but the hallway running from front to back, was confirmed in his impression that strict discipline ruled in that household. The room was orderly and speckless, the few pictures hung mathematically level, the flowers in a bowl on the table were fresh and well displayed.

'And what is the business that brings you and Mr Trent down so unexpectedly?' Mrs Landell enquired. 'Is it some new point about the valuation of the property, perhaps?' She looked from one to the other of them with round blue eyes.

Selby looked at her with an expression that was new in Trent's experience of that genial, rather sybaritic man of law. He was now serious, cool and hard.

'No, Mrs Landell; nothing to do with that,' Selby said. 'I am sorry to tell you I have reason to believe that your husband made another will not long ago, and that it is in this house. If there is such a will, and if it is in order legally, it will of course supersede the will made shortly after your marriage.'

Mrs Landell's first emotion on hearing this statement was to be seen in a look of obviously genuine amazement. Her eyes and mouth opened together, and her hands fell on the arms of her chair. The feeling that succeeded, which she did her best to control, was as plainly one of anger and incredulity.

'I don't believe a word of it,' she said sharply. 'It is quite impossible. My husband certainly did not see his solicitor, or any other lawyer, for a long time before his death. When he did see Mr Snow, I was always present. If he made another will, I must have known about it. The idea is absurd. Why should he have wanted to make another will?'

Selby shrugged. 'That I cannot say, Mrs Landell. The question does not arise. But if he had wanted to, he could make a will without a lawyer's assistance, and if it complied with the requirements of the law it would be a valid will. The position is that, as his legal adviser and executor of the will of which we know, I am bound to satisfy myself that there is no later will, if I have grounds for thinking that there is one. And I have grounds for thinking so.'

Mrs Landell made a derisive sound. 'Have you really? And grounds for thinking it is in this house, too? Well, I can tell you that it isn't. I have been through every single paper in the place, I have looked carefully everywhere, and there is no such thing.'

'There was nothing locked up then?' Selby suggested.

'Of course not,' Mrs Landell snapped. 'My husband had no secrets from me.'

Selby coughed. 'It may be so. All the same, Mrs Landell, I shall have to satisfy myself on the point. The law is very strict about matters of this kind, and I must make a search on my own account.'

'And suppose I say I will not allow it? This is all my property now, and I am not obliged to let anyone come rummaging about for something that isn't there.'

Again Selby coughed. 'That is not exactly the position, Mrs Landell. When a person dies, having made a will appointing an executor, his property vests at once in that executor, and it remains entirely in his control until the estate has been distributed as the will directs. The will on which you are relying, and which is the only one at present positively known to exist, appointed my partner and myself executors. We must act in that capacity, unless and until a later will comes to light. I hope that is quite clear.'

This information appeared, as Selby put it later, to take the wind completely out of Mrs Landell's sails. She sat in frowning silence, mastering her feelings, for a few moments, then rose to her feet.

'Very well,' she said. 'If what you tell me is correct, it seems you can do as you like, and I cannot prevent you wasting your time. Where will you begin your search?'

'I think,' Selby said, 'the best place to make a start would be the room where he spent most of his time when by himself. There is such a room, I suppose?'

She went to the door. 'I will show you the study,' she said, not looking at either of them. 'Your friend had better come too, as you say you want him to assist you.'

She led the way across the hall to another room, with a french window opening on the lawn behind the house. Before this stood a large writing-table, old-fashioned and solid like the rest of the furniture, which included three bookcases of bird's-eye maple. Not wasting time, Selby and Trent went each to one of the bookcases, while Mrs Landell looked on implacably from the doorway.

'*Annales Thucydidei et Xenophontei*,' read Selby in an undertone, glancing up and down the shelves. '*Miscellanea Critica*, by Cobet— give me the *Rural Rides*, for choice. I say, Phil, I seem to have come to the wrong shop. *Palæographia Græca*, by Montfaucon—I had an idea that was a place where they used to break chaps on the wheel in Paris. Greek plays—rows and rows of them. How are you getting on?'

'I am on the trail, I believe,' Trent answered. 'This is all English poetry—but not arranged in any order. Aha! What do I see?' He pulled out a thin red volume. 'One of the best-looking books that was ever printed and bound.' He was turning the pages rapidly. 'Here we are—the Ocean Chart. But no longer "a perfect and absolute blank".'

He handed the book to Selby, who scanned attentively the page at which it was opened. 'Beautiful writing, isn't it?' he remarked. 'Not much larger than smallish print, and quite as legible. Hm! Hm!' He frowned over the minute script, nodding approval from time to time; then looked up. 'Yes, this is all right. Everything clear, and the attestation clause quite in order—that's what gets 'em, very often.'

Mrs Landell, whose existence Selby appeared to have forgotten for the moment, now spoke in a strangled voice. 'Do you mean to tell me that there is a will written in that book?'

'I beg your pardon,' the lawyer said with studied politeness. 'Yes, Mrs Landell, this is the will for which I was looking. It is very brief, but quite clearly expressed, and properly executed and witnessed. The witnesses are Mabel Catherine Wheeler and Ida Florence Kirkby, both domestic servants, resident in this house.'

'They dared to do that behind my back!' Mrs Landell raged. 'It's a conspiracy!'

Selby shook his head. 'There is no question here of an agreement to carry out some hurtful purpose,' he said. 'The witnesses appear to have signed their names at the request of their employer, and they were under no obligation to mention the matter to any other person. Possibly he requested them not to do so; it makes no difference. As for the provisions of the will, it begins by bequeathing the sum of ten thousand pounds, free of legacy duty, to yourself——'

'What!' screamed Mrs Landell.

'Ten thousand pounds, free of legacy duty,' Selby repeated calmly. 'It gives fifty pounds each to my partner and myself, in consideration of our acting as executors—that, you may remember, was provided by the previous will. And all the rest of the testator's property goes to his nephew, Robert Spencer Landell, of 27 Longland Road, Blackheath, in the county of Kent.'

The last vestige of self-control departed from Mrs Landell as the words were spoken. Choking with fury and trembling violently, she snatched the book from Selby's hand, ripped out the inscribed page, and tore it across again and again. 'Now what are you going to do?' she gasped.

'The question is, what you are going to do,' Selby returned with perfect coolness. 'If you destroy that will beyond repair, you commit a felony which is punishable by penal servitude. Besides that, the will could still be proved; I am acquainted with its contents, and can swear to them. The witnesses can swear that it was executed. Mr Trent and I can swear to what has just taken place. If you will take my advice, Mrs Landell, you will give me back those bits of paper. If they can be pieced together into a legible document, the Court will not refuse to recognize it, and I may be able to save you from being prosecuted—I shall do my best. And there is another thing. As matters stand now, I must ask you to consider your arrangements for the future. There is no hurry, naturally; I shall not press you in any way; but you realize that while you continue living here you do so on sufferance, and that the place must be taken over by Mr Robert Landell in due course.'

Mrs Landell was sobered at last. Very pale, and staring fixedly at Selby, she flung the pieces of the will on the writing-table and walked rapidly from the room.

'I had no idea you could be such a brute, Arthur,' Trent remarked as he drove the car Londonwards through the Berkshire levels.

Selby said nothing.

'The accused made no reply,' Trent observed. 'Perhaps you didn't notice that you were being brutal, with those icy little legal lectures of yours, and your drawing out the agony in that study until you had her almost at screaming-point even before the blow fell.'

Selby glanced at him. 'Yes, I noticed all that. I don't think I am a vindictive man, Phil, but she made me see red. In spite of what she said, it's clear to me that she suspected he might have made another will at some time. She looked for it high and low. If she had found it she would undoubtedly have suppressed it. And her husband had no secrets from her! And whenever Snow was there she was always present! Can you imagine what it was like being dominated and bullied by a harpy like that?'

'Ghastly,' Trent agreed. 'But look here, Arthur; if he could get the two maids to witness the will, and keep quiet about it, why couldn't he have made it on an ordinary sheet of paper and enclosed it in a letter to your firm, and got either Mabel Catherine or Ida Florence to post it secretly?'

Selby shook his head. 'I thought of that. Probably he didn't dare take the risk of the girl being caught with the letter by her mistress. If that had happened, the fat *would* have been in the fire. Besides, we should have acknowledged the letter, and she would have opened our reply and read it. Reading all his correspondence would have been part of the treatment, you may be sure. No, Phil: I liked old Landell, and I meant to hurt. Sorry; but there it is.'

'I wasn't objecting to your being brutal,' Trent said. 'I felt just like you, and you had my unstinted moral support all the time. I particularly liked that passage when you reminded her that she could be slung out on her ear whenever you chose.'

'She's devilish lucky, really,' Selby said. 'She can live fairly comfortably on the income from her legacy if she likes. And she can marry again, God help us all! Landell got back on her in the end; but he did it like a gentleman.'

'So did you,' Trent said. 'A very nice little job of torturing, I should call it.'

Selby's smile was bitter. 'It only lasted minutes,' he said. 'Not years.'

Tokay of the Comet Year

H. Warner Allen

EVEN Mr Clerihew had to admit that Manton's pride in his wines was justified. He himself could scarcely have set before his most honoured guests bottles so rare and precious. Connoisseur and wine merchant, Mr Clerihew had a tiny shop hidden away in an old-fashioned court, and there was nothing to show its purpose but a collection of ancient wine-bottles in the curved bow-window. He was no ordinary wine merchant. He dealt only in rarities, and throughout the freemasonry of wine-lovers his name was known as the greatest specialist in those exquisite wines which, the perfect produce of nature and man, give to a year a golden number in the calendar of Bacchus. In these evil days, when phylloxera has wrought ruin among the vineyards, one could still find at Clerihew's a magnum, or even a jeroboam, of those glorious Médocs made before the scourge struck France. Clerihew himself employed a veritable secret service to keep him informed of any cellars through-out the world where really precious wines were stored, and he was always first on the spot with a lavish offer if some connoisseur was forced, by death or misfortune, to part with his prized bottles.

The band of true wine-lovers is small, but it is select. The highest in the land were happy to know Clerihew and to lunch with him in the little panelled room behind the shop, where for centuries his ancestors had offered the simplest of good food and the perfection of wine to their friends and customers. Clerihew, whose gentle manner concealed an adventurous spirit and remarkable shrewd-ness, was a discreet, sympathetic, and silent listener, and many a secret of State was confided to his judgement by the men who had learnt to trust him. Sandy-haired and rather bald, he wore round spectacles, which gave to his cherubic countenance an expression of Pickwickian innocence. On one subject alone was he talkative, and even sometimes pontifical. He would talk of the noble wines he collected with the passionate enthusiasm of a collector.

Manton had descended on Clerihew from the United States with the best of introductions from friends and customers, recommending him as an oil magnate of unlimited wealth with a reverent enthusiasm for wine. Incidentally, he was referred to as a leader of the American Anti-Communist League, whose mission to Europe was concerned with establishing a world-wide alliance against Bolshevism. Manton was a big man with a big laugh and a loud voice, clean-shaven in American fashion, though his long, curling, iron-grey hair suggested aestheticism.

Manton had wanted to meet Sir Philip Carmichael, the Foreign Secretary, less, he explained, to discuss this anti-Bolshevist business than to submit to the Minister's world-renowned palate certain rare wines which had come into Manton's possession in the course of an adventurous life. At first Clerihew was a little doubtful about the sincerity of this American's taste for wines, a rare accomplishment among his countrymen. However, the man seemed sincere in his worship of Bacchus, and Clerihew arranged for him to meet Sir Philip over a beautiful magnum of Margaux 1871. It was then that Manton had demanded his revenge, and invited them both to a symposium of wine, which, he declared, would challenge perfection.

Mr Clerihew had been uneasy about these boasted wines. A challenge of the kind so often ended in a tragic anti-climax. Manton had, no doubt, read Sir Philip's treatise on hock and claret—he quoted it glibly—but could he, in a world sadly impoverished in noble wines, have turned the money that he clearly had in abundance into the most 'precious stuff' sold by a vintner? His doubts were increased when he learned that there were to be lady guests. No one enjoyed, in a modest admiring way, feminine society more than Mr Clerihew, but he held that its enjoyment clashed with the appreciation of ancient wine. However, his doubts proved groundless. Manton kept his word. He had a charming house in Hill Street, and his cook was excellent. The little party, too, was well chosen—Sir Philip and his daughter, Helen Carmichael, who brought with her a very attractive friend, Lady Erica Montague, Manton, and Clerihew himself. Manton had insisted that good wine could only be appreciated in fair company, and Helen and Lady Erica were very good to look at. Helen, Clerihew had known since she was a child. It was the first time he had met her friend, a very pretty blonde with dark, appealing eyes, whose vivacity was emphasized by a slight foreign accent. A Russian by birth, she was, he gathered, the widow of a British officer.

'I am giving you first a hock,' said Mr Manton, 'a Steinberg Cabinet of 1868, that I am sure you will appreciate.'

Sir Philip, after a single sip, burst into an enthusiastic encomium. Mr Clerihew was longer in pronouncing judgement. It was truly a Steinberg Cabinet of 1868, and, what was more, a wine he instantly recognized. There were two bottles of it still stored in his cellar, and it was strange, very strange, that anyone else should be able to offer it to his guests.

'It is,' he said at last, 'a very beautiful wine. Would it be indiscreet to ask you where you found it?'

'Oh,' said Manton, airily, 'in my humble way, as you know, I am a collector of rare wines. I believe this Steinberg Cabinet was once in the Rothschild cellars. One of my agents bought it for me in Paris.'

Mr Clerihew looked a little puzzled, and in silence returned to his glass and plate. A magnum of Lafite 1864, the greatest claret of our time, followed the superb hock, a cumulation of excellences which Mr Clerihew secretly thought inartistic.

Finally, with the dessert, there came a Tokay. Manton poured out the precious wine himself, and, as he raised his glass, he challenged Mr Clerihew.

'I do not think,' he said, 'that there exists in the whole world a more wonderful Tokay. Perhaps Mr Clerihew, whose palate is world-renowned, will name it for us and tell us all about it.'

Mr Clerihew modestly emphasized the shortcomings of his palate, and the capricious errors to which every wine-lover's taste was subject. With expert ease, he set the wine swirling round his glass, and, after a deep inhalation of its bouquet, he took a sip that he rolled thoughtfully round his tongue.

'A very old and wonderful Tokay Essence,' he said, pontifically, 'a veritable attar of grapes. You know that Tokay Essence is made only in the best years, when the choicest grapes are left upon the vines until they are dried almost to raisins. These picked grapes are piled in a vat and left unpressed for twenty-four hours. Under their own weight a little, a very little, juice is squeezed out, and this rich and rare liquid alone produces Tokay Essence, a restorative for Emperors. As to this wine, with some confidence I would name it as Tokay Essence of 1811, the legendary year of the Comet which produced the most wonderful vintage of the nineteenth century, and which, according to the superstitious, foreshadowed the retreat from Moscow.'

Mr Clerihew paused. A sudden inspiration made him add: 'If I am right, I think I could name also the illustrious cellars from which this wine came.'

Manton was too busy with his own glass to reply. After a just perceptible delay and hesitation he answered: 'I am afraid that, for once, our admirable Mr Clerihew has made a mistake. Like Homer, he has nodded. This wine, noble as it is, cannot quite lay claim to the honour of the Comet year. I am not quite sure of its vintage— 1823, I think, and it came from the cellars of the Emperor of Austria.'

Mr Clerihew accepted the correction with less confusion than might have been expected.

Engrossed as he was in appreciating the rare wines and in giving shape to a strange idea that these wines had given him, Mr Clerihew took part in the conversation at the table in rather an absent-minded way. He noticed vaguely a curious alteration in Lady Erica's behaviour. Manton had obviously been captivated by her beauty as soon as he saw her. They talked with great animation about the crimes of Communism. Rumour at the time was busy with the cunning and the cruelty of Azeff, the masked chief of the Ogpu, a man of many disguises and of many women, who, it was said, concealed his features even from his closest subordinates. Then Manton changed the subject and tried to make the conversation more personal to them both, more confidential, but Lady Erica had kept him at arm's length.

A metamorphosis, however, took place during the ceremony of the Lafite '64, the greatest claret that our generation has known. Before, she had been cold and distant, seemed to have a distaste for

Manton. After—Mr Clerihew permitted himself a vulgarism—she was all over him. It might have been the wine, or it might not. When Manton turned towards her, she leaned towards him and shamelessly used those dark eyes that contrasted so fascinatingly with her fairness. Finally, there was the incident of the library. After dinner, Manton had invited his guests to stray about the house and see his pictures, and he and Lady Erica stayed behind for a few moments in the library. Mr Clerihew, gazing vacantly at a still life in the hall, fancied that he heard a little scuffle in the library, a smothered laugh, and, he imagined, a kiss. Certainly both Lady Erica and Manton were smoothing their hair when they came through the door.

The party broke up about half an hour before midnight, and Mr Clerihew sat up in his bedroom for some time before he went to bed, worrying his head over Manton's wines. Next morning he spent an hour studying the books of his firm, which were almost an encyclopedia of the greatest wines of the last century, but he could find no information concerning Steinberg Cabinet 1868 or Tokay Essence 1811 to relieve his anxiety.

His meditation was interrupted by the appearance of a tall man in top hat and morning coat who stumbled into the room with every appearance of excitement and distress. It was the first time that Clerihew had seen that philosophical and Olympian wine-lover, Sir Philip Carmichael, the Foreign Secretary, show the smallest symptom of agitation.

'Clerihew!' he exclaimed. 'Terrible news! Manton was murdered last night just after we left him. Poison, the police think.'

'Manton murdered!' said Clerihew, and he followed the words with a long whistle.

But neither murders nor, for that matter, a natural cataclysm could make Clerihew forget his courtly manners. Without more ado, he drew up a chair for Sir Philip and insisted on the Foreign Secretary taking a mouthful of the 1830 Cognac.

'No wonder you are worried and distressed. There is nothing like the ethers and esters of a really old brandy for restoring calmness.'

Sir Philip took a sip, but even that exquisite liquid could not prevail against his nervous disturbance. He swallowed it as though it were medicine.

'But that is not the worst,' said Sir Philip. 'The draft of the Baltic Treaty has disappeared.'

Mr Clerihew showed no surprise, but nodded sympathetically.

'It is evidently a double Bolshevist *coup*. They murdered Manton because he was one of their worst enemies, and because he was helping us guard that Baltic Treaty, which is all-important to them. You know Manton was one of the big men in the American Anti-Bolshevist League. Of course you know, as you introduced him to me. As a matter of fact, he was down at my country house all day yesterday, helping me devise an absolutely safe hiding-place for the draft, as I had taken it down there for the Christmas holidays. Now they have stolen the Treaty and killed Manton. All our efforts to obtain a balance of power in the Baltic have gone west, and it may mean war. How England can keep out I cannot see.'

'Dear, oh, dear,' clucked Mr Clerihew.

'If they hadn't killed poor Manton, I could have gone to him. He was the only man who could have recovered that Treaty. He was up to all the Bolshevist tricks. The Americans have a wonderful organization, and, of course, they have far more money to spend than our people. They have photographs and descriptions, and, often enough, fingerprints of thousands of Soviet agents. Recently, when there was a leakage in the Foreign Office, the police could make nothing of it, but Manton, with extraordinary astuteness, trapped the Communist spy almost at once.'

'I wonder,' said Mr Clerihew, reflectively, 'I wonder.'

There was something in Mr Clerihew's tone which surprised even the distracted Sir Philip, and he was about to ask what he wondered when their conversation was interrupted by a detective from Scotland Yard. Sir Philip declared that he must leave at once for the Foreign Office, and after his departure Mr Clerihew was careful to confirm the obvious impression of Mr Park, the detective, that he could not possibly throw any light on the mystery of Manton's death. Mr Park's mind was made up. The affair was a Communist outrage, and the only way to find the murderer was to round up the Reds. An adroit question or two provided Mr Clerihew with a few further details as to the murder. Manton had been found sitting at a table in his study on the ground floor, which was opposite the dining-room. There was a bottle of Tokay on the table and two glasses. One of the glasses was half full of Tokay, while the other,

which was believed to have contained poison, had only a few drops
left in it.

'There seems no reason for suicide,' said the detective, 'and, if so,
why two glasses?' There were no fingerprints except those of the
murdered man. The analysts were at work, and the doctors believed
that Manton could not have died much after one a.m.

After the detective had left, Mr Clerihew went to the telephone and
summoned, from a neighbouring hotel, a young Englishman named
Lewis, who from time to time acted as his agent in smelling out rare
wines in the Near East. He had lately undertaken a dangerous
mission in quest of the precious liquid, for Clerihew had sent him
to try to tap the resources of the one great cellar that after the War
still remained overflowing with the most glorious wines. He had
returned empty-handed, though he had gathered information that
might one day lead, with the aid of diplomacy and corruption, to
the transference of some of these wines from the East to Clerihew's
cellar.

'Hock, Steinberg Cabinet 1868, Fuder 4569,' said Clerihew, in
an awed whisper. 'Claret, a double magnum of Lafite 1864, and
Tokay of the Comet year 1811. Could they come from anywhere
else?'

Lewis shook his head, and, dropping his voice and glancing round
the little room as if he was afraid of being overheard, he said: 'I told
you what it cost me to have a glimpse of the cellar-book. I saw those
very wines you mention taken out in the name of——'

He paused and wrote something on a slip of paper. Clerihew
glanced at it, tore it hastily up into tiny pieces, and dropped them
into the fire.

'Since that is so,' said Mr Clerihew, slowly to himself as Mr
Lewis departed, 'the only question that remains is, where is the
Baltic Treaty?'

A few more minutes' thought, a short study of a reference in
Who's Who, and, with the determination of a man who has taken a
final resolution, he put on top hat and coat and disappeared through
the side door.

He drove to a fashionable bridge club, and kept the taxi waiting.
Lady Erica had confessed the previous evening that she spent most

of her afternoons there, and Mr Clerihew suspected that that day
she would not change her habits. His guess was right, for after a
wait which seemed so long that he began to grudge the ticking of
the taxi clock outside, she came down and greeted him with a *grande
dame* air that seemed a trifle exaggerated.

'So sorry to keep you waiting, but I had to finish my rubber.
What a terrible business about poor Mr Manton! I had a long
interview with a detective this morning, but I could not give him
any help. Of course, it must be those dreadful Bolsheviks.'

'I came to ask you to take a little drive with me,' said Mr
Clerihew, meekly, turning down his eyes in honest surprise that he
should be speaking on such terms to so resplendent a being.

Lady Erica raised her eyebrows.

'I thought that I might be of service to you, that I might relieve
you of an inconvenient document, and see that it is conveyed to the
proper quarter,' he went on.

For a moment she gasped and stuttered. Then, in a flash, she
pulled herself together, and Mr Clerihew felt for an instant that he
had strayed into a tiger's den.

'No, no, no,' he said, deprecatingly. 'I have only come as a friend.
I want to help you. An execution is not a crime.'

Lady Erica looked the little wine merchant up and down. The
night before she had hardly noticed him even as a blot on the
landscape, had summed him up as something of a bore who *would*
talk about wines. Now she was struck by his apparent admiration
for herself, and his air of good-humoured kindness. She felt he was
eminently safe. So, protesting feebly, for form's sake, that she did
not understand, she allowed herself to be guided to the cab and
heard Mr Clerihew instruct the driver to go round and round the
Park until further orders.

Mr Clerihew enjoyed in silence for a time the unwonted pride of
driving with a peculiarly beautiful woman at his side.

At last he cleared his throat and said, quietly: 'How jolly this is!
Even in winter the Park is delightful. I suppose you have the
document on you?'

Lady Erica was silent.

'Of course you have it. I will look out of the window while you
produce it. Think what a relief it will be to be rid of that burden on
your conscience and to know that it is sure to go to the right

quarter. Do not be afraid of me. I only want to help you, and I cannot blame you for what you did last night.'

Mr Clerihew looked out of the window. Lady Erica hesitated for a time, divided between the fear of a trap and the confidence that the little man's simplicity gave her. Then there was a rustle of silk and a minute later she tapped Mr Clerihew on the arm.

'Here it is.'

Without a glance at it, he stowed away in the capacious pocket of his overcoat the Baltic Treaty.

'Now,' said Mr Clerihew, benignly, 'we can talk frankly. Remember that I am on your side, my dear, and you can count on me. Am I right in thinking that you have good reason to hate the Bolsheviks?'

'They murdered my husband and all those I loved best,' said Lady Erica, in a low voice.

'I thought that there must be something of the kind. I understand it all now, but I should like to know what there was in the claret that told you that Manton was—or, rather, was not what he professed to be.'

'The claret had nothing to do with it, though I suppose I was drinking it when I noticed that the top joint of the little finger of Manton's left hand was missing. A woman in Riga—she had been his mistress—told me that the man I had been looking for so long had just such a finger, and, as a second sign, she told me that his left ear was deformed, a mere caricature of an ear. I could not see his ear, because, as you know, he wore his hair long enough to cover it, but I felt sure that I had found my man. He wanted to make love to me, and I encouraged him.

'Later, in the library, I made my guess a certainty by letting him kiss me. It was unpleasant'—Lady Erica shuddered—'I should have preferred a slug or an orang-utan, but it gave me an opportunity to push his hair aside and see his ear. Then I knew it was Azeff. He fell into my trap quickly enough, begged me to come back and taste a second glass of Tokay—the elixir of love, he called it—after you had all gone, and slipped his latch-key into my hand. You can guess the rest.'

'For curiosity's sake,' said Mr Clerihew, 'I should like to know a few more details.'

'When I was with my husband in Russia, I grew accustomed to wearing round my neck a little bottle full of painless and deadly poison. Azeff had told me that the servants would be all in bed by midnight, and a quarter of an hour after I came back, opened the door with the latch-key, and went into the library. I found him sitting there, reading that document you have in your pocket. He poured out the Tokay into two glasses that were standing on the table. He still had that document in his hand—I found out afterwards what it was—and he turned his back to hide it away in his desk. It is difficult to make passionate love with an important document in one hand. That gave me my opportunity, and all the contents of my bottle went into his glass. He came back and drank it with some silly mumble about the elixir of love. I touched my wine with my lips and watched him fall back silently and painlessly. Then, on an impulse, I went to the desk and found the paper he had been reading, and as I was sure that he could have no right to it, I took it away. That is how I killed Azeff. But how did you know anything about it?'

'My dear lady, I knew nothing about it until that man offered us his Steinberg Cabinet of 1868. I recognized it at once as belonging to a very famous cask. The Rhine wine-growers ferment their hocks in small casks, pressing their choicest grapes in one, their second best in a second, and so on, so that they have from the same vineyard a number of wines of varying qualities distinguished by a cask number known only to the initiated. The finest hock that this world has ever known came in 1868 from Fuder 4569, which was, in point of fact, only half a cask. My father, with the greatest trouble, succeeded in purchasing two dozen bottles for a fabulous sum. All the rest went to the Russian Imperial cellars. The Rothschilds never had any of it. Again, the Tokay was Tokay Essence of 1811, as I said. A hundred bottles or so of the Comet year Tokay were discovered just before the War walled up in a cellar in Hungary. My firm purchased a few bottles for an enormous sum, and again the rest went to the Tsar. You will understand that when I tasted those wines I guessed at once that they came from the Imperial cellars. When Manton lied about them I knew that something was wrong.'

'But surely,' said Lady Erica, 'the Tsar's wines have long ago been drunk?'

'I am coming to that,' Mr Clerihew replied. 'I search the whole world for rare wines, and it struck me some time ago that the only cellars which contained the wines I wanted were the Imperial cellars of Russia. I discovered that the wines were still there, tended by the cellarmen of the Empire as if they formed a museum, and that only the true-Red Commissar was allowed to draw upon them. So I was pretty sure that Manton had obtained his marvellous wines from the Tsar's cellars, and I naturally asked myself who was the man who could dispose of these Imperial wines. The answer was easy: only some Soviet Commissar engaged on Soviet business. Today I learnt from my agent, who has been trying to purchase the Imperial wines, and who had actually seen the cellar-book, which is still kept up to date, that the very wines that we drank last night had been issued to Azeff, chief of the Ogpu. I concluded that Manton was either Azeff himself or at least some high official in the Ogpu. Sir Philip Carmichael's fame as a connoisseur and wine-lover is world-wide. A spy who wanted to make his acquaintance could have no better introduction than those precious bottles. Azeff's reputation for audacity made it quite probable that he had come in person to steal the draft of the Baltic Treaty, a knowledge of which was of vital importance to the Soviet.'

'But how did I come into it?'

'Knowing your history as written in *Who's Who*, I did not find it hard to guess at Azeff's fate. Azeff had been down at Sir Philip's country house to help him contrive a safe place for the Baltic Treaty, and he naturally took the opportunity of stealing it. I felt sure you must have taken it, as otherwise the police would have found it in his house. So I eagerly grasped the chance of helping one of those fascinating young women whom I so rarely meet.'

Perhaps Lady Erica misunderstood Mr Clerihew's tribute to her charm. At any rate, she began, indignantly: 'Please understand I regret nothing. I have killed the man who murdered——'

Mr Clerihew held up a shocked hand. 'Lady Erica, I beg you. As I said before, an execution is not a crime. What I propose is that I shall take the Treaty back to Sir Philip, warning him under seal of confidence that Manton was Azeff. He will realize at once that his own reputation demands that the whole matter shall be hushed up as soon as possible, and even in a democratic State there are ways and means of suppressing inquiry when the interests of the country are at stake.'

At this point Lady Erica, whose nerves had been more tightly strained than Mr Clerihew imagined, broke down, and began to sob on his shoulder. History does not recount how Mr Clerihew comforted her, but, as he drove down to see Sir Philip Carmichael at the Foreign Office in a taxi with a clock marking colossal sums, he wrote down in his notebook, rather conceitedly and pedantically: 'The knowledge of wine that maketh glad the heart of man is sometimes a responsibility as well as a privilege, but in either form it is very agreeable.'

II

LEGAL NICETIES

Novelist, short-story writer, playwright, essayist, and critic, *W. Somerset Maugham* (1874–1965) was one of the most accomplished pre-modernist writers of this century. Like Arnold Bennett he seemed to revel in hard work; yet though as prolific, his novels do not—unlike those of the older writer—have that whiff of the machine-shop about them. His first book *Liza of Lambeth* (1897) was spurned by some critics of the day as too offensively naturalistic, though it did well enough to allow him to take up writing full time. He had a wry humour—best revealed in the self-deprecatory *Ashenden* (1928), his fictionalized account of, in his own words, his 'uncommonly useless' and at times catastrophic exploits working for British Intelligence during the First World War—but could be unneccessarily cruel when the mood took him: the novelist Hugh Walpole, for instance, was mercilessly guyed in *Cakes And Ale* (1930). An inveterate traveller, he went several times around the world and spent long periods in the Pacific region and China; he had an acute sense of place which he was able to draw on successfully years afterwards in both his fiction and non-fiction. Although his contributions to the *Strand* were few (in all, seven stories) they spanned over forty years; the first, 'A Point of Law', appeared in 1903, the last, 'The Kite', in 1946. For 'A Point of Law' Maugham was paid £20, which enabled him to take a much-needed holiday on the Riviera during a particularly grim period in his life.

Will Scott (*fl.* 1920–55) was an incorrigible scribbler for the down-market weeklies and a master of the twelve-hundred-word comic sketch. Hardly a week went by, during the 1920s, without something by him appearing in the *Humorist* or *Passing Show* (before the latter was turned into a general-interest rival to *Answers* and *Tit-*

Bits). His slicker work he sold to the smart and glossy society journals like the *Sketch*, the *Tatler*, and the *Sphere*. Scott broke into the *Strand* in 1934, thereafter selling the magazine nearly thirty stories over the next dozen years, most of which display the confident precision of the craftsman; not a few, like 'Not Guilty', have an amoral tinge to them that lifts them wholly out of the ruck.

A Point of Law

W. Somerset Maugham

WHEN I feel more than usually poor (on a rainy day, for instance, when opulent stockbrokers roll swiftly in electric broughams, or when some friend in bleak March weather tells me he is starting that very night for Monte Carlo) I make my will; it gives me a peculiar satisfaction to leave my worldly goods, such as they are, to persons who will not in the least care to receive them, and I like the obsequious air of the clerk who blows my name up a tube to the family solicitor. It is an amusement which costs me nothing, for Mr Addishaw, the senior partner in the eminently respectable firm of Addishaw, Jones, and Braham, knows my foible; he is aware also that a solicitor's bill is the last I should ever pay, and I have warned him that if ever he sends it I will write a satiric story which shall hold him up to the ridicule of all his neighbours on Brixton Hill. What accounts he prepares after my demise do not in the smallest degree perturb me; my executors and he may fight it out between them.

One day, then, I walked down the Strand, feeling very wretched after a cheap luncheon in a crowded Italian restaurant (a crust of bread and a glass of water may be rendered appetizing by hunger and a keen sense of the romantic, but who can survey without despondency a cut off the joint, half cold and ill-cooked, and boiled potatoes?), and, jostled by hurrying persons, I meditated on the hollowness and the folly of the world. I felt certain that Mr Addishaw at this hour would be disengaged, and it seemed an occasion upon which his services were eminently desirable; it would comfort me just then to prepare for the inevitable dissolution. I turned the corner and soon found myself at the handsome edifice, with its array of polished brass-plates and its general look of prosperity, wherein the firm for many years had rented offices.

'Can I see Mr Addishaw?' I enquired.

And in a moment I was shown upstairs into the sumptuous apartment which the good gentleman inhabited. He had evidently just lunched, and with him the meal had without doubt been satisfactory; for he sat in the armchair generally reserved for clients, toasting his toes at the cheerful fire, and with great content smoked his cigar. There was so much self-satisfaction about his red face that the mere sight of him cheered me; and the benevolence of his snowy whiskers impressed me more than ever before with a sense of his extreme worth.

'You look as if you read the Lessons in church every Sunday morning, Mr Addishaw,' I said, when I shook hands with him. 'I've come to make my will.'

'Ah, well,' he answered, 'I have nothing to do for ten minutes. I don't mind wasting a little time.'

'You must sit at your desk,' I insisted, 'or I sha'n't feel that I'm getting my money's worth.'

Patiently he changed his seat, and with some elaboration I gave a list of all the bequests I wished to make.

'And now,' said I, 'we come to my wines, spirits, and liqueurs.'

'Good gracious me!' he cried; 'I didn't know that you had started a cellar. You are becoming a man of substance. I will tell my wife to ask for your new book at Mudie's.'

'Your generosity overwhelms me,' I retorted. 'Some day, I venture to hope, you will go so far as to buy a second-hand copy of one of my works. But I have no cellar. The wine in my flat is kept in a cupboard along with the coats and hats, the electric meter, my priceless manuscripts, and several pairs of old boots. I have no wines, spirits, and liqueurs, but I wish to leave them to somebody, so that future generations may imagine that writers in the twentieth century lived as luxuriously as butchers and peers of the realm and mountebanks.'

Somewhat astonished at this harangue Mr Addishaw wrote as I desired; then a pale young clerk was sent for and together the legal gentlemen witnessed my signature.

'And now,' said I, 'I will light a cigar to complete the illusion that I am a man of means, and bid you good afternoon.'

Mr Addishaw returned to his armchair by the fire and, feeling apparently very good-humoured, asked me to remain for a few minutes; he had taken the only comfortable seat in the room, but I drew up the writing-chair and sat down.

'Wills are odd things,' said Mr Addishaw, in a meditative manner. 'Only the other day I had to deal with the testament of the late Lord Justice Drysden; and it was so ill-composed that no one could make head or tail of it. But his eldest son happened to be a solicitor, and he said to the rest of the family: "I'm going to arrange this matter as I consider right, and if you don't agree I'll throw the whole thing into Chancery and you'll none of you get a penny!" The family were not too pleased, for their brother thought fit to order the affair in a manner not altogether disadvantageous to himself; but I advised them to submit. My father and my grandfather were solicitors before me, so I think I have law more or less in the blood; and I've always taught my children two things. I think if they know them they can't come to much harm in the world.'

'And what are they?' I asked.

'Never tell a lie and never go to law.'

Mr Addishaw rose slowly from his chair and went to the door.

'If anyone wishes to see me, Drayton, say that I shall be disengaged in a quarter of an hour,' he called to his clerk.

Then, with a little smile which sent his honest red face into a number of puckers, he took from a cupboard a bottle, well coated with dust, and two wine-glasses.

'What is this?' I asked.

'Well, I'm an old man,' he answered, 'and I keep to some customs of the profession which these young sparks of today have given up. I always have a bottle of port in my room, and sometimes when I don't feel very well I drink a glass or two.'

He poured out the wine and looked at it with a smile of infinite content. He lifted it to his nose and closed his eyes as though he were contemplating some pious mystery. He sipped it and then nodded to me three times with a look full of meaning.

'And yet there are total abstainers in the world!' he exclaimed.

He emptied the glass, sighed, refilled it, and sat down.

'Talking of wills, I said the last word in a matter this morning which has interested me a good deal; and, if you like, I will tell you the story, because it shows how sometimes by pure chance that ass, the law, may work so as to protect the innocent and punish the contriving.

'One of the oldest clients of my firm is the family of Daubernoon, north-country squires, who have held immense estates in Westmorland since the good old days of King Henry VIII. They were not a saving race, so that in personalty they never left anything worth speaking of, but they always took care to keep the property unencumbered; and even now, when land is worth so little and the landlord finds it as difficult as the farmer to make both ends meet, their estates bring in the goodly income of six thousand a year.

'Roger Daubernoon, the late squire, injured his spine in a hunting accident, and it would have been a mercy if he had killed himself outright, since he lingered for twenty years, a cripple and an invalid who required incessant care. His wife died shortly afterwards and he was left with an only daughter, in whose charge he placed himself. A man used to an active, busy life, in illness he grew querulous and selfish, and it seemed to him quite natural that Kate Daubernoon, then a girl of twenty, should devote her life to his comfort. A skilful nurse, she became so necessary to him that he could not face the thought that one day she might leave him; he was devoured by the fear that she would marry, and he refused, pretexting his ill-health, to have visitors at the Manor. He grew petulant and angry if to go to some party she abandoned him for a couple of hours, and finally Miss Daubernoon resigned herself to a cloistral life. Year in, year out, she remained in close attendance on her father, partly from affection, but more for duty's sake; she looked after the house, walked by the squire's bath-chair, read to him, and never once left home. She saw no one but the villagers, by whom for her charitable kindness she was adored, the parson and his wife, the doctor, and twice a year myself.

'And she grew old. Miss Daubernoon had never been beautiful, she had never been even pretty; and the stealthy years, the monotonous life, robbed her of the country freshness which in early youth had made up for other deficiencies. As year by year I went up to Westmorland to see Mr Daubernoon, I was distressed to note the difference in his daughter; and before her time she grew prim and old-maidish. She ceased to regret the joyous life of the world, growing so accustomed to the narrow circle wherein vegetably she existed that I think nothing at last would have induced her to withdraw from it. Finally, when I was staying in the house at Christmas, two years ago, the village doctor came privately to see me. He told me that Miss Daubernoon had been ill through the autumn and now, to his dismay, he had discovered that she was phthisical.

'"You know what our winters are here," he said to me; "if she does not go away it will probably kill her."

'I went to her at the doctor's request, and used the persuasions which with him had been quite useless. But she would listen to nothing.

'"I know that I am ill," she answered, "but I cannot leave my father. Do you see no change in him since you were last here?"

'I was obliged to confess that I did; the long years of suffering had broken down at last that iron frame, and even the most inexperienced could see that now the end could not be far off.

'"It would kill my father at once to move him. It would kill him also if I went away."

'"But do you think you have a right to place your own life in such danger?"

'"I am willing to take the risk."

'I knew her obstinate character, and I felt I could never induce her to change her mind, so I went straight to Mr Daubernoon himself.

'"I think you should know that Kate is dangerously ill," I said. "She has consumption, and the only thing that can save her is to winter abroad."

'"Who says so?" he asked.

'There was no astonishment in his manner, so that I wondered whether he had divined the illness of Miss Daubernoon, or whether in his utter selfishness he was indifferent to it. I mentioned Dr Hobley's name.

'"Twenty years ago he said I couldn't live six months," answered Mr Daubernoon. "He's a nervous old woman. Kate's as strong and well as you are."

'"Would you like a specialist to come from Liverpool to see her?"

'"Oh, those doctors always back one another up. A specialist would only frighten Kate."

'I saw that he would never allow himself to be persuaded that his daughter needed attention, and I spoke more sternly to him.

'"Mr Daubernoon," I said, "if your daughter dies the responsibility will be yours."

'Then a cruel look came into his worn, thin face—a look I had never seen before, and a hardness filled his eyes that was horrible.

'"After all, I can only last six months. When I'm dead she can do what she likes. *Après moi le déluge.*"

'I did not answer, appalled by the sick man's cruel selfishness; the poor girl had sacrificed her youth to him, her hopes of being wife and mother; and now he wanted her very life. And she was ready to give it.

'Mr Daubernoon lived four months longer than he said, for the autumn had arrived when a telegram came saying that he was dead. It was sent by Dr Hobley, who bade me come to Westmorland at once.

'But when I arrived it was the change in Miss Daubernoon that shocked me most. Those final months had worked havoc with her, so that it was impossible not to see that she was very ill. She was thin and haggard, her hair was streaked with grey, and she coughed constantly. She seemed ten years older than when I had last seen her, and, though she was no more than forty, looked almost an elderly woman.

'"I'm very much alarmed at the change in Miss Daubernoon," I told the doctor. "What do you think?"

'"She's dying, Mr Addishaw," he answered; "she can't live another year."

'"Fortunately, now she can go away."

'"She can do that, but it won't save her. It's too late."

'After the funeral Miss Daubernoon came to me and said she wished to have a talk on business matters.

'"Never mind about business," I said; "I can arrange all that. What you must do is to get down to Italy before the cold weather comes."

'"That is what I mean to do," she answered. "I think I should tell you"—she hesitated and looked down, a faint blush colouring her pallid cheeks—"I think I should tell you that I am going to be married at once."

'"What!" I cried. "But you're not fit to marry; you're as ill as you can be."

'"I think I have six months to live. I want to be happy. It's only because I'm so ill that I cannot wait. We are to be married in London in a week."

'For a moment I was silent, not knowing what to say. Then I asked to whom she was engaged.

'"Mr Ralph Mason," she answered, shortly. "You met him last time you were here. We have been devoted to one another for the last two years."

'I could not remember anyone of that name, and I enquired, somewhat curtly, when I should have the pleasure of renewing my acquaintance with this gentleman.

'"He's now coming towards us," she said, and a look of radiant happiness came into her face.

'I saw walking along the garden path through which we sauntered a tall young man in a frock-coat, a tall hat, and patent leather boots. In a moment I recognized him.

'"But that is the land-agent's clerk?"

'"Yes," she said.

'He was certainly a very handsome man, with a beautiful moustache and the dashing air of a counter-jumper trying to ape the gentleman. I should think he was fifteen years younger than Miss Daubernoon, and this was enough to surprise me; but the most amazing part of it all was that her pride—you know what the pride is of people in that particular class of life—should have allowed her to think of marriage with such a person. And when I knew him better I found to my dismay that there was in him no redeeming trait; he was merely a very ordinary, common, provincial tradesman, with nothing but his rather vulgar good looks to recommend him. And when I compared his strapping vigour with Miss Daubernoon's old, sickly weakness, I could not doubt that he was merely an adventurer of the very worst class. I said nothing at the time, but later, finding myself alone with her, I did not hesitate to speak plainly.

'"Why do you suppose Mr Mason wishes to marry you?" I asked.

'A painful, timid look came into her eyes, so that I almost repented my words, but it seemed a duty to be outspoken at all costs to save her much future pain.

'"I think he loves me," she answered.

'"My dear, I don't want to hurt you, but I must tell you the truth. You can't believe that this young man really cares for you. You're very ill."

'"I'm dying," she interrupted.

'"You're ever so much older than he is. Good heavens! look at yourself in the glass. Ask yourself if he can possibly have fallen in love with you. And there's one palpable reason why he wishes to marry you. Can't you see that it's your money he wants, and for your money's sake he's willing to—to put up with you?"

'Hot tears ran down her cheeks, so that I felt hatefully cruel, but something had to be done to stop such an insane marriage.

'"Don't remind me that I'm old and plain," she said. "Do you think I can't feel it? But I know he loves me for myself, and even if he doesn't I will marry him. The only thing that has kept me alive is my love for him, and, after all, I have such a little while to live that you might let me spend it as happily as I can."

'"And do you think you can be happy with him? Do you think he'll have the patience to wait for your death? My poor lady, you don't know what may be in store for you. At present he's nice enough to you, and apparently you don't mind if he's common and vulgar; but when you're once safely married do you think he'll take the trouble to pretend he loves you? You must be mad."

'She began to cry, silently, so that for the life of me I could not go on, and I resolved instead to speak with Ralph Mason himself. I made enquiries in the neighbouring market-town, and I was scarcely surprised to discover that his character was thoroughly bad. He was known to be a hard drinker, violent in temper, unscrupulous; his friends said he was a good sportsman, which meant, apparently, that he attended all the race-meetings he could and betted more heavily than his means allowed. A sort of provincial Lothario, various tales were brought me of his exploits; and his good looks, his supercilious charm of manner, appeared to make women an easy conquest. I cannot tell you how alarmed I was when I learnt for what sort of a man it was that Miss Daubernoon had conceived such a passionate infatuation; but his very depravity made it just possible that he would accept certain proposals that I had in mind. I telegraphed to Robert Daubernoon, an officer on half-pay with a large family, a cousin of the late squire's and Kate's only relative and natural heir; and on receiving his answer invited Ralph Mason to call on me.

'"I want to talk to you as a business man," I said. "When Miss Daubernoon told me she wished to marry you, I ventured to make certain enquiries; and I have heard a good deal about you."

'He was going to speak, but I begged him to listen quietly till I had finished. With scoundrels I have always found it best to speak to the point; a certain cynical frankness often puts them at their ease, so that much time and verbiage are spared.

'"You know as well as I do that Miss Daubernoon is dying, and I dare say you will not think it necessary to pretend to me that you are in love with her. You cannot seriously wish to marry her, and I am authorized to offer you an annuity of two thousand a year if you will put off your marriage indefinitely."

'He looked at me and stroked his handsome moustache, and presently he gave a mocking smile.

'"You are a solicitor, Mr Addishaw?" he asked.

'"Yes."

'"And presumably a man of business?"

'I was inclined to call him an impertinent jackanapes, but refrained.

'"And granting that all you say is true, and I don't love Kate Daubernoon, and wish to marry her solely because I think she can only live a few months, at the end of which I shall find myself a rich man—do you think I should be such a fool as to accept your offer?"

'"I thought it possible, when you considered that the money was as safe as the Bank of England, while otherwise you are dependent on your wife's will, which may be altered."

'"I'm not afraid of that."

'"And also that you would be behaving more or less like a gentleman. Her own doctor has told me that marriage is bound to kill her almost at once. Don't you think what you're doing is very cruel?"

'"I'm a business man, too, Mr Addishaw," he answered.

'He broke off the conversation abruptly, and I felt I had done harm rather than good, for soon I found that Miss Daubernoon knew what I had said. I do not know what account of the affair Ralph Mason gave her, but I can imagine that my behaviour was painted in the darkest colours, while his own shone with all the heroic virtues. Miss Daubernoon, harassed by her father's death and funeral, for two or three days was too ill to leave her room, and only Ralph Mason was allowed to see her. She wrote me a note.

'"I did not mind what you said to me," she wrote, "but I am indignant and deeply distressed that you should have attempted to turn Ralph from me. I think your interference impertinent. I address you now no longer as a friend, but merely as my solicitor, and I beg you to prepare at once, for my signature, a will leaving absolutely everything of which I die possessed to Ralph Mason."

'I dare say I am not a man of very easy temper, and with some heat I replied that she might get another solicitor to prepare this will for her; I would have nothing to do with it. And that evening, without seeing her again, I started for London.

'Three days later I heard from Dr Hobley that they had left Daubernoon, though Kate was much too ill to travel; they were married at a registry office in Marylebone, and next day crossed the Channel on their way to Italy.

'There was a good deal of work connected with the estate of the late Roger Daubernoon. He had left rather a large legacy to his cousin Robert and smaller sums to various servants and dependents, so that practically all his personalty was absorbed. Stocks and shares had to be sold, consequently I was in somewhat frequent correspondence with Mrs Mason, but her letters were always very short, referring merely to the business on hand, so that I could not tell whether she was ill or well, happy or wretched. I hoped with all my heart that these last months of her life went smoothly, I hoped the man was kind to her, and at least took the trouble to conceal from his wife that he waited impatiently for her death. Poor thing, I trust she preserved to the last the illusion which had given her the only joy her life had known; I was no longer angry with her, but very, very sorry.

'Then one day, in the spring, my clerk whistled up that Mr Ralph Mason wished to see me. I knew at once that the poor woman was dead. He came in; and though in the country he had dressed himself preposterously in a frock-coat and a tall hat, now he wore a rather loud check suit and a bowler; a black tie was his only sign of mourning. And I had never felt such an antipathy for this swell-mobsman. I hated his handsome military bearing, his smart counter-jumper looks, and the scent on his handkerchief. There was a superciliousness in his manner which told me I should have to pay for all I had said of him; he, of course, was now the squire, and I was a humble solicitor. I knew I should not long keep the business of the house of Daubernoon, and upon my word I was not sorry. I had no wish to deal with a man of that stamp.

'I did not rise from my chair as he came in.

'"Good morning," I said. "Pray be seated."

'"I have come to see you on business," he answered, insolently. "My wife died in Rome on the 24th of last March, and you are executor of her will."

'I felt expressions of regret would be out of place, and I could imagine the satisfaction the man took in his freedom.

'"I hope you were not unkind to her," I said.

'"I told you I'd come solely on business. I have brought the will in my pocket. It was by my wish that you were appointed executor."

'I understood what a revengeful pleasure he took in the thought that I must deliver over to him the vast estates of the Daubernoons. Silently I took the will, which was very short, written on a sheet of notepaper.

I, Kate Daubernoon of the Manor, Daubernoon, hereby revoke all former wills and testamentary dispositions made by me, and declare this to be my last will and testament. I appoint James Addishaw, of 103, Lancaster Place, London, to be the executor of this my will. I give all my real and personal property whatsoever to Ralph Mason. In witness whereof I have set my hand to this my will the 10th day of September, 1902.

KATE DAUBERNOON.

'It was written in her own hand and duly witnessed by two servants at the Manor. I could hardly believe my eyes.

'"How did you get the form?" I asked.

'"I have some knowledge of law," he answered.

'"That I can scarcely believe." My heart beat with excitement, but I did not wish to let him see my triumph too quickly. "Is this the only will your wife made?"

'"Yes."

'"Are you sure there is no later one?"

'"Absolutely positive."

'"Have you observed the date? Three days before your marriage."

'"The will was made on the very day that you sent for me and offered me two thousand a year to give her up."

'There was a ring of exultation in his voice, but I answered very quietly, "You would have been wise to accept it."

'"Do you think so?" he laughed.

'"Because this will is invalid. Marriage annuls all testamentary dispositions previously made, and this piece of paper is absolutely worthless."

'I shall never forget the look that came into his face, the green pallor that spread across his cheeks, discolouring his very lips; at first he could not understand, the blow was too unexpected.

'"What do you mean?" he cried. "It's not true."

'"You may take the will to any solicitor you choose."

'"You old wretch!" he hissed.

'"If you're not civil I shall send for my clerks to kick you downstairs."

'He reached out his hand for the will and I handed it to him; he read it through once more.

'"Do you mean to say I get nothing?"

'"Not exactly. Your wife died intestate; her real property goes to Robert Daubernoon, the heir-at-law. You, as her husband, get the personalty."

'"But she meant to leave me everything."

'"I dare say. But the fact remains that she left you nothing at all."

'"I get the money and the furniture of the Manor. I shall go there at once."

'"Pardon me; I shall telegraph to the servants not to admit you. The house has no longer anything to do with you. And as for the furniture, I should remind you that there your wife had only a life interest; her father never expected her to marry, and, anxious that it should not be disturbed, left it to Robert Daubernoon."

'As I spoke I thought how Ralph Mason must have looked at the old pictures and seen them going one by one under the hammer at Christie's; they would have fetched a goodly sum. I think this last shock broke him, for he asked me in quite another tone how much money there was.

'"You know that as well as I do," was my reply. "Mr Daubernoon's legacies took a great deal. There can be very little left. You may feel sure that what there is shall be duly handed to you."

'I stood up and opened the door for him to go out. He looked up defiantly.

'"Well, I'll fight you," he said.

'"You'll find no one fool enough to take up the case," I answered, scornfully.

'He looked at me as though gladly he would have seized me by the throat; he glanced round the room for something on which to wreak his passion, but apparently nothing offered, and with a kind of stifled groan he went out. And he departed to think over the utter frustration of all his schemes, a bad man and a clever man, and that ass, the law, had beaten him.

'I settled up everything as quickly as I could. I found a good many bills owing, and these I paid; the journey to Italy had cost a great deal, and my own account was not a small one. There was even less money due to the estate than I expected, for Mrs Mason had died immediately before quarter-day. This morning I was able to write to her husband, sending him a cheque for the amount, less legacy duty, to which he was entitled. I can imagine his feelings when he looked at it, for the exact sum was forty-three pounds seven shillings and threepence halfpenny.'

Not Guilty

Will Scott

THROUGH the steamed windows she noticed the rain running like
a tiny waterfall off the peak of the taxi-driver's cap as he twisted
round to open the door. And how the beating raindrops close to the
lamps looked like thick white ropes, and those farther away like thin
grey wires. Silly things to notice, at such a time. . . . Her fare
ready, she got out quickly, lowering her head against the storm as
she handed the man his money.

'Thank you very much. Much obliged. Shocking night, isn't it?'

'Yes.'

'Regular second flood! Good-night, Mrs Clifford.'

'Good-night.'

The taxi rattled away through the rain as Christine Clifford
hurried up the storm-churned path to the front door. There was a
light, she observed, in the lounge, and another one beyond in the
little room they had always called the Cubby Hole. Steven was
home, and that would mean no waiting. Well, all the better. Get it
over.

She let herself in. A waste of time to ring. This was Thursday,
Venner and Mrs Venner's weekly night at the pictures. Ring? What
on earth had made her think of that? This was her home. But the
thought showed how far matters had gone.

The rain streaming from her clothes, she closed the outer door
behind her and made her way along the hall to the lounge. The
door was open. She went in. The lounge was unoccupied; for
which, now that it had come to it, she was thankful. Breathing
space . . . A minute to think.

She sat down on a leather-covered chair next to the desk.

As many another before her, and in the same words, she was later to reflect that it is funny how things turn out. If the upper left drawer of the desk had been closed it would have been a different story that she lived to tell. The drawer was open, a couple of inches, and inside it something shone.

From sheer surprise and for no other reason she took it out. A revolver. Steven's? How came Steven to possess a revolver? And why? This was something new. Why a revolver? And had she ever really known her husband at all?

A door squeaked. The door of the Cubby Hole. How well she knew the sound. She looked up, and there was Steven.

'Christine!'

'Well?'

Steven Clifford frowned, an unfriendly frown. It was the sort of welcome she had half expected.

'I thought you were in Monte Carlo,' he said.

'I've come back.'

'Why?'

'Babette.'

His eyes narrowed, but did not move from hers.

'Go on,' he said.

'It seems I was the last to know,' said Christine. 'All the time you have been making a fool of me I have been making a fool of myself.'

He did not speak.

'I—I want you to give her up.'

But still he did not speak.

'Did you hear me, Steven?'

'Yes.'

'Well?'

'I can't give her up.'

'You mean you won't?'

'I mean what I say. I can't.'

'But you can give me up?'

She flushed and then went cold, so cold that the weapon on which her hand still rested, warmed by her grasp, seemed to burn her and make her again aware of it. And then Steven said the wrong thing.

'You've had two years of me. What do you want—eternity?'

The wrong thing because it gave her the chance to say the right thing—the smart thing, the apt thing; and she had never been used to saying the apt thing.

'Do *you*?' she cried; and the words themselves made her raise the revolver and point it at him.

'For God's sake, you damned little fool, put that down!' Steven Clifford cried.

There was no thinking. Things seemed to happen themselves. He was rushing towards her, his face livid with fury. There was a crash and a spurt and from the panelling above the portrait over the fireplace a little cloud of sawdust appeared and faded. Steven stopped and came on again. There seemed only one thing to do, and she did it.

And then he was lying there still, in front of the desk, and she seemed to realize only presently that she had killed him.

The odd thing was that it had very little to do with her. She had not meant to kill him. She had meant anything. Or what had she meant? At first, when she first came in—what? Not this. But this had happened. There he was. Dead . . .

Slowly she sat again on the leather chair. Steven was dead. The revolver was in her hand. Steven had been shot. *She* had shot him. Things would have to be done.

She decided to go. It appeared the logical thing to do. Why should she suffer more for Steven than she had suffered already? But from where she sat to the door, and from the door down the hall to the outer door, was that trail of muddy footprints to show she had been here. Oh—and yes! the taximan . . .

Go . . . Easier to say than to do. They would find her footprints and interview the taximan, and the taximan would tell how he had brought her from the station to the house. And then she would suffer again—die because of him as she had lived for him—giving everything, to the end.

She flushed with the indignity of the thought. Justice? Justice was cold, impersonal; justice was nobody. She was warm and living and . . . cheated. Even a vixen fought for life. Reptiles. *Anything* fought for life. And she was living.

It felt like waking up. She began to do things, as after a sleep. The right things, too, they seemed to be; at once, instinctively.

Fingerprints, to start with. Well, she had read all about that in books. She took out her handkerchief and wiped the revolver clean. Then she stooped and forced the thing into his grasp, closing his fingers round it. The action made her shudder, but it was soon over.

She rose and turned to the door. Stopped . . .

The right things they seemed to be, instinctively. But at the very beginning this was not right. 'Suicide of Steven Clifford.' And there were her footprints. And, somewhere, the taximan.

Suicide of Steven Clifford. And she had been here in the room. There was evidence. Yes, lucky she had thought of that. It meant that she had found the body. And having found the body—what?

Of course!

She turned back to the desk, sat and pulled the telephone towards her. How should she put it? 'This is Mrs Steven Clifford. Will you come at once, please. Something terrible has happened to my husband. He's committed suicide.'

Yes. Yes, something like that.

She put her hand on the receiver. It shook as she did so, rattled the instrument so much that the bell tinkled—tinkled like a warning. From above the portrait over the fireplace a tiny hole, a pale spot on the dark panel, looked down like an eye.

The first bullet . . .

They would find that hole. And then they would know. *Suicide* of Steven Clifford? No, that was hopeless now.

They would say—why had he fired *behind* him at the panel? Ridiculous. Men always fell forward in the direction of the shot, when they were killed. She had read that, too, somewhere. And he was facing the door to the hall. That first bullet in the panel gave the whole game away. It meant *someone else*, shooting from the direction of the hall. And the two bullets were from the one revolver—the revolver in Steven's hand. It didn't make sense. They'd find out the truth in five minutes.

Christine drew her hand away from the telephone and let it sink to her lap. It had all seemed so easy and now it seemed so difficult—almost impossible.

Something pink on his desk caught her eye. A cheque for four thousand pounds, made payable to Steven. Something to do with his business. And he was in perfect health, in the prime of life, with the woman he wanted—Babette.

No, not suicide. They'd soon see that.

The bullet hole over the fireplace. They would find the bullet hole. They were certain to find the bullet hole.

Well, then—what? The first thing was to make sure they didn't find the bullet hole. How? Plug it with brown paper, stain the brown paper with ink? But if their eyes happened to catch that she was done for. She stared across the room and saw a way. Not, perhaps, the perfect way, but the only way.

She rose to cross the room and stopped again, remembering something just in time. Damp mud still clung to her shoes. Each time she moved she made fresh footprints, and footprints near the fireplace would draw their attention to the fireplace, from the fireplace to the wall.

Quickly she slipped her feet out of her shoes, and in her stockings crossed the floor. She pulled a tall chair round, climbed up, and stared at the bullet hole. It was half an inch above the portrait and about an inch from the centre. She lifted the picture from its hook. She knew that hook; had been in the room on the day it was first screwed there. Little had she thought, then . . .

She rested the portrait on the mantelpiece and unscrewed the hook. This she inserted in the bullet hole and twisted it home. She gave it a pull. It held. On it she hung the portrait.

Then she climbed down from the tall chair, put it back in its place, and looked up. No hole was visible in the panel now. The bullet hole carried the hook; the original hole was hidden behind the portrait. That seemed all right. There were tiny specks of sawdust on the mantelpiece. She blew them away.

Now what? Standing quite still, she attempted to go over everything.

If not suicide, then murder. And the revolver was in Steven's hand. She removed it and placed it in the desk. He had been shot . . . and he was facing the door. Shot from the direction of the door. And there were her footprints. They proved she had walked as far as the desk. No further. But as far as the desk.

Her body shaking, she stood over Steven and noted carefully the details of his crumpled figure. Slowly she turned him round until he faced the open door of the Cubby Hole. She flung out his left hand, bent his right knee under his left leg. Then she rose and looked at him for a full minute. Yes; she could see nothing wrong with that.

The door of the Cubby Hole . . . She crossed the room and looked in, entered the Cubby Hole. With her handkerchief round her fingers she raised the window an inch or two. He could have been shot by somebody looking through the open window.

Yes. The bullet would tear through the open doorway of the lounge and strike him down as he stood in front of his desk.

Yes . . . And the other bullet?

She returned to the lounge, opened the door to the hall, went back to the Cubby Hole door, and raised her hand. She took the 'sight' along her finger. Yes, the other bullet would have crashed through the third panel of the hall window, to lose itself some-where—anywhere—in the garden.

From her handbag she took a nail-file, went again into the hall, stabbed at the third pane with the nail-file, watched the jagged pieces of glass fall out. And felt the rain drive in.

Then back to the desk. There was the revolver. Wiping it again, she took it into the Cubby Hole and dropped it out of the window. She heard it splash into the muddy garden bed beneath. She went back into the lounge.

Everything seemed right now. He had been shot by somebody standing outside the Cubby Hole window. Two bullets had been fired. The first had gone through the hall window. The second had killed Steven. She had come in, come to the desk, found Steven, telephoned for the police.

She had come to the desk but no further. There was evidence . . .

She moved behind the desk to the leather chair, sat and put on her shoes, looked around. Had she forgotten anything?

Yes! Her first action on finding him would have been to turn him over and see if he still lived. She sank on one knee and turned him over; then rose and picked up the telephone.

'Police!' she gasped.

Soon a voice spoke to her.

'This is Mrs Steven Clifford,' she said. 'Will you come at once, please. Something terrible has happened to my husband. I think he's been murdered.'

She hung up the receiver and stood shaking, staring up at the portrait over the fireplace. Now they could come and arrest her. The sooner the better.

Very much the better . . .

Detective-Inspector Bryce could see just what had happened. It was, if you happened to be Inspector Noakes, as plain as the nose on your face.

Somebody had poked the revolver through the Cubby Hole window and fired. Two shots. The first had missed, smashing the window in the hall. The second had got him.

'And without wishing to speak ill of the dead,' added Detective-Inspector Bryce, 'I'm surprised he didn't stop one years ago. The things we've heard about Steven Clifford! There'll be plenty of people to think the world's a better place now he's out of it.'

'Including——?' Noakes prompted.

'Ah!' said Bryce. 'That's the bit we've got to come to. You say there are no footprints outside on the gravel path from the window of the little room there?'

'What can you expect on a night like this? Ten seconds of this rain would pound any footprint out of existence. Thinking——?'

'What I'm thinking is this,' Bryce answered. 'Her footprints here show that she came no further than the desk. He was shot from the direction of that little room, and the absence of scorching means he was shot at a distance. And she doesn't appear to have been over there at all. At any rate—*not that time.*'

Noakes twisted his brow into rows of crazy lines and stared at his superior.

'I mean,' Bryce went on, 'suppose she comes in, dries her shoes carefully on the mat outside, enters this room, gets the gun, goes over there to the little room—or as far as the door—shoots him, gets out of the window of the little room, drops the gun, comes round by the gravel path to the front door, comes in again, this time *doesn't* dry her shoes, goes to the desk, leaving footprints to show that's as far as she *did* go, "finds" the body and telephones us?'

'Ye-es . . .' said Noakes. 'Takes a bit of thinking out. For her, I mean.'

'The point is,' Bryce reminded him, 'has anybody else been here?'

'Which we've got to find out.'

'Which we *will*.'

'Ye-es . . .'

There's this revue woman he's had in tow. It's an open secret. Everybody knows about her, and his wife must. She's supposed to be in Monte Carlo and we find her here. Does that mean something?'

'She can come home when she likes.'

'Quite. But where's her luggage?'

'Left at the station?'

'If you like. But there isn't even a suitcase. Looks as if she hadn't meant to stay, doesn't it? She comes home, but not to stay. *Home*, mind. All the way from Monte Carlo. All right. What has she come for?'

'H'm.'

'Well, we've got to have something to start on.'

'She *did* 'phone us, you know,' Noakes reminded him. '*And* suggested murder. If she had the place to herself, why didn't she clean the gun, put it in his hand, and suggest suicide?'

Bryce picked up a pink slip from Steven Clifford's desk.

'Here's a cheque for four thousand. He was in the prime of life, prosperous, leading just the sort of life he wanted to lead. If he'd been broke—well, maybe. But this cheque's dated yesterday. How *are* you going to make it look like suicide?'

'She could have destroyed the cheque.'

'But not the transaction, whatever it was. That would have come to light in a couple of days.'

'Do women think of these things?'

'Do we know that she didn't?'

'You're assuming . . .'

'I'm assuming nothing. But she's the only one to hand so far. Where did you put her?'

'Dining-room.'

'Well, come on. Let's see if she's got something else to say for herself.'

To the statement she had already volunteered Christine Clifford was apparently prepared to add any details they required. She had, she said, planned to stay in Monte Carlo until the end of the month, but she had decided suddenly to come home two days ago.

'Was there any particular reason for your change of plan, Mrs Clifford?' Bryce asked.

Without moving her eyes from his and without a moment's hesitation she replied:

'Yes. Rumours had come to my ears about my husband and another woman. In the circumstances letters were out of the question. And time might have been important. I came home at once to tax him with it.'

'Without your luggage?'

'I left that at the station, in case I should not be staying here.'

'Which you thought likely?'

'Which I thought likely.'

'I see. . . . You got out of the taxi and came straight in here?'

'Yes.'

'Was your husband surprised to see you?'

She did not answer. She sat looking at him, still without confusion. But she did not answer.

('Why,' thought Bryce, 'doesn't she say "I found him dead" quickly? Does she *want* me to arrest her?')

'I have already explained,' she said at last, 'he was dead when I came in.'

('Oh, *was* he!' thought Bryce.) 'H'm . . .' he murmured aloud. 'Was there any sign of anybody else about the house when you came in?'

'No.'

'Nor outside, when you left the taxi?'

'No.'

'Do you know of anybody who would have been likely to kill your husband?'

'No.'

No every time . . .

('Damn it!' thought Bryce, '*does* she want me to arrest her?')

'Do you recognize the revolver?' he asked.

'Yes. It is my husband's.'

'You are certain?'

'Positive.'

'So that whoever shot him would have to come into the house to get the weapon.'

'That is what it looks like.'

'Yes. . . . The two servants are out?'

'Venner and Mrs Venner? Yes, always on this night. As they are man and wife they always have their night off together.'

'You knew they would be out, when you came?'

'Oh yes.'

'Thank you.'

The doctor came. A man with a camera came. And with one thing and another it was turned midnight before Bryce and Noakes had a minute to compare notes together.

'What I don't understand,' said Bryce, 'is why she's trying to run her neck into it. May be fed up with life, now he's gone. Ought to be chirpy about it, after what she knew, but you never can tell with women. Honestly, if I arrested her I think she'd be glad.'

Twelve hours later he arrested her.

Nearly nine weeks afterwards Venner sat in his little kitchen over an early edition of the evening newspaper, a cup of steaming tea by his side.

'Read it out,' said Mrs Venner.

Venner read it out.

'"Evidence," Sir Morgan continued, "we must have. It has been said in this court that motive and opportunity have been proved. Ladies and gentlemen, I submit that this is not sufficient. The accused may have *wanted* to kill her husband. She may have had the chance to kill him. The question you have to answer is: *Did* she kill him?

'"An unpopular ruler may be shot in the streets of his capital, with five hundred angry subjects about him, all within shooting distance. Each has the motive; each has the opportunity. But to know that is to know just not quite enough. Evidence—*proof*—is required before the right man can be picked out from the five hundred. I hope this illustration makes my meaning clear.

'"The half-hearted theory, for which the prosecution itself shows little enthusiasm, that the accused climbed out of the window, walked along the gravel path, re-entered the house—this time taking care to leave footprints only as far as the desk—and pretended to find the body; this half-hearted theory is fantastic. There were, as you know, no footprints on that gravel path. In such a downpour there could not be. *But*—there was gravel on that gravel path— yellow gravel—and she brought no gravel into the house that night.

Her footprints were there in the room, but they were clean of gravel. She walked only from the taxi.

'"Where, then, is the evidence we seek? Evidence we must have, circumstantial though it may be—but evidence. Where is the evidence here? I submit there is none—not a tittle—that the accused ever stood in that part of the room from which the fatal shot was fired. You may think this; you may think that. You do not *know*. There is *no evidence*."'

Venner looked up and coughed.

'There's a bit here at the end,' he said, and read on: '"The case is expected to end late this afternoon."'

He glanced at his watch.

'Six o'clock.'

'The wireless!' whispered Mrs Venner.

Venner put the newspaper aside, crossed the room to his primitive set, and switched it on. Then he and his wife stood breathless, waiting.

'. . . colder than of late; some showers. . . . First news. Copyright reserved. The Clifford Case. A remarkable demonstration was witnessed at the Central Criminal Court this afternoon at the close of the trial of Mrs Christine Clifford on a charge of murdering her husband. After the jury had returned their verdict of Not Guilty . . .'

'Thank God!' murmured Venner. And hurried to get brandy for his wife.

For a fortnight in Torquay, Christine Clifford hid from eyes and tongues and cameras. Everybody thought that the house would be sold; that she would go away for good. But at the end of the fortnight the home that had been her home and Steven Clifford's was opened up again and she came back. It was a Tuesday, early in the evening, and Venner and Mrs Venner were at the door to welcome her with congratulations. She was home and, by the Venners, *wanted*. She remembered the last time. . . .

She dined alone and told Venner she would take coffee in the lounge. At which Venner opened his discreet eyes wider than they were usually opened. Not yet since her return had Mrs Clifford been into the lounge. Of course, Venner admitted to himself, since she was keeping on the house the lounge would be lived in; would have to be. But just *now*, on the first night . . .

'I will light the gas fire, madam,' he said.

Presently she went into the lounge. Venner was by the door, the gas fire lit.

'Thank you, Venner,' she said.

He was still by the door.

It seemed much the same, though strangely far away; not so much a room she was in as a picture she was looking at. The door to the Cubby Hole was closed, the desk was in the same place. There was no pink cheque on the desk now. She wondered where it had gone, and promptly forgot it. She found herself looking for footprints, but they were gone. In front of the gas fire was an easy chair, a small stand, richly carved, by its side. She sat down.

Venner was still by the door . . .

'What is it, Venner?' she asked softly.

'Well, madam——'

He was looking at the portrait over the fireplace. She, too, looked up at it, then back at Venner. His discreet eyes were again opened wider than usually. Something above the portrait was puzzling him.

'Yes?'

'That—that's very strange, madam!'

'Strange, Venner?'

'The picture, madam—over the fireplace there. It—it's slightly out of centre. It isn't in the middle of the panel. I don't remember noticing that before. I'm sure it used not to be like that—I'd have noticed it. I hung the picture there myself, madam, when we came here four years ago. I feel positive——'

'You are right, Venner. The picture is out of centre. It has been moved.'

'Moved, madam? But who——?'

'Get the step-ladder, Venner.'

'Yes, madam.'

Funny business. Moved. Why? And who moved it? But whoever moved it—why? And when? Queer he'd never noticed it before. How long had it been like that?

Venner wondered his way out to the kitchen and wondered his way back again with the step-ladder. Mrs Clifford had moved from the fireplace. She was sitting now close to the desk.

'The—step-ladder, madam.'

'Yes. Take the picture down, Venner.'

'Very good, madam.'

Funny business, and getting funnier. Why was she so quiet? Pale, too. *Very* queer. Could it have anything to do with . . .

Venner climbed up the ladder and lifted the portrait off its hook.

'And now what, Venner?' Mrs Clifford asked.

'It's very strange, madam, I must say. There are two holes here. The screw has been moved to a fresh place and the picture lifted. I'm sure I haven't done it. Nor Mrs Venner, madam. I can't understand it in the least. There's been nobody else. Except the police. And they——'

'It's not really very puzzling, Venner,' she interrupted. 'That was the hole that was made by the first bullet.'

'The—first . . .'

'I'm afraid I'm not much good with firearms. The first shot went very wide.'

Venner's mouth fell open. He had to put out his hand to keep his balance on the top of the step-ladder.

'*You*, madam?'

'Yes, Venner. You can put the picture back. And you might as well move the screw to its original position. You see—it doesn't matter now.'

Venner, his mind numbed, obeyed orders, then came down the step-ladder and waited.

'You can take the step-ladder away,' said Christine. 'Then come back. Before—before you tell your wife.'

Still mechanically, Venner obeyed orders. Soon he was back, looking very self-conscious.

'You will understand, Venner,' she said, 'why I had to hide that. If they had found that tiny bullet hole they would have known at once that he was shot from over there, where my footprints were. So I raised the picture and . . . turned him round, and they believed it.'

'You could have—gone away, madam,' suggested Venner.

'No, Venner. That would have done no good. I had one hope only.'

'Yes, madam?'

'To be arrested and tried.'

This was beyond Venner.

'I gave a plain denial, but offered no defence,' Christine went on. 'They arrested me because of my husband's revolver, because of my knowledge of his life apart from me, because of my motive, because of my presence here, because of a dozen things. They did not arrest me *because of the bullet hole*—and that was my only chance. To be arrested and tried before anybody noticed that bullet hole. To be arrested and tried . . . and acquitted. Acquitted, Venner.'

'Yes, madam.'

'You see?'

'I—well . . .'

'They had theories; they had no real evidence. That bullet hole is evidence. It is proof. And sooner or later—perhaps sooner—it was bound to be discovered. By whoever bought or rented the house. By whoever cleaned the wall or the picture. If I had put them off with a tale of a strange man lurking about the house, or of make-believe threats my husband was supposed to receive—if I had delayed them, that hole might have been found before my arrest. And then . . . Now, you see?'

'Yes, madam.'

'I put no obstacle in their way. They took me. There was no one else to take. And the verdict was Not Guilty.'

'Yes, madam.'

'And by the law of the land nobody can be tried twice for that crime. You knew that, Venner?'

'Yes, madam.'

'Not Guilty—and always now it will remain Not Guilty. Nothing can ever alter that.'

'No, madam.'

She looked at him.

'The bullet hole does not matter now.'

'No, madam.'

'You have been with us a long time, Venner; you and Mrs Venner. I don't know if this is going to alter things—what you will care to do about it. . . .'

Venner, close to the door, shuffled, glanced at Christine, rubbed his hands together, looked away, opened the door, and went out.

She sat there a moment, then rose; smiled, sighed, stared at something a thousand miles away behind the gas fire, lifted the lid of the cigarette box on the table, took out a cigarette and lit it.

Three minutes later Venner was back, carrying a tray.

'Your coffee, madam.'

'Thank you, Venner.'

III

THE TWIST

Sapper (Herman Cyril McNeile, 1888–1937) found fame and a considerable fortune writing headlong thrillers about Bulldog Drummond, his ex-Army plug-ugly who was determined to do anything but opt for the quiet life. His books sold in their hundreds of thousands during the inter-war years. Like a good many other writers of the time, Sapper (a great purloiner of plots) was deeply impressed by the Grimpen Mire sequence in Conan Doyle's *The Hound of the Baskervilles*, which resurfaced, in one form or another, in a number of his own works. His series detective was Ronald Standish ('Sherlock Holmes in cricketing togs', as someone once remarked), many of whose exploits appeared in the *Strand*; many though did not, Reeves Shaw rejecting them as being 'really . . . too close' to those of Doyle. A careless writer, he frequently had trouble with his characters' identities, especially those of his heroines whose names sometimes changed during the course of a single chapter. Nevertheless, when on form, and especially in his shorter fiction, he was a natural story-teller, particularly adept at the shock-ending story (his model here was O. Henry). 'The Idol's Eye' is an early crime story, written soon after Sapper retired from the Royal Engineers (rank, lieutenant-colonel) and cleverly utilizing a supernatural plot device.

In the days before radio and rapid transportation *Seamark* (Austin J. Small, *fl.* 1919–29) roamed the wastelands of the world—mainly the Yukon and up to the Arctic Circle, but also around the Pacific, across the Kalahari, and through West Africa's fever-belt ('the white man's grave'). He served in the Royal Navy during the First World War and was in several actions, notably the attack on the German submarine pens at Zeebrugge. He was a prolific short-story writer for the fiction magazines of the early 1920s, at one stage appearing in *20-Story Magazine* under his own name as well as his somewhat obscure pseudonym (*1*. Landmark visible from the sea, navigational guide; *2*. a coastline's upper tidal limit). He put a great deal of his own experience of the gruelling side of life into his stories, which are vivid and vigorously told, with just the right amount of sentiment and melodrama to appeal to his audience. Coming under the spell of the thriller writer Edgar Wallace he began to write of vast global conspiracies and insane criminals who used super-science to gain their ends (*Master Vorst* [1926]; *The Man they couldn't Arrest* [1927]; *The Avenging Ray* [1930]) but died under miserable circumstances, gassing himself just when success was within his grasp, due to a depressive condition and his increasingly wretched marriage. 'The Perfect Crime' was his only contribution to the *Strand*.

During the 1920s and 1930s *Augustus Muir* (*fl.* 1925–54) divided his time between journalism and thriller writing. He was a dependable feature-writer who turned up in a variety of periodicals and newspapers, in this role often writing lengthy pieces for the *Strand* that are characterized by a skilful and attractive deployment of facts and figures and a dry wit. It is possible he was on the staff, since some of his articles are little more than exercises in in-house puffery (an enthusiastic piece on Reeves Shaw and his humorous weekly the *Humorist*, to which Muir also contributed, reveals much about the editor and his chief writers and artists but fails to mention that its offices were just down the corridor). Time has taken its revenge on at least one of his articles: in 1930 he wrote a fulsome piece about his visit to 'A Treasure-House of Books', the home of Thomas J. Wise, the greatest bibliophile of his day—soon to be brought down by John Carter and Graham Pollard as the greatest humbug, forger, and literary scoundrel of his day. Muir wrote a score of detective novels, two under the pseudonym 'Austin Moore'. 'The Intruder' was one of a series of 'Five Minute' short-shorts to which several writers contributed.

Richard Keverne (C. J. W. Hosken, 1882–1950) was for most of his working life a journalist. During the First World War he joined the Royal Flying Corps, serving through to the Armistice. He was on the staff of the *Daily Mirror* for seventeen years, using his pseudonym to write over a dozen well-received detective novels in his spare time, as well as three as Clifford Hosken, his real name. Together with 'Henry Wade' (Sir Henry Aubrey-Fletcher) he was instrumental in the success of the publisher Constable's 'Crime Line', which during the 1930s was especially strong, issuing all of Keverne's and Wade's output, as well as detective stories by E. C. Bentley, H. Warner Allen, and David Magarshack (later translator of Dostoevsky). Though not unappealing, Keverne's style was on the whole penny-plain, becoming twopence-coloured only when he turned to the eighteenth century for inspiration, writing a number of engaging crime stories set on and around the High Toby and utilizing his extensive knowledge of coaching days and ways: his classic on the subject, *Tales of Old Inns: The History, Legend and Romance of Some of Our Older Hostelries* (1927; revised by the adventure writer Hammond Innes in 1947), kept him in small cigars till he died. 'Cast-Iron Alibi' features Inspector Artifex, a character about whom Keverne wrote several short stories and three novellas (the latter forming the book *Artifex Intervenes* [1934]).

The Idol's Eye

Sapper

'PERSONALLY, I don't consider there's a word of truth in the whole thing' said Denton, dogmatically. 'All this mystery and spook stunt was started by hysterical old women, and has been kept alive by professional knaves, who fill their pockets at the expense of fools.'

He drained his port, and glared round the table as if challenging anyone to dispute his assertion.

'There was a silly old aunt of mine,' he continued, thrusting his heavy-featured face forward, 'who bought a house down Camberley way two or three years ago. Admirable house: just suited the old lady. Special room facing south for the canaries and parrots, and all that sort of thing.' He helped himself to another glass of port. 'She hadn't been in the house a fortnight before the servants gave notice. They weren't going to stop on, they said, in a house where noises were heard at strange hours of the night, and where the clothes were snatched off the cook's bed. So the old thing wrote to me—I was managing her affairs for her—and asked what she should do. I told her that I'd come down and deal with the noises, and that if anyone started pulling my bedclothes off he'd get a thick ear for his trouble.'

Denton laughed, and, leaning back in his chair, thrust his hands into his trousers pockets. 'Of course there were noises,' he continued. 'Show me any house—especially an old one—where there ain't noises at night. The stairs creaked—stairs always do: boards in the passages contracted a bit and made a noise—boards always do. And as for the cook's bedclothes, having once seen the cook I didn't wonder they came off in the night. She must have weighed twenty stone, and nothing less than full-size double sheets could have been expected to remain tucked in. But do you suppose it was any good pointing these things out to the old dear? Not on your life! All she said to me was: "Harry, my boy: there are agencies at work in this world of which we have no knowledge. You may not be able to feel with them; some of us can. And it is written in the Book that they are evil."'

Again Denton laughed coarsely. 'Twaddle! Bunkum! The only agent that she felt was the house agent, who was charmed at the prospect of a second commission so soon.'

'She moved, did she?' said Lethbridge, our host.

'Of course she did,' jeered Denton. 'And the last I heard of the house was that it had been taken by a retired grocer with a large family who were perfectly happy there.' He thumped his fist on the table. 'The whole thing is entirely imagination. If you sit at the end of a dark passage, when the moon is throwing fantastic shadows, and imagine hard enough that you're going to see a ghost, you probably will. At least you'll fancy you see something. But that's not a ghost. There's nothing really there. You might as well say that the figures you see in a dream are real.'

'Which raises a very big question, doesn't it?' said Mansfrey, thoughtfully. He was a quiet man with spectacles, who had so far taken little part in the conversation.

'Even granted that what you say is correct, and I do not dispute it, you cannot dismiss imagination in quite the same manner as you do a dream. It may well be that half the so-called ghosts which people see or hear are merely imagination: but the result on the people is the same as if they were there in reality.' His blue eyes were fixed on Denton mildly, and he blinked once or twice. 'It takes all sorts to make a world, and everyone is not so completely devoid of imagination as you are, Denton.'

'I don't know that I am completely devoid of imagination,' said Denton. 'I can see as far into a brick wall as most men, where a business proposition is concerned. But if you mean that I'm never likely to see a ghost, you're quite right.' He was staring at Mansfrey, and his face was a little flushed. It struck me as he sat there half-sprawling over the table, what a coarse animal he was. And yet rumour had it that he was very popular with a certain type of woman.

Mansfrey sipped his port, and a slight smile played round his lips. Lethbridge noticed it and made a movement as if to join the ladies. For Mansfrey's smile was deliberately provocative, and Denton was not a congenial companion if provoked—especially after three glasses of port. His voice, loud enough at ordinary times, became louder: the bully in him, which was never far from the surface, flared out.

'Ghosts,' said Mansfrey, gently, 'are the least of the results of imagination. Even if you did see one, Denton, I don't expect it would worry you much.' His mild blue eyes were again fixed on the other man. 'It is not that manifestation of the power of mind that I was particularly thinking of.'

Denton gave a sneering laugh. 'Then what was it?' he asked. 'Trying to walk between two lamp-posts and finding there was only one?'

'Personally,' answered Mansfrey, 'I have never suffered that way.' Lethbridge looked at me uncomfortably, but Mansfrey was speaking again. 'It was the power of mind over matter with regard to bodily ailments that I was thinking of.'

'Good heavens,' jeered Denton, 'you don't mean to say that you're a Christian Scientist?'

'Up to a point, certainly,' answered the other. 'If it is possible, and we know on indisputable proof that it is, for a man to deliberately decide to die when there is nothing the matter with him, and having come to that decision to sit down on the ground and put it into effect—surely the contrary must be still more feasible. For in the case of the native who dies, his mind is acting against nature: in the case of the man who tries to cure himself his mind is acting with nature.'

'Those natives who die in that manner have always been seen by somebody else's brother-in-law,' answered Denton. 'I'll believe it, Mansfrey, when I see it for myself.'

'I doubt if you would,' said Mansfrey. 'You'd say the man was malingering even when he was in his coffin.'

Once again I glanced at Lethbridge. It almost seemed as if Mansfrey, usually the mildest of men, was deliberately going out of his way to annoy Denton.

'And I suppose,' he continued, after a pause, 'that you absolutely disbelieve in the ill luck that goes with certain houses and other inanimate objects—such as the Maga diamond, for instance?'

'Absolutely,' answered Denton. 'And if I had the money I would pay a thousand pounds to anyone who would prove me wrong——' Then he laughed. 'I thought you were reputed to be a scientist, Mansfrey! Funny sort of science, isn't it. Do you honestly mean to tell me that you believe a bit of carbon like the Maga diamond has the power to bring bad luck to its owner?'

'The last four owners have died violent deaths,' remarked Mansfrey, quietly.

Denton snorted. 'Coincidence,' he cried. 'Good heavens! man, you're talking like an hysterical nursemaid.'

'When up against the standard of pure knowledge,' returned Mansfrey, mildly, 'quite a number of people talk like hysterical nursemaids. When one reflects how little one knows, I sometimes wonder why even the cleverest man ever speaks at all.' He started fumbling in his waistcoat pocket. 'But talking of the Maga diamond, I've got something here that might interest you.'

He produced a little chamois-leather bag, and untied the string that kept it closed. Then before our astonished gaze he tipped out on to the tablecloth what appeared to be a large ruby. It was a cut stone, and in the light it glowed and scintillated with a thousand red flames.

'Pretty thing, isn't it?' said Mansfrey.

'My dear fellow,' cried Lethbridge, leaning forward, 'is it real? If so, it must be worth a fortune. I'm some judge of precious stones, but I've never dreamed of anything to approach that.'

'Glass,' laughed its owner. 'A particularly beautiful tint of red glass. No—it's not a historic jewel that I've got here, Lethbridge, but something which bears on what we have been discussing.' His mild eyes once more sought Denton's face. 'This piece of glass, so the story runs, was originally the eye of an idol in one of the most sacred shrines in Lhasa. The Tibetans, as you know, are a very religious race—and this particular idol was apparently the "big noise" amongst all their gods. Some young fools, on a shooting trip, managed to get to Lhasa—no mean feat, incidentally, in itself—and not content with that they violated this most sacred temple, and stole the eye of the god.'

Denton gave a shout of laughter. 'Good lads,' he cried. 'That's the stuff to give the troops.'

Mansfrey looked at him gravely. 'They were discovered by the priests,' he continued, 'and had to run for their lives. All quite usual, you see: the good old historic story of fiction. Even the curse comes in, so as not to spoil the sequence. I, of course, have only heard it fifteenth hand, but I give it to you as I got it. The thing is harmless, unless allowed to remain in the hand, or up against a man's bare flesh for a certain length of time. How long I don't know. The sailor I got it from was a bit vague himself—all he wanted to do was to get rid of it as quickly as he could. But if, so the yarn goes, it remains for this necessary period of time in a man's hand or up against him somewhere—the man dies.'

Denton shook with amusement. 'And do you believe that twaddle?' he demanded.

'I don't know,' said Mansfrey, slowly. 'There are one or two very strange stories about it.' He prodded the glass gently with his finger, and the ruby lights shivered and danced till it seemed as if it was on fire. 'A Danish sailor stole it from the man who sold it to me, on the voyage home. He was an enormously powerful, healthy fellow, but he was found dead the next morning with the thing inside his shirt. My sailor friend got it from a Chinaman in Chefoo. The Chink's assistant had recently stolen it out of his master's shop. He had been found dead with it in his hand, and the Chink was frightened.' Mansfrey smiled, and put the bit of glass back in its bag. 'Just two yarns of many, and they're all the same. Anybody who holds it, or lets it touch him for too long, dies. And dies to all appearances a natural death.'

'And you really believe that twaddle?' said Denton, again, even more offensively than before.

Mansfrey shrugged his shoulders. 'I don't know whether I do or don't,' he answered. 'I myself have tested the thing; and as far as I can see, it is just a piece of ordinary red glass, but——' Again he shrugged his shoulders, and then replaced the leather bag in his pocket.

'Do you mean to say that you've been too frightened to hold the thing in your hand and prove that it's rot?' cried Denton. He turned to Lethbridge. 'Well, I'm hanged! And in the twentieth century. Chuck the bauble over here, Mansfrey. I'll sleep with it in my hand tonight, and give it back to you tomorrow morning at breakfast.'

But Mansfrey shook his head. 'Oh, no, Denton,' he said, 'most certainly not. If anything *did* happen, I should never forgive myself.'

The opposition only served to make Denton more determined than ever, and more objectionably rude into the bargain. Personally, I had been surprised at Mansfrey carrying such a thing about with him—it did not fit in with what I knew of the man at all; but I was even more surprised at his reluctance to allow Denton to have it. It was preposterous that he could really believe there was any danger to be feared from holding a piece of coloured glass in one's hand, and yet for five or ten minutes he remained obdurate.

Then, suddenly, he gave in. 'Very well, Denton,' he remarked, 'you shall have it. But don't say I didn't warn you.'

Denton laughed. 'If your preposterous stories were to be believed, and came true in my case, I gather I shouldn't be in a condition to say much. But my ghost shall come and haunt you, Mansfrey. I'll pull off your bedclothes, and rattle chains in the passages.'

We all laughed, and shortly after Lethbridge rose. As he got to the door he paused and looked at us doubtfully. 'Of course it's all rot, and only a joke—but I think we might as well postpone telling the ladies until Denton gives it back tomorrow at breakfast. My wife is such a nervous woman, don't you know. Probably come running along to your room, Denton, every half-hour to see that you're still snoring.'

Denton gave one of his usual bellows, and in a few minutes we had all settled down to bridge.

It was Denton himself who insisted on his hand being tied up with a pocket handkerchief. The four of us were standing talking in his room before turning in: in fact, Mansfrey had already completed the first part of his toilet by donning a smoking jacket of striking design.

'Bring out your bally bit of glass, my boy,' boomed Denton, jovially, 'and put it right there.' He held out a hand like a leg of mutton. 'Then I'll close my fist, and afterwards you tie my hand with a handkerchief, so that I can't open it in the night.'

But the idol's eye was not immediately forthcoming. 'I tell you candidly, Denton,' said Mansfrey, 'I wish you'd give it up. I don't believe myself that there *is* anything in it, but somehow——' His eyes were blinking very fast behind his spectacles; he seemd the picture of frightened indecision.

Denton laughed and clapped him on the back; and to be clapped on the back by Denton is rather like being kicked by a mule. I have had experience of both, and I know.

'You funny little man,' he cried, and prepared to do it again, until Mansfrey discreetly withdrew out of range. 'You funny little man—blinking away there like a startled owl. You know, Lethbridge, I do really believe that he fancies there's something in his blessed old glass eye from Lhasa. Give it to me, you silly ass,' he said to Mansfrey. 'I'll show you.' To say that Denton's speech was thick would be to exaggerate, but as I sat on the edge of his dressing-table, smoking a cigarette, I could not help recalling that, though Lethbridge and I had each had one whisky and soda during the evening, while Mansfrey had drunk only plain Vichy, the tantalus was nearly empty when we came to bed. Denton was, in fact, in a condition when, for peace all round, it was better not to annoy him.

Apparently the same idea had struck Lethbridge, for he turned to Mansfrey and nodded his head. 'Give it to him, old boy, and let's get to bed. I'm dog tired.'

'Very well,' answered Mansfrey. 'I'll get it. It is in my waistcoat pocket.'

Slowly, almost reluctantly, he left the room, and went along the passage to his own. While we waited, Denton got into his pyjamas, and by the time Mansfrey returned he was already in bed.

'Here it is,' said Mansfrey, holding out the little bag. 'But I wish you wouldn't, Denton.'

'Oh! confound you and your wishes,' said Denton, irritably, stretching out his hand. 'Put it there, little man, put it there.'

The piece of glass rolled out of the bag, and lay for a moment glittering scarlet in Denton's huge palm. Then his fingers closed over it, and Lethbridge tied a handkerchief round his fist.

'I'll give it back to you at breakfast, Mansfrey,' he said, turning over on his side. 'And you can prepare to be roasted, my lad, properly roasted. Good-night, you fellows: turn out the light, one of you, as you go.'

I closed the door behind me, and strolled towards my own room. It was next to Mansfrey's, and I stopped for a moment talking to him.

'What a great animal that fellow is,' I remarked.

He did not reply at once, and I glanced at him. He was standing quite still, with his pale blue eyes fixed on Denton's room, from which already I fancied I heard the snores of the heavy sleeper.

'Animal is not a bad description of him,' he answered, thoughtfully. 'Not at all bad. Good night.'

He stepped inside his door and closed it, and it was only as I switched off my own light that it struck me that Mansfrey's eyes had never blinked as he stood looking at Denton's door. And blinking was a chronic affliction of his.

I seemed only to have been asleep a few minutes when I was awakened by the light being switched on. Lethbridge was standing by my bed, looking white and shaken.

'My God! man,' he said, as I blinked up at him. 'He's dead!'

'Who is?' I cried foolishly, sitting up in bed.

'Why, Denton,' he answered, and the whole thing came back to my mind.

'Denton dead!' I looked at him horror-struck. 'He can't be, man: there must be some mistake.'

'I wish to God there was,' he answered hoarsely. 'Mansfrey's with him now—almost off his head.'

I reached for my dressing-gown, and glanced at the time. It was just half-past four.

'I'll never forgive myself,' he went on, as I searched for my slippers. 'That fool story of Mansfrey's made a sort of impression on me, and I couldn't sleep. After a while I got out of bed and went to Denton's room. I listened outside, and you know how he used to snore. There wasn't a sound: absolute silence.' He wiped his forehead with a shaking hand. 'I don't know—but I got uneasy. I opened the door and went in. Still not a sound. Then I switched on the light.' Lethbridge shuddered. 'There he was, lying in bed, absolutely motionless. I went over to him, and put my hand on his heart. Not a movement: he was dead.'

I stared at him speechlessly, and then together we went towards Denton's room. The door was ajar, and as we pushed it open Mansfrey, who was standing by the dead man, turned his white, stricken face towards us.

'Not a trace of life,' he whispered. 'Not a trace.' He ran his hands through his hair, blinking at us despairingly. 'What a fool I was, what an utter fool, to show him that thing.'

'Oh! rot, man,' said Lethbridge, roughly. 'It can't have been that paltry bit of red glass. He's dead now, poor fellow, but he was a gross liver, and there's no getting away from the fact that he drank too much last night. Probably heart failure.'

But Mansfrey only shook his head, and stared miserably out of the window to where the first faint streaks of dawn were showing in the sky.

'The point is, what we're going to do now,' went on Lethbridge. He held up the hand holding the idol's eye, and then let it fall again with a shudder.

'Ring up a doctor at once,' said Mansfrey. 'He's dead, but you must send for one.'

'Yes,' said Lethbridge, slowly, 'I suppose we must. Er—the only thing is—er——' he looked awkwardly from Mansfrey to me, 'this—er—bit of glass. You know what local people are, and the sort of things that—er—may be said. I mean, it will be a little hard to account for the poor fellow being found dead with this bauble in his hand, all tied up like this. The papers will get hold of it, and we shall have a crowd of confounded reporters buzzing round, trying to nose out a story.'

Mansfrey blinked at him in silence. 'You suggest,' he said at length, 'that we should take it out of his hand?'

'I do,' said Lethbridge, eagerly. 'After all, the poor chap's dead, and we've got the living to consider. It's bad enough having a death in the house at all: it'll be perfectly awful if it's turned into a nine days' newspaper wonder. I mean, it isn't as if there was any question of foul play,' he glanced apologetically at Mansfrey: 'we all of us are equally concerned, and it *can* only be a very strange and gruesome coincidence. What do you say, Mayhew?'

'I quite agree,' I answered. At the time I was engaged in a big deal, and I was certainly not anxious for notoriety—even of a reflected nature—in the papers. 'I suggest that we remove the stone, and that we destroy it forthwith by smashing it to pieces and throwing the bits into the pond.'

Lethbridge gave a sigh of relief, and started to unfasten the handkerchief. 'One moment,' interrupted Mansfrey. 'With all due regard for both your interests, my case is not quite the same as yours. We are not all equally concerned. The thing is mine: I gave it to him.' He blinked at us apologetically. 'I've got to think of the years to come, when the momentary unpleasantness will be forgotten, and you two—almost unconsciously—may begin to wonder whether it *was* a coincidence.' He silenced our quick expressions of denial with a smile. 'You may,' he said, 'and I prefer not to risk it. And so I will only agree to your proposal on one condition, and that is that one or other of you send the thing to some good analytical chemist and have it tested. I *know* that it is glass: I want you to *know* it too.'

'Right,' said Lethbridge, who would willingly have promised anything, so long as he was allowed to remove the glass eye. 'I quite see your point of view, Mansfrey.' He was busy untying the knot in the handkerchief. 'Perhaps Mayhew will take it up tomorrow to town with him, when he goes.'

At length the handkerchief was removed, and with obvious distaste Lethbridge forced back the fingers. There lay the glass, clouded a little by the moisture of the dead man's hand—but still glittering with its devilish red light. Then suddenly the arm relaxed and the idol's eye rolled on to the carpet.

'My God!' said Lethbridge, hoarsely, 'put the vile thing away, Mansfrey, and let's send for a doctor.'

'The bag is on my table,' he answered. 'I'll put it in.' With his handkerchief he picked the thing up, and carried it away.

Lethbridge turned to me. 'I don't often drink at this hour of the night,' he said, 'but when I've rung up the doctor, I'm going to open a bottle of brandy. I want it.'

We tidied up the clothes, and with a last look at the great body lying motionless on the bed, we went out softly, locking the door behind us.

An hour later the doctor came and made his examination. By this time, of course, the whole house knew, and there was no question of any more sleep. The women had forgathered in Mrs Lethbridge's room, and we three men waited for the doctor downstairs. He came, after only a short time in the dead man's room, and helped himself to a cup of tea.

'It may be necessary,' he said, 'to hold a post-mortem. You say that he was perfectly fit last night?'

'Perfectly,' said Lethbridge.

'Forgive my putting the question,' continued the doctor, 'but did he have much to drink?'

'He was always a very heavy drinker and eater,' answered Lethbridge, and both Mansfrey and I nodded in agreement.

'So I should have imagined,' commented the doctor. 'I have no doubt in my mind that, though he looked a strong, healthy man, we shall find he was pretty rotten inside. Brought on by over-indulgence, you know. He was essentially the type that becomes liable to fits later in life. Most unpleasant for you, Mr Lethbridge. I'll do everything I can to spare you unnecessary inconvenience. But I'm afraid we shall have to have a post-mortem. You see, there's no obvious cause of death.'

Lethbridge saw him to the door, and shortly after we heard his car drive off.

'May Heaven be praised,' said Lethbridge, coming back into the room, 'that we took that glass thing out of his hand, and that we didn't mention it to the women last night.' He sat down and wiped his forehead. 'Chuck that brandy over, Mansfrey; I want another.'

Thus ended the tragic house-party. At nine o'clock I left for town, with the idol's eye in my pocket. I took it to a chemist and asked him to submit it to any tests he liked, and tell me what it was. Later in the evening I called for it, and he handed it back across the counter.

'As far as I can see, sir,' he remarked, 'it is simply a piece of ordinary red glass, of not the slightest value save for its rather peculiar shape.'

I thanked him and took it home with me. The next day I returned it to Mansfrey with a brief note containing the chemist's report, and a suggestion that he should drop it into the Thames.

Lethbridge sent me a cutting from the local paper giving an account of the inquest and the result of the post-mortem.

'Death from natural causes,' was the verdict; and gradually, in the stress of reconstructing a business which had suffered badly during the war, the matter passed from my head. Occasionally the strange coincidence came back to my mind and worried me: occasionally I even wondered whether, indeed, there was some deadly power in that piece of red glass: whether in a far-off Tibetan temple strange priests, performing their sinister rites round a sightless idol, kept count in some mysterious way of their god's revenge. Then I would laugh to myself and recall the doctor's words when he had made his brief examination of Denton—'We shall find he was pretty rotten inside.'

And so, but for a strange freak of fate, the matter would have ended and passed into the limbo of forgotten things. Instead of which—but the devil of it all is, I don't know what to do.

Two days ago I wandered casually into Jones's curio shop just off the Strand. At times I have picked up quite good bits of stuff there, and I frequently drop in on the chance of a bargain.

'I've got the very thing for you, Mr Mayhew,' he said as soon as he saw me. 'A couple of bits of old Sheffield. Just wait while I get them.'

He disappeared into the back of the shop and left me alone. I strolled round, looking at his stuff, and in corner I found a peculiarly ugly carved table standing on three gimcrack legs. Ordinarily, I should merely have shuddered and passed on: but something made me stop and look at it a little more closely. Its proud designer, presumably in order to finish it off tastefully, had cut four holes in the top, and into these four holes he had placed four pieces of coloured glass—yellow, blue, green, and red. Mechanically I touched them, and to my surprise I found the red one was loose. Still quite mechanically I worked it about, and finally took it out.

A minute later Jones found me staring dazedly at something in my hand, which, even in the dim light of the shop, glowed and scintillated like a giant ruby.

'Here are those two bits of plate, Mr Mayhew,' he remarked. Then he saw what I had in my hand, and glanced at he table. 'Don't worry about that. It's been loose ever since I got it. I must seccotine it in some day.'

'Tell me, Mr Jones,' I endeavoured to speak quite calmly, 'where did you get this from?'

'What—that table? A Mr Mansfrey asked me to try and sell it for him months ago: you know, the gentleman who's just written that book on poisons. Not that I've got any hope of obliging him, for it's a horrible-looking thing, I think.'

A thousand wild thoughts were rushing through my brain as I stood there, with the dealer watching me curiously. If that bit of red glass came out of a table, it had never adorned an idol's face in Tibet. And as it *had* come out of a table, it proved that Mansfrey had lied. Why?

'I will take that table,' I said to the astounded dealer. 'I'll give you five pounds for it. Send it round at once.'

'Shall I put that red thing in, sir,' he asked.

'No,' I answered. 'I'll keep this.'

I strode out of the shop and into the Strand. Why had Mansfrey gone to the trouble of inventing that long tissue of falsehood? Why? The question rang ceaselessly through my brain. Why should a writer on poisons and an able, clever man—I had heard of Mansfrey's new book—take the trouble to lie steadily throughout an evening, unless he had some object in view?

I turned into my club, and sat down to try and puzzle things out. And the more I thought of it the less I liked it.

At length I rose and, going to a table, wrote a note to Mansfrey asking him to come round and see me at my flat. He came last night—and as I said before, I don't know what to do.

Straight in front of him as he came into the room I had placed the table. The hole for the red glass was empty, the piece itself was in the centre of the mantelpiece. He stopped abruptly and stared at the little table: then he turned and the gleaming red thing in front of the clock caught his eyes. Then he looked at me, blinking placidly with a faint smile on his face.

'I didn't know you knew Jones,' he said, sinking into an easy chair, and lighting a cigarette.

'I should like an explanation, Mansfrey,' I remarked, sternly.

'What of? Denton's death? My dear fellow—surely it was quite obvious from the first. I killed him.' He still blinked at me with his mild blue eyes.

'You killed him!' I almost shouted.

'Hush, hush!' He held up a deprecating hand. 'Not so loud, please. Of course I killed him, as I had always intended to do. He was one of the type of carrion who was not fit to live. He ruined my sister!' For a moment he had ceased blinking: then he went on again quite calmly. 'But why should I weary you with personal history? Is there anything else you'd like to know?'

'A lot,' I said. 'Of course, your reason is a big extenuating circumstance, and undoubtedly Denton was a blackguardly cad—but that does not excuse you, Mansfrey, for murdering him.'

'I absolutely disagree,' he returned, gently. 'The law would have given me no redress, so I had to make my own.'

'Of course,' I said, after a pause, 'I shall have to tell Scotland Yard. I mean, I can't possibly condone such a thing.'

He smiled peacefully and shook his head. 'I don't think I would if I were you,' he murmured. 'Who was it who begged Denton not to take the idol's eye in his hand——?' He glanced at the glass on the mantelpiece. 'It bore a striking resemblance to that thing you've got there, now I come to look at it. But, who was it? Why, me. Who overruled me? Well—neither you nor Lethbridge backed me up, anyway. Who was it suggested removing it before the doctor came? I think I am right in saying it was Lethbridge. Who insisted on a chemical analysis? I did. Who had it carried out? You, and I have the chemist's report in my desk. What was the result of the post-mortem and the coroner's inquest? Death from natural causes: no trace of poison.' He blinked on placidly. 'Oh! no, my friend, I don't quite see you going to Scotland Yard. In the extremely improbable event of that august body not regarding you as a lunatic, you would inevitably, and Lethbridge also, be regarded as my accomplices in the matter. You see, between you, in all innocence, you compromised yourselves very awkwardly—very awkwardly indeed.' He rose to go.

'How did you kill him?' I demanded.

'A rare and little-known poison,' he answered. 'You'll find something about it in my new book. Probably the most deadly in the world, for it leaves no trace. It kills by shock, which induces heart failure. I dipped that glass—er—I mean the idol's eye, which is so like that bit of glass—into a solution of the poison before putting it in his hand. Then the next morning I dipped it in another solution. You considerately left it with me for some hours—a minute was all I required. From experiments I have carried out on animals, I should think he died in about half an hour. Er—good-night.'

The door closed behind him, and I sat staring at the red bauble glittering in the light. Then in a fit of rage I took it to the window and hurled it into the street below. It broke into a thousand fragments, and Mansfrey—who had just left the front door—looked up and smiled. 'Er—good-night,' he called, and I could imagine those blue eyes blinking mildly.

And the devil of it all is, as I mentioned previously—I don't know what to do.

The Perfect Crime

Seamark

MR JEROLD POGARTY evolved and committed the Perfect Crime. The capitals are excusable, for no less a critic than the Attorney-General himself, in rising to state the case for the Crown, thus described Mr Pogarty's experiment.

It was a gem, a shining example of the higher art of transgression: a crime so perfectly conceived, so scrupulously prepared, and so immaculately carried out that it placed Mr Jerold Pogarty, at a stroke, in a high place among the world's master criminals. As a work of art it stands: the lesser lights reverence it as a guide and a model upon which to mould their own efforts, and at least one company promoter raises his hat even now whenever the name of Pogarty is mentioned.

It was the only criminal offence Mr Pogarty ever committed in his life. He spent two critically delightful years in its consummation, although he could have finished the matter off in a couple of minutes had he wished. But he preferred the years to the minutes, which is why he attained perfection.

It succeeded brilliantly.

And yet it failed. It failed so lamentably and so needlessly that, in the awful moment when the crash came and the Law gazed into his eyes, stark and malignant, Mr Jerold Pogarty laughed, laughed hysterically at the comedy of his own error.

It is a disturbing, yet nevertheless unassailable, fact that every man has, at some time or another, seriously contemplated committing one really worth-while crime, one that would place him and his family for ever beyond the harassing worry of the great struggle.

He has done that just as assuredly as he has, at some time or another, seriously contemplated the question of suicide.

Where Mr Pogarty differed, utterly and entirely, from the vast majority was that he was one of the infinitesimal few who possessed the ability, the callousness, the courage, *and* the opportunity to transmute the thought into the deed. And he proceeded to do so with the same calm, orderly dignity that characterized every other action of his smooth, unruffled life.

He began committing his crime on a Saturday, exactly two years before he actually took up his pen and wrote a few figures on the wrong side of the legal line. On that day several things happened to Mr Pogarty that had never happened before.

To begin with, Mr Pogarty got to the bank that morning an hour late. That had never happened before. For twenty years, fifteen minutes to ten had always seen Mr Pogarty hanging up his hat on his own private peg. There was never more than a few seconds in it either way. Why should there be? Mr Pogarty always caught the same train, and the bank was only three hundred and forty-seven steps from the station.

But that morning there had been a suicide on the train, and that had never happened before. Some poor half-demented creature, battered and beaten in the great struggle and lacking one of the essentials for committing one really worth-while job, had suddenly grasped up at a courage big enough to do the biggest job of all.

Mr Pogarty gazed at the open door. He muttered 'Dear *me!*' and gazed dully round as though to assure himself that the compartment really was empty.

He mechanically pulled the communication cord—and he had never done that before. Because he was the sole witness, he was requested by a policeman to 'just pop round to the station, sir, just for a few minutes, if you don't mind, sir—just a mere formality, you know, sir, just to make out a proper statement, sir'.

Mr Pogarty popped round to the station, by the side of a walking uniform—and that had never happened before.

He discovered that policemen are a ponderously decent set of fellows, albeit nearly as much addicted to immovable routines as he was himself.

They made him an hour late. They insisted on making him an

hour late. They insisted on doing that as calmly and as sincerely as they apologized for so doing.

He went up the bank steps slowly, passed in through a palatial temple of counters and columns, counting-houses and cash, and went into his own private office. As he closed the door he caught the warning whisper of a junior clerk to his chum: "Shh! boys. Old Pogarty has turned up!'

His hat stopped half-way to the peg.

Old Pogarty! He felt a cold, clammy hand sliding all over his skin. Old Pogarty! He had never heard himself called that before. For a painful moment the power of thought slid out of his brain, and his face went tense as though he awaited the horrific explosion of a shell he had already seen drop. Then he stared Destiny straight in the eyes. And Destiny laughed at him.

He saw himself standing, bareheaded and bewildered, at the grim half-way house on the crest of the hill. It was labelled the Abattoir of Illusions, the Slaughterhouse of Dreams. Behind him, all the grand hopes, the splendid ambitions, the shining ideals of youth streamed away to a far horizon. There they lay, resplendent, magnificent, a glorious panoply, woven of cloth-of-gold on the precious loom of youth, all ablaze with the brilliance, the bloom, and the beauty of the days when his life was young. And it was fading fast! His frightened eyes saw it receding hour by hour, dimming and flattening to a dull, dead monotone of memory. Like the glorious, golden confidence of youth, it was dying; in a little while it would be gone—gone beyond all dreaming and desiring. It became a dreadfully silent procession of shattered illusions, hollow ambitions, and broken ideals, slipping back inexorably into the shadows. And ahead lay the sunset. Full and square in the path he must tread, the great plain went falling away, unchecked, remorseless, to where the red embers of the dying fires lit up the journey's end. He stood, gazing wild-eyed at the tragedy of life.

And Destiny hugged itself at the spectacle, Destiny being privileged to see the funny side of the man standing in the borderland of forty.

'Go to, old fool!' it tittered. 'What are you but old? Hair gone, teeth gone, vigour gone, digestion going, rheumatism coming, you'll be an old 'un in no time. Don't stare at me like that—hundreds and thousands of myriad millions have fought their way up that side of the hill, and they *all* shy at the sunset. Death? Why, man, there are so many countless impis of dead in the soil that the bread you ate this morning was grown in the dust of the dead. That cocky little devil who called you "Old Pogarty" just now—he will be a back number himself almost before he knows what's what. That's the only little bit of satisfaction you get out of this business. Excuse me laughing, won't you, but you *do* look a silly fish standing there with your mouth open. But there, they all do. Right down through the ages I've stood here, watching the millions pass. Armies of them, legions of them, all fighting and struggling like mad to get a look over the top of that hill. And they all rear up and plunge like startled horses when they get their first sight of the sunset. Tee hee! Pass along there, old fool; make way for the millions yet to come. This is where you *wish*!'

Mr Pogarty's hat completed its journey. He stood and stared at it for a moment, not quite certain as to how it got there. Then he sat down very gingerly to think things out. Man is by nature a selfish animal. At a crisis he is apt to think in terms of personal possessions. Mr Pogarty did. Somewhat to his own surprise, he found that nine-tenths of his were abstract. Even so, they were beyond price.

Twenty years of faithful service in the throne-rooms of cash and credit. A few hundreds put by for the rainy day that came along every now and then to remind him of others coming. A brilliantly yet unconsciously established reputation for absolute dependability, honesty, and sobriety. A bachelorhood equally solidly founded. A meticulous brain. A perfect knowledge of every phase and facet of the working system of the bank. A board that might, or might not, bestow on him 'some little token of appreciation, some little memento of the high esteem, admiration, and regard in which the whole of the directorate had always held him, throughout the long years of his, etc., etc.,' when the time came for them to kick him a little further down the road to the sunset. ·

Three was a lot more, too; such as a horror of genteel poverty.

It was at that moment that Mr Pogarty's criminal complex functioned. As a criminal, he passed from the potential to the intentional. The idea of committing one magnificent declension, which until then had been wholly subconscious and subservient, suddenly became definite. It became a reality, one of his personal possessions.

Mr Pogarty was not a little perturbed at the brutal casualness of it. His amazed brain demanded a reaction, a touch of the humdrum, to bring it to earth. He found himself signing his name on a pile of letters and documents. They had been placed on his desk for that purpose. That had been his first job in the morning for years and years, putting his signature to a great sheaf of papers and things. They were all perfectly in order, of course. They always were. The secretaries saw to that. A long mechanical succession of signatures went crawling along under a long succession of 'Yours faithfully'.

Pogarty's was rather a neat signature, he thought. It looked well. The quaint little flourish to the initial 'J' and the trim little pull-back loop of the final 'y' created the necessary incisiveness about a signature that was known and honoured throughout banking circles all over the City.

While he was writing he began to visualize the absurd simplicity of the idea that had lain dormant at the back of his mind ever since he first detected the weaknesses in the bank's system. 'No banking system can be perfect,' he assured himself, 'for the simple reason that the final balance is struck in figures instead of actual gold-weight in the opposite scale-pan. And figures will always be open to jugglery.'

He began to toy with his idea. He fondled it as would a connoisseur some priceless old art treasure. All the weekend he pondered it, turning it this way and that, testing odd little bits of it, working out minor little details of it with the analytical delicacy of a chess master proving out a problem game. He studied it, inspected it, examined it piece by piece, put it under the microscope of his meticulous brain, turned it upside down and inside out, reassembled the whole scheme and mentally rehearsed the final working out of each incident. Then he ascended to the pinnacle of intentional criminality. He made it his hobby.

His perfect idea became his pastime and his recreation, his first and only love. He revelled in it. His hours of ease were spent in sublimating it to the highest pitch of perfection. His plan deserved it, for he had found the means of effectually eliminating that bugbear of all criminals, the hue and cry. He wanted to live his subsequent life at his ease, without having to experience the slightest qualm or fear. And he knew that it could be done.

He decided on the most suitable amount to negotiate.

'Forty thousand pounds,' he murmured, speculatively. 'That is the ideal figure. It is the lowest I shall require and the highest I can utilize without making a bulge in the market elsewhere. Most decidedly, forty thousand is the ideal figure.'

Having arrived at that decision, he took a prolonged look at himself in the glass. Certainly that young blighter of a junior had been a trifle premature. Mr Jerold Pogarty did not look old. He was dapper, neat, natty, and as straight as a backboard. His complexion was clear and his eyes as bright and keen as steel. Admittedly he was semi-bald and his teeth were a bit groggy, but he wore his clothes exceptionally well, and there was not a trace of what one might call elderly-spread below his waistcoat. He had a small sandy-buff moustache which suited him admirably. The wee touch of pomposity in his manner became him as naturally as did his morning coat and white spats.

Mr Jerold Pogarty decided that that particular identity should slowly wane in Threadneedle Street and be transported bodily, except the moustache, to his future home, which he decided would be St Albans, as being a quiet, exclusive little place and within half an hour of town. That was only one brilliant facet of his idea. He was to manufacture a false identity right under the board's nose and live an artificial life before their eyes. His real self he proposed to efface and reserve for his own subsequent use later on in St Albans. The next morning he turned up at the bank wearing spectacles. They were plain glass lenses, but his friends were not to know that. So they just looked at him and shook their sympathetic heads.

From that moment Mr Jerold Pogarty, of Norwood and Threadneedle Street, became half of himself. That is, he became one of two entirely separate and distinct personalities. The one went to the bank regularly every morning, performed his duties in the same suave, faultless manner, lunched at the same table with the same friends, went home at the same time, and never lapsed from punctuality again. The only notable change in him was that slowly but surely his eyesight failed. Strength by strength he found it necessary to increase the magnifying power of his lenses until,

before many months had sped, he blinked wistfully at the directorate from behind a couple of pebbles a quarter of an inch thick. But
when he was alone he pushed them up on to his forehead, and at
other times, unless he was being addressed personally, he closed his
eyes, for Mr Pogarty was proudly jealous of his vision.

Later on other changes appeared in him, or became noticeable for
the first time. His knees had lost their spring. He was apt to stand
just a trifle bent, as though his tendons were feeling the years, and
he shuffled ever such a trifle when he walked. These were the most
marked of the other perfectly portrayed little signs of age creeping
upon the body of Mr Pogarty. But he also spoke mumblingly
because his teeth were out, and Colonel Calhoun, of the board, was
'quite certain the old devil had put on four inches and a stone since
last year'.

Sir Wilmot shrugged. 'Well, well, that's the way of life, Colonel.
We all come to it, you know. Though I must say I always admired
old Pogarty's figure—sort of hoped I might wear half as well when
the fifties loomed ahead. But he certainly has cracked up. His teeth
have all gone to pot too.'

'Um—looks bad. Not quite the thing. Man can't talk decently to
our class of clients. Not quite the thing. Looks bad.'

'Yes, well, there it is. His articulation, I know, is painfully senile,
but I understand he has some miserable affection of the gums. They
are so beastly soft and tender it is absolutely impossible for him to
wear false teeth. Poor old boy has my sympathy, but—ah!—as you
say.'

The other half of Mr Jerold Pogarty remained exactly as the real
Mr Pogarty always was. The only thing that changd in *him* was his
name, which was Mr Wilfrid Wilderson. He was a smart, neat,
dapper little gentleman with a delightful little place down at St
Albans. He fell quite in love with the old city; he loved its quiet
peace and the tasteful tone of its residential quarters. Indeed, his
one regret was that his wretchedly plebeian business imposed
necessary absences upon him, for Mr Wilfrid Wilderson was a dried
fruit importer with many business connections at what he was
pleased to call the smelly end of the Mediterranean.

For two years without a break he sedulously cultivated the
atmosphere of his new entity. Two years was the lowest limit of
time in which he considered he could safely accomplish the meta-

morphosis. He took a meticulous delight in its gradual development, while the new conception of *Old* Pogarty as gradually materialized at the bank.

Each evening Mr Jerold Pogarty, of Norwood and Threadneedle Street, got into a first-class compartment of the fast train down from St Pancras, and half an hour later Mr Wilfrid Wilderson, of St Albans and the smelly end of the Mediterranean, got out.

Towards the end of the second year it was a very shuffling figure that got in; a figure that was over at the knees, decidedly stout, spoke with labial senility, wore a little sandy-buff moustache, and bumped into piles of luggage in spite of very strong glasses. He always got into an empty compartment, an easy task these days. On the way down he unwound a great many swathes of very fine silk from around his person, swathes that had been added to month by month with studied care. He took off his sandy-buff moustache, discarded his pebble glasses, inserted a double set of very perfect false teeth, squared his shoulders, straightened his knees, and dapper little Mr Wilfrid Wilderson got out.

In St Albans he established his own perfectly regulated menage. He paid his rent, rates, and taxes there, had a bank account there, posted letters and circulars to himself there, called himself up now and then on the telephone, and on several occasions telegraphed to himself to go in a hurry to the smelly end of the Mediterranean. He entertained his own little circle of friends there, and was entertained in return. He was barbered and tailored and haberdashed there, and registered his vote in the Council elections. He wrote letters to the local press and prevailed upon Inspector Gorrel, of the local police, to keep his eyes on his little place during his necessary absences.

Inspector Gorrel liked him very much indeed. 'A very nice old party,' he declared in the mess-room. 'We could do with a few more like him in the city. Gave me a tenner for the fund with all the pleasure in the world, he did. "What's that, my dear Gorrel," he says; "the Police Orphange? Most decidedly I will give you something. Mustn't let the little kiddies suffer, must we? I'd like to make it more, but this wretched Smyrna business has played the deuce with dried fruit," he says. "I think I shall make it an annual subscription; come along and see me every year," he says, and handed me over a tenner as though it was no more than a "tanner".'

'Good old sport. Dried fruits, is he?'

'Yes. Travels a goodish deal where that stuff grows. That's why he has to go away sometimes. But he says he is retiring very soon, and maybe will settle down here permanently.'

He always stayed in St Albans overnight and had breakfast about eight o'clock. His housekeeper was a quiet, staid old soul who superintended such matters for him with comfortable care. Except at weekends he never troubled her again till after tea. He had friends in Harpenden, Luton, Hitchin, Watford, and all the little country towns around, whom he was frequently visiting. His housekeeper could testify to that.

But after breakfasting Mr Wilfrid Wilderson did not go out paying duty calls. He caught the nine o'clock fast train to St Pancras, *en route* for Threadneedle Street, and a day's labour that was an absolute model of dignified propriety.

He took a very real delight in perfecting his two personalities. They lived in his heart as completely as a masterpiece lives in the soul of an artist. Throughout the long course of the two years he applied himself with infinite care to the detection of weaknesses or possibilities of improvements in his plan. Thus one day it appeared that old Pogarty's hearing was not what it used to be. He had developed an annoying habit of saying 'Eh?' with his hand behind his ear when juniors spoke to him, and 'I beg your pardon?' when addressed by the board. That came about after overhearing a chance remark of Gorrel's to the station sergeant. 'Eyes like an 'awk and ears like a pointer, he has,' whispered that gentleman with proprietary pride when Wilderson stopped him in the street to give him another subscription to the Police Orphange Fund. He saw in the remark yet another opportunity of creating another alibi of contrast; and so Mr Jerold Pogarty began going deaf.

He had moved from his flat at Norwood to a comfortable hotel in the neighbourhood, so that his sudden change of habits should give no cause for comment. Night after night and month after month he made the trip to St Albans with unfailing regularity. On quarter days and at the end of the financial year, when the bank worked at high pressure until far into the night, Mr Wilderson was called away to the smelly end of the Mediterranean. But at all other times he cultivated the society of St Albans. He showed himself there as much as possible, became a patron of various entertainments and movements, rented a pew in the beautiful Abbey there, and even founded a Wilderson Challenge Shield to be competed for annually by the local football teams.

Thus with elegant care and effortless skill he established a thousand witnesses at one end of the line who could swear on oath that Mr Wilfrid Wilderson, smart, dapper, alert little Mr Wilfrid Wilderson, had been an honoured and respected citizen of St Albans for at least two years to their definite knowledge; and that he hadn't left the town for months on end. While at the other end almost as many were quite convinced that poor old Pogarty, who, alas! was failing fast, had discharged his skilled and arduous duties faithfully and well at the bank for as long as they could remember.

The only possible weakness was the train. It was the one connecting link that, unfortunately, could not be eliminated. He had thought of making the journey by car, stopping at some lonely point on the road, and getting into it to change, but that would have created an even more notable link at the garage. Furthermore, it would necessitate his learning to drive a car, an expedient which, at his time of life, would be indiscreet, to say the least. So the train it had to be; and his season ticket was held in the name of Wilderson.

The last and final preparation occasioned him a good deal of thoughtful study. It concerned the demise of Mr Jerold Pogarty. The ideal location for that old boy's tragic exit had long been firmly fixed in his mind. It was an ideal place; there was not the slightest shadow of a doubt of it. That little strip of coast where England peeps across at the Isle of Wight carried features that dovetailed in perfectly with every single one of his requirements.

He spent his summer holidays there for two years running, maturing his plans and perfecting his arrangements without the slightest suspicion of haste or hurry. He took Gosport as his centre. From there he hired out little sailing dinghies and went for long invigorating trips down the green waters of the Solent, going right up close to the mammoth homing liners. He lowered the little stuns'l, stood up in the boat, and cheered lustily as the splendid vessels swung grandly past him and rounded the point for Southampton.

The boatmen smiled at him. He was a quaint little figure, old Mr Pogarty. Some said he had the sea in his blood, but it had been denied him. Office stools chained him, and he didn't find out until it was too late that he was born of the old woman of the sea. But he certainly had an abounding, exulting pride in the great ships that came in from the far ends of the oceans.

Even after his plans were all complete and ready for fulfilment, he still dallied with his scheme. He was obsessed with the skill and the beauty of it. It titillated his artistic sense to a point of quiet rapture. He thought of it as a beautifully constructed machine, waiting stationary, ready at a touch on the master-key to slip smoothly into a veritable poem of motion.

He waited for the summer, and then pressed the master-key. On that day he took up his pen and wrote a few figures on the wrong side of the legal line. The thing was simplicity itself, merely the writing of the right figures in the wrong ledgers. Mr Pogarty went down to the strong room with the ledgers and returned without them. In his inside pocket were forty thousand pounds in notes and bearer bonds.

He sat in his chair appalled at the simplicity of crime. He was one of the eight men in that building privileged to enter the vaults.

'My dear Mr Wilderson,' he said judicially to himself, 'isn't it amazing what simple, tiny, insignificant little actions can make a man a criminal! The mere twitching of a finger—the gallows! A simple Yes instead of an equally simple No in a Court of Law— Dartmoor. The mere inscription of the right figures in the wrong sequence—a living tomb of isolation in a sepulchre of silence. Awful to contemplate.'

'I have long pondered the same painful thought,' smiled Mr Wilderson, his fingertips pressed benignly together. 'Modern progress seems to have created a system wherein it is easier to commit sin than to prevent it. That, in my humble estimation, is a crime in itself. Think! It is easier to commit a murder, or perjury, or to steal forty thousand pounds than it is to do something really normal, like getting married or having a tooth out. Now, I should never have the courage to get married. It is all very queer and enigmatic—more so, my dear Pogarty, after one has peeped over and seen the sunset.'

During the next few days Mr Jerold Pogarty negotiated the notes without a hitch and without raising the slightest suspicion. The whole thing was done with the utmost discretion.

*

On the following Saturday afternoon he made his fall from grace irrevocable. He dropped a letter into the pillar-box, a pitiful, pleading letter that was addressed to the board. He heard the letter drop, and his heart missed a beat, for he realized that letters, once posted, proceed inexorably to their appointed address. No effort of his could regain possession of that letter.

The letter pleaded for forgiveness, prayed for a little charity of thought. He was getting old and something must have gone wrong in his head. Excuses were beyond him; he himself did not know how it had all happened. His confession was utter and complete. Gambling was not for old brains; it had demanded subtler faculties than he possessed. But he had just been jolted into sanity; he had made a slip, a ghastly blunder in his figure jugglery that made discovery inevitable. Forgive—and try to think well of him. It was not he, it was his miserable old brain that had betrayed him. He was taking what he humbly ventured to submit was the bravest course, the course that would give the dear old bank the least trouble and pain. He mentioned one or two little matters that would require immediate attention on Monday morning, and finished the missive with the neat little signature they knew so well.

'Dear *me*!' he reflected. 'That is the last time I shall ever sign that name. Most extraordinary, after the thousands and thousands of times I have written that name.'

The mail train bore him swiftly to Portsmouth. He crossed over to the Isle of Wight. Early in the morning he booked a bathing cabin for the day. He went in, donned a bathing suit, dressed again, lit the spirit stove, and went out, leaving his suitcase and a flask of hot tea in the cabin. He hung the key on a piece of string round his neck.

He returned to Gosport by motor-boat. In an hour's time the great *Berengaria* was due. The boatmen smiled when the decayed old gentleman asked for a boat. They gave him one and he left thirty pounds deposit on it as he always did—'just in case anything went wrong, for he really wasn't very much of a sailor, you know, and he wouldn't like them to lose by it.' He made a round of the marine store dealers and fishing tackle shops and bought a couple of lead sinkers at each.

The boatmen waved him a merry hand as the old 'Cheership Party' sailed off. When well out into the fairway he took off his boots and dropped them overboard. Then he took off his collar and tie, waistcoat, shirt, and vest, attached sinkers to them, and watched them sink into the shimmering deeps. 'Good-bye, Mr Pogarty,' he murmured, as they sank out of sight. Then, dressed only in jacket, trousers, hat, and socks, but apparently fully clad, he slid away down Channel till he came opposite his bathing hut, where he backed and filled till the *Berengaria* swung into view.

She came on, riding majestically by in a colossal tiering of decks and boats and smoking funnels. He let the sail fall and stood up to wave his hat as the splendid thing swept by, less than thirty yards abeam. She passed. Suddenly those on the high decks clutched at the rails in horror. The old gentleman in the dinghy was in a bad way. He had got caught in the mammoth suck of the great liner and was spinning in the backwash. His boat was tossing desperately. Horrors, he was over!

Bells clanged in the soul of the mammoth. She stopped. A lifeboat struck the water with a sudden splash. Strong arms at the end of strong oars thrust madly towards the pathetic little cockle-shell that lay keel up in the water. They circled and searched and rowed around for over half an hour. Keen eyes peered over the face of the waters, every little bit of weed and wood that broke the surface was chased and scrutinized. For over half an hour they rowed and searched. But they neither rescued nor found the body of Mr Jerold Pogarty. All they found was his hat.

The lifeboat was recalled and the *Berengaria* proceeded on her way, to report the little tragedy to the shore authorities higher up in Southampton Water.

Mr Pogarty listened with a thankful heart to the screw-beats of the liner. He was under the boat, clinging calmly to the centre thwart, breathing easily and deeply with his head a foot out of water inside the overturned hull.

He waited until the thud of the propellers diminished to a faint monody of sound far away in the back blocks of the Channel. He passed away the time in ridding himself of his other clothes. The socks were an awkward business, but he got them off at last. He dropped a lead sinker in each, tied them together at the tops, and let them go. The trousers and jacket went down with the remainder of the weights in the pockets. He tore the little sandy-buff moustache to shreds and put them in his mouth. He unfastened the swimming belt from the centre thwart and adjusted it. Then he dived out from under the hull.

Once well away from the boat, he ejected the moustache and turned all his attentions towards the Isle of Wight shore half a mile away. It took him nearly two hours with long and frequent rests, and he was chilled to the bone by the time he was mingling with the Sunday afternoon crowd bathing from the beach. It was an intense effort of will-power, but he stayed in among them for another ten minutes before edging in towards the sands. He emerged, in his bathing suit, a quiet, normal holiday-maker, coming in after a pleasant afternoon's swim.

He went into his hut, his whole body one vast ache of weary coldness. He almost fainted with the violence of the reaction of the heated interior of the hut. He collapsed on a chair and rested, sipping hot tea from the flask to get the biting flavour of the sea-water off his palate.

After a vigorous towelling he dressed. There was every mortal thing he wanted in the suit-case, right down to hair pomade, cash, and the Sunday paper—and a telescope. Through the glass he saw that the *Berengaria* had lost little time in reporting the accident. A clutter of small boats jostled about round the overturned craft. But they never found the poor old chap's body. He must have sunk like a log, they said.

Mr Wilfrid Wilderson, immaculately dressed, gay and debonair, went out on to the beach, mixed with the crowd, and read his paper. He returned his bathing hut key and after a couple of days' delightful sauntering round Cowes and Ryde went back to St Albans.

Not until he got into the train at Portsmouth did the reaction set in. He trembled like an aspen. But it was the trembling of a great and thrilling pride at the beauty of the thing he had done. Not only had he succeeded magnificently—the Monday and Tuesday morning papers told him how perfect that success had been—but he had smacked Destiny's face. Boldly, openly, and flatly he had landed fair and square on its jeering cheek.

In St Albans he entered into the fullness of his desires. On the fruits of the Perfect Crime he lived as he had always longed to live—the life of a perfect gentleman in an aura of utter bliss and contentment. Mr Jerold Pogarty was dead and forgotten. Mr Wilfrid Wilderson continued his calm, orderly way without a qualm or a tremor.

The weeks and the months slipped by. They passed on the oiled wheels of delectable pleasure and tasteful ease. He retired from business and settled down permanently in St Albans. He withdrew the name of Wilfrid Wilderson, Ltd from the various trade directories in which it had appeared for over two years. He bought a beautiful car to run him up to town whenever he felt that way inclined—he had a very natural aversion to the railway. He presented his challenge shield when the winter drew into the spring, and he celebrated his definite retirement from business by giving Gorrel an extra contribution to the Orphanage Fund.

Inspector Gorrel was delighted. He was secretary of the local branch of the fund, and he tried to express his clumsy thanks as he stowed the five ten-pound notes in the crown of his cap. Mr Wilfrid Wilderson signed the subscription list and smilingly pushed it across to him.

'Please don't thank me, inspector,' he murmured. 'I am sincerely pleased to be able to be of any little assistance. The police are a jolly fine set of fellows and I'm delighted to help you in any little way in my humble power. Besides which, the orphanage is a very worthy——'

He broke off and stared at the inspector. Gorrel, white-faced and almost nervous, was standing over him with a pair of terrible-looking handcuffs in his fingers.

'What—what on earth—what is the matter, inspector?' stammered Wilderson.

'Sorry I am—sir——' muttered Gorrel, apologetically. For the life of him he couldn't help that 'sir'.

'But—but—what——'

'Look!' Gorrel held out the subscription list with a shaking hand.

Wilderson looked—and looked again. He began to laugh hysterically.

Mr Wilfrid Wilderson had signed the wrong name.

The Intruder

Augustus Muir

AVOIDING the long avenue, he quickly came near to the house. He knew how to move in the dark without making a sound, and he emerged from the shrubbery and paused for a moment on the margin of the lawn, then went across and examined the windows. Presently he gave a little chuckle: for one of them was unfastened.

His feet were silent on the grass as he hurried back to the trees, and a tiny pocket-lamp flashed in his hand. From the road there came an answering signal; and the man stole back to the house.

He allowed several minutes to pass before he pushed open the window. The curtains had been drawn close, and he slipped through between them and peered around the room.

It was in darkness; but on the open hearth he could see the embers of a log fire. And then suddenly the light was snapped on. A tall man in a dinner-jacket was standing beside the desk. In the glow from the reading-lamp the newcomer could see he had reddish hair, a firm jaw, and cool blue eyes.

'Why not come in?' His voice was restrained. 'I've been listening to you with interest.'

The man beside the curtains was taken aback, but only for a moment. 'Put 'em up!' One of his hands was in his coat pocket, and there was a jutting ridge of cloth.

The man in the dinner-jacket smiled.

'By the looks of you,' he said, 'you aren't such a fool as to carry a gun. If a burglar is caught with a loaded weapon on him, the penalty is rather heavy—you know that as well as I do. So that bluff cuts no ice with me.'

At the window, the intruder laughed and gave a shrug. 'A pretty cool one, aren't you?' he began, but the tall man had swiftly reached to the desk and picked up a small revolver.

'Come here and sit down! I'm going to telephone the police.'

The short man took a step forward. 'Have a heart, guv'nor! You got me guessing just now—got me fair, you did. . . .'

'Sit down!' The muzzle of the weapon did not waver. 'Have a heart? For cool insolence, that takes some beating. There's only one place for a fellow of your kidney, and that's a nice comfortable cell.'

He glanced towards the door as a young woman came into the library. She stopped; a white hand went up to her cheek; and then she walked slowly forward. There was a puzzled look in her big dark eyes. 'Who is this?'

'I think he'd better answer that himself,' said the tall man. 'Out with it—what's your name?'

'Joe, sir.'

'Joe what? . . . Won't say, eh? Well, I don't suppose the police will take long to find out. He looks as if he'd been at this game for years.'

Joe turned to the girl. 'I been going straight, lady—I been straight for a twelve-month. This ain't been my usual lay. It's the truth I'm telling you.'

Her brow was wrinkled, and she seemed to have a trick of pouting her lips when she was perplexed. 'I'm afraid I don't understand.'

'Don't listen to him!' said the tall man sharply, but Joe insisted on trying to explain:

'Con stuff—that was my market. Finding a mug and rooking him. . . . Well, what's a mug for? If a con man don't lift a mug's brass, somebody else does. It's the way of the world, lady.'

'Joe's right, you know.' She nodded to the tall man. There was a faint smile in her eyes now; she seemed to have regained her self-possession. 'If you're a con man, as you call it——'

'Not for twelve months, Miss. I been straight, I tell you.' He glanced round the library, and his small bright eyes came to rest upon a safe in the corner. 'It's years since I took a chance on this game. Not that I didn't know my job—a slick hand, I was, with the pipe and bottle. . . . Sorry, Miss; how could you know that. Blow-pipe and a tube of gas. But I chucked that when I lined up with my old Dutch, bless her.'

'Then what are you doing here now?'

'Hard times for the likes of me, Miss. Out of a job, and got two nippers. That ain't——'

'I've had enough of this,' interrupted the other man. 'I'm going to 'phone the police.'

'Just a moment,' she pleaded. 'I want to hear what he's got to say.'

'I ain't got much, lady!' Joe continued. 'Among my pals they say the only harm a bloke can do is to get pinched. I've said it myself. But I ain't saying it now. For why? I'll tell you. I reads in a paper about the pearl necklace the young squire is going to give his fiancy for her birthday. Keep the missus and kids for months and no stint, that would. . . . If I'd known you before I come, Miss, it ain't here you'd find me now. The noospaper said it's your birthday tomorrow—and . . .'

'It's true.' She came nearer to him. 'Shall I tell you? My mother is giving a dance, and Harry and I slipped away because he wanted to show me the pearls tonight. We must hurry back in a few minutes. Now you know why you've been unlucky.' Suddenly she turned round and took the tall man's wrist in both her hands. 'Don't call the police, Harry!'

'Are you expecting me to sympathize with a crook who came after the very necklace——'

'That's the whole point!' she pleaded. 'He's admitted everything—and he's sorry. He's got a wife and two kiddies——'

'And an oily tongue!' said the tall man grimly. 'He can spin a yarn.' There was a frown on his face as he watched her go over to Joe and open her bag.

'I want you to promise me something,' she said gently. 'If we don't call the police, will you keep straight for another year? Harry and I will be married by that time. Come to me at this house a year from now—the eve of my birthday—and I'll have another little gift for you.'

Joe pulled off his hat and crushed it under his arm, then unfolded the note she had given him.

'A fiver, lady!' He gave a whistle.

'Quiet,' she admonished. 'You'll waken the servants. Now go—and I'm counting on you to keep your promise.'

'Thank you, Miss—and bless you!' Joe trousered the banknote.

'May you be very happy with—him!' After a final glance at the man who still stood scowling beside the desk, he slipped out through the window.

The moment he had gone, the girl drew the curtains close, while her companion pulled a small kit of tools from below the desk. 'We'd better get a move on,' he said. 'We've only got two hours to get into this damned safe!'

He worked for several minutes, and then the girl remarked:

'I thought I'd seen that fellow Joe before, but I'm hanged if I can place him.'

'Detective-Inspector Joe Gilmour of Scotland Yard is the name,' said a voice from the window. 'Sorry about the sob story—I had to give my Sergeant time to collect my other men.' He chuckled. 'And thank you, Miss—thank you for the fiver even if it *is* a dud. . . .'

Cast-Iron Alibi

Richard Keverne

'MISS CAMPBELL,' the maid announced, and the Chief Constable rose.

'Er—good afternoon,' he said as the door closed. 'Won't you please sit down.'

'No. I won't sit down, thank you,' the girl said. 'What I have to say to you will only take a very few moments. But thank you very much for seeing me.'

'Not at all. Not at all,' the Chief Constable replied, feeling unaccountably embarrassed. He turned to a note on his desk. 'When you telephoned this morning you said that you had something of importance to tell me confidentially. Well—you'd really better sit down. We can talk so much more easily if you do.' He smiled.

'Very well.' She took the chair he indicated and he sank back into his own. 'What I have to say, Major Godfrey, is this. I want you to know that I am Enid Cameron but, for obvious reasons, I have changed my name.'

'Enid Cameron?' he repeated frowning. 'Enid Cameron?'

'Yes. The woman who was sentenced to three years at the Old Bailey in nineteen-thirty-eight——'

'Of course; I remember, the——'

'The woman cat burglar I think they called me. Something bright and stupid like that.' She gave a bitter little laugh. 'But that doesn't matter now.'

Miles Godfrey's face hardened. He became official.

'Well, madam?' he said more coldly. But he eyed the slim fair-haired girl before him with intense interest. He remembered her sensational case.

'I have come to tell you that I have been offered employment as a lady gardener by some people called Powell at Grove Lodge, Mersden Magna, about five miles from here, I think.'

He nodded.

'I am on my way to see them now. But whether I accept the job depends on you.'

'On me? How do you mean?' Godfrey spoke less severely. He was growing more interested.

'On whether you are going to send your policemen nosing about making enquiries about me. If so—I shan't take it.'

'But——' he began.

'That's what happened in the last job I had,' she interrupted. 'I was doing farm work in the South Riding. I believe I was giving satisfaction and I liked the work. Then the police began asking clumsy questions about me. Some kind person—I don't know who, but someone evidently had recognized me—had sent them an anonymous letter. Anyhow, it was enough. I left before the farmer sacked me. Now is that going to happen again here?'

She stared at him defiantly, and Miles Godfrey was, for the moment, at a loss to know what to answer.

'Tell me a little more—if you wish to,' he said after a brief silence.

'I'll tell you this,' she answered with savage bitterness, 'not that I expect you to believe it, but—I've learned my lesson. If this sort of persecution goes on, there's only one end to it. No, no, no: I'm not going back into the ways of crime as you people call it. I can think of nothing more horrible than what I suffered in prison. Nothing.' She shuddered. 'I'm too much of a coward to risk that again. But—if one cannot earn a living, there is only one alternative——'

'Now, now, don't talk like that,' the Chief Constable interrupted rather fatuously. 'There's no reason why you shouldn't earn an honest living.'

'Yes there is: you and your system. That's why I'm here. I thought if I came and told you everything—at once—at least I might have a decent chance. Haven't I—purged—my offence, as you call it?' She threw out her hands in a despairing gesture. 'And it's no crime to change your name, is it?' An attractive touch of Scottish accent was creeping into her voice. 'And if you must know,' she added fiercely, 'Elizabeth Campbell is my name. Enid Cameron wasn't. I've told none of your people that before. Major Godfrey, won't you promise that I may have this chance?'

Miles Godfrey moved uneasily in his chair. He was a kindly, conscientious man, but many years of police work had shaken his faith in penitent criminal nature. His head told him that there was something wrong here; his heart that it might be the outside chance: the woman's protestations seemed to be genuine.

'Madam,' he said at last, 'I can promise you this. If you don't worry us, my men shall not worry you.'

'You mean it?' she asked eagerly.

'I do.' He spoke gravely. 'And I wish you well in your new life, and I hope it will succeed. I think you were wise to do what you have done. I dare say from time to time you may see me at the Powells' at Mersden Magna. But believe me, if we should meet there, we shall do so as strangers. I can say no more but I wish you good luck.'

The girl rose abruptly.

'Thank you,' she answered simply.

'I'll see you out,' he said, and extended his hand.

She hesitated before she took it, then, 'Thank you for that too,' she said.

The Chief Constable watched her as she hurried away, down the drive, then he wandered into his garden. Miles Godfrey found much consolation in his garden.

He was uncertain in his mind. After half an hour's pottering among his roses he had still come to no decision. Over tea he mentioned the Powells casually to his wife.

'Those new people at Mersden Magna,' he said, 'have they bought the house, do you know?'

'No, dear. They've taken it for three years, so Mrs Powell was saying. They were bombed out of their own home—near Worthing, I think she said.'

'That's bad. Did they lose a lot?'

'Very nearly everything. It must be heart-breaking. Still they're very plucky. I think you'd like them. Mr Powell seemed a most intelligent man. Very quiet. He was in the Indian Woods and Forests he told me.'

'Rotten luck losing your furniture like that,' Godfrey said. 'Lucky to get off with their lives, though. I hope they have got something more than his pension to live on.'

'I shouldn't think much,' Mrs Godfrey said. Miles Godfrey listened attentively; his wife had a flair for assessing other people's finances. 'But they're sensible about it. They're living very quietly. She's tremendously keen on the garden. I took to them both.'

'Next time I'm that way I must look in,' Godfrey said.

His wife had answered one question he had been asking himself. On the face of it the Powells would not seem to be the sort of people to possess the kind of jewellery which, as he remembered, had been Enid Cameron's special line in crime.

He asked another question later that day, for his head still told him that there was something wrong about Elizabeth Campbell.

From his study after dinner, he telephoned the Chief Constable of the South Riding. He knew him slightly, a hard-bitten Yorkshire-man named Ackroyd. He rang his private house.

'Look here, Ackroyd,' he said when he had recalled himself to him. 'This is more a personal than a professional enquiry. Have you had that woman Enid Cameron in your part of the world lately?'

'Enid Cameron? Oh yes, I know who you mean. Why? Has she been giving you any trouble?'

'None at all,' Miles Godfrey said. 'Did she give you any?'

'No. But someone sent us an anonymous letter to say she was working on a farm at Copley under the name of Campbell. We made a routine enquiry apparently and I hear she cleared off.'

'Enquiry produce anything?'

'Nothing at all except a kick from the farmer she was working for. I hear he told off one of my sergeants who made the enquiry for losing him a good hand. That's how I came to hear about it.'

'How long had she been there?'

'Only a few weeks, as I remember. One of these women's land organizations sent her.'

'And so far as you know everything was satisfactory?'

'Perfectly. Why: what's your interest?'

'Can't tell you now. Just a mild hunch, that's all. Thanks very much, Ackroyd. Keeping busy?'

'Yes. Jerry sees to that. He's been rather too active our way. You had much trouble?'

They discussed air raids for a few moments before they rang off, and Godfrey was easier in mind about Elizabeth Campbell when he went to bed. At least her story had been true.

But not entirely easy. The presence of a skilled and notorious jewel thief in his county was no matter to be regarded lightly. And that he had promised that his men should not worry her if she did not worry them did not relieve him of the responsibility of keeping an eye on her.

Miles Godfrey turned up the report of her trial in the county paper when he was in Norminster next day.

The report was a full one, for the 'Woman Cat Burglar' case had made a big sensation at the time. His memory of the main details of the case, he found, was very fairly accurate. Enid Cameron had been seen coming down the fire escape of a block of flats near Knightsbridge. When they caught her she had some fifteen thousand pounds' worth of jewellery on her, the property of an Argentine meat magnate's wife.

She had had bad luck. She had jumped the last few feet and twisted her ankle, otherwise it seemed she might have got clear away. But there were certain other points that particularly engaged the Chief Constable's attention. The girl had been dressed in man's clothes at the time. When she had been found guilty she asked for two other similar crimes to be taken into consideration. That, to Godfrey, looked as if she were an old hand. Yet, as was stated by Inspector Artifex of Scotland Yard who had charge of the case, nothing was known against her, nor had he been able to discover anything of her history.

The judge referred to that in passing sentence. 'Although you have elected to tell the police nothing of your upbringing or your past history it is clear to me that you are a woman of education and culture,' he had said. 'That fact adds a gravity to your crime. . . .' Miles Godfrey returnd to his office at the Shire Hall more interested than ever in Elizabeth Campbell.

He was getting a kick out of this case; he admitted it frankly. He was going on with it.

'I find I shall have to go up to London tomorrow,' he told his wife at dinner, 'and I may have to stay overnight.'

'Oh, I do hope there won't be a raid,' she said anxiously. 'Don't stay unless you must.'

'I won't,' he reassured her.

Godfrey had determined to have an unofficial talk with Inspector Artifex. He knew several men at the Yard who would give him an introduction, and he was lucky. Artifex was in the building when he called.

An Inspector Marchant who had been in Norminster on a murder inquiry recently introduced him.

'Major Godfrey wants to know something about your pal Enid Cameron,' he said. 'Not professionally but he's interested in the lady's history.'

'So was I,' Artifex said with a sour grin. 'And she took mighty good care that I shouldn't know anything about it. Come along this way, sir, and I'll tell you what I can.'

They went through a bare, cold corridor to Artifex's room. He was a middle-aged man with a deeply lined face that suggested an old-time actor, and he shook his head slowly when Godfrey said, 'So you never found out who she was.'

'Never. Never even knew where she was living. Nothing on her; not even a laundry mark. And,' Artifex smiled, 'she always told me I never would find out. But she was a lady right enough.'

'Really,' Godfrey commented non-commitally.

'Yes. Charming manners. Used to apologize to me for the trouble she was giving. Last thing she said to me was, "I'd like to thank you for all your kindness."' Artifex's lined face wrinkled with amusement. 'And the funny part about it was I believe she meant it. Attractive little devil. Has a pretty Scotch accent.'

'Indeed? At least we may assume, then, she's Scotch,' Miles Godfrey said humorously.

'Well, I wouldn't even bet on that,' Artifex responded.

'Fingerprints didn't help you?'

'No. No record of them.'

'Think she was an old hand?'

'Damned sure of it. I could name six or seven jobs I'm absolutely sure she did. but we couldn't prove it. Same methods. Same stuff—first-class jewels.'

'She admitted to two other cases, didn't she?'

'Yes.' Again Artifex's face wrinkled. 'And that was clever too. The only two I think I might have proved. Stopped us making more enquiries about them, her confessing. It's my belief we might have got on to who she was if we'd gone a bit further.'

'Seems to have been a clever young woman.'

'Clever as a cart-load of monkeys.'

'What's your own opinion, Inspector?' Godfrey asked.

'Me? Well, I think she was working for someone else. They fixed up the jobs for her and she did 'em. And I've a very shrewd suspicion I know who the other parties were. I'd risk a bet it was the Cummings, but I was never able to connect them up.'

'The Cummings?'

'Don't suppose you'd know them, sir. Two of them, man and woman. As clever a pair of fences as you'd want to meet. Archie Cummings is inside at the moment. The woman was in Dublin last I heard of her. Shouldn't be surprised if Enid was there too. If so the Irish police will have some trouble soon.'

'Enid Cameron's been out some time now, I suppose.'

'Nine months or more I should say. She'd get her full remission. As a matter of fact I was only talking to Mr Weston about her a week or two ago. He was prison chaplain at Wensbury when she was inside. He was interested in her too. Said everybody liked her there. Gave no trouble. Used to work in the garden. They were sorry to lose her.'

'And now,' Godfrey said, 'she's at large.'

'Yes, but we'll hear about her soon.'

'You don't think she's likely to go straight?'

'Mr Weston thought so, but then chaplains always do,' Artifex said cynically. 'That's their job. But in my experience, I'm afraid not, Major. You see, with that type it's the excitement they like, and they can't resist it for long. Now a girl like that would probably have a decent little packet put away. And friends to go to. Well, when she came out she'd want a good time. If there hadn't been a war, she'd have gone abroad, and when she'd spent her packet, she'd have to start earning more. If you want my opinion, if she isn't in Ireland she'll turn up somewhere outside London—some safe area where the rich bomb dodgers have gone. Devonshire perhaps, or Wales. That's where her sort of stuff is now. I don't think she's likely to come to your part. You're not safe enough. But if she does, you keep an eye on her. I know her—the little—er, lady.'

'I will, Inspector,' Godfrey said with a laugh.

Miles Godfrey was home in time for dinner that night. As they sat down to the table, his wife said. 'Mrs Powell, you know, those new people at Mersden Magna, called this afternoon. She's asked us to go over next Wednesday. They're having a few people in for sherry. I said I was sure you'd come if you could. It would be such a good opportunity for you to meet him. About six she said.'

'Good idea. I'll go,' Godfrey said casually.

Grove Lodge was a smallish place; a square, featureless white-washed mid-Victorian house set in a big garden. Godfrey knew it well.

It was nearly seven o'clock when he arrived. His wife had come earlier. The lawn was dotted with garden chairs, and Powell had fixed up a long table for drinks and things under a big chestnut tree near the house. Miles Godfrey eyed the guests with interest as he stood talking for a few moments to his hosts. He knew most of them.

'You'll find Mrs Godfrey over there in the shade, I think,' Mrs Powell said. 'It's so dreadfully hot still. This new time is quite absurd, don't you think?'

'I like it. It can never be too hot for me,' her husband put in. He was a tall, spare, sallow man who looked as if he had lived in the tropics most of his life.

'If you have a moment later on, I must get you to show me your garden and your roses, Mrs Powell,' Miles Godfrey said before he drifted away. 'Roses are rather a hobby of mine.'

'I should love to,' she said. 'But I'm afraid you won't think much of mine.'

'I'm sure I shall,' he laughed.

He strolled across the lawn in search of his wife, but before he reached her he had stopped many times to talk to acquaintances.

While he was chatting with the local parson, he heard a voice behind him saying, 'May I give you another glass of sherry, sir?' and he turned to face Elizabeth Campbell.

She was dressed simply in a plain linen frock and she carried a tray of glasses. Her eyes met his without the slightest trace of recognition.

'Thank you,' he said, exchanging his empty glass for a full one. 'Thank you very much.'

She moved over to another group of guests and Godfrey asked innocently, 'Who's the lady, padre?'

'That? Oh, she's the Powells' gardener. A real treasure, according to Mrs Powell. A lady, you know.'

'So I judge,' Godfrey said. 'If she knows anything about gardening, they're lucky to get her. My man's called up and I can't find anyone who's any good. Have to do most of the work myself.'

'I believe she's really most competent,' the parson responded. 'Curious what strange occupations ladies are taking up in these days.'

'Very curious,' Godfrey agreed.

He saw Miss Campbell moving among the guests with her tray. She offered him sandwiches a little later on, again without any trace of self-consciousness, and he found that she was causing a good deal of interest among the women.

His wife spoke of her. 'We ought to try to get a woman to do the garden, Miles,' she said. 'So clever of the Powells to think of it. This land army, you know.' Mrs Godfrey was always rather vague.

Presently Miles Godfrey met the girl again.

The guests were beginning to leave and Mrs Powell came to redeem her promise to show him round the garden. They were at the far end of the kitchen garden when he caught sight of her. She was watering a long bed.

'Hallo; what have you got coming on there?' he asked.

'I'm afraid I don't know,' Mrs Powell said. 'I just can't get excited about vegetables. I know I ought to, but I leave that to my husband and Miss Campbell.' She called, 'What are those things, Miss Campbell?'

The girl raised her head.

'Green peas, madam,' she answered, and Godfrey put in cheerily, 'Pretty late, aren't they? I hope you have more luck with late peas than I do. Mine always get mildewed.'

'They need a lot of care and water,' the girl said, 'but I've generally been fairly fortunate with them.'

'This is Miss Campbell, who has come to look after our garden,' Mrs Powell stated, as though she felt that some form of introduction were required.

'Miss Campbell's been good enough to look after my thirst already,' Godfry said with a smile, and the girl smiled in return. 'What kind of peas have you got there.' he went on, his gardener's interest aroused.

'They're Beechy's Wonder,' she answered.

'Beechy's Wonder—I never heard of them. I must try them. Is it too late to sow now, Miss Campbell?'

'Oh no—you can sow up till the end of the month certainly.'

'Where can I buy them? Did you get them locally?'

Major Miles Godfrey had forgotten for the moment that he was a policeman keeping a tactful eye on a dangerous crook. He was only eager to try these new late peas he had just heard of.

'No, sir. I got them from an Edinburgh firm for Mr Powell. They're quite well known in Scotland.'

'Haven't we some seed we could give Major Godfrey,' Mrs Powell said.

'Plenty, madam.'

'No, no; I mustn't rob you like that,' Godfrey protested half-heartedly.

'Robbery—nonsense, Major. We should be only too pleased. Miss Campbell, get some, will you?'

The girl went off towards a tool shed and Godfrey and his hostess followed slowly.

'Very competent young woman you've got hold of, Mrs Powell,' he said.

'Yes, isn't she? So helpful. She'll do anything. But you know it's rather—embarrassing at times.'

'Embarrassing? How do you mean?'

'Well, you can see she's a lady, but she insists upon being treated like a servant and calling me "madam" and my husband "sir". It's so silly, I think, in these days.'

'Yes. I suppose it is. Still it might be more awkward the other way. Does she live in the house?'

'No. She has lodgings in the village.'

'How did you manage to find her?'

'Through the woman's land army or something. It was my husband's idea. She'd been doing farm work in Yorkshire, but she found it a little too hard. Oh, there you are, Miss Campbell.'

The girl had emerged from the shed, a big packet in her hand.

But Godfrey protested.

'No, no; I only want a few, really,' he said. 'Just enough for a short row. Here,'—he drew an envelope from his pocket—'just put me in a few there, will you, Miss Campbell. That's ample, thank you.'

'I'm in luck,' he told his wife when they joined her. 'I've seen a charming garden, a charming lady gardener, and I've been given some peas that I'm assured we can sow now and eat in the autumn.'

It was not until he was changing for dinner that Miles Godfrey really remembered that he was a policeman again. When he took the precious envelope from his pocket he saw on it three grimy but perfect prints where the girl's fingers had held it.

It was funny how things like that came your way when you didn't need them.

Next morning, when he opened his *Times* at breakfast a headline caught his eyes. 'Daring Jewel Robbery', it ran. Miles Godfrey read the story with an intense and growing interest, for every detail of the crime screamed Enid Cameron.

The robbery had taken place in a country house in Gloucestershire. As the brief report told, a case containing pearls and other jewels worth twenty thousand pounds had been taken from the bedroom of the wife of a wealthy stockbroker on the previous night. The owner stated that she had seen her jewels immediately before coming down to dinner at eight. When she had gone up after listening to the wireless news, about half-past nine, they had gone. It was suggested that the theft had occurred during the news period and that the burglar had gained access to the room by scaling a water pipe leading to an adjoining bathroom.

Godfrey frowned as he made a mental calculation. From Mersden Magna to the Gloucestershire house must be the best part of a hundred and fifty miles—possibly more. In a very fast car it would take fully four hours and he had been talking to Enid Cameron at half-past seven, a bit later if anything. That ruled her out absolutely. He himself could give her a cast-iron alibi. The frown faded. Miles Godfrey was glad, very glad.

But, as he thought it over a little later on, this was going to make it devilish awkward for her. The Gloucesterhire police and probably the Yard would already be looking for her, unless they were fools.

They'd soon get a line on her from the South Riding constabulary, and then—the odds were they'd trace her to Mersden Magna before long. Poor little devil! Despite her complete alibi she'd lose her job. Godfrey tried to work out what would be the wisest action for him to take. Obviously he must do something. He determined to have a word with Artifex.

But Artifex forestalled him. He was on the telephone to the Shire Hall immediately after lunch.

'Well, sir, I wasn't far wrong, was I?' he said. 'Enid Cameron's turned up again. You've seen the case in the papers, I expect.'

'That Gloucestershire business?'

'Yes.'

'So you think that was her job?'

'Sure of it. Her stuff, her methods. No one else could have done it. I told you she'd turn up soon in some safe area where the good jewellery has gone to.'

'Are you on the case, Inspector?'

'Yes, sir. The county police called us in about an hour ago. I'm going down, this evening, but I wanted a word with you first.'

'Oh, why?' Godfrey affected surprise. 'Think we can help you at all?'

'Well——' Artifex spoke humorously. '—I had just an idea that perhaps you had a reason for our talk the other day. Of course I may be wrong.'

'I'm not sure you're not,' Godfrey responded. 'Tell me, Inspector: are the newspaper facts correct—about time, I mean?'

'No doubt of that, sir. The county police are satisfied. Just the sort of thing she would do. Choose the news time. She'd know servants and everybody else would be listening then. Give her a clear twenty minutes and Enid doesn't want more than that.'

'Think you'll get her?'

'Shouldn't be surprised. But it's the gang she works with I want. And they're not going to find it so easy to get rid of the stuff now. There's no pushing it abroad like there used to be.'

'No, I suppose not. Well, what do you want us to do?'

'Know anything about her, sir?'

'Yes,' Godfrey said slowly. 'Something you won't like.'

'What's that, sir?'

'That I'm absolutely certain she didn't do that job.'

'How's that?' Artifex seemed annoyed. 'How can you be certain, sir?'

'Because, Inspector, I myself can give her an alibi——'

'What?' Artifex interjected.

'Yes. A cast-iron one. Look here: this is for your ear only. Enid Cameron *is* going straight and I know where she is; I've been keeping an eye on her for some time.'

'Good lord!'

'I don't want you to waste your time looking for her, and I don't want her to lose her job by having enquiries made about her. I know that she was a hundred and fifty miles from the place in Gloucestershire after half-past seven last night, and unless your times are wrong she couldn't have done it. That's good enough, isn't it?'

'Well, sir, if you say so I must believe it,' Artifex replied dubiously.

'Still, you might make quite sure of your times, Inspector, and if they are wrong, I'll do a further check this end. Meanwhile I'll send you a present.'

'A present, sir?'

'Yes. I know you think I'm mistaken, so I'll send you something to put your mind at rest. Three beautiful fingerprints. If I put the letter on the three o'clock train, it will be at Liverpool Street at four fifty-five. Have it met and give me a ring when you've checked them. I'll be here till six.'

When at length he rang off, Miles Godfrey was mildly amused; Artifex was so obviously reluctant to believe that Enid Cameron could not have committed the burglary. He was looking forward with some interest to the inspector's discomfiture when he rang later.

Artifex rang at about a quarter to six.

'Well, are you satisfied, Inspector?' Godfrey asked with a chuckle.

'No, sir; I'm not.'

'What! Didn't you identify the fingerprints?'

'Yes, sir: we know them.'

'Then what's the catch? Times wrong?'

'I can't explain now, sir. I'm just coming down to see you and I've got to rush if I'm to catch the six-fifteen. Would you have an eye kept on the lady? I want to ask her a question or two when I come. Where can I find you, sir.'

'Me? You'd better come here. To the Shire Hall. I'll come back.'

'Thank you, sir.' Artifex ran off, and Miles Godfrey sat frowning at the telephone on his desk for some time.

He was not happy. Unless Artifex was being unnecessarily officious, it looked as if, somehow, he'd made a blunder. Yet for the life of him Miles Godfrey could not see how. Enid Cameron's alibi was cast iron—even if the Gloucestershire burglary had taken place at midnight. Still, he had his duty to do. It was going to be very hard luck on her, but if he handled the matter himself he might make it a bit easier for her.

Godfrey decided to go out to Mersden Magna at once, improvise some excuse—something about those late peas, beg some more perhaps—and see the girl.

As he went to his car, he came face to face with Mrs Powell. He would gladly have avoided her, but she stopped him.

'Good afternoon, Major Godfrey,' she said brightly. 'What a dreary place Norminister is on early closing day.'

'Yes, it is pretty dead,' he responded.

She went on. 'I'd forgotten it was Thursday. I had to come in to bring Miss Campbell to the station——'

'Miss Campbell—your excellent lady gardener—you're not losing her, I hope, Mrs Powell.' Godfrey was suddenly very anxious.

'Oh, no. She's only going to London for a couple of nights. She has a sister who's a Waaf or an At or something. I never can remember these funny names. She's stationed in the Midlands and she's got leave unexpectedly and she wired Miss Campbell to know if she could meet her in London for a celebration. Of course we said she could go, though it is a nuisance, so I ran her in in the car. And I thought I'd do some shopping before I went back and I discovered it's your horrible early closing day.'

'How very annoying,' Godfrey said with enormous conviction. 'It's very kind of you to let the girl go. But I suppose one could hardly say "no". What train was she getting?'

'The six-twenty, I think it is. I left her at the car park. She said she had plenty of time to walk to the station, and I went on to find all the shops shut.'

Norminster's early closing day still rankled badly. Godfrey was sympathetic again. He bade her goodbye rather abruptly and turned back to the Shire Hall.

'Ask Superintendent Ford to come to my room at once,' he told the constable at the door, and a minute later he was speaking urgently to Ford.

'There's an Inspector Artifex of the CID coming down here to see me. He's catching the six-fifteen from Liverpool Street. You've got to communicate with him somehow. Ring the Yard. Ring the Railway Police at the station. Say I'm going to London on the six-twenty and ask him to wait for me at Liverpool Street. I'll look for him at the barrier. Say it's most urgent. He'll understand. That quit clear, Ford?'

'Quite, sir.'

'Right.'

Then Miles Godfrey made a dash for Norminster station.

He reached it just as the train came in and observed, with relief, Elizabeth Campbell among the crowd on the platform. Presently he saw her enter the dining-car and he made his way to a compartment at the front of the train.

There was only one stop on the journey and Godfrey satisfied himself that she had not left the train there. Indeed, he was growing altogether more satisfied as the journey proceeded. He was still convinced that the girl could not possibly have committed the Gloucestershire crime, but if Artifex had to interrogate her it was far better that he should do so in London than in Mersden Magna. The Powells need know nothing whatever about it.

As they ran slowly into the terminus, Godfrey's fingers were on the handle of the carriage door. He was on the platform before the train had stopped. At the barrier he looked for Artifex and saw him standing some little way back from the gate.

'I'm glad you got my message in time,' he said as he joined him. 'The girl's on this train. I only heard just in time to catch it. Her story is that she's come up to spend a couple of nights with a sister who's a Waaf or something on leave. I have no reason to doubt it or believe it. But I thought I'd better come along myself. No time to explain to any of my men.'

'Very wise, sir. Thank you very much,' Artifex said, his eyes fixed on the passengers beginning to crowd through the gates.

'There she is. Know her?' Godfrey went on as he caught sight of Elizabeth Campbell coming to the gate, carrying a small suitcase.

'I know her,' Artifex said in an odd tone.

'And—there's the sister, I assume.'

A girl in uniform was greeting her. They kissed, then began to move slowly off.

'Thank you, sir. Thank you very much,' Artifex said with apparent irrelevance. He went towards her, Godfrey close on his heels.

'Good evening, Miss Cameron,' he said, politely raising his hat, 'I think you'll remember me.'

The two girls stopped instantly. Godfrey's eyes were on Elizabeth Campbell. He saw her face harden. It was a couple of seconds before he realized that Artifex was not addressing her. It was the girl in uniform to whom he had spoken.

The girl in uniform said in a staccato tone, 'Yes. What do you want?'

'I want you to come along to Scotland Yard with me and answer a few questions,' Artifex said blandly. Then he turned to Miss Campbell.

'I am a police officer and I believe you to be Margaret Cummings,' he began. 'I must——'

'What!' Godfrey exclaimed.

'Very clever, aren't you?' the girl sneered, glaring at him while Artifex went on in official phrases quite unperturbed.

'Well, we got the stuff, sir,' Artifex said to Miles Godfrey an hour later. 'In a suitcase at Liverpool Street. We found the cloakroom ticket on Cameron. But she very nearly got away with it. I should have had to accept your alibi if it hadn't been for those fingerprints. I should never have troubled to look for her. And I'll admit when we found those prints were Margaret Cummings' I couldn't quite see what the game was. But, by gad, it was smart.' He smiled appreciatively. 'I wonder whose brainwave it was. Fifty-fifty, I shouldn't wonder; not much to choose between them for artfulness. But it's a new one on me.'

'A new one! It's a new one on me too,' Miles Godfrey said frowning. 'And, damn it all, Artifex, I admit I don't quite see it all yet. Do you imagine this woman Cummings would have had the nerve to go back to Mersden Magna?'

'No, sir: much too clever for that. But she'd covered her tracks.

Have a look at that: we found it on Cameron, it's in her writing. That would have been posted by now if we hadn't caught her,' Artifex added.

Miles Godfrey took a letter addressed to himself. It ran:

When I read about that robbery in Gloucestershire in the papers this morning I knew it was no good going on. The police are bound to say I did it and your men will be coming to question me, so I'm going away again. You know I didn't do it, so do lots of people, but that wouldn't have mattered.

'Will you explain everything to Mr and Mrs Powell. It doesn't matter now. But I'd like them to know that you knew about me. Thank them for their kindness and say I'm sorry. And thank you for yours.—ELIZABETH CAMPBELL.

'Of all the infernal little hypocrites!' Godfrey exclaimed angrily.

'Oh, but cunning, very cunning,' Artifex broke in. 'She fades out and leaves the alibi stronger than ever. Thought of everything. Cleared herself. If it hadn't been for you, sir, they'd have walked clean away with the stuff.'

Major Miles Godfrey gave an enigmatic grunt.

IV

ROGUES, KNAVES AND FORTUNE-HUNTERS

Grandson of the biologist T. H. Huxley, grand-nephew of the poet and critic Matthew Arnold, nephew of the novelist Mrs Humphry Ward, *Aldous Huxley* (1894–1963) began his career as a writer of witty, brittle novels of London society while on the staff of the *Athenaeum* under Middleton Murry. Great things were expected of him. A pessimist as far as the future of humanity went, his revulsion against man and manners led him to write his 'Utopian' satire *Brave New World* (1932), once hugely admired, and feared, now regarded as a prophetic failure. He turned to mysticism and his books, both fiction and non-fiction, became increasingly didactic. Never afraid to experiment (in life as in his novels), his experiences with mescalin, as recorded in *The Doors of Perception* (1954), strongly influenced the psychedelic generation of the 1960s. His oft-reprinted murder story 'The Gioconda Smile' is a dark little masterpiece; 'A Deal in Old Masters' shows a lighter, though still cynical, touch.

A. J. Alan (Leslie Harrison Lambert, 1883–1941) was, in the opinion of the critic Kenelm Foss, the initiator of the BBC accent. A career civil servant at the Foreign Office, Alan found unlooked-for fame as a radio story-teller, his languid yet slightly fussy tones (preserved in the BBC Sound Archives and on at least one 78 rpm record) precisely suiting his material. His speciality was the shaggy-dog story, exemplified by the very first story he told, 'My Adventure in Jermyn Street' (originally broadcast on 31 January 1924), in which the narrator is sent tickets to a play, meets a mysterious woman, is taken to a flat in Jermyn Street, is left alone and subsequently discovers that the apartment is empty, the rest of the rooms dust-sheeted, the woman (not a ghost) vanished. There is no explanation. Plainly put, it is hard to see his stories' attractions. And yet the manner of his delivery—diffident, amused, perplexed, self-depre-catory, entirely un-ironic—still charms and engages; and though he sounded as though (the professional raconteur) he was creating the story as he spoke, every word was carefully scripted, every pause, every chuckle, every clearing of the throat flagged in red. He was skilled at the twist-ending tale and wrote a number of atmospheric supernatural stories. When translated into print his work was just as diverting. Most of his output, at least up to 1932, was collected in *Good Evening, Everyone!* (1928) and *A. J. Alan: His Second Book* (1932). 'Private Water', uncollected until now, is a beguiling example of his idiosyncratic style.

Though on the staff of *The Times* for eighteen years and editor of *The Times Literary Supplement* from 1938 to 1944, D. L. *Murray* (1888–1962) yet found time to produce a volume of early Victorian social history, a biography of Disraeli, three novels, and five immense, and immensely entertaining, historical novels of the type that would now be labelled 'blockbusters'. When he left *The Times* his output slowed somewhat: from 1945 to 1961 he wrote a mere seven novels and a life of the composer Franz Lehar (with the theatre historian W. Macqueen-Pope). After taking a First at Oxford, Murray was attached to the War Office during the First World War in the Intelligence Department. He was on the *Athenaeum* as drama critic at the same time as Aldous Huxley. An early novel, *Stardust* (1931), was a highly elaborate extravaganza involving murder, blackmail, bankruptcy, White Slave trafficking, and torture, all set against the colourful backdrop of the sawdust ring. Murray's talents as an exhaustive researcher into the minutiae of the past were impressively displayed in his historical fictions, in which were packed not only sights, sounds, smells, and immense social detail but the most labyrinthine plots. Set in England and the Crimea, *Trum-peter, Sound!* (1933), his most celebrated work, is a vivid and engross-ing novel (Russian spies, duels, a false marriage, Wellington's funeral, young hero thwarted from gaining his rightful inheritance) having as its centre-piece a panoramic retelling of the Charge of the Light Brigade. In 'A Gift from the Nabob', a tale of impudent roguery, Murray proved he could work just as well on a miniature canvas.

Literary maverick, egotist, and *poseur*, *J. Maclaren-Ross* (1912–64) for many embodied the spirit of Fitzrovia during the 1940s. A distinctive figure, with his dark glasses, fur coat, and gold-knobbed cane, he had a disconcerting habit of challenging to a duel those he felt had crossed him (generally speaking most who knew him). Maclaren-Ross (the 'J' might have stood for Julian but no one seems entirely certain) was brought up in France and spent some time as a vacuum-cleaner salesman in the 1930s (sardonically fictionalized in *Of Love and Hunger* [1947]); during the war quantities of his short stories were published in the 'little magazines' of the day: *Horizon*, *Penguin New Writing*, *Lilliput*, *Printer's Pie*, *English Story*. He rarely wrote in any person other than the first and his picaresque tales were mainly anecdotal, written at times in a jocular slang. He wrote of other-ranks and squaddies, the Soho drinking classes, on-the-edge literary types, all groups to which he had at one time or another belonged. He was an incisive critic, a parodist of some genius, had an unparalleled knowledge of the novels of the twentieth century (the plot for even the most obscure of which he could summon up in a trice), and a fondness, even admiration, for pulp fiction and fictioneers, particularly the writers of Sexton Blake thrillers. In his 'Dance to the Music of Time' novel sequence Anthony Powell has painted a more or less faithful portrait of Maclaren-Ross as 'X. Trapnel'. 'The Episcopal Seal' is the tale of an irresistible rogue.

A Deal in Old Masters

Aldous Huxley

'Pictures,' said Mr Bigger; 'you want to see some pictures? Well, we have a very interesting mixed exhibition of modern stuff in our galleries at the moment. French and English, you know.'

The customer held up his hand, shook his head. 'No, no. Nothing modern for me,' he declared, in his pleasant northern English. 'I want real pictures, old pictures. Rembrandt and Sir Joshua Reynolds and that sort of thing.'

'Perfectly.' Mr Bigger nodded. 'Old Masters. Oh, of course we deal in the old as well as the modern.'

'The fact is,' said the other, 'that I've just bought a rather large house—a Manor House,' he added, in impressive tones.

Mr Bigger smiled; there was an ingenuousness about this simple-minded fellow which was most engaging. He wondered how the man had made his money. 'A Manor House.' The way he had said it was really charming. Here was a man who had worked his way up from serfdom to the lordship of a manor, from the broad base of the feudal pyramid to the narrow summit. His own history and all the history of classes had been implicit in that awed proud emphasis on the 'Manor'. But the stranger was running on; Mr Bigger could not allow his thoughts to wander further. 'In a house of this style,' he was saying, 'and with a position like mine to keep up, one must have a few pictures. Old Masters, you know; Rembrandts and What's-his-names.'

'Of course,' said Mr Bigger, 'an Old Master is a symbol of social superiority.'

'That's just it,' cried the other, beaming; 'you've said just what I wanted to say.'

Mr Bigger bowed and smiled. It was delightful to find someone who took one's little ironies as sober seriousness.

'Of course, we should only need Old Masters downstairs, in the reception-room. It would be too much of a good thing to have them in the bedrooms too.'

'Altogether too much of a good thing,' Mr Bigger assented.

'As a matter of fact,' the Lord of the Manor went on, 'my daughter—she does a bit of sketching. And very pretty it is. I'm having some of her things framed to hang in the bedrooms. It's useful having an artist in the family. Saves you buying pictures. But, of course, we must have something old downstairs.'

'I think I have exactly what you want.' Mr Bigger got up and rang the bell. 'My daughter does a little sketching'—he pictured a large blonde barmaidish personage, thirty-one and not yet married, running a bit to seed. His secretary appeared at the door. 'Bring me the Venetian portrait, Miss Pratt, the one in the back room. You know which I mean.'

'You're very snug in here,' said the Lord of the Manor. 'Business good, I hope.'

Mr Bigger sighed. 'The slump,' he said. 'We art dealers feel it worse than anyone.'

'Ah, the slump.' The Lord of the Manor chuckled. 'I foresaw it all the time. Some people seemed to think the good times were going to last for ever. What fools! I sold out of everything at the crest of the wave. That's why I can buy pictures now.'

Mr Bigger laughed too. This was the right sort of customer. 'Wish I'd had anything to sell out during the boom,' he said.

The Lord of the Manor laughed till the tears rolled down his cheeks. He was still laughing when Miss Pratt re-entered the room. She carried a picture, shieldwise, in her two hands, before her.

'Put it on the easel, Miss Pratt,' said Mr Bigger. 'Now,' he turned to the Lord of the Manor, 'what do you think of that?'

The picture that stood on the easel before them was a half-length portrait. Plump-faced, white-skinned, high-bosomed in her deeply scalloped dress of blue silk, the subject of the picture seemed a typical Italian lady of the middle eighteenth century. A little complacent smile curved the pouting lips and in one hand she held a black mask, as though she had just taken it off after a day of carnival.

'Very nice,' said the Lord of the Manor; but he added, doubtfully, 'It isn't very like Rembrandt, is it? It's all so clear and bright. Generally in Old Masters you can never see anything at all, they're so dark and foggy.'

'Very true,' said Mr Bigger. 'But not all Old Masters are like Rembrandt.'

'I suppose not.' The Lord of the Manor seemed hardly to be convinced.

'This is eighteenth-century Venetian. Their colour was always luminous. Giangolini was the painter. He died young, you know. Not more than half a dozen of his pictures are known. And this is one.'

The Lord of the Manor nodded. He could appreciate the value of rarity.

'One notices at a first glance the influence of Longhi,' Mr Bigger went on, airily. 'And there is something of the morbidezza of Rosalba in the painting of the face.'

The Lord of the Manor was looking uncomfortably from Mr Bigger to the picture and from the picture to Mr Bigger. There is nothing so embarrassing as to be talked at by someone possessing more knowledge than you do. Mr Bigger pressed his advantage.

'Curious,' he went on, 'that one sees nothing of Tiepolo's manner in this. Don't you think so?'

The Lord of the Manor nodded. His face wore a gloomy expression. The corners of his baby's mouth drooped. One almost expected him to burst into tears.

'It's pleasant,' said Mr Bigger, relenting at last, 'to talk to somebody who really knows about painting. So few people do.'

'Well, I can't say I've ever gone into the subject very deeply,' said the Lord of the Manor, modestly. 'But I know what I like when I see it.' His face brightened again, as he felt himself on safer ground.

'A natural instinct,' said Mr Bigger. 'That's a very precious gift. I could see by your face that you had it; I could see that the moment you came into the gallery.'

The Lord of the Manor was delighted. 'Really now,' he said. He felt himself growing larger, more important. 'Really.' He cocked his head critically on one side. 'Yes. I must say I think that's a very fine bit of painting. Very fine. But the fact is, I should rather have liked a more historical piece, if you know what I mean. Something more ancestor-like, you know. A portrait of somebody with a story—like Anne Boleyn, or Nell Gwynn, or the Duke of Wellington, or someone like that.'

'But, my dear sir, I was just going to tell you. This picture has a story.' Mr Bigger leaned forward and tapped the Lord of the Manor on the knee. His eyes twinkled with benevolent and amused brightness under his bushy eyebrows. There was a knowing kindliness in his smile. 'A most remarkable story is connected with the painting of that picture.'

'You don't say so?' The Lord of the Manor raised his eyebrows.

Mr Bigger leaned back in his chair. 'The lady you see there,' he said, indicating the portrait with a wave of the hand, 'was the wife of the fourth Earl Hurtmore. The family is now extinct. The ninth Earl died only last year. I got this picture when the house was sold up. It's sad to see the passing of these old ancestral homes.' Mr Bigger sighed. The Lord of the Manor looked solemn, as though he were in church. There was a moment's silence; then Mr Bigger went on in a changed tone. 'From his portraits, which I have seen, the fourth Earl seems to have been a long-faced, gloomy, grey-looking fellow. One can never imagine him young; he was the sort of man who looks permanently fifty. His chief interests in life were music and Roman antiquities. There's one portrait of him holding an ivory flute in one hand and resting the other on a fragment of Roman carving. He spent at least half his life travelling in Italy, looking for antiques and listening to music. When he was about fifty-five, he suddenly decided that it was about time to get married. This was the lady of his choice.' Mr Bigger pointed to the picture. 'His money and his title must have made up for many deficiencies. One can't imagine, from her appearance, that Lady Hurtmore took a great deal of interest in Roman antiquities. Nor, I should think, did she care much for the science and history of music. She liked clothes, she liked society, she liked gambling, she liked flirting, she liked enjoying herself. It doesn't seem that the newly wedded couple got on too well. But still, they avoided an open breach. A year after the marriage Lord Hurtmore decided to pay another visit to Italy. They reached Venice in the early autumn. For Lord Hurtmore, Venice meant unlimited music. It meant Galuppi's daily concerts at the orphange of the Misericordia. It meant Piccini at Santa Maria. It meant new operas at the San Moise; it meant delicious cantatas at a hundred churches. It meant private concerts of amateurs; it meant Porpora and the finest singers in Europe; it meant Tartini and the greatest violinists. For Lady Hurtmore, Venice meant something rather different. It meant gambling at the Ridotto, masked balls, gay supper parties—all the delights of the most amusing city in the world. Living their separate lives, both might have been happy here in Venice almost indefinitely. But one day Lord Hurtmore had the disastrous idea of having his wife's portrait painted. Young Giangolini was recommended to him as the promising, the coming painter. Lady Hurtmore began her sittings. Giangolini was handsome and dashing, Giangolini was young. He had an amorous technique as perfect as his artistic technique. Lady Hurtmore would have been more than human if she had been able to resist him. She was not more than human.'

'None of us are, eh?' The Lord of the Manor dug his finger into Mr Bigger's ribs and laughed.

Politely, Mr Bigger joined in his mirth; when it had subsided, he went on. 'In the end they decided to run away together across the border. They would live at Vienna—live on the Hurtmore family jewels, which the lady would be careful to pack in her suit-case. They were worth upwards of twenty thousand, the Hurtmore jewels; and in Vienna, under Maria-Theresa, one could live handsomely on the interest of twenty thousand.

'The arrangements were easily made. Giangolini had a friend who did everything for them—got them passports under an assumed name, hired horses to be in waiting on the mainland, placed his gondola at their disposal. They decided to flee on the day of the last sitting. The day came. Lord Hurtmore, according to his usual custom, brought his wife to Giangolini's studio in a gondola, left her there, perched on the high-backed model's throne, and went off again to listen to Galuppi's concert at the Misericordia. It was the time of full carnival. Even in broad daylight people went about in masks. Lady Hurtmore wore one of black silk—you see her holding it, there, in the portrait. Her husband, though he was no reveller and disapproved of carnival junketings, preferred to conform to the grotesque fashion of his neighbours rather than attract attention to himself by not conforming.

'The long black cloak, the huge three-cornered black hat, the
long-nosed mask of white paper were the ordinary attire of every
Venetian gentleman in these carnival weeks. Lord Hurtmore did
not care to be conspicuous; he wore the same. There must have
been something richly absurd and incongruous in the spectacle of
this grave and solemn-faced English milord dressed in the clown's
uniform of a gay Venetian masker. "Pantaloon in the clothes of
Pulcinella," was how the lovers described him to one another; the
old dotard of the eternal comedy dressed up as the clown. Well, this
morning, as I have said, Lord Hurtmore came as usual in his hired
gondola, bringing his lady with him. And she in her turn was
bringing, under the folds of her capacious cloak, a little leather box
wherein, snug on their silken bed, reposed the Hurtmore jewels.
Seated in the dark little cabin of the gondola they watched the
churches, the richly fretted palazzi, the high mean houses gliding
past them. From under his Punch's mask Lord Hurtmore's voice
spoke gravely, slowly, imperturbably.

'"The learned Father Martini," he said, "has promised to do me
the honour of coming to dine with us tomorrow. I doubt if any man
knows more of musical history than he. I will ask you to be at pains
to do him special honour."

'"You may be sure I will, my lord." She could hardly contain the
laughing excitement that bubbled up within her. Tomorrow at
dinner-time she would be far away—over the frontier, beyond
Gorizia, galloping along the Vienna road. Poor old Pantaloon! But
no, she wasn't in the least sorry for him. After all, he had his music,
he had his odds and ends of broken marble. Under her cloak she
clutched the jewel-case more tightly. How intoxicatingly amusing
her secret was!'

Mr Bigger clasped his hands and pressed them dramatically over his
heart. He was enjoying himself. He turned his long, foxy nose
towards the Lord of the Manor, and smiled benevolently. The Lord
of the Manor for his part was all attention.

'Well?' he inquired.

Mr Bigger unclasped his hands, and let them fall on to his knees.

'Well,' he said, 'the gondola draws up at Giangolini's door, Lord
Hurtmore helps his wife out, leads her up to the painter's great
room on the first floor, commits her into his charge with his usual

polite formula, and then goes off to hear Galuppi's morning concert
at the Misericordia. The lovers have a good two hours to make their
final preparations.

'Old Pantaloon safely out of sight, up pops the painter's useful
friend, masked and cloaked like everyone else in the streets and on
the canals of this carnival Venice. There follow embracements and
hand-shakings and laughter all round; everything has been so
marvellously successful, not a suspicion roused. From under Lady
Hurtmore's cloak comes the jewel-case. She opens it, and there are
loud Italian exclamations of astonishment and admiration. The
brilliants, the pearls, the great Hurtmore emeralds, the ruby clasps,
the diamond earrings—all these bright, glittering things are lovingly
examined, knowingly handled. Fifty thousand sequins at the least
is the estimate of the useful friend. The two lovers throw themselves
ecstatically into one another's arms.

'The useful friend interrupts them; there are still a few last things
to be done. They must go and sign for their passports at the
Ministry of Police. Oh, a mere formality; but still it has to be done.
He will go out at the same time and sell one of the lady's diamonds
to provide the necessary funds for the journey.'

Mr Bigger paused to light a cigarette. He blew a cloud of smoke,
and went on.

'So they set out, all in their masks and capes, the useful friend in
one direction, the painter and his mistress in another. Ah, love in
Venice!' Mr Bigger turned up his eyes in ecstasy. 'Have you ever been
in Venice and in love, sir?' he enquired of the Lord of the Manor.

'Never further than Dieppe,' said the Lord of the Manor, shaking
his head.

'Ah, then you've missed one of life's great experiences. You can
never fully and completely understand what must have been the
sensations of little Lady Hurtmore and the artist as they glided
down the long canals, gazing at one another through the eye-holes
of their masks. Sometimes, perhaps, they kissed—though it would
have been difficult to do that without unmasking, and there was
always the danger that someone might have recognized their naked
faces through the windows of their little cabin. No, on the whole,'
Mr Bigger concluded, reflectively, 'I expect they confined themselves to looking at one another. But in Venice, drowsing along the
canals, one can almost be satisfied with looking—just looking.'

He caressed the air with his hand and let his voice droop away into silence. He took two or three puffs at his cigarette without saying anything. When he went on, his voice was very quiet and even.

'About half an hour after they had gone, a gondola drew up at Giangolini's door and a man in a paper mask, wrapped in a black cloak and wearing on his head the inevitable three-cornered hat, got out and went upstairs to the painter's room. It was empty. The portrait smiled sweetly and a little fatuously from the easel. But no painter stood before it and the model's throne was untenanted. The long-nosed mask looked about the room with an expressionless curiosity. The wandering glance came to rest at last on the jewel-case that stood where the lovers had carelessly left it, open on the table. Deep-set and darkly shadowed behind the grotesque mask, the eyes dwelt long and fixedly on this object. Long-nosed Pulcinella seemed to be wrapt in meditation.

'A few minutes later there was the sound of footsteps on the stairs, of two voices laughing togther. The masker turned away to look out of the window. Behind him the door opened noisily; drunk with excitement, with gay laughable irresponsibility, the lovers burst in.

'"Aha, *caro amico!* Back already. What luck with the diamond?"

'The cloaked figure at the window did not stir; Giangolini rattled gaily on. There had been no trouble whatever about the signatures, no questions asked; he had the passports in his pocket. They could start at once.

'Lady Hurtmore suddenly began to laugh uncontrollably; she couldn't stop.

'"What's the matter?" asked Giangolini, laughing too.

'"I was thinking," she gasped between the paroxysms of her mirth, "I was thinking of old Pantalone sitting at the Misericordia, solemn as an owl, listening"—she almost choked, and the words came out shrill and forced as though she were speaking through tears—"listening to old Galuppi's boring old cantatas."

'The man at the window turned round. "Unfortunately, madam," he said, "the learned maestro was indisposed this morning. There was no concert." He took off his mask. "And so I took the liberty of returning earlier than usual." The long, grey, unsmiling face of Lord Hurtmore confronted them.

'The lovers stared at him for a moment speechlessly. Lady Hurtmore put her hand to her heart; it had given a fearful jump, and she felt a horrible sensation in the pit of her stomach. Poor Giangolini had gone as white as his paper mask. Even in these days of *cicisbei*, of official gentlemen friends, there were cases on record of outraged and jealous husbands resorting to homicide. He was unarmed, but goodness only knew what weapons of destruction were concealed under that enigmatic black cloak. But Lord Hurtmore did nothing brutal or undignified. Gravely and calmly, as he did everything, he walked over to the table, picked up the jewel-case, closed it with the greatest care, and saying: "My box, I think," put it in his pocket and walked out of the room. The lovers were left looking questioningly at one another.'

There was a silence.

'What happened then?' asked the Lord of the Manor.

'The anti-climax,' Mr Bigger replied, shaking his head mournfully. 'Giangolini had bargained to elope with fifty thousand sequins. Lady Hurtmore didn't, on reflection, much relish the idea of love in a cottage. Woman's place, she decided at last, is in the home—with the family jewels. But would Lord Hurtmore see the matter in precisely the same light? That was the question, the alarming, disquieting question. She decided to go and see for herself.

'She got back just in time for dinner. "His Illustrissimous Excellency is waiting in the dining-room," said the major-domo. The tall doors were flung open before her; she swam in majestically, chin held high—but with what a terror in her soul! Her husband was standing by the fireplace. He advanced to meet her.

'"I was expecting you, madam," he said, and led her to her place.

'That was the only reference he ever made to the incident. In the afternoon he sent a servant to fetch the portrait from the painter's studio. It formed part of their baggage when, a month later, they set out for England. The story has been passed down with the picture from one generation to the next. I had it from an old friend of the family when I bought the portrait last year.'

Mr Bigger threw his cigarette end into the grate. He flattered himself that he had told that tale very well.

'Very interesting,' said the Lord of the Manor, 'very interesting indeed. Quite historical, isn't it? One could hardly do better with Nell Gwynn or Anne Boleyn, could one?'

Mr Bigger smiled vaguely, distantly. He was thinking of Venice—the Russian countess staying in his pension, the tufted tree in the courtyard outside his bedroom, that strong, hot scent she used (it made you catch your breath when you first smelt it), and there was the bathing on the Lido, and the gondola, and the dome of the Salute against the hazy sky, looking just as it looked when Guardi painted it. How enormously long ago and far away it all seemed now! He was hardly more than a boy then; it had been his first great adventure. He woke up with a start from his reverie.

The Lord of the Manor was speaking. 'How much now would you want for that picture?' he asked. His tone was detached, off-hand; he was a rare one for bargaining.

'Well,' said Mr Bigger, quitting with reluctance the Russian countess, the paradisaical Venice of five-and-twenty years ago, 'I've asked as much as a thousand for less important works than this. But I don't mind letting this go to you for seven-fifty.'

The Lord of the Manor whistled. 'Seven-fifty,' he repeated. 'It's too much.'

'But, my dear sir,' Mr Bigger protested, 'think what you'd have to pay for a Rembrandt of this size and quality—twenty thousand at least. Seven hundred and fifty isn't at all too much. On the contrary, it's very little considering the importance of the picture you're getting. You have a good enough judgement to see that this is a very fine work of art.'

'Oh, I'm not denying that,' said the Lord of the Manor. 'All I say is that seven-fifty's a lot of money. Whe-ew! I'm glad my daughter does sketching. Think if I'd had to furnish the bedrooms with pictures at seven-fifty a time!' He laughed.

Mr Bigger smiled. 'You must also remember,' he said, 'that you're making a very good investment. Late Venetians are going up. If I had any capital to spare——' The door opened and Miss Pratt's blonde and frizzy head popped in.

'Mr Crowley wants to know if he can see you, Mr Bigger.'

Mr Bigger frowned. 'Tell him to wait,' he said, irritably. He coughed and turned back to the Lord of the Manor. 'If I had any capital to spare, I'd put it all into late Venetians. Every penny.'

He wondered, as he said the words, how often he had told people that he'd put all his capital, if he had any, into primitives, cubism, nigger sculpture, Japanese prints . . .

In the end the Lord of the Manor wrote him a cheque for six hundred and eighty.

'You might let me have a typewritten copy of the story,' he said, as he put on his hat. 'It would be a good tale to tell one's guests at dinner, don't you think. I'd like to have the details quite correct.'

'Oh, of course, of course,' said Mr Bigger, 'the details are most important.'

He ushered the little round man to the door. 'Good morning. Good morning.' He was gone.

A tall, pale youth with side whiskers appeared in the doorway. His eyes were dark and melancholy; his expression, his general appearance, were romantic and at the same time a little pitiable. It was young Crowley, the painter.

'Sorry to have kept you waiting,' said Mr Bigger. 'What did you want to see me for?'

Mr Crowley looked embarrassed, he hesitated. How he hated having to do this sort of thing! 'The fact is,' he said at last, 'I'm horribly short of money. I wondered if perhaps you wouldn't mind—if it would be convenient to you—to pay me for that thing I did for you the other day. I'm awfully sorry to bother you like this.'

'Not at all, my dear fellow.' Mr Bigger felt sorry for this wretched creature who didn't know how to look after himself. Poor young Crowley was as helpless as a baby, 'How much did we settle it was to be?'

'Twenty pounds, I think it was,' said Mr Crowley, timidly.

Mr Bigger took out his pocket-book. 'We'll make it twenty-five,' he said.

'Oh, no, really, I couldn't. Thanks very much.' Mr Crowley blushed like a girl. 'I suppose you wouldn't like to have a show of some of my landscapes, would you?' he asked, emboldened by Mr Bigger's air of benevolence.

'No, no. Nothing of your own.' Mr Bigger shook his head inexorably.

'There's no money in modern stuff. But I'll take any number of those sham Old Masters of yours.' He drummed with his fingers on Lady Hurtmore's sleekly painted shoulder. 'Try another Venetian,' he added. 'This one was a great success.'

Private Water

A. J. Alan

THERE's a man in the Department where I work who's a great friend of mine—in spite of the fact that we share a room—and this story's all about him. He says he doesn't mind, but in order not to identify him too closely I'm just going to call him Henry.

It all began one morning a few months ago when he staggered into the office with a huge great iron thing like the wheel of a traction engine. I said, 'What in the world's that?'

He said, 'Oh, didn't you know? I've had a country cottage given me and this is the base of a petrol engine I've bought to pump the water out of the well with because it's too much fag to do it by hand.'

He went on to say that he wasn't going to use the iron base as he thought a concrete bed would be better.

This was the first I'd heard of this cottage because I'd been away on leave, but it was apparently somewhere in Norfolk and it had been given him by his mother.

He *did* tell me how *she'd* come by it, but I've forgotten. The point is that she didn't want it herself so she'd passed it on to Henry.

He was rather vague as to its exact position as he'd only been down once, by road, but it seemed quite a decent sort of place. It was furnished after a fashion, so he said, but it would want a whole lot doing to it, so they were going down each weekend and getting it into shape by degrees.

As time went on I naturally heard a good deal about how things were going.

You do when you are in the same office as a man, and I couldn't help noticing that everything that could go wrong was doing, and when I say everything, I mean everything. It was almost uncanny. The most complete chapter of accidents happened in connection with the well, so I'll just quote it as an example.

This well was bang in the middle of the lawn and it looked quite decorative, but Mrs Henry struck at the idea of installing a pump and a blooming great petrol engine alongside it. So what they decided to do was to sink the pump in the ground close to the well and stick the engine right away to the side, somewhere.

The engine was to transmit its power to the pump along a series of wheels and belts. These were to be down out of sight in a trench.

Well, first of all the concrete bed for the engine kept on cracking. The local builder must have got his quantities wrong. Anyway, he had to remake it three times before it would stand up to its job.

Then, one of the driving wheels in the trench was mounted slightly out of true and every now and then its belt came off. This, of course, whizzed along and fouled all the other belts, and they said 'let's *all* go down the trench,' and the poor old pump got the lot.

Then again, about the engine. It occurred to the Henrys that it would be bad for it to stand out in all weathers without a thing on, as it were, so they got hold of some match-boarding and felt, and built a sort of chicken-house round it, and they tell me it looked very fine, but not for long. That completely disappeared. Someone must have come along during the week and taken it away.

Even *that* wasn't the end of their hydraulic troubles. When they'd finally got the whole arrangement working and actual water was being produced, they thought they'd better have some of it analysed, and the answer was three per cent of organic matter. Luckily it turned out to be only a dead rabbit, but coming on the top of everything else it did really look more than mere chance.

I said to Henry: 'Norfolk doesn't seem to want you. Whom have you been annoying?' He said, 'We can't have been annoying anyone because there isn't another house in sight,' but he agreed that it was all very strange.

However, by the middle of April they seemed to have overcome the last of their troubles and they went down and achieved a completely enjoyable weekend; but it was so quiet in the evenings that they thought a wireless set might liven things up a bit. Would

I go down and help him install it? I said I would and we all drove down on the following Saturday. We both had to go to the office in the morning (I forget why), and we didn't arrive until late in the afternoon.

A perfectly gorgeous spot, but rather difficult to describe—its position, I mean. You approached it down a long lane all overgrown with grass which appeared to lead straight into a small river, but just before we took the final plunge there was a gate on the right-hand side and Henry said 'Here we are.'

His domain consisted of two cottages knocked into one, with a lawn in front, and past the bottom of this lawn flowed the river. At the back of the cottages there was a sort of barn place which they used as a garage. I'm telling you all this because the general lay-out is rather important.

First of all we had tea, and then I thought we'd better get the aerial up in case it turned wet. So we set to work. We didn't have to bother about a mast because there was a convenient tree down by the river, but even so it took longer than we expected—jobs like that always do—and it was pretty nearly dark before we'd finished.

Just as I was beginning to climb down the tree for the last time I noticed a light shining not far off, not more than a few hundred yards anyway. I thought it was strange because Henry had said there was nothing within miles of them, so I called out 'What's that light over there?' Henry couldn't see it from the ground and said, 'What light?' but just then there were loud cries of 'Dinner' from the house and the subject dropped.

Afterwards we connected up the set and got quite good signals, even without a proper earth; all we had was a few feet of wire lying on the grass, but Mrs Henry didn't like that in case it got left there permanently.

So Henry said 'All right. There's some wire netting in the loft over the garage. We could bury that. Let's go and get it.' I murmured 'Must we?' but they didn't hear, and along we went with an electric torch and climbed the ladder into this infernal loft.

We located the netting all right, but to get at it we had to move a lot of old planks and things, and underneath we came across a great long thing done up in canvas. We undid it and it turned out to be a canoe, a Candian canoe, complete with two paddles.

This was a distinct find, although there was no saying what condition it might be in, but we said 'Good oh' and lowered it through the trapdoor on chance.

By the time we'd buried the wire netting it was ten o'clock and we all went to bed. Now I'm not used to going to bed at ten, and the result was that next morning I was wide awake at six. I got up and looked at the weather. Not a cloud in the sky or a breath of wind. I decided that it would be a sin to stay frowsting in bed a moment longer, and not only that. My room was next to the bathroom, and I was terrified that Henry might come along and sing in it—so I strolled down and had a look at the river and that immediately reminded me of the canoe.

I went and fetched it from outside the garage and put it in the water, and to my great surprise it didn't leak. So I got in and paddled away down stream. Not that there *was* much stream—you could hardly tell which way it was flowing. It meandered about (like my stories), and after I'd gone a few hundred yards and was meaning to turn back, I came to a place where there was a chain across. There was also a notice board which said 'PRIVATE WATER'. That settled it. It was a perfect morning for trespassing so I scraped under the chain and went on. No one seemed to mind except numerous water-fowl which got up and flew away, uttering piercing cries. I expect they didn't like the colour of my pyjamas. Evidently provincial birds.

A minute or two later the river took a sharp turn to the left and led into quite a large sheet of water. By large I mean about half a mile long and a couple of hundred yards wide, and it wasn't till then that it struck me that this must be one of the smaller 'Broads'.

Across the middle of this 'Broad' there was a winding row of posts apparently to mark the course of the river, but it occurred to me that it ought to have been able to find its way without that.

Anyhow, I followed the posts and got through a narrow opening on the far side into a still larger river. By the way, before I actually went through the opening I noticed a peculiar sort of hut standing near the edge of the lake. It had got a coke stove outside it, and, as far as one could see, the flue of the stove went deliberately in at one end of the hut and came out at the other. Leaning up against the wall of this hut were several sacks which I put down as containing coke for the stove. They were a bit light in colour, but perhaps they were young ones. And then I got through into the main river. A few yards down stream, immediately to my right, there was a large wherry moored against the bank. A wherry, by the way, is a sort of sailing barge, got up pretty.

I hadn't spotted her before because the river bank was too high and they'd taken the mast out of her. She was evidently there for keeps, from the look of her moorings, but lying astern of her was an extremely serviceable motor-boat. I should have liked to have gone on board her and had a look round, but hanging up in the bows there was a large flat fish, obviously maturing for bait, which was quite unapproachable, so I paddled frantically out of range and back to breakfast.

Henry met me when I landed and said, 'Where've *you* been?' I said, 'I've been to trace what that light was I saw last night.' He said, 'Oh, really, what was it?' (not a bit interested) and I said, 'If you *must* know it was a piece of fish hanging up to ripen on board a motor-boat out in the river there.' He still didn't seem impressed. He simply said, 'I'm glad you've got back because our infernal pump's gone wrong again.' Putting it right took us till goodness knows when, but somewhere about six a small boy turned up from the outer world with a message about some eggs. He also mentioned that there'd been a mail-van robbery in the neighbourhood the afternoon before. I immediately thought of my row of pale-coloured sacks.

I said, 'Splendid. I can tell you where the swag is,' and then I absolutely made them listen to my tale of adventure in the morning, and I put it to them: I said, 'Why don't we go along in the canoe tonight and fetch one of these sacks, and make sure?' Well, Henry thought it would be quite a good scheme, so after dinner off we went, just he and I.

It was pitch dark, but you can always see on the water, and we got to the hut and found that the sacks were still there. We chose a nice fat one and solemnly carted it all the way back to the cottage. But when we opened it in the middle of the sitting-room floor, all we found inside was a whole lot of dried leaves. Rather a sell, on the face of it, but Henry said, 'Yes, but what *is* this stuff?' And we tried various things and finally burnt a bit. That left no room for doubt at all. It was tobacco. Whereupon I had one of my brilliant ideas. I said, 'If I'm right we are on to a far bigger show than a mail-

van robbery. That river over there is the Ant. The Ant runs into
the Bure. The Bure and the Yare meet and run into the sea at
Yarmouth.

'Now, let's assume, just for the sake of argument, that this feller
in the wherry goes in for smuggling. He starts off by making a
reputation for himself as a fisherman. He can get to Yarmouth in an
hour in his motor-boat, and he goes in and out at all sorts of odd
times until no one ever takes any notice of him. Very well.

'As soon as he gets to that stage he goes out every now and then,
ostensibly after bloater, and meets another motor-boat somewhere
out to sea. This other motor-boat may have come from Belgium, or
anywhere you like, with a cargo of tobacco. He picks up this cargo
and brings it back here—miles inland. In due course he puts it
ashore at the foot of your lane, and it goes up to London by lorry.
That's why everything's gone wrong here. He naturally doesn't
want anyone living right at his back door.'

I admit that this seemed a hopelessly far-fetched theory, but how
else could you explain a quarter of a ton of tobacco in an out-of-the-
way place like that? Anyway, we couldn't explain it, and then we
began to get rather indignant. Not that we objected to smuggling
per se. Why, I remember once coming ashore at Chatham so stuffed
out with what my friends were going to smoke during a week's
leave that they had to carry me on a stretcher, but that was
different—it was War Time.

However, this was a clear case of unfair competition with home
industries (and we all had shares in the Imperial Tobacco Company), and we were just discussing what we ought to do about it
when there was a ring at the bell, and lo and behold it was a
policeman. Mind you this was hardly a coincidence. He'd been
round the Saturday before selling tickets for some country police
fête, and he'd called about that. At all events we said 'Come in,
you're just the man we want.' So we sat him down and gave him a
drink, and then we produced the sack and said, 'What do you think
that is?' He just looked at it and said, 'I *know* what it is—it's
tobacco. Where did you get it?'

So I started to tell him about the wherry, and all that; and he
said, 'Oh yes, that belongs to Mr de Vuyker, a Dutch gentleman—
we know all about him.' I said, 'Do you also know that he smuggles
tobacco?' and he burst out laughing. He said, 'Smuggles it! He

doesn't have to smuggle it, he *grows* it. He's got sixteen acres under cultivation on the other side of the river. Didn't you see his drying shed?' and of course I had, only I didn't know what it was.

Well, you can imagine how foolish we felt. Our bobby was evidently conversant with the technical side of the business and he went on to explain that the stuff we'd brought away was actually waste which couldn't be used, but it had to be disposed of in some particular way under the eagle eye of an excise officer otherwise duty would have to be paid on it.

Henry said, 'Does that mean we've got to take this rotten stuff back?' and Robert was afraid that it *did* mean exactly that. The worst of it was that we should have to do it that night because we were making a very early start next morning.

So Robert was given what they call 'the other half', and duly seen off, and then Henry and I got into the canoe and paddled all the way to de Vuyker's shed with this blessed sack. When we eventually got back to the cottage we found Mrs Henry pacing nervously backwards and forwards on the lawn. She said, 'I'm so glad you've come because there's something funny going on further up the lane—the weirdest noises are being made.' We could hear them ourselves. Strange odd crashes at regular intervals. So we went along to investigate and found that it was friend Robert still trying to get on to his bicycle.

Quite astounding. I thought policemen were like firemen and that it didn't matter *what* you gave them, but they can't be. He was awfully pleased to see us and said that if we'd only hold his bicycle still while he mounted, and then give him a push he'd be quite all right, but I said, 'No, my lad I think not.' I should hate to get a policeman into trouble, and there was no doubt that we were, in some measure, responsible for his unfortunate condition. That being so, we felt we ought to do the right thing by him, so while Henry was getting the car out, I brushed him down and found his helmet, and then we took him and his bicycle home.

Next morning we all came back to London, I having had a most amusing time—so much so, in fact, that I'd brought away a little memento of it. As you may possibly imagine I hadn't entirely swallowed the policeman's explanation of the sack of tobacco, and while the Henrys were seeing him off the night before I'd had another look at it.

The top layer certainly was rubbish, stalks and so on, but once you got down below that the whole of the rest of the sack was stuffed tight with neat bundles of unbroken leaves tied up with cotton.

Well, I'd taken out one of these bundles and kept it, and when I left the office that evening I went and called on my tobacconist. I planked my bundle down in front of him and said, 'What's that.'

He proceeded to do various things to it. He first of all cut the cotton and breathed on the edges. Then he fanned out the leaves and smelt them and said, 'That's very fine.' I asked him what it was worth. He said, 'Well, it all depends. Without the duty, it's worth about sixpence a pound, but *with* the duty it's about ten shillings.' (Isn't it iniquitous?)

I next asked him whether it could be grown in England, and he laughed. He said, 'Good gracious no, that's the very best Virginia pipe tobacco. Can you get any more?'

I said, 'Yes—rath*er*. The next dark weekend.'

A Gift from the Nabob

D. L. Murray

BEAU BRUMMELL rose from his chair in annoyance—the lady had fainted.

He was still turning her black pearl in his fingers beneath the scrutiny of his lorgnon, and his insolent lips were still stamped with the grimace that said more plainly than words, 'Your gem, ma'am, is spurious.'

That look had been enough to send Miss Vandeleur to the carpet of her drawing-room, where she lay prettily pathetic, with her eyes closed, her corkscrew curls tumbled, and her slender ankles showing beneath her flounced Regency skirt.

Mr Brummell moved his hand to the bell-pull, and then decided to summon no servant. Himself he flung open the long windows that gave upon Brighton front, and let in the sea air. With his own elegant hand he sprinkled her with water from a vase and, when her eyelids fluttered open again, assisted her to the sofa.

'It was such a shock to me,' she whispered. 'That pearl is all my fortune.'

'But I said nothing, ma'am!'

'Your look was enough: it told all. Yet the Nabob of Ruttlipore gave that pearl to my late father, the Collector for the District. He swore it was his greatest treasure, the Eye of the Goddess Kali in the Temple!'

'Even a Nabob, ma'am, may not be immune from deceitfulness. But I am only an *amateur* of precious stones. Let me take it to some competent jeweller for his opinion.'

'By no means!' She almost snatched the jewel from his palm and clapped it into her reticule. 'Not a soul in Brighton, Mr Brummell, must know that my black pearl is spurious. You do not matter, since you are a gentleman and would not betray me. But I cannot pay for this house I have taken for the season, I cannot even meet my tradesmen's bills, unless I can sell the Nabob's pearl. . . . Would it be very wicked in me, Mr Brummell, to ask you how this may still be done?' She shot him a glance from her large, brown eyes that might have pierced even his stiff shirt-frill.

'Good God, ma'am, I don't know what it is you demand of me?'

'Only an introduction. Some rich gentleman . . . short-sighted, it will be best . . . and very foolish.'

'Rich . . . short-sighted . . . and very foolish!' drawled the Beau. 'I see no one to fill the role but my friend, Wales. . . . And he certainly would never miss the money.'

'And where, pray, does this Mr Wales reside?'

'The Prince of Wales,' retorted Brummell with acerbity. 'Don't you know your social ABC, Miss Vandeleur?'

'Alas! I am an orphan, only three weeks home from India, without a friend! That is why I ventured to send for the celebrated Mr Brummell, though a stranger.'

'And let me tell you, ma'am, that only charms like yours could excuse such an unheard of liberty.' He leered in a fashion that was meant to be complimentary, but gave him rather too much the air of a sandy Mephistopheles.

'But would his Royal Highness, the Prince Regent, buy my black pearl?'

'He has very small discrimination in jewellery.'

'But would he permit me to approach him?'

'He has very great discrimination in females.'

Miss Vandeleur smiled. 'But I should require a presentation.'

'Gad, ma'am, if you will walk in the Promenade Grove any Tuesday night without a mask, you will need no formal presentation to Prinney. He is sure to be there with his friends.'

'Of whom you are one?'

'I do not boast of it.' He took snuff with a disdainful nostril.

'Shall we be partners, Mr Brummell? They tell me you are crippled with gaming debts. . . . You shall have half what I get.'

The Beau stood up stiff as a poker. 'That which may be reckoned a peccadillo, ma'am, in a pretty woman, thrown upon her wits, would be a damning lapse of taste in a gentleman. I am surprised at you.'

'Then you reduce me to beggary . . . and despair!' The brown eyes brimmed over.

Brummell relented. 'I never could resist the artillery of such *beaux yeux* as yours,' he said. 'I will do this much for you, and for the pleasure of making a fool of Prinney. If you will be in the Grove on Tuesday, wearing the pearl in your scarf, I will direct his Royal Highness's attention to you, Miss Vandeleur.'

'Why the devil do you keep peeping into that arbour, Brummell?' The Prince Regent, who had been propelling his swollen bulk along the Promenade Grove, with the aid of a cane and his friend's arm, stopped in the middle of the path between the rows of blue and red fairy-lamps. He was incognito, and attended only, at a score of paces' distance, by a couple of prize-fighters.

'I fancied, sir, I recognized a lady of my acquaintance in there.'

The Prince stooped with an effort and peered between the branches. 'A devilish pretty woman, and alone!' he wheezed. 'What is that odd piece of jewellery in her scarf?'

'It is said to be a black pearl, sir, given to her father, who was in the East India Company's service, by a Nabob.'

'Two rare jewels, hey? Come, you shall present me to her, simply as a gentleman of your acquaintance.'

'She cannot fail to recognize you, sir.'

'What if she should? Curse you, do you think I am too old for a frolic? Take me to her at once; it is a command.'

Discretion suggested to Mr Brummell the wisdom of slipping out of the arbour very soon after the introductions had been made. For about a quarter of an hour he sauntered up and down the alley outside, until at last he saw the Prince issue from the screen of leaves and beckon to him.

'This is a sad story, Brummell, curse me if it isn't,' said the Regent with sympathetic tears filling the wrinkles of his encrimsoned cheeks. 'Poor little woman! Alone in the world, without a penny to call her own . . . except this magnificent jewel.'

He unclenched his podgy fist and rolled the Nabob's pearl about on it.

'How can we bear, Brummell, to neglect in this scandalous fashion the families of those who are building up our empire in the East? It is a d——d shame. . . . She tells me she would be willing to part with this for five hundred guineas, if I'd pay her within the hour to meet some creditor at daybreak.' He held the pearl up to the nearest lamp. 'It is not dear for such a rarity.'

Brummell gave a dry laugh. 'It is a bargain, sir! If the pearl is genuine.'

'Not genuine?' The Prince's eyes goggled behind their fat. 'But why shouldn't it be genuine? Her tears are not those of a deceiver, and damme, I think I have some knowledge and use of precious stones. I've a mind to buy it from her, out of kindness.'

'Better take another opinion, sir. Cuffey the jeweller——'

'Have you lost your wits?' cried the Prince peevishly. 'Once let Cuffey get wind that there is a jewel like this in Brighton and he'll find a way to outbid me for it. I shall have to pay thousands then to get it. No, sir, I'll back my own fancy for once, begad! She shall have her guineas this very night, as she asks!'

Late the next morning the Prince in a gilt-tasselled nightcap was lying abed in his Chinese Pavilion, now toying with the black pearl, now watching the fashionable parade upon the Steyne outside, a spectacle he was able to enjoy without stirring from his pillow by an ingenious arrangement of looking-glasses.

Suddenly he uttered an incredulous exclamation. His mirror had shown him the astounding sight of Beau Brummell hurrying towards the palace hatless and with the ends of his cravat flying loose. 'Gad!' he exclaimed, 'it must mean a War or a Revolution . . . or that someone else has invented a new style of neckcloth!'

His curiosity was so stirred that he conceded Mr Brummell's prayer for an audience without a moment's waiting. He had never seen the stoical Beau so moved before as he poured out his dreadful news.

'I blame myself, sir, for introducing the baggage to your notice. She proves to be an adventuress, a common swindler who has fled by the Newhaven boat in the early hours of this morning.' (Mr Brummell, in fact, had ordered the coach himself, tucked Miss Vandeleur snugly into it, and given her a paternal tap on the cheek before letting her go with all her guineas intact.)

'What is that to me?' demanded the Prince, his fiery face creasing into irritable puckers. 'Unless—Good God, Brummell, you don't suggest that the Nabob's black pearl——'

'May I examine it, sir? You gave me no opportunity last night.' Brummell drew out his lorgnon, picked up the pearl and after a few moments' examination gave a significant grimace.

The Regent fell back with a choking sound on his pillows. 'Brandy!' he gasped, and the Beau hastened to fill a glass from a decanter by the bedside. For a moment he had feared a fit.

'I said nothing, sir!' he remonstrated.

'Your look was enough. By gad, it told all! And besides, everyone knows you're a connoisseur of stones, damn you!' The Prince tugged at the bell-pull till it came away in his hand. 'Make after that woman! Stop her embarking!'

'Too late, I fear, sir. And besides, your Royal Highness knows there is something worse than being duped out of five hundred guineas.'

'What is that, Brummell?'

'Ridicule, sir! the King, or the King's representative, can do no wrong, even in appraising a jewel.'

'You're right, Brummell. Not a soul must know, especially not Cuffey! They'd never stop laughing at me.'

'The pearl, sir, might make a pretty ornament, even though undoubtedly spurious.'

'Keep it yourself then, and wear it in your shirt-frill if you're so damned taken with it. . . . Only take it and yourself out of my sight now!'

Mr Brummell obeyed. And later that day, after the Regent had made one of his erratic and unexpected flights from Brighton back to the capital, the Beau was to be seen parading the Steyne in the full enjoyment of the breeze from the sea.

'One can work wonders with a look,' he told himself as his fingers strayed again and again to his shirt-front. There, duskily gleaming, reposed the gift of the Nabob of Ruttlipore to Miss Vandeleur's father—a black pearl, once the Eye of the Goddess Kali, and worth, so a visit to Cuffey the jeweller that afternoon had confirmed Mr Brummell in thinking, not less than five thousand guineas.

The Episcopal Seal

J. Maclaren-Ross

BISHOP THURLOW looked both bloated and seedy. No disrespect to the Church: he wasn't really a Bishop, although this was his Christian name and there had been a Bishop somewhere way back in his family, so that his background was episcopal in its general tone and influenced him, no doubt, in choosing the profession he ultimately adopted.

I believe, too, that at one time he had been intended for Holy Orders and had studied for some months at a Theological College; but the Bishop seldom spoke of his past: he was a man who lived predominantly in the present.

I first ran across him in the Sink, in Soho. This café, now closed down by the police, had, at the time I'm writing about, something of the status of a club, but without any tiresome regulations. There was a cellar down below where gambling went on for those who could afford it and a room at ground level with coffee and a few chess-sets provided for those who could not.

The Bishop was sitting in the upstairs room playing chess when I came in. He sat on a sofa directly underneath the mural, painted by a pacifist, of Christ crucified wearing a gas-mask, which was afterwards daubed over with whitewash by the new proprietor whose way of life caused the police to close the place down.

A cup of tea stood on the table beside him. Tea cost twopence in the Sink; coffee cost sixpence. I also ordered tea, waving aside the stunted grey Greek waiter who rushed threateningly towards me with a cry of 'coffee'.

The usual clientele was present: the bearded man who cast

horoscopes, the one-armed ex-Serviceman who recited Shakespeare to theatre queues, a group of Indians talking about post-dated cheques.

Among these was Krishna. He rolled his eyes round in my direction and winked slowly, smiling and smoothing back his hair at the same time with both hands.

I sat down at a table next to the Bishop. His opponent, a small man who looked like a betting-clerk, was plainly in difficulties. All his pieces were pinned, and even as I looked across, the Bishop discovered check.

'Mate next move,' he murmured; there was no way out; he sat back benevolently, with his hands clasped over his stomach, while the small man peered in desperation down at the board.

'That's foxed it,' he seemed to say. The Bishop without replying held out a plump, inexorable palm. Half a crown changed hands: the Bishop caused this to vanish, with something of a conjurer's celerity, into his waistcoat pocket.

'Have another?'

The little man paid no attention to this. Cramming on a bowler, he rushed incontinently out of the café. The Bishop, smiling gently, set up the pieces again and leant over towards me. 'Care for a game, young man?'

'Not just now, thanks.'

'We could play for a small stake, if you wish. Half a crown?'

'No, really. Not today.'

'Sixpence then. You wouldn't refuse? The humble tanner.'

'No.'

The Bishop sighed: 'I'm sorry I can't tempt you.' His stomach shook softly with the sigh; his hands trembled a little over the Staunton men; he said: 'I'll give you pawn and move.'

'Nothing doing.'

'A knight.'

'No. You're too strong a player for me.'

'Nonsense. Nonsense, my dear boy. I talk a good middle game.'

He smiled at me with sparse, discoloured teeth; a rough grey stubble glinted along his distended cheeks over his sagging jowls. He gave me up as a bad job. Something at the next table caught his attention: the Indians were advising the youngest member of their group to write dunning his uncle in Ceylon for twenty quid.

'But how shall I go about it?' the young Indian was saying. 'What shall I say?'

'A cable,' the Bishop cut in quickly. The Indians looked round. 'Costs more, but it's quicker. If I may offer the benefit of my experience.'

'Thank you,' the young Indian said.

'And put on it: *Beg assistance*.'

The Bishop raised an episcopal forefinger; 'That's all. Short and sweet. It never fails.' He rose to his feet, pushing past the chess-board and the cup of cooling tea: 'Mind you, when it comes off, I shall expect my cut. Ten per cent—for the consultation. This day week.'

He waddled out. All his clothes had been made for a taller man: the black stained jacket hung down well below his hips, the trousers had been turned up twice. I watched him pass through the door into the street, lifting his feet sideways with caution, as a duck walks.

Krishna came over, patting his yellow neck-cloth into place. 'Any news?' he said. He meant: 'Have you any money?' I said: 'No,' and then: 'Who was that?'

'Oh, Thurlow. The Bishop. He's a South Kensington man. Rarely up this way.'

'What's he do for a living?'

'Vicars,' Krishna said. 'He does vicars.'

'Vicars?'

'Yes. You know—funds.'

'But is there any money in that?'

'Two quid a time, I believe. I've never done it myself, but I know a woman who did six vicars in one day.'

'Twelve quid. Seems incredible.'

'Quite a feat,' Krishna said. 'Of course the Bishop put her on to them: he took his ten per cent.'

'We might try that some time.'

'No,' Krishna said.

About a fortnight later I met the Bishop again. I found him standing beside me in a pub, at lunch-time.

'How are things in Kensington?' I asked him.

'Terrible, young man; absolutely appalling. I have been obliged to—evacuate.'

'Not bomb damage, I hope?'

'Unfortunately, no. If it were bomb damage I should be able to claim—at some distant date. Have you the price of a bitter on you, young man?'

'I have, but that's about all.'

'Straitened circumstances?' the Bishop said. 'Financial necessity?'

'In a nutshell,' I said. 'Did you get your cut from that Indian boy?'

'Of course. My formula never fails. But alas, with the increased cost of living, money goes nowhere these days.'

'Nowhere,' I said.

'Look at the price of drink.'

'Indeed.'

The Bishop shook his head: baldness in the exact centre of it gave the effect of a tonsure. He gulped at the glass of bitter and shuddered all over. He was plainly recovering from a bout and in a bad way.

He said: 'But never despair, my boy, I might be able to assist you. . . . Let me see . . . have you any living relatives? An uncle? Beg assistance?'

'No.'

'Alone in the world, eh?'

'Yes.'

'Never mind, there are other ways. . . . I think that if you could afford a further bitter, I could put you on to something good.'

'It's not vicars?'

'No, no. You wouldn't do for vicars; you're not the type, dear boy. No, I was thinking of the Indigent City Fathers' Fund.'

'What's that?'

'Another bitter first. To lubricate the workings of the mind.'

'All right.'

The Bishop grabbed the glass and took another huge swallow, but this time he did not shudder. He said: 'It's called the City Fathers' Fund for the Indigent, actually. I think you'd qualify admirably. All you have to say is that at one time you were employed in the City.'

'But I never have been.'

'Come come,' the Bishop said sharply. 'A little *nous*, dear boy. You must be prepared to practise a small innocent deception. I'd imagined you to be a young man of resource.'

'Supposing they find out?'

'They won't. What's the time?'

'That clock says a quarter to two.'

'We can just do it,' the Bishop said. 'How much ready cash have you?'

'Five bob.'

'That's ample,' swallowing his bitter. 'Come with me.'

We walked out, up Percy Street, the Bishop's black jacket flapping round his hips as he trotted along beside me.

'Quick; this taxi!'

We climbed in. I could see my five bob going down the drain. I said: 'Why not a bus?'

'No time. Besides,' the Bishop's jowls jolted a little as we jerked past the Negroes in American suitings on the corner by Better Books, round Cambridge Circus and down towards the Strand, 'a taxi is excellent to relax in. Soothes the mind, allows you to prepare in comparative calm for the ordeal ahead.'

'What ordeal?'

'The ordeal of life, dear boy,' the Bishop said gently, glancing out through the window at a clock in Trafalgar Square. 'We'll have five minutes in hand.'

'I don't like this at all,' I said.

'Stop fussing, dear boy. Abandon yourself—to blessed peace.'

The Bishop closed his eyes and leaned back on the padded seat: he said no more. The taxi wound its way in and out of the labyrinthian purlieus of the City. Suddenly the Bishop's eyes flew open; he leaned forward and banged on the glass.

'Stop round this corner.'

We got out and I paid the fare. That left me half a crown. 'This way,' the Bishop said. A portal loomed up, with Doric columns on either side. 'In here.' The Bishop pushed me ahead of him into a hall full of statuary, up a flight of broad stone steps. On the first landing was a door bearing the name of the Fund; it stood half open on a room full of wooden benches facing an empty magisterial throne raised upon a dais. A few disreputable figures—one of them in actual rags—were huddled dejectedly together on the front bench. Behind these sat the small bowler-hatted man whom the Bishop had beaten at chess.

At sight of him the Bishop frowned. 'That scrounger Stubbs. What right has he——' But at that moment a clock chimed and a door at the back of the room opened. Everyone stood up: it was like being in Court when the magistrate comes in. And, indeed, the man who had just entered had an air almost as magisterial as the throne on to which he now climbed. He wore a gold watch-chain and a wing collar—he might have been the Lord Mayor of London himself. An official in some kind of gown accompanied him, carrying a sheaf of forms which were dished round to all of us.

While we were filling these in, the magisterial man stared up at the ceiling, stroking his chin judicially. He had the look of one about to have his shoes shined; the elevation of his throne and the semi-crouching posture of one of the tramps in the front row contributed to this impression.

The crouching tramp was first man in. A bell rang and his name was called out. He stumbled through an incredibly tall story of one-time employment in the City. The magisterial man cut this short half-way. One or two leading questions deflated the tramp: the official escorted him to the door empty-handed. Then for a time the magisterial man toyed with the other tramps: one in particular he put through a terrific grilling.

I panicked at this and made a move to bolt. But the Bishop clutched at my arm. 'Take no notice,' he hissed; 'it's a put-up job. They are all actors!'

'Actors?'

'Paid by the Fund to discourage impostors.'

Meanwhile tramp after tramp had been disposed of: the last one was dismissed in a voice like the crack of a whip. I sweated; it was Stubbs's turn. He stood up. He was sweating too.

'He'll get nothing,' the Bishop hissed malignantly into my ear.

He was right. The magisterial man made short work of Stubbs. He shuffled out after the tramps; the Bishop pinched my arm with pleasure. He leaned across to see what I'd written on my form. A look of horror came over his face; he pointed to the entry opposite 'Profession'. I'd put down 'Author'. The Bishop made frantic signs, but it was too late to change anything; the offical in the gown had already taken the form out of my hand and the Bishop was on his feet answering questions. He described himself as an auctioneer, which surprised me. A tale of hard luck and wartime unemployment followed. The magisterial man rubbed his chin on the sharp edge of the wing-collar.

'Surely I've seen your face before.'

'Alas, sir,' the Bishop said unctuously, 'force of circumstance caused me to apply to you once before. A long time ago.'

'How long?'

'1942. You will find the entry in your records, sir.'

'H'm. All right. Wait there.'

My name was called and I stood up; my knees knocked together. The magisterial man frowned at the form that had been handed up to him.

He said: 'You're an author?'

'Yes, sir.'

'Have you ever been employed in the City of London?'

'Not exactly, sir.'

'How d'you mean, not exactly?'

'Well, I've published a lot in magazines. Their offices are round about the City. Fleet Street and so on.'

'Give me some addresses, please.'

I did. One of them was bang in the City itself, there was no denying that. I had the magisterial man bottled. He hitched at his collar and drummed on the arms of his throne.

'All right. If you'll wait there a moment.'

The official in the gown went out and came back with a bag. It contained pound notes: we signed receipts for three quid apiece, clutching these in our hands we made for the door; the Bishop almost fell downstairs in his hurry.

'Quick!' he said. 'Across the way! While they're still open.'

In the pub he ordered Scotch and, what's more, paid for it himself. 'Well, dear boy, you did it. Congratulations! I'd never have thought up that author stunt. I *said* you were a young man of resource and, mark you, I am rarely wrong.'

'Another drink?'

'That wouldn't come amiss. By the way, before I forget. My cut.'

'Of course.' I hadn't had time to get change: I held out one of my quids.

'Very handsome of you, dear boy.' It vanished seemingly into thin air, or at any rate into his pocket.

'Oh, I say. I didn't mean the whole quid.'

'Now now, dear boy,' the Bishop said reproachfully. 'Never go back on a good deed once it's done. After all, we so seldom get the opportunity . . . look, I'll pay for the drinks.'

'Fair enough.'

'Better times!' the Bishop raised his glass. 'You wouldn't care to do a vicar with me this afternoon.'

'No, thanks.'

'You're sure?'

'Absolutely.'

'A game of chess then. The Sink.'

'Why not? This pub's shutting.'

At chess the Bishop won another five bob off me: he was in fine fettle. Stubbs was there. The Bishop gave him a baleful glare.

'I'm glad he got his deserts, the dirty skunk. Sneaking off down there while my back was turned, when it was I who put him on to it . . . the ingratitude . . . you can have no conception.' He craned his neck at the clock. 'But it's late, I must go.'

'A vicar?'

'No no, my wife. One has certain responsibilities . . . the weaker sex. . . .'

I had not envisaged him as a married man. I wondered what sort of woman the wife could be. And then one evening I met her; in a pub, naturally. She stood beside the Bishop at the bar: she was twice his size. A slattern. Sort of gypsy. Coarse black hair, lot of bangles, and a moustache. And half-seas-over to boot.

The Bishop had a clot of dried blood on his cheek; he looked shamefaced and subdued. 'Haven't seen you around lately,' I said to him.

'No; I've been farming.'

I was staggered. 'Farming?'

'Chalk Farm.' He giggled. 'The agricultural life.'

The wife broke in harshly. 'Who the hell's this?'

'A friend. Doris, may I introduce . . .'

'Go to hell. Gimme a cigarette.'

'I'm afraid, my love, you've smoked my last. Perhaps, dear boy, you could oblige . . .'

I produced my packet; and, moreover, having money at the time, bought a round of drinks. The wife's manner immediately softened: she gave me a glittering smile, full of gold. It was a Hampstead pub, and when it closed I went back with them to Chalk Farm.

They lived in a basement. Horrible place, smelling of the wife's stale scent. She changed at once into a kimono and slippers and started to have a row with her husband over some stuff of hers he'd pawned.

'But, my love, we've got to live. Look, I've got a new scheme.'

He opened a drawer and took out a large map of London, with various districts marked in ink, like a vacuum-cleaner salesman's territory-plan. The marked portions represented vicars: the Bishop was planning a mass attack all over London.

'This one at Highgate's particularly promising. He goes up to a fiver, I believe. We could all of us try him.'

The wife sniffed. 'It'd better come off.'

'My love, have you ever known me fail?'

I stayed the night. A mattress on the floor in the kitchen. Just as I was dozing off, another row broke out. A scream and a crash of crockery. After that there was a lull, except for the scampering of mice across the kitchen floor.

At seven next morning an alarm-clock went off and hostilities were resumed.

The wife's voice said: 'Wake up, you lazy hound. Where are the cigarettes?'

'My love, I haven't any.'

'Get some then and make it snappy. Do you want to go to prison?'

'Please, my love, have a heart. Give me another five minutes.'

'I've enough on you to hang you.'

'Don't say such things, I implore you.'

'Then get me some cigarettes.'

Of course, he came in to me. 'Why d'you put up with it?' I asked him.

'My dear boy, I couldn't do without Doris. Why, I'd be lost without her. Irrevocably lost.'

He went away with my cigarettes and I went back to sleep again. When I woke there was a council of war going on. The Bishop had his map out and was sketching out the day's operations. He was a different man: a general, a leader; even his wife listened meekly and nodded assent at the districts and vicars assigned to her. A thin mousy-looking woman had joined them and was also taking instructions.

'Not a drop to drink, mind you, until after the first two vicars. Then you may indulge in a glass of bitter, but no more. Now, have we enough between us for the first taxi?'

He attempted to enrol me in his canvassing group, but without success. He said: 'Very sad, dear boy; you'd have made a likely recruit. Never mind, however. It's your loss. . . .'

I did not see him again for some months. Then he turned up at the Sink, and I was shocked at his appearance. He had never been a man who shaved closely, but now a positive fringe of grey whisker sprouted raggedly round his chin, like the beard of a shrimp, and his eyes looked as though their red rims had been turned inside out. His overcoat came down to his heels and the sleeves covered up his hands. Even his voice had lost its former tone of unctuous authority; it sounded cracked and hoarse as he said: 'Dear boy, I'm on the run.'

'Duns?'

'Worse than that.'

'The police?'

He nodded. 'A hunted man.'

'But what have you done?'

'Get me a cup of coffee and I'll tell you.'

He did. Here is the story.

Doris, his wife, had been married before. The stepson, Gavin, was 21. Suddenly he came home on leave. He wore steel spectacles and was in the Pioneer Corps. A studious type: the Bishop enrolled him at once, and the boy proved an enthusiastic pupil. When asked if he could do vicars, he replied: 'Can a duck swim.' And indeed he took to the life like a duck to water. Vicars inaccessible even to the astute Bishop coughed up quids wholesale. He did the magisterial man as well. He sent cables to obscure relatives saying Beg Assistance, and received replies in solid cash.

Unfortunately, he was so absorbed in his new profession that he overstayed his leave. Twenty-one days went by and he was posted as a deserter. Pretty soon, while he was on his way to do a vicar in Watford, the police picked him up. He returned to face a court martial.

Doris didn't care for this. She blamed the Bishop for leading the boy astray. The Bishop had qualms too: he felt he had to get Gavin out of the mess. So he wrote a letter to the commanding officer saying that Gavin had been detained on parish duties for the church, and signed it *The Bishop of Thurlow*. Worse still, he got hold of a Bishop's ring from somewhere—he claimed it had belonged to his ancestor—and set the episcopal seal under his signature.

The CO saw through this letter and passed it on to the police. The police now wanted urgently to interview the Bishop of Thurlow. Forced to quit Chalk Farm, he was without beer, boots, or home. Doris had gone to ground with her mother, who hated the Bishop and wouldn't allow him inside the house.

The possibility of prison terrified the Bishop: he was going to pieces: it was the hold Doris had had over him all these years. 'It'll break me up, I know it will. Can't you do anything to help, dear boy?'

I couldn't; I was passing through one of my moneyless periods. I couldn't even lend him enough to get a bed in a doss-house.

'Never mind,' the Bishop said, pulling himself together with an effort. 'Never despair, dear boy. I will try to get into a Turkish bath—on credit.'

He rose; he gave a ragged smile. He raised one hand, the fingers crossed: it was a benediction. Then he waddled out web-footed, and the door of the Sink closed behind him gently.

The police caught up with him quite soon; he got nine months.

And when I met him in the street a fortnight ago I hardly recognized him. Prison hadn't broken him up, after all; the very reverse. He looked five years younger. His eyes weren't bloodshot, his face was smooth and urbane, his hands no longer trembled, and he seemed on the whole less fat.

· 'Where have you been all this time?' I asked him tactfully.

'Staying in the country.'

'What was it like?'

'The air was excellent, the food was palatable, but the service was abominable. I shall not go there again.'

V

MOSTLY MURDER

A comic writer of genius, *W. W. Jacobs* (1863–1943) began his working life, after passing the Civil Service examination, in the Savings Bank Department of the Post Office. Unlike Trollope, who laboured long and hard in the postal service (though in a largely peripatetic role), Jacobs felt that this was not his natural habitat. At the age of twenty he started selling humorous 'fillers' to the weeklies and in the early 1890s was writing for the national magazines, such as *Chambers' Journal*, *Harper's Magazine* (the British version), and Jerome K. Jerome's *Idler*. In 1897, now an established author—his first volume of short stories having come out a year earlier, and the firm of Pearson about to issue his novella *The Skipper's Wooing*—he sent two stories to George Newnes' revolutionary but ill-fated four-colour weekly *The Million* that were noticed by Greenhough Smith; thereafter most of Jacobs' output was published in the *Strand*. His early fees must have come as a distinct shock. He wrote four stories in 1898 (the first year he appeared) and was paid around £75 a story: £300 for the year. As the average wage was well below £150, and as Jacobs was still working for the Post Office, quite suddenly income tax became something of a problem (by 1917 he was being paid £350 per story). He finally left the Post Office in 1900, his output slowing down from 1920 onwards; by then he was a wealthy man. A staunch Conservative and arch-opponent of the Welfare State ('I'd hate a lot of clever people . . . doing me good. Damn their eyes!'), the one cross he had to bear was his vigorously feminist wife Agnes (twenty years his junior) who hurled bricks through windows and wrote anarchical letters to the press, which Jacobs was forever trying to suppress; H. G. Wells drew a not entirely flattering portrait of her as the eponymous heroine of *The Wife of Sir Isaac Harman* (1914). In many of his comic stories viragos with rolling-pins play their part. None, however, was as malevolent as Hannah in 'The Interruption', which exhibits Jacobs' darker side.

In the main, the thrillers of *Edgar Wallace* (1875–1932) contained few elements of pure deduction or ratiocination in the Holmesean tradition (indeed, Wallace had little time for Holmes or his creator, lampooning the former in many of his stories and publicly feuding with the latter over Doyle's attachment to Spiritualism); they were, instead, characterized by an unflagging pace, a good deal of low-life comedy, and a succession of dramatic shocks. Although he wrote few stories for the *Strand*, for the Newnes organization as a whole Wallace probably worked far harder than for any other publisher, and for a considerably longer period. Some of his earliest short stories, after he had been sacked from the *Daily Mail* in 1907, appeared in the *Strand*'s all-fiction stable-mate the *Grand Magazine*. Over a period of twenty-two years, from 1907 through to 1929, he wrote five serials for the *Grand* and sixty-seven short stories— including quantities about 'Sanders of the River' as well as the eight tales later collected in *The Mind of Mr J. G. Reeder* (1925), the nearest to pure deductive detective fiction he composed. In 1910 Wallace despairingly sold Newnes all rights to his failure *The Four Just Men*, which the firm then turned into a small goldmine, keeping it continuously in print for nearly thirty years, with Wallace almost certainly receiving not a penny from the proceeds. He bore no grudge; there was always another novel, another series of shorts. To the *Strand* itself, from 1914 to 1931, he sold just twenty-four stories, but these included (a neat revenge, perhaps?) half a dozen 'Four Just Men' tales which later became two-thirds of *The Law of the Four Just Men* (1921), the book which opened the door to the publishers Hodder & Stoughton, who, within five years, had transformed Wallace from a failing middle-aged crime writer into one of the richest, most successful, and best-loved writers of the day. 'The Chobham Affair' is late Wallace, though certainly none the worse for that.

Hylton Cleaver (1891–1961) was a prolific concocter of boys' fiction who wrote unusually well-crafted crime stories for adults on the side. His first sale was made in 1913, at the age of 22, to *The Captain*, Newnes' superior monthly for boys on which P. G.

Wodehouse had cut his writing teeth in the early 1900s. Cleaver concentrated on supplying serials and 'completes' to all the best boys' papers—*The Captain*, *Boys' Own Paper*, *Chums*—but wrote as well for the Amalgamated Press's rather more downmarket weekly *Modern Boy* (home, during the 1930s, of W. E. Johns' Biggles, and Robert Murray Graydon's fantastical character Captain Justice, who bore more than a passing resemblance to C. J. Cutcliffe-Hyne's fiery little adventurer Captain Kettle). Cleaver published a large number of boys' books together with several adult novels. A playwright, mainly for repertory companies and London's 'outer circuit', in later life he became a sports writer for the *Evening Standard* (his autobiography, published in the 1950s, was entitled *Sporting Rhapsody*). Although he contributed a couple of tales to the *Strand* just after the First World War, his output increased through the 1930s, when 'By Kind Permission of the Murdered Man', an ingenious 'perfect crime' tale, appeared.

An industrious writer, *Marguerite Steen* (1894–1975) published nearly fifty books in a career that spanned forty years: contemporary novels, biographies, plays, and, especially, long historical sagas of which the 'Flood Family' trilogy is her most celebrated. The best-known novel in the sequence is the first, *The Sun is My Undoing* (1941), a tremendous bestseller which, however, is more than simply a vivid page-turner about the flourishing port of Bristol 200 years ago. The Floods are slavers, and while recounting their energetic exploits Steen examines the social and moral conflicts raised by their ugly trade. Before taking up writing Steen qualified as a Froebel teacher and taught dance and proto-eurhythmics for three years in Halifax immediately after the end of the First World War. She took to the stage, touring with the Fred Terry-Julia Neilson company, and was befriended by the elderly Ellen Terry and the novelist Hugh Walpole, who both persuaded her to pursue a career in writing. Steen's first novel (which was not a success) appeared in 1926. She later wrote a study of Walpole (1933) as well as a history of the Terry family (1962). In 'In View of the Audience' she skilfully creates an atmosphere of chilly terror.

Quentin Reynolds (*fl.* 1924–70) was the very epitome of the heavy-weight, muscular-prosed American journalist. A junior boxing champion and crack swimmer, he graduated from university in 1924, spent some time at law school, then plunged into the bustling New York newspaper world as sports writer, rewrite man, and reporter. On returning from assignment in Germany in 1933 he joined the staff of the high-circulation periodical *Collier's*, for which he wrote descriptive pieces and fiction. In London during the early stages of the Blitz, he wrote the commentary for one of the most famous and influential propaganda films made during the war, *England Can Take It*, which had a salutary effect on American opinion when released. A war reporter covering most of the African and Italian campaigns, as well as those in the Pacific, he successfully sued the Hearst corporation for libel in 1954 for accusing him of being 'yellow' and 'an absentee war correspondent', gaining what was then the largest libel award made in America ($175,000). Reynolds wrote a useful history of the leading American periodical and pulp-magazine publishers Street & Smith, *The Fiction Factory* (1955). 'The Man Who Dreamed Too Much' is a racily written and effective tale of revenge.

About *Loel Yeo* no information is to be gleaned apart from the fact that he (she?) wrote a single story, 'Inquest', for the *Strand* in 1932. Perhaps the author was the same Yeo (no given name appended) who published a number of light sketches on the war (gathered from the *Daily Mail*, *Punch*, and *Outlook*) under the title *Soldier Man* in 1917? And perhaps not. Loel Yeo does not appear to have written anything else for any other magazine of the day, and this, to say the least, is odd. Whoever he was, and whether or not Loel Yeo was his real name (anagramatically, it doesn't make much sense), he could write. And not merely competently, either. There is assurance in the style, an authoritative building-up of tension, convincing characterization, a telling use of irony. No wonder Dorothy L. Sayers, a fine judge of good writing, snapped 'Inquest' up in 1934 for her third and final volume of *Great Short Stories of Detection*, *Mystery and Horror*.

The Interruption

W. W. Jacobs

THE last of the funeral guests had gone and Spencer Goddard, in decent black, sat alone in his small, well-furnished study. There was a queer sense of freedom in the house since the coffin had left it; the coffin which was now hidden in its solitary grave beneath the yellow earth. The air, which for the last three days had seemed stale and contaminated, now smelt fresh and clean. He went to the open window and, looking into the fading light of the autumn day, took a deep breath.

He closed the window and, stooping down, put a match to the fire, and, dropping into his easy chair, sat listening to the cheery crackle of the wood. At the age of thirty-eight he had turned over a fresh page. Life, free and unencumbered, was before him. His dead wife's money was at last his, to spend as he pleased instead of being doled out in reluctant driblets.

He turned at a step at the door and his face assumed the appearance of gravity and sadness it had worn for the last four days. The cook, with the same air of decorous grief, entered the room quietly and, crossing to the mantelpiece, placed upon it a photograph.

'I thought you'd like to have it, sir,' she said, in a low voice, 'to remind you.'

Goddard thanked her, and, rising, took it in his hand and stood regarding it. He noticed with satisfaction that his hand was absolutely steady.

'It is a very good likeness—till she was taken ill,' continued the woman. 'I never saw anybody change so sudden.'

'The nature of her disease, Hannah,' said her master.

The woman nodded, and, dabbing at her eyes with her handkerchief, stood regarding him.

'Is there anything you want?' he enquired, after a time.

She shook her head. 'I can't believe she's gone,' she said, in a low voice. 'Every now and then I have a queer feeling that she's still here——'

'It's your nerves,' said her master, sharply.

'——and wanting to tell me something.'

By a great effort Goddard refrained from looking at her.

'Nerves,' he said again. 'Perhaps you ought to have a little holiday. It has been a great strain upon you.'

'You, too, sir,' said the woman, respectfully. 'Waiting on her hand and foot as you have done, I can't think how you stood it. If you'd only had a nurse——'

'I preferred to do it myself, Hannah,' said her master. 'If I had had a nurse it would have alarmed her.'

The woman assented. 'And they are always peeking and prying into what doesn't concern them,' she added. 'Always think they know more than the doctors do.'

Goddard turned a slow look upon her. The tall, angular figure was standing in an attitude of respectful attention; the cold slaty-brown eyes were cast down, the sullen face expressionless.

'She couldn't have had a better doctor,' he said, looking at the fire again. 'No man could have done more for her.'

'And nobody could have done more for her than you did, sir,' was the reply. 'There's few husbands that would have done what you did.'

Goddard stiffened in his chair. 'That will do, Hannah,' he said, curtly.

'Or done it so well,' said the woman, with measured slowness.

With a strange, sinking sensation, her master paused to regain his control. Then he turned and eyed her steadily. 'Thank you,' he said, slowly; 'you mean well, but at present I cannot discuss it.'

For some time after the door had closed behind her he sat in deep thought. The feeling of well-being of a few minutes before had vanished, leaving in its place an apprehension which he refused to consider, but which would not be allayed. He thought over his actions of the last few weeks, carefully, and could remember no flaw. His wife's illness, the doctor's diagnosis, his own solicitous care, were all in keeping with the ordinary. He tried to remember the woman's exact words—her manner. Something had shown him Fear. What?

He could have laughed at his fears next morning. The dining-room was full of sunshine and the fragrance of coffee and bacon was in the air. Better still, a worried and commonplace Hannah. Worried over two eggs with false birth-certificates, over the vendor of which she became almost lyrical.

'The bacon is excellent,' said her smiling master, 'so is the coffee; but your coffee always is.'

Hannah smiled in return, and, taking fresh eggs from a rosy-cheeked maid, put them before him.

A pipe, followed by a brisk walk, cheered him still further. He came home glowing with exercise and again possessed with that sense of freedom and freshness. He went into the garden—now his own—and planned alterations.

After lunch he went over the house. The windows of his wife's bedroom were open and the room neat and airy. His glance wandered from the made-up bed to the brightly polished furniture. Then he went to the dressing-table and opened the drawers, searching each in turn. With the exception of a few odds and ends they were empty. He went out on to the landing and called for Hannah.

'Do you know whether your mistress locked up any of her things?' he enquired.

'What things?' said the woman.

'Well, her jewellery mostly.'

'Oh!' Hannah smiled. 'She gave it all to me,' she said, quietly.

Goddard checked an exclamation. His heart was beating nervously, but he spoke sternly.

'When?'

'Just before she died—of gastro-enteritis,' said the woman.

There was a long silence. He turned and with great care mechanically closed the drawers of the dressing-table. The tilted glass showed him the pallor of his face, and he spoke without turning round.

'That is all right, then,' he said, huskily. 'I only wanted to know what had become of it. I thought, perhaps, Milly——'

Hannah shook her head. 'Milly's all right,' she said, with a strange smile. 'She's as honest as we are. Is there anything more you want, sir?'

She closed the door behind her with the quietness of the well-trained servant; Goddard, steadying himself with his hand on the rail of the bed, stood looking into the future.

The days passed monotonously, as they pass with a man in prison. Gone was the sense of freedom and the idea of a wider life. Instead of a cell, a house with ten rooms—but Hannah, the jailer, guarding each one. Respectful and attentive, the model servant, he saw in every word a threat against his liberty—his life. In the sullen face and cold eyes he saw her knowledge of power; in her solicitude for his comfort and approval, a sardonic jest. It was the master playing at being the servant. The years of unwilling servitude were over, but she felt her way carefully with infinite zest in the game. Warped and bitter, with a cleverness which had never before had scope, she had entered into her kingdom. She took it little by little, savouring every morsel.

'I hope I've done right, sir,' she said one morning. 'I have given Milly notice.'

Goddard looked up from his paper. 'Isn't she satisfactory?' he enquired.

'Not to my thinking, sir,' said the woman. 'And she says she is coming to see you about it. I told her that would be no good.'

'I had better see her and hear what she has to say,' said her master.

'Of course, if you wish to,' said Hannah; 'only, after giving her notice, if she doesn't go I shall. I should be sorry to go—I've been very comfortable here—but it's either her or me.'

'I should be sorry to lose you,' said Goddard in a hopeless voice.

'Thank you, sir,' said Hannah. 'I'm sure I've tried to do my best. I've been with you some time now—and I know all your little ways. I expect I understand you better than anybody else would. I do all I can to make you comfortable.'

'Very well, I leave it to you,' said Goddard in a voice which strove to be brisk and commanding. 'You have my permission to dismiss her.'

'There's another thing I wanted to see you about,' said Hannah;

'my wages. I was going to ask for a rise, seeing that I'm really housekeeper here now.'

'Certainly,' said her master, considering, 'that only seems fair. Let me see—what are you getting?'

'Thirty-six.'

Goddard reflected for a moment and then turned with a benevolent smile. 'Very well,' he said, cordially, 'I'll make it forty-two. That's ten shillings a month more.'

'I was thinking of a hundred,' said Hannah, dryly.

The significance of the demand appalled him. 'Rather a big jump,' he said at last. 'I really don't know that I——'

'It doesn't matter,' said Hannah. 'I thought I was worth it—to you—that's all. You know best. Some people might think I was worth *two* hundred. That's a bigger jump, but after all a big jump is better than——'

She broke off and tittered. Goddard eyed her.

'——than a big drop,' she concluded.

Her master's face set. The lips almost disappeared and something came into the pale eyes that was revolting. Still eyeing her, he rose and approached her. She stood her ground and met him eye to eye.

'You are jocular,' he said at last.

'Short life and a merry one,' said the woman.

'Mine or yours?'

'Both, perhaps,' was the reply.

'If—if I give you a hundred,' said Goddard, moistening his lips, 'that ought to make your life merrier, at any rate.'

Hannah nodded. 'Merry and long, perhaps,' she said, slowly. 'I'm careful, you know—very careful.'

'I am sure you are,' said Goddard, his face relaxing.

'Careful what I eat and drink, I mean,' said the woman, eyeing him steadily.

'That is wise,' he said, slowly. 'I am myself—that is why I am paying a good cook a large salary. But don't overdo things, Hannah; don't kill the goose that lays the golden eggs.'

'I am not likely to do that,' she said, coldly. 'Live and let live; that is my motto. Some people have different ones. But I'm careful; nobody won't catch me napping. I've left a letter with my sister, in case.'

Goddard turned slowly and in a casual fashion put the flowers straight in a bowl on the table, and, wandering to the window, looked out. His face was white again and his hands trembled.

'To be opened after my death,' continued Hannah. 'I don't believe in doctors—not after what I've seen of them—I don't think they know enough; so if I die I shall be examined. I've given good reasons.'

'And suppose,' said Goddard, coming from the window, 'suppose she is curious, and opens it before you die?'

'We must chance that,' said Hannah, shrugging her shoulders; 'but I don't think she will. I sealed it up with sealing-wax, with a mark on it.'

'She might open it and say nothing about it,' persisted her master.

An unwholesome grin spread slowly over Hannah's features. 'I should know it soon enough,' she declared, boisterously, 'and so would other people. Lord! there would be an upset! Chidham would have something to talk about for once. We should be in the paper—both of us.'

Goddard forced a smile. 'Dear me!' he said, gently. 'Your pen seems to be a dangerous weapon, Hannah, but I hope that the need to open it will not happen for another fifty years. You look well and strong.'

The woman nodded. 'I don't take up my troubles before they come,' she said, with a satisfied air; 'but there's no harm in trying to prevent them coming. Prevention is better than cure.'

'Exactly,' said her master; 'and, by the way, there's no need for this little financial arrangement to be known by anybody else. I might become unpopular with my neighbours for setting a bad example. Of course, I am giving you this sum because I really think you are worth it.'

'I'm sure you do,' said Hannah. 'I'm not sure I ain't worth more, but this'll do to go on with. I shall get a girl for less than we are paying Milly, and that'll be another little bit extra for me.'

'Certainly,' said Goddard, and smiled again.

'Come to think of it,' said Hannah, pausing at the door, 'I ain't sure I shall get anybody else; then there'll be more than ever for me. If I do the work I might as well have the money.'

Her master nodded, and, left to himself, sat down to think out a position which was as intolerable as it was dangerous. At a great risk he had escaped from the dominion of one woman only to fall, bound and helpless, into the hands of another. However vague and unconvincing the suspicions of Hannah might be, they would be sufficient. Evidence could be unearthed. Cold with fear one moment, and hot with fury the next, he sought in vain for some avenue of escape. It was his brain against that of a cunning, illiterate fool; a fool whose malicious stupidity only added to his danger. And she drank. With largely increased wages she would drink more and his very life might depend upon a hiccuped boast. It was clear that she was enjoying her supremacy; later on her vanity would urge her to display it before others. He might have to obey the crack of her whip before witnesses, and that would cut off all possibility of escape.

He sat with his head in his hands. There must be a way out and he must find it. Soon. He must find it before gossip began; before the changed position of master and servant lent colour to her story when that story became known. Shaking with fury, he thought of her lean, ugly throat and the joy of choking her life out with his fingers. He started suddenly, and took a quick breath. No, not fingers—a rope.

Bright and cheerful outside and with his friends, in the house he was quiet and submissive. Milly had gone, and, if the service was poorer and the rooms neglected, he gave no sign. If a bell remained unanswered he made no complaint, and to studied insolence turned the other cheek of politeness. When at this tribute to her power the woman smiled, he smiled in return. A smile which, for all its disarming softness, left her vaguely uneasy.

'I'm not afraid of you,' she said once, with a menacing air.

'I hope not,' said Goddard in a slightly surprised voice.

'Some people might be, but I'm not,' she declared. 'If anything happened to me——'

'Nothing could happen to such a careful woman as you are,' he said, smiling again. 'You ought to live to ninety—with luck.'

It was clear to him that the situation was getting on his nerves. Unremembered but terrible dreams haunted his sleep. Dreams in which some great, inevitable disaster was always pressing upon him, although he could never discover what it was. Each morning he awoke unrefreshed to face another day of torment. He could not meet the woman's eyes for fear of revealing the threat that was in his own.

Delay was dangerous and foolish. He had thought out every move in that contest of wits which was to remove the shadow of the rope from his own neck and place it about that of the woman. There was a little risk, but the stake was a big one. He had but to set the ball rolling and others would keep it on its course. It was time to act.

He came in a little jaded from his afternoon walk, and left his tea untouched. He ate but little dinner, and, sitting hunched up over the fire, told the woman that he had taken a slight chill. Her concern, he felt grimly, might have been greater if she had known the cause.

He was no better next day, and after lunch called in to consult his doctor. He left with a clean bill of health except for a slight digestive derangement, the remedy for which he took away with him in a bottle. For two days he swallowed one tablespoonful three times a day in water, without result, then he took to his bed.

'A day or two in bed won't hurt you,' said the doctor. 'Show me that tongue of yours again.'

'But what is the matter with me, Roberts?' enquired the patient.

The doctor pondered. 'Nothing to trouble about—nerves a bit wrong—digestion a little bit impaired. You'll be all right in a day or two.'

Goddard nodded. So far, so good; Roberts had not outlived his usefulness. He smiled grimly after the doctor had left at the surprise he was preparing for him. A little rough on Roberts and his professional reputation, perhaps, but these things could not be avoided.

He lay back and visualized the programme. A day or two longer, getting gradually worse, then a little sickness. After that a nervous, somewhat shamefaced patient hinting at things. His food had a queer taste—he felt worse after taking it; he knew it was ridiculous, still—there was some of his beef-tea he had put aside, perhaps the doctor would like to examine it? and the medicine? Secretions too; perhaps he would like to see those?

Propped on his elbow, he stared fixedly at the wall. There would be a trace—a faint trace—of arsenic in the secretions. There would be more than a trace in the other things. An attempt to poison him would be clearly indicated, and—his wife's symptoms had resembled his own—let Hannah get out of the web he was spinning if she could. As for the letter she had threatened him with, let her produce it; it could only recoil upon herself. Fifty letters could not save her from the doom he was preparing for her. It was her life or his, and he would show no mercy.

For three days he doctored himself with sedulous care, watching himself anxiously the while. His nerve was going and he knew it. Before him was the strain of the discovery, the arrest, and the trial. The gruesome business of his wife's death. A long business. He would wait no longer, and he would open the proceedings with dramatic suddenness.

It was between nine and ten o'clock at night when he rang his bell, and it was not until he had rung four times that he heard the heavy steps of Hannah mounting the stairs.

'What d'you want?' she demanded, standing in the doorway.

'I'm very ill,' he said, gasping. 'Run for the doctor. Quick!'

The woman stared at him in genuine amazement. 'What, at this time o'night?' she exclaimed. 'Not likely.'

'I'm dying!' said Goddard in a broken voice.

'Not you,' she said, roughly. 'You'll be better in the morning.'

'I'm dying,' he repeated. 'Go—for—the—doctor.'

The woman hesitated. The rain beat in heavy squalls against the window, and the doctor's house was a mile distant on the lonely road. She glanced at the figure on the bed.

'I should catch my death o' cold,' she grumbled.

She stood sullenly regarding him. He certainly looked very ill, and his death would by no means benefit her. She listened, scowling, to the wind and the rain.

'All right,' she said at last, and went noisily from the room.

His face set in a mirthless smile, he heard her bustling about below. The front-door slammed violently and he was alone.

He waited for a few minutes and then, getting out of bed, put on his dressing-gown and set about his preparations. With a steady hand he added a little white powder to the remains of his beef-tea and to the contents of his bottle of medicine. He stood listening a moment at some faint sound from below, and, having satisfied himself, lit a candle and made his way to Hannah's room. For a space he stood irresolute, looking about him. Then he opened one of the drawers and, placing the broken packet of powder under a pile of clothing at the back, made his way back to bed.

He was disturbed to find that he was trembling with excitement and nervousness. He longed for tobacco, but that was impossible. To reassure himself he began to rehearse his conversation with the doctor, and again he thought over every possible complication. The scene with the woman would be terrible; he would have to be too ill to take any part in it. The less he said the better. Others would do all that was necessary.

He lay for a long time listening to the sound of the wind and the rain. Inside, the house seemed unusually quiet, and with an odd sensation he suddenly realized that it was the first time he had been alone in it since his wife's death. He remembered that she would have to be disturbed. The thought was unwelcome. He did not want her to be disturbed. Let the dead sleep.

He sat up in bed and drew his watch from beneath the pillow. Hannah ought to have been back before; in any case she could not be long now. At any moment he might hear her key in the lock. He lay down again and reminded himself that things were shaping well. He had shaped them, and some of the satisfaction of the artist was his.

The silence was oppressive. The house seemed to be listening, waiting. He looked at his watch again and wondered, with a curse, what had happened to the woman. It was clear that the doctor must be out, but that was no reason for her delay. It was close on midnight, and the atmosphere of the house seemed in some strange fashion to be brooding and hostile.

In a lull in the wind he thought he heard footsteps outside, and his face cleared as he sat up listening for the sound of the key in the door below. In another moment the woman would be in the house and the fears engendered by a disordered fancy would have flown. The sound of the steps had ceased, but he could hear no sound of entrance. Until all hope had gone, he sat listening. He was certain he had heard footsteps. Whose?

Trembling and haggard he sat waiting, assailed by a crowd of murmuring fears. One whispered that he had failed and would have to pay the penalty of failing; that he had gambled with Death and lost.

By a strong effort he fought down these fancies and, closing his eyes, tried to compose himself to rest. It was evident now that the doctor was out and that Hannah was waiting to return with him in his car. He was frightening himself for nothing. At any moment he might hear the sound of their arrival.

He heard something else, and, sitting up suddenly, tried to think what it was and what had caused it. It was a very faint sound— stealthy. Holding his breath, he waited for it to be repeated. He heard it again, the mere ghost of a sound—the whisper of a sound, but significant as most whispers are.

He wiped his brow with his sleeve and told himself firmly that it was nerves, and nothing but nerves; but, against his will, he still listened. He fancied now that the sound came from his wife's room, the other side of the landing. It increased in loudness and became more insistent, but with his eyes fixed on the door of his room he still kept himself in hand, and tried to listen instead to the wind and the rain.

For a time he heard nothing but that. Then there came a scraping, scurrying noise from his wife's room, and a sudden, terrific crash.

With a loud scream his nerve broke, and springing from the bed he sped downstairs and, flinging open the front-door, dashed into the night. The door, caught by the wind, slammed behind him.

With his hand holding the garden gate open, ready for further flight, he stood sobbing for breath. His bare feet were bruised and the rain was very cold, but he took no heed. Then he ran a little way along the road and stood for some time, hoping and listening.

He came back slowly. The wind was bitter and he was soaked to the skin. In desperation he made his way back to the house, only to find the door closed. The porch gave a little protection from the rain, but none from the wind, and, shaking in every limb, he leaned in abject misery against the door. He pulled himself together after a time and stumbled round to the back-door. Locked! And all the lower windows were shuttered. He made his way back to the porch and, crouching there in hopeless misery, waited for the woman to return.

He had a dim memory when he awoke of somebody questioning him, and then of being half-pushed, half-carried upstairs to bed. There was something wrong with his head and his chest and he was trembling violently, and very cold. Somebody was speaking.

'You must have taken leave of your senses,' said the voice of Hannah. 'I thought you were dead.'

He forced his eyes to open. 'Doctor,' he muttered, 'doctor.'

'Out on a bad case,' said Hannah. 'I waited till I was tired of waiting, and then came along. Good thing for you I did. He'll be round first thing this morning. He ought to be here now.'

She bustled about, tidying up the room, his leaden eyes following her as she collected the beef-tea and other things on a tray and carried them out.

'Nice thing I did yesterday,' she remarked, as she came back. 'Left the missus's bedroom window open. When I opened the door this morning I found that beautiful Chippidale glass of hers had blown off the table and smashed to pieces. Did you hear it?'

Goddard made no reply. In a confused fashion he was trying to think. Accident or not, the fall of the glass had served its purpose. Were there such things as accidents? Or was Life a puzzle—a puzzle into which every piece was made to fit? Fear and the wind . . . no: conscience and the wind . . . had saved the woman. He must get the powder back from her drawer . . . before she discovered it and denounced him. The medicine . . . he must remember not to take it . . .

He was very ill, seriously ill. He must have taken a chill owing to that panic flight into the garden. Why didn't the doctor come? He had come . . . at last . . . he was doing something to his chest . . . it was cold . . .

Again . . . the doctor . . . there was something he wanted to tell him . . . Hannah and a powder . . . what was it?

Later on he remembered, together with other things that he had hoped to forget. He lay watching an endless procession of memories, broken at times by a glance at the doctor, the nurse, and Hannah, who were all standing near the bed regarding him. They had been there a long time, and they were all very quiet. The last time he looked at Hannah was the first time for months that he had looked at her without loathing and hatred. Then he knew that he was dying.

The Chobham Affair

Edgar Wallace

THERE was a man who had a way with women, especially women who had not graduated in the more worldly school of experience. His name was Alphonse Riebiera, and he described himself as a Spaniard, though his passport was issued by a South American republic. Sometimes he presented visiting cards which were inscribed:

LE MARQUIS DE RIEBIERA

but that was only on very special occasions.

He was young, with an olive complexion, faultless features, and showed his two rows of dazzling white teeth when he smiled. He found it convenient to change his appearance. For example: when he was a hired dancer attached to the personnel of an Egyptian hotel he wore little side-whiskers, which oddly enough exaggerated his youthfulness; in the casino at Enghien, where by some means he secured the position of croupier, he was decorated with a little black moustache. Staid, sober, and unimaginative spectators of his many adventures were irritably amazed that women said anything to him, but then it is notoriously difficult for any man, even an unimaginative man, to discover attractive qualities in successful lovers.

And yet the most unlikely women came under his spell and had to regret it. There arrived a time when he became a patron of the gambling establishments where he had been the most humble and the least trusted of servants, when he lived royally in hotels where he once was hired at so many piastres per dance. Diamonds came to his spotless shirt front, pretty manicurists tended his nails and received fees larger than his one-time dancing partners had slipped shyly into his hand.

There are certain gross men who play interminable dominoes in the cheaper cafés that abound on the unfashionable side of the Seine who are amazing news centres. They know how the oddest people live, and they were very plain spoken when they discussed Alphonse. They could tell you, though Heaven knows how the information came to them, of fat registered letters that came to him in his flat in the Boulevard Haussmann. Registered letters stuffed with money and despairing letters that said in effect (and in various languages): 'I can send you no more—this is the last.' But they did send more.

Alphonse had developed a well-organized business. He would leave for London, or Rome, or Amsterdam, or Vienna, or even Athens, arriving at his destination by sleeping-car, drive to the best hotel, hire a luxurious suite—and telephone. Usually the unhappy lady met him by appointment, tearful, hysterically furious, bitter, insulting, but always remunerative.

For when Alphonse read extracts from the letters they had sent to him in the day of the Great Glamour and told them what their husbands' income was almost to a pound, lira, franc, or guilder, they reconsidered their decision to tell their husbands everything, and Alphonse went back to Paris with his allowance.

This was his method with the bigger game; sometimes he announced his coming visit with a letter discreetly worded, which made personal application unnecessary. He was not very much afraid of husbands or brothers; the philosophy which had germinated from his experience made him contemptuous of human nature. He believed that most people were cowards and lived in fear of their lives, and greater fear of their reputations. He carried two silver-plated revolvers, one in each hip-pocket. They had prettily damascened barrels and ivory handles carved in the likeness of nymphs. He bought them in Cairo from a man who smuggled cocaine from Vienna.

Alphonse had some twenty 'clients' on his books, and added to them as opportunity arose. Of the twenty, five were gold mines (he thought of them as such), the remainder were silver mines.

There was a silver mine living in England, a very lovely, rather sad-looking girl, who was happily married except when she thought of Alphonse. She loved her husband and hated herself, and hated Alphonse intensely and impotently. Having a fortune of her own she could pay—therefore she paid.

Then in a fit of desperate revolt she wrote saying, 'This is the last, etc.' Alphonse was amused. He waited until September, when the next allowance was due, and it did not come. Nor in October, nor November. In December he wrote to her; he did not wish to go to England in December, for England is very gloomy and foggy, and it was so much nicer in Egypt. But business was business.

His letter reached its address when the woman to whom it was addressed was on a visit to her aunt in Long Island. She had been born an American. Alphonse had not written in answer to her letter; she had sailed for New York feeling safe.

Her husband, whose initial was the same as his wife's, opened the letter by accident and read it through very carefully. He was no fool. He did not regard the wife he wooed as an outcast; what happened before his marriage was her business—what happened now was his.

And he understood these wild dreams of hers, and her wild uncontrollable weeping for no reason at all, and he knew what the future held for her. He went to Paris and made enquiries: he sought the company of the gross men who play dominoes and heard much that was interesting.

Alphonse arrived in London and telephoned from a call-box. Madam was not at home. A typewritten letter came to him, making an appointment for the Wednesday. It was, of course, for a secret rendezvous. The affair ran normally.

He passed his time pleasantly in the days of waiting. Bought a new Spanza car of the latest model, arranged for its transportation to Paris, and in the meantime amused himself by driving it.

At the appointed hour he arrived, knocked at the door of the house, and was admitted . . .

Riebiera, green of face, shaking at the knees, surrendered his two ornamented pistols without a fight——

At eight o'clock on Christmas morning Superintendent Oakington was called from his warm bed by telephone, and was told the news.

A milkman, driving across Chobham Common, had seen a car standing a little off the road. It was apparently a new car, and must have been standing in its position all night. There were three inches of snow on its roof; beneath the body of the car the bracken was green.

An arresting sight even for a milkman, who at seven o'clock on a wintry morning had no other thought than to supply the needs of his customers as quickly as possible and return at the earliest moment to his own home and the festivities and feastings proper to the day.

He got out of the Ford he was driving and stamped through the snow. He saw a man lying face downwards, and in his grey hand a silver-barrelled revolver. He was dead. And then the startled milkman saw the second man. His face was invisible. It lay under a thick white mask of snow that made his pinched features grotesque and hideous.

The milkman ran back to his car and drove towards a police-station.

Mr Oakington was on the spot within an hour of being called. There were a dozen policemen grouped around the car and the shapes in the snow: the reporters, thank God, had not arrived.

Late in the afternoon the Superintendent put a call through to one man who might help in a moment of profound bewilderment.

Archibald Lenton was the most promising of Treasury Juniors that the Bar had known for years. The Common Law Bar lifts its delicate nose at lawyers who are interested in criminal cases to the exclusion of other practice. But Archie Lenton survived the unspoken disapproval of his brethren, and concentrating on this unsavoury aspect of the Law was both a successful advocate and an authority on certain types of crime, for he had written a textbook which was accepted as authoritative.

An hour later he was in the Superintendent's room at Scotland Yard, listening to the story.

'We've identified both men. One is a foreigner, a man from the Argentine, so far as I can discover from his passport, named Alphonse or Alphonso Riebiera. He lives in Paris and has been in this country for about a week.'

'Well off?'

'Very, I should say. We found about two hundred pounds in his pocket. He was staying at the Nederland Hotel, and bought a car for twelve hundred pounds only last Friday, paying cash. That is the car we found near the body. I've been on the 'phone to Paris and he is suspected there of being a blackmailer. The police have searched and sealed his flat, but found no documents of any kind. He is evidently the sort of man who keeps his business under his hat.'

'He was shot, you say? How many times?'

'Once, through the head. The other man was killed in exactly the same way. There was a trace of blood in the car, but nothing else.'

Mr Lenton jotted down a note on a pad of paper.

'Who was the other man?' he asked.

'That's the queerest thing of all—an old acquaintance of yours.'

'Mine? Who on earth——?'

'Do you remember a fellow you defended on a murder charge—Joe Stackett?'

'At Exeter, good Lord, yes! Was that the man?'

'We've identified him from his fingerprints. As a matter of fact, we were after Joe—he's an expert car thief who only came out of prison last week. He got away with a car yesterday morning, but abandoned it after a chase and slipped through the fingers of the Flying Squad. Last night he pinched an old car from a second-hand dealer and was spotted and chased. We found the car abandoned in Tooting. He was never seen again until he was picked up on Chobham Common.'

Archie Lenton leant back in his chair and stared thoughtfully at the ceiling.

'He stole the Spanza—the owner jumped on the running board and there was a fight——' he began, but the Superintendent shook his head.

'Where did he get his gun? English criminals do not carry guns. And they weren't ordinary revolvers. Silver-plated, ivory butts carved with girls' figures—both identical. There were fifty pounds in Joe's pocket; they are consecutive numbers to those found in Riebiera's pocket-book. If he'd stolen them he'd have taken the lot. Joe wouldn't stop at murder, you know that, Mr Lenton. He killed that old woman in Exeter, although he was acquitted. Riebiera must have given him the fifty——'

A telephone bell rang; the Superintendent drew the instrument towards him and listened. After ten minutes of a conversation which was confined, so far as Oakington was concerned, to a dozen brief questions, he put down the receiver.

'One of my officers has traced the movements of the car: it was seen standing outside a house in Tooting. It was there at nine-forty-five, and was seen by a postman. If you feel like spending Christmas night doing a little bit of detective work, we'll go down and see the place.'

They arrived half an hour later at a house in a very respectable neighbourhood. The two detectives who waited their coming had obtained the keys but had not gone inside. The house was for sale and was standing empty. It was the property of two old maiden ladies, who had placed the premises in an agent's hands when they had moved into the country.

The appearance of the car before an empty house had aroused the interest of the postman. He had seen no lights in the windows and decided that the car was owned by one of the guests at the next-door house.

Oakington opened the door and switched on the light. Strangely enough, the old ladies had not had the current disconnected, though they were notoriously mean. The passage was bare, except for a pair of bead curtains which hung from an arched support to the ceiling.

The front room drew blank. It was in one of the back rooms on the ground floor that they found evidence of the crime. There was blood on the bare planks of the floor and in the grate a litter of ashes.

'Somebody has burnt papers—I smelt it when I came into the room,' said Lenton.

He knelt before the grate and lifted a handful of fine ashes carefully.

'And these have been stirred up until there isn't an ash big enough to hold a word,' he said.

He examined the blood prints and made a careful scrutiny of the walls. The window was covered with a shutter.

'That kept the light from getting out,' he said, 'and the sound of the shot getting out. There is nothing else here.'

The detective sergeant who was inspecting the other rooms returned with the news that a kitchen window had been forced. There was one muddy print on the kitchen table which was under the window and a rough attempt had been made to obliterate this. Behind the house was a large garden, and behind that an allotment. It would be easy to reach and enter the house without exciting attention.

'But if Stackett was being chased by the police why should he come here?' he asked.

'His car was found abandoned not more than two hundred yards from here,' explained Oakington. 'He may have entered the house in the hope of finding something valuable, and have been surprised by Riebiera.'

Archie Lenton laughed softly.

'I can give you a better theory than that,' he said, and for the greater part of the night he wrote carefully and convincingly, reconstructing the crime, giving the most minute details.

That account is still preserved at Scotland Yard, and there are many highly placed officials who swear by it.

And yet something altogether different happened on the night of that 24th of December . . .

The streets were greasy. The car-lines abominably so. Stackett's mean little car slithered and skidded alarmingly. He had been in a bad temper when he started out on his hungry quest; he grew sour and savage with the evening passing on with nothing to show for his discomfort.

The suburban high street was crowded too; tram-cars moved at a crawl, their bells clanging pathetically; street vendors had their stalls jammed end to end on either side of the thoroughfare; stalls green and red with holly wreaths and untidy bunches of mistletoe; there were butcher stalls, raucous auctioneers holding masses of raw beef and roaring their offers; vegetable stalls; stalls piled high with plates, and cups and saucers, gaudy dishes and glassware, shining in the rays of the powerful acetylene lamps.

The car skidded. There was a crash and a scream. Breaking crockery has an alarming sound. A yell from the stall-owner; Stackett straightened his machine and darted between a tram-car and a trolley.

'Hi, you!'

He twisted his wheel, almost knocked down the policeman who came to intercept him, and swung into a dark side street, his foot clamped on the accelerator. He turned to the right and the left, to the right again. Here was a long suburban road; houses monotonously alike on either side, terribly dreary brick boxes where men and women and children lived, were born, paid rent, and died. A mile further on he passed the gateway of the cemetery where they found the rest which was their supreme reward for living at all.

The police whistle had followed him for less than a quarter of a mile. He had passed a policeman running towards the sound—anyway, flatties never worried Stackett. Some of his ill-humour passed in the amusement which the sight of the running copper brought.

Bringing the noisy little car to a standstill by the side of the road, he got down and, relighting the cigarette he had so carefully extinguished, gazed glumly at the stained and battered mudguard which was shivering and shaking under the pulsations of the engine . . .

Through that same greasy street came a motor-cyclist, muffled to the chin, his goggles dangling about his neck. He pulled up his shining wheel near the policeman on point duty and, supporting his balance with one foot in the muddy road, asked questions.

'Yes, sergeant,' said the policeman. 'I saw him. He went down there. As a matter of fact, I was going to pinch him for driving to the common danger, but he hopped it.'

'That's Joe Stackett,' nodded Sergeant Kenton, of the CID. 'A thin-faced man with a pointed nose?'

The point-duty policeman had not seen the face behind the windscreen, but he had seen the car, and that he described accurately.

'Stolen from Elmer's garage. At least, Elmer will say so, but he probably provided it. Dumped stuff. Which way did you say?'

The policeman indicated, and the sergeant kicked his engine to life and went chug-chugging down the dark street.

He missed Mr Stackett by a piece of bad luck—bad luck for everybody, including Mr Stackett, who was at the beginning of his amazing adventure.

Switching off the engine, he had continued on foot. About fifty yards away was the wide opening of a road superior in class to any he had traversed. Even the dreariest suburb has its West-end, and here were villas standing on their own acres; very sedate villas, with porches and porch lamps in wrought-iron and oddly coloured glass, and shaven lawns, and rose gardens swathed in matting, and no two villas were alike. At the far end he saw a red light, and his heart leapt with joy: Christmas—it was to be Christmas after all, with good food and lashings of drink and other manifestations of happiness and comfort peculiarly attractive to Joe Stackett.

Even in the darkness it looked like a car worth stealing. He saw somebody near the machine, and stopped. It was difficult to tell in the gloom whether the person near the car had got in or had come out. He listened. There came to him neither the slam of the driver's door nor the whine of the self-starter. He came a little closer, walked boldly on, his restless eyes moving left and right for danger. All the houses were occupied. Bright lights illuminated the casement cloth which covered the windows. He heard the sound of respectable revelry and two gramophones playing dance tunes. But his eyes always came back to the polished limousine at the door of the end house. There was no light there. It was completely dark, from the gabled attic to the ground floor.

He quickened his pace. It was a Spanza. His heart leapt at the recognition. For a Spanza is a car for which there is a ready sale. You can get as much as a hundred pounds for a new one. They are popular amongst Eurasians and wealthy Hindus. Binky Jones, who was the best car fence in London, would pay him cash, not less than sixty. In a week's time that car would be crated and on its way to India, there to be resold at a handsome profit.

The driver's door was wide open. He heard the soft purr of the engine. He slid into the driver's seat, closed the door noiselessly, and almost without as much as a whine the Spanza moved on.

It was a new one, brand new . . . A hundred at least.

Gathering speed, he passed to the end of the road, came to a wide common, and skirted it. Presently he was in another shopping street, but he knew too much to turn back towards London. He would take the open country for it, work round through Esher and come into London by the Portsmouth Road. The art of car stealing is to move as quickly as possible from the police division where the machine is stolen, and may be instantly reported, to a 'foreign' division, which will not know of the theft until hours after.

There might be all sorts of extra pickings. There was a big luggage trunk behind, and possibly a few knick-knacks in the body of the car itself. At a suitable moment he would make a leisurely search. At the moment he headed for Epsom, turning back to hit the Kingston by-pass. Sleet fell—snow and rain together. He set the screen-wiper working, and began to hum a little tune. The Kingston by-pass was deserted. It was too unpleasant a night for much traffic.

Mr Stackett was debating what would be the best place to make his search when he felt an unpleasant draught behind him. He had noticed there was a sliding window separating the interior of the car from the driver's seat, which had possibly worked loose. He put up his hand to push it close.

'Drive on! Don't turn round, or I'll blow your head off!'

Involuntarily he half-turned to see the gaping muzzle of an automatic, and in his agitation put his foot on the brake. The car skidded from one side of the road to the other, half-turned, and recovered.

'Drive on, I am telling you,' said a metallic voice. 'When you reach the Portsmouth Road turn and bear towards Weybridge. If you attempt to stop I will shoot you. Is that clear?'

Joe Stackett's teeth were chattering. He could not articulate the 'yes'. All that he could do was to nod. He went on nodding for half a mile before he realized what he was doing.

No further word came from the interior of the car until they passed the racecourse; then unexpectedly the voice gave a new direction:

'Turn left towards Leatherhead.'

The driver obeyed.

They came to a stretch of common. Stackett, who knew the country well, realized the complete isolation of the spot.

'Slow down, pull in to the left. . . . There is no dip there. You can switch on your lights.'

The car slid and bumped over the uneven ground, the wheels crunched through beds of bracken. . . .

'Stop.'

The door behind him opened. The man got out. He jerked open the driver's door.

'Step down,' he said. 'Turn out your lights first. Have you got a gun?'

'Gun? Why the hell should I have a gun?' stammered the car thief.

He was focused all the time in a ring of light from a very bright electric torch which the passenger had turned upon him.

'You are an act of Providence.'

Stackett could not see the face of the speaker. He saw only the gun in the hand, for the stranger kept this well in the light.

'Look inside the car.'

Stackett looked and almost collapsed: there was a figure huddled in one corner of the seat—the figure of a man. He saw something else—a bicycle jammed into the car, one wheel touching the roof, the other on the floor. He saw the man's white face. . . . Dead! A slim, rather short man, with dark hair and a dark moustache, a foreigner. There was a little red hole in his temple.

'Pull him out,' commanded the voice sharply.

Stackett shrank back, but a powerful hand pushed him towards the car.

'Pull him out!'

With his face moist with cold perspiration, the car thief obeyed; put his hands under the armpits of the inanimate figure, dragged him out, and laid him on the bracken.

'He's dead,' he whimpered.

'Completely,' said the other.

Suddenly he switched off his electric torch. Far away came a gleam of light on the road, coming swiftly towards them. It was a car moving towards Esher. It passed.

'I saw you coming just after I had got the body into the car. There wasn't time to get back to the house. I'd hoped you were just an ordinary pedestrian. When I saw you get into the car I guessed pretty well your vocation. What is your name?'

'Joseph Stackett.'

'Stackett?' The light flashed on his face again. 'How wonderful! Do you remember the Exeter Assizes? The old woman you killed with a hammer? I defended you!'

Joe's eyes were wide open. He stared past the light at the dim grey thing that was a face.

'Mr Lenton?' he said, hoarsely. 'Good God, sir!'

'You murdered her in cold blood for a few paltry shillings, and you would have been dead now, Stackett, if I hadn't found a flaw in the evidence. You expected to die, didn't you? You remember how we used to talk in Exeter Jail about the trap that would not work when they tried to hang a murderer and the ghoulish satisfaction you had that you would stand on the same trap?'

Joe Stackett grinned uncomfortably.

'And I meant it, sir,' he said, 'but you can't try a man twice——' Then his eyes dropped to the figure at his feet—the dapper little man with a black moustache, with a red hole in his temple.

Lenton leant over the dead man, took out a pocket-case from the inside of the jacket, and at his leisure detached ten five-pound notes from the fat packet of them.

'Put those in your pocket.'

He obeyed, wondering what service would be required of him, wondered more why the pocket-book with its precious notes was returned to the dead man's pocket.

Lenton looked back along the road. Snow was falling now, real snow. It came down in small particles, falling so thickly that it seemed that a fog lay on the land.

'You fit into this perfectly—a man unfit to live. There is fate in this meeting.'

'I don't know what you mean by fate.'

Joe Stackett grew bold; he had to deal with a lawyer and a gentleman who, in a criminal sense, was his inferior. The money obviously had been given to him to keep his mouth shut.

'What have you been doing, Mr Lenton? That's bad, ain't it? This fellow's dead and——'

Then in a flash he realized the monetary value of the situation and he grew immediately bold.

'This job's going to cost you something, guv'nor,' he said, and he dropped his hand suddenly to his hip.

He must have seen the pencil of flame that came from the other's hand. He could have felt nothing, for he was dead before he sprawled over the body on the ground.

Mr Archibald Lenton examined the revolver by the light of his lamp, opened the breech and closed it again. Stooping, he laid it near the hand of the little man with the black moustache and, lifting the body of Joe Stackett, dragged it towards the car and let it drop. Bending down, he clasped the still warm hands about the butt of another pistol. Then, at his leisure, he took the bicycle from the interior of the car and carried it back to the road. It was already white and fine snow was falling in sheets.

Mr Lenton went on and reached his home two hours later, when the bells of the local church were ringing musically.

There was a cable waiting for him from his wife.

'A Happy Christmas to you, darling.'

He was ridiculously pleased that she had remembered to send the wire—he was very fond of his wife.

By Kind Permission of the Murdered Man

Hylton Cleaver

ARCHING his back a little, dipping his pen with an annoying preciseness into the ink, Stephen P. H. Moreton began to write neatly in the journal which he had always kept under lock and key. He would fill several pages, and when he had finished he would cut these pages out and post them; then nobody could get at them but the authorities.

At the top of the page he wrote:

'Whosoever first reads this statement is advised to take it without delay to Scotland Yard. The reasons will be obvious.' Then he signed his name, and did so with a certain flourish and some pride, because in a very little while his name would be exceedingly well known. Or so he hoped.

After that he began his statement, and this is what he wrote:

There is a weekend party in progress here and it is not a great success; for one thing, there is at it a man whom everyone dislikes, to wit, myself. I have been told that I am something between an excellent anarchist and a villainous king, and I still recall that tribute with self-satisfaction. But the failure of this house-party can be traced far beyond my presence. It is due in great part to the persistent inability of modern people to amuse themselves, coupled with their insatiable desire for entertainment.

There seems to be only one topic of conversation: 'What are we going to do now?' And nobody can give any answer without starting disagreement.

This is a country house, and my sisters—poor crushed women—are hostesses, my weak-willed brother and myself are hosts, and for once the party was my own idea; this has taken everybody by surprise, and they are wondering why I suggested it, and what they are supposed to do. They are all sitting about and waiting for something to happen, and sometimes they catch me eyeing them, which makes them feel uncomfortable. My power to make people feel uncomfortable is a great source of amusement to me, especially in trains.

If they only knew it, I suggested this party because I myself wanted to be entertained, and for a very good reason. Three months ago I was sentenced to death by a man who pronounced judgement in a consulting-room in Upper Wimpole Street. Kindly but firmly he diagnosed a tumour on the brain, and when he found what type of man I was, and that I insisted on the truth, he allowed me to drag out of him the essential fact that three months was likely to see the end of me. Well, those three months are up to the day, and I had earmarked this as my last weekend. Instead of turning out a wonderful party for my benefit, the whole affair is falling singularly flat. Of course they know nothing of this, beyond the fact that periodically I have headaches; to these they put down my nasty temper. If I were addicted to self-pity I should think the failure of this party a rather pathetic thing. Fortunately, I dislike pity of any sort, but can stand anyone's pity better than my own.

I have come indoors because I can see that my hand is to be forced. They cannot amuse themselves and they will not amuse me. I am host, and so as my last gesture I must make plans against my will for the entertainment of my own guests, in which case it shall be the best I can provide. The weekend, in spite of their incompetence, shall be unforgettable. There shall be a murder.

I have never trusted other people to do for me the things I could do better for myself, and I do not see why the leading character in a murder case should necessarily be the murderer; the whole thing is surely better devised if he be the murdered man; if, in fact, he has carried out all the arrangements to suit his own requirements, with what they call a good sense of the theatre.

I am due to die, and I do not like facing the probability that I shall do so in an untidy manner, by passing out in a Tube train or falling down in the street. I cannot bear the thought of lying about waiting to be identified, whilst a morbid crowd peers down at me pending the arrival of the ambulance. I prefer to end it myself and in my own way. I will be found dramatically dead, and the guests need ask no longer 'What shall we do?' They can apply themselves to the exciting task of eluding the keen suspicion, that they *have done something*—namely, *this*. It isn't going to look like suicide.

In a sense I suppose my demise will mean the end of the party; but not immediately, and not, at all events, tonight. The police will see that nobody leaves until they are satisfied, and this will be a matter of some difficulty, because this is a party at which anybody might quite easily and willingly have killed me. On which of them, I wonder, will the guilt be fastened?

Arthur Bush has written me a letter, saying: 'One day I believe I shall choke you, Stephen; and how I shall enjoy it!'

Then there is Barbara Cardell. I am attracted to women who think me repulsive; they signify a challenge which I seldom decline. I am not addicted to amours of a facile sort, but I enjoy the experience of capturing a woman who is terrified of my touch. For this reason I gladly admit in this last chapter of my diary that Barbara Cardell has been responsible for my most thrilling recent moments; not long ago *she* breathed in my ear: 'If you don't let me alone I'll kill you.'

Tom, my own younger brother, owes me packets of money, and he is white with indignation this afternoon because I have been telling people so, and there is a girl here whom he wanted to impress. And there is Mrs Hartley Case, who has a weakness for unpleasant men. A curious woman and, I am afraid, a spiteful one.

The question will be asked why I should write this statement. The fact is, I don't want things to go to the point of hanging, and I would rather feel that I had been delightfully clever. This confession will therefore be discovered in just the right time, and he or she will be saved from the gallows by the very man they despised.

The difficulty is what to do with these pages when I have cut them out. Before now, rather than carry valuable documents about with me, I have posted them to myelf, but if I posted these they would be opened too soon after my death; the same would apply if

I addressed the letter to one of my guests or to the police, and so I have decided on an ingenious idea. I will entrust them to the postal authorities for some time by addressing the envelope to an imaginary person at an imaginary address; in due course the envelope will be scrawled across and returned to the Dead Letter Office, where it will be opened prior to its return to me; and this will occur, I calculate, in anything from three days to three weeks—certainly before a hanging could take place.

The next question, naturally, is the cause of death.

I must rule out any method usually employed in suicide, and this precludes drowning, gas, hanging, and poison. I must aim at sudden death, and the poison used by a murderer is generally gradual and most unpleasant.

This practically limits me to shooting.

I have a revolver, but there are two objections to the use of it.

The first is the fact that self-shooting is self-evident by the nature of the bullet-hole, and the second is the difficulty of disposing of the revolver.

So, I must either create evidence of a struggle, or I must be shot in the back.

Can a man shoot himself in the back?

Experiments have satisfied me that it is none too easy to shoot oneself in the back of the head, but not too difficult to do so in the back of the body. On the other hand, a shot in the small of the back is not necessarily fatal or instantaneous, so I must make sure that the bullet goes slap through my heart. Having achieved this end, how am I to release my fingers from the revolver, and erase the fingerprints? I could guard against the latter problem by wearing gloves, but I can't help feeling that I should look rather silly lying dead in gloves. And, in any case, how am I to dispose of the revolver?

I have turned this over in my mind innumerable times, and have hit upon and discarded all kinds of schemes. I have thought of fixing the revolver into some kind of niche or grip, and operating it by a string, but the revolver would remain where it was and would be easily spotted.

Then I thought of shooting myself alongside a bucket of white-wash in the hope that as my finger pulled the trigger and my hand relaxed its grip the revolver would drop into the bucket and would

not be found for some days. You would be surprised at the curious
ways in which one's mind works on a problem of this sort, and the
far-fetched ideas that have struck me. You see, I want to hide the
revolver merely for a day or two. Eventually, it must, of course, be
found, wherever it is, but in the meantime I shall at least have
entertained the guests. I cannot outline here all the ways and means
I have examined, and, in any case, one of my headaches is coming
on, and so I must be quick. I should hate to think that I were to be
found after all this preparation, lying on the carpet with this
unfinished statement on my table, and the pen beside it. But I have
arrived at this conclusion, and though it sounds at first rather like
the contraption of a caricaturist, I must devise some kind of pulley
or strong spring which, as my hand slackens its grip before
becoming rigid, will jerk the revolver out of my fingers, flinging it
somewhere else.

If I can devise some kind of strong, elastic band, or coil spring,
and fit the revolver to one end of it, I could stretch this to the
uttermost at the moment of firing, certain that as the tension of my
hand relaxed the revolver would be jerked away. I have felt so
confident that this idea must not be lightly dismissed that I have
been looking about in the workshops and garage for a spare spring,
or something that would serve the purpose. The next problem is, to
what is the *other* end of this spring or pulley to be attached, so that
it will not be seen too easily? If I shot myself in the open I could
arrange for the revolver to be flung by it over a hedge or a wall, or
even up into a tree, but I am beginning to feel that it will be safest
to have it dragged out of my hand into some *recess*. The most
sensible place seems to me to be the loft in the workshops. I can
attach one end of a spring to a ring in a rafter just out of sight,
lengthen this with a piece of cord, and so arrange my position that
the revolver will be shot up into the loft and left there, the moment
I fall. In fact, this plan so pleases me that I am sure I shall find some
way of working it out when I get there. In any case those who read
this letter will judge whether I have been successful in getting rid of
the gun, and I hope I shall give them a run for their money. If only
I could devise a sort of nightmare catapult, I could have the revolver
sent a tremendous distance, and my only regret then would be that
I should never be able to see it travelling.

This, then, is my farewell, and I go without remorse.

I am not unamused at the belief that the disclosures in this letter will embarrass one or two of those mentioned. I dare say I shall be found with a twisted smile on my lips and my eyes turned towards the revolver's hiding place, though they won't realize that my expression is their one important clue. At any rate, no one can say my brain was affected; nobody, surely, ever planned an entertainment so meticulously as the perfect host. The only possibilities of error which I foresee are the failure of the revolver to hide itself, and the remote chance that this letter may be delivered to an empty house and left to lie there indefinitely.

STEPHEN P. H. MORETON

'I wish,' said Pamela Viner to her husband, 'somebody would very sweetly tell me what persuaded us to come here.'

'The fact,' replied her husband, 'that like everybody else we are sorry for his sisters. And the only thing is to put up with him and to pretend he isn't here.'

'You might as well try to pretend you hadn't seen a ghost sit down in a vacant place at dinner. Stephen is the official spectre at any feast he sits at. He's one of those men you never see till you're on top of him and then he always makes you jump. Perhaps you men don't notice the way he has of trying to make nice women hate him by the way he looks at them out of the corner of his eye.'

'One day,' said Billy, 'someone will fill up his eye for him, and it may yet be me.'

He paused and felt for his cigarette case.

'Come up to the house. They're slow bringing out the drinks, and that's one thing you ought at least to get plenty of at this place.'

It was precisely twenty minutes after the Viners had gone in that everybody heard a sudden echoing report which was at first put down as a car backfiring. After a moment somebody did add:

'Or it may be Hugh Macfarlane after his blessed rabbits. In which case he must have hit one for the first time: he didn't let it have both barrels.'

The guests continued, after that, to lounge about and to toy with cocktails, conversation being slow and a little forced, for when people are bored they are inclined to attempt ambiguous and pseudo-clever answers to the most ordinary questions; anything to create a little laughter.

It was dark, and one or two were settling down to bridge or billiards when the Moretons' chauffeur, coming back to duty and going towards the garage, stopped at the workshop for some tools, and switched on the light. There he remained with a stare, at first startled, then morbidly fascinated. Slowly he advanced across the uncovered flooring and halted, with stooping shoulders and limp arms, peering down at closer quarters until, against his inclination, he forced himself to reach down and touch that sprawling body; he had an unpleasant feeling that if it moved or emitted a sound of any sort he would catch at his breath and fall over backwards.

But it didn't move, and it made no sound. He tried to turn it over, and realized the significance of its dead weight; then his eyes became fascinated by the hole in Mr Stephen's back and the blood-soaked area round it, and he looked down at his own fingers in distaste. Breathing heavily, he straightened and scuttled out of that building, and he ran all the way along the gravel to the house.

Some of them came running back; at least, they started running, but as they neared the workshop it seemed as though, considering the man was dead, this showed some vague disrespect, and they dropped to a rapid and determined walk, pushed in one by one, and collected in the doorway, whilst Tom Moreton went weirdly ahead and dropped upon one knee. From the back Billy Viner said: 'We heard a shot, you know. This, then, is what it was . . . we thought it was a car . . . or Hugh Macfarlane shooting rabbits.'

And Arthur Bush, going ahead to stand by Tom, said, almost curtly, because he spoke in a curt way when disturbed:

'I suppose he didn't shoot himself?'

From the back Mrs Hartley Case, who was very still and very white, replied:

'He certainly never needed to do that. Anyone would have saved him the trouble.'

'No man,' said Billy Viner, 'shoots himself in the back. He must have been doing something here, and somebody surprised him, and fired before he could turn.'

'Stephen,' said Mrs Hartley Case, 'had a flair, of course, for turning his back on people.'

Tom, white and shaky, turned Stephen over; there *was* a twisted smile on his lips and his eyes *were* open.

'Better leave everything,' said Tom. 'See that my sisters don't come here. Will somebody go and telephone? We'll have to get the police, and tell them to bring a doctor. Better keep everything as it is, or the place will be all over fingerprints.'

The guests and the family had been collected in the big room on the ground floor. They were confronted by two plain-clothes representatives of the police, and an inspector and a constable in uniform. The constable kept dutifully in the background, staring at his superiors. The county superintendent was proceeding with his questions as if a murder were a necessary and important part of anybody's daily life, and must be briskly faced.

There were no tears. Stephen's sisters had been inured by life with him, and they stood at the back, dry-eyed and old before their years, crushed and apologetic. They heard the police fix the time of the shot and catechize each guest as to his movements at that time; they checked these notes up as far as possible, and made little notes and now and then corrections.

Before the guests were allowed to disperse even for a short time, the police carried out a careful search of the house, workshop, and grounds. They were looking for a revolver. In the workshop they also looked for other clues, but found nothing to intrigue them, and the body was removed after photographs had been taken; then they locked the workshop. In the dark they examined the paths, but the gravel had by now been generally kicked about, and the superintendent had to resign himself in the end to the probability that this would be a lengthy business. There were a rain water-butt, a smouldering bonfire, bushes, and ditches to be searched with every care. This would go on all night and all tomorrow.

The guests sat up late, talking. In general they could say little, but in private they said a lot; and they supposed the police would get somebody in the end. Murder always came out, and they expected it would turn out to be one of them, but which? The more inquisitive kept looking for guilty expressions on the faces of the others, but people have very different ways of showing or concealing their emotions. To one extent they were unanimous, and so were the police. He obviously hadn't killed himself. This was a triumph of the first order for the ingenuity of Stephen Moreton, and one can imagine him still grinning where he lay.

Next day the police dragged the pond, and Stephen's revolver was found at the bottom of it.

That day the police held another little court. The revolver, for everyone to see, lay upon the table.

Did anyone identify it?

Tom Moreton identified it. It was Stephen's own revolver. So far as Tom knew it had never been out of Stephen's keeping. Why had Stephen carried a revolver? Was it licensed? No, Tom believed it wasn't licensed. So far as he knew Stephen preferred to carry it unofficially and risk the consequences; he carried it, Tom supposed, because he had made many enemies.

Were any of his enemies among this party?

Tom shrugged. He imagined they were everywhere. The superintendent pointed out two interesting facts. The revolver was Stephen's own, only one bullet had been fired from it, and that had proved to be the bullet which had been extracted from the body and compared with the rifling and the calibre of the revolver. The police began to take a grimmer interest; there was rubbing of chins and scratching of hard heads. They intended to find out, come what might, who had known that there was that revolver in the house. This was their great mistake and Stephen's great success. They should have tried to find out how Stephen could have died by his own hand in the workshop, and yet transferred the revolver to the duck-pond.

Days passed and they were no nearer a solution. The guests went to their homes. The space given to the mystery in the papers grew noticeably less; soon a mere paragraph reminded readers that the police were pursuing their enquiries. Scotland Yard had been called in, so far without result. The guests met one another sometimes at lunch or tea and talked the whole thing over. They even telephoned when they heard rumours, but these were always only rumours.

And then the great day for Stephen dawned, and a clerk in the Dead Letter Office at the GPO arrived, in the course of routine, at what appeared to be an ordinary letter, 'incorrectly addressed' to a person 'not known'. He opened the letter to note the name and address of the sender, and found the last few pages neatly cut out of Stephen's journal. He then beheld the cautionary lines that Stephen had written first; so he rose from his desk, and went to bend over another clerk's desk, where they read the script together, after which the first clerk solemnly proceeded down the room and took it to his chief.

Eventually that document reached the police, they studied it with incredulous comprehension, and then they looked at one another, and they said:

'Did you see any spring or pulley in the rafters—and besides, how did he fling it into the *pond*—thirty or forty yards away? Look here, we'd better go down there again and check this up——'

And a fast car was ordered.

Two of the guests at that weekend party met later in the week. These were Hugh Macfarlane and Billy Viner, and it was Hugh who called on Viner.

He said: 'Have you seen the early evening papers, Viner? There's an extraordinary headline and a letter published—parts of it at any rate—supposed to have been written by Stephen.'

'Yes,' Viner said, 'I've seen it, and I read the letter.'

'It's a confession—unless they've cut out bits that alter the whole sense of it.'

'Oh, yes, it's a confession, and it's typical of Stephen. The only thing nobody can explain is how he got the revolver flung so far away, and what he did it *with*.'

Hugh had been walking restlessly about the room; he stopped now with feet apart and hands on hips, looking at Viner seriously.

'Well, he took pains enough to make it foolproof. The only error he foresaw was that the letter might not be opened in time—that and the doubts he had about getting rid of the revolver. But he was all right there. The gun disappeared all right and the letter turned up at the proper time. Do you know what he entirely overlooked, though?'

Viner shook his head. He was eyeing Macfarlane curiously. He thought Macfarlane looked rather strained.

'There's something I want to tell you, Viner. I'd like to tell somebody and you're a chap I can trust. I was the last chap to see Stephen alive. I know more than I told them.'

'I dare say we all do.'

'But this is vital—and I've got to tell someone now. I don't know whether you know it, but I'm in love with Barbara Cardell.'

Viner looked at him quizzically. 'You surprise me.'

'I am, Viner—I have been for ages. And because of what she told me *I'd* gone that day to try to find Stephen and have it out with him. I was going through the garden in a hell of a temper when I noticed him go into the workshop, and as he didn't come out I followed him and stood in the doorway and looked in. I realize now that he was fiddling with a cord, and in fact a spring was left on the bench and could be seen there afterwards, though nobody thought anything of it. I couldn't see what he was doing then, and so I just said:

'"Stephen——"

'He didn't look round. He simply answered in that beastly voice of his:

'"Please go away, I'm busy."

'But I said "Stephen" again, a bit more impatiently, and then I snapped, "I want to talk to you about Barbara Cardell," and at that he said, in the sort of mutter of anyone who's very busy doing something:

'"I can't imagine anybody having much to say about that young woman."

'As he said that, Viner, I saw something lying on a table. It was his revolver, and something induced me to pick it up. I was going to show I meant business, and so I held it with a distinct satisfaction at the idea of it pointing at him, and said:

'"You'd better turn round, Stephen."

'And then he seemed to think that over and suddenly he gave an uncanny gurgle, like a man going a little mad, but he lifted his head a little and seemed to stare in front of him, and then he said:

'"Good Lord, have you picked up my revolver?"

'I didn't answer, and he went on: "Now, that's the one possibility I never thought of . . . *never*. In that case, *by all means shoot*. Shoot now. Right in the back, but for your own sake and mine do shoot to kill. I don't want to be winged or lamed and left here for you to have another shot at . . . and don't ever say after this that I had no sense of humour."

'I waited. I *couldn't* shoot, and when he realized I was dithering and wanting him to look at me, he suddenly snapped out: "Go on, for pity's sake, get on with it. You never keep men waiting on the gallows! Try to remember, man alive, what you've come here for. You've come about a girl . . . if you don't shoot I'll have to tell you some of the things I did. You don't want me to *drive* you to it, do you? Or do you? Good Heavens, I'll tell you some things about her if you like!" And he did, Viner, all sorts of terrible things.'

Hugh stopped and came close to Viner.

'*I* know now what he was doing. . . . It *wasn't the truth* . . . he was telling me all that to drive me to it; he wanted me to fit in with the whole scheme like the last part of a jigsaw puzzle . . . and so *he drove me to it*. He stood there, with his back to me, and kept on talking—getting more scandalous all the time—and suddenly something snapped in me, and I fired, all in a second. I did fire—and now I realize I hit him just where he wanted to be hit. . . . And he crumpled up and gurgled once, then dropped and lay there, and I stayed just long enough to make sure he was dead, then I got out of it, and I got rid of the revolver. And when they were cross-examining me afterwards I told the police I was with Barbara at that time and she said that was so.'

Viner was at his sideboard pouring out stiff whiskies, and now he turned and he grimly handed one to Hugh.

'Better drink this, and pull yourself together. You've told somebody now and you'll feel better. But remember this much. Never in your life get tight. When men get tight they talk. This will die down and be forgotten; you'll be as right as rain, as long as you can keep from talking. You had the great satisfaction of shooting a man who deserved it, and you're going to get away with it—by kind permission of the man you shot.'

He nodded and he motioned to the glass.

'Go on—drink that—and then forget it.'

In View of the Audience

Marguerite Steen

GEORGE BREWSTER picked up his hat, gloves, walking-stick, a seven-and-sixpenny thriller and, finally, himself from the floor of the first-class compartment, assembled the units with as much dignity as he could muster, decided that dignity, in the circumstances, was a little ridiculous, and ended by grinning at the solitary witness of the pantomime turn which he, involuntarily, had provided.

'A near thing,' he admitted, regarding with sympathy the remains of what had been, a few seconds previously, a goodish hat, and now, owing to his own ill-timed impetuosity, more nearly resembled a grey felt pancake than anything he could remember having seen before.

'Ah, yes—awfully near!' gasped the little man, who sat at the further end of the compartment. To look at him, one might have imagined that it was he, rather than George Brewster, who had just succeeded, at imminent risk to life and limb, in boarding the train as the end carriages swung past the platform. His smooth, straw-coloured face was overlaid with pallor, and he blinked his eyelids so rapidly that it was not until some time had passed that Brewster had the opportunity of noticing that the eyes themselves were rather remarkable, of a surprisingly light turquoise blue.

'Excuse me,' murmured the little man, a few moments later. 'Would you mind—so very much—if we had the windows *both* up for a minute or two? We're just coming to the tunnel.'

'Pleasure,' mumbled George Brewster, dropping his paper to comply with the timid request. 'Afraid I gave you rather a shock,' he roared, above the tunnel thunder of the train.

'Oh, not at all,' came the protestant squeak of the other's voice. They did not attempt to pursue the conversation further until the train ran again into open country; when, to Brewster's surprise, the little man ventured, diffidently:

'I suppose—that is to say—would you care for me to lend you a brush? The floors of these carriages are not kept as they ought to be—by any manner of means.'

'Good lord, no, they aren't, are they?' said Brewster, perceiving for the first time the abominable smear of dust down the crease of his trousers. 'I'd be very much obliged—if you've got such a thing handy.'

His companion opened a dressing bag and produced a brush, which Brewster proceeded to put to its proper use.

'By the way,' he said, carelessly, while so employed, 'have you any idea what time this train gets into Crewe?'

'Crewe?' repeated the little man, with a puzzled stare. 'Did you say Crewe? Dear me, I'm very sorry; I'm afraid this isn't the Crewe train at all. How very unfortunate!'

Swaying with the train, Brewster gaped speechlessly.

'The first stop,' explained the little man, punctiliously, 'is at a place called Coalford, in the Midlands. It's rather an odd run, this one,' he went on in a conversational voice. 'In fact, one might call it an example of the pleasing whimsy which now and again takes possession even of the railway companies! One can hardly understand why a place like Coalford should have a non-stop special of its own. We leave the main line at Stafford——'

'Good lord, man,' gasped George Brewster, weakly, 'are you certain? The Crewe train always starts from that platform.'

'Not now,' corrected the other. 'Dear, dear me, I'm so sorry about it!' He seemed to adopt the whole affair as a matter of personal oversight. 'Really,' he continued with deep concern, 'you could hardly be coming to a more unfortunate place than Coalford! There's no main-line train for three hours after this gets in——'

'I suppose I can get a car,' interrupted Brewster, scowlingly.

'You may,' said the little man, doubtfully, 'or you may not. I, personally, should be very sorry to entrust myself to any of Coalford's means of locomotion for a long-distance journey. I'm terribly afraid—you see, Coalford is a dreadfully primitive place. In fact, it's quite a frightful place. A sort of little down-and-out industrial town. I've just bought a theatre there,' he concluded, startlingly.

In spite of his anger and perturbation, Brewster could not help being arrested by the final words. They completed his conviction that his travelling companion, although pleasant, was slightly mad. It was annoying to be shut up with a mad person for an hour and a half—it must be at least that before they got into the Midlands. He said, huffily:

'Sounds rather a venture, doesn't it? I didn't think any provincial theatres were flourishing at present; and if the place is as you describe——!'

'It was very cheap,' confessed his companion, naïvely. 'And I've got an idea of turning it into a picture-house. I think if we could manage to get hold of one or two really good films—one of Maureen Maguire's, for instance——'

The frown on George Brewster's forehead smoothed itself away, and the irritation from his mind. His whole soul expanded with a ridiculous brotherliness towards the man whom, a few seconds before, he had regarded as an unmitigated bore. It is an incontrovertible fact that the average person regards any purveyor of unpleasant news with a feeling of unjust resentment, and in this respect George Brewster was very average. But, in common with ninety per cent of the audiences who had seen the Magnificent All-British Super-Drama, *Piccadilly Princess*, he was convinced that he was in love with the heroine, Maureen Maguire; and the mention of the lady of his heart, the totally unexpected opportunity it afforded of discoursing upon a topic near his soul, completely banished his former unworthy thoughts of his companion.

'You certainly ought to make money with Maureen Maguire,' he agreed, eagerly. 'Now, tell me: have you ever noticed——'

'I like drama,' put in the little man, dreamily.

'She's got the whole lot of them whacked for drama!' beamed George Brewster. 'Shearer, Garbo, Dietrich——'

'I wasn't thinking of screen drama, I'm afraid,' was the disappointing response. 'The drama of real life: that's the thing for me. I'm afraid I don't think a great deal of film drama: in fact, I'm not interested in films, as films, at all.'

'Your point of view is interesting,' said George Brewster, a trifle stiffly, for he resented being arrested in full flight upon a topic on which he felt he could do himself justice. 'You know, it's curious,' he could not help adding, 'but I should never have connected you with the theatre in any way—acting, or management.'

'I never looked well in an astrachan collar,' smiled the little man, wanly. 'And cigars make me sick.' He paused to extract a card from his note-case, which he handed to George Brewster. 'Not,' he added, with an air of modest disclaimer, 'that it will convey anything to you.'

George made the polite noises one uses to disguise the fact that a name actually does convey nothing at all. 'Henry Morpeth' was engraved upon the card, and an address that one connects vaguely with the region about Portman Square. He volunteered the information that his own name was Brewster—George Brewster; which was received by his companion with a courteous inclination of the head.

'No, I suppose I don't look much like a manager,' said Mr Morpeth, regretfully. 'Although,' he added, 'I once wrote a play. Still, that doesn't make one a manager, does it?'

Brewster agreed it didn't. By now he was quite convinced that Henry Morpeth, if not positively crazy, was definitely feeble-minded. To humour him, he asked, on the kindly contemptuous note that one adopts towards the breed:

'Ever have your play produced?'

'Oh, yes,' said Mr Morpeth, gently. 'Maureen Maguire played in it. That would be—let me see—twenty years ago.'

George Brewster nearly shot out of his seat: an involuntary betrayal of his feelings which was not lost upon Mr Morpeth.

'Wonderful woman,' he murmured, the smile playing once more across his pale, somewhat foolish-looking face. 'One of the immortals, I should say—really—what? Naturally I was very much in love with her. She was about eighteen at the time; I a trifle older—well, maybe nine or ten years older. Romantic, you know, like all young men in those days.'

A kind of depression had fallen upon George Brewster; he made the simultaneous discovery that his feet were cold and that he was thirsty. He was, also, furious with himself for having been such a muttonheaded idiot as to get on the wrong train and ready to gnash his teeth at the prospect of spending three hours in such a place as Henry Morpeth had described.

'Perhaps,' said Mr Morpeth, diffidently, 'if you have nothing better to do—that is, if you really can't find a means of getting away from Coalford until the main-line connection comes in—you might care to look at my newly acquired property with me?'

Brewster grunted conventional thanks and dug his hands in his pockets. He began, under his breath, in a mournful, valedictory fashion, to whistle the first bars of the theme-song from *Piccadilly Princess*.

'Of course,' continued Mr Morpeth, 'it may be no good at all. Quite useless. Only fit to be pulled down. Deterioration, you know, and all that. Dry rot. Rats. What?'

Involuntarily, Brewster ceased his whistling and stared.

'Do you mean to say you've bought a theatre—in a place like Coalford—without the slightest idea what condition it is in?' He began, against his will, to find something interesting in what looked like large-scale idiocy.

'It really was *very* cheap,' deprecated Mr Morpeth. 'I happened to hear it was for sale—and I had a little money by me—so I instructed my solicitors to buy. You see, they couldn't ask very much for a property that had been lying empty getting on for twenty years; could they?'

'I should say not,' snorted Mr Brewster, his commercial instinct rising in outrage in the presence of such foolishness.

'No,' said Mr Morpeth, thoughtfully. 'It's really very queer. You never know which way a thing like that will strike the public. You know what people are: how they'll go and stare for hours at the outside of a house where a crime's been committed. It might, of course, have been the making of the place. Instead—for some reason or other—they simply sheered off. Funny, isn't it?'

'Something queer took place in the theatre?' suggested Brewster, as the other broke off.

'Oh, yes. Really. Devilish queer,' murmured the little man, softly; he wiped away the vapour with his cuff, and stared through the window at a rain-sodden landscape. 'Horrid weather we're having, for the time of year, don't you think?'

A very odd feeling began to creep over George Brewster. He was not an imaginative young man, neither was he given to apprehensions; yet the rhythmical beat of the wheels over the metals suddenly seemed, to his startled fancy, to be charged with some kind of mysterious purpose, faintly sinister, that crystallized in the innocuous person of his travelling companion.

He leaned back in his corner and scowled forensically at the profile of Henry Morpeth. Any less suggestive personality could hardly be imagined; a small, quiet, conventional-looking man, with a middle-class timorousness in the parting of his hair. The last person on earth, one would have said, to indulge any impulse, prudent or imprudent; cautious, humble, self-effacing, of comfortable but not excessive means. Possibly a retired Government official; his age might be anywhere between thirty-five and fifty-five. His face was smooth and unlined, but the skin itself had a look almost of antiquity. A furious curiosity took possession of George Brewster, which he controlled in his next remark.

'So you're thinking of turning it into a picture-house?'

'Well, yes, rather; if it isn't too dilapidated to do anything with at all. You see, it struck me it would be amusing to fetch Maureen Maguire back into the place where I first met her—twenty years ago.'

Again the cold, uncomfortable twinge passed through George Brewster. Apart from the shock experienced by a young man when he learns that the charmer whom he has regarded as being in the heyday of her youth and beauty is approaching her fortieth year, there was something—some hidden shade of meaning that seemed to slide beneath his companion's mild words.

'I suppose, Mr Brewster, you never by any chance happened to write a play?' The little man's voice was apologetic, as though he felt that he was, merely by making the suggestion, attributing a wholly unjustifiable indiscretion to his unknown companion.

'Well, no,' said Brewster. 'What sort of a play was it?' he added, with an effort; he did not really want to know, but Morpeth was making so obvious an effort to be agreeable one could not but meet him half way.

'Oh, it was really a very bad play,' he confessed, hastily. 'Very bad indeed. It was supposed to be a thriller. It was, in fact, a sort of pot-pourri of all the thrillers I had ever read. I was, in fact, I still am, very fond of thrillers; a taste, I venture to think, you share with me?' he added, with a questioning glance at the book which lay between them.

'I must say I enjoy a good detective yarn as much as anything,' admitted Brewster, uneasily, without knowing why.

'Only, of course, nothing that happens in books is ever quite so interesting as real life,' qualified Mr Morpeth. 'To begin with, the mystery, if there is a mystery, is always solved. Now—perhaps you won't agree with me—the best mysteries are those for which there is no possible solution.'

Brewster frowned; he had an orderly and business-like mind; he detested leaving a thing unfinished. He disagreed, verbally, with Mr Morpeth.

'Well, perhaps I'm wrong,' said the latter, obligingly. 'But I confess to a great weakness for the unsolved mystery. It always— how shall I put it?—*gratified* my sense of—well, I dare say it sounds ridiculous, but if I might call it my artistic sense?—that the affair at the Coalford Theatre Royal was never cleared up: in spite of the fact that everybody in the audience saw it take place—just as clearly as I can see you now.' He gave a little apologetic cough—his whole life seemed to be tuned to a key of apology—and concluded, 'But no doubt I'm boring you. All rather before your time—what? Let's see—we shall be in in a quarter of an hour or so. Singularly unattractive scenery, what?'

A sordid panorama, common to the coal-mining districts, lay about them; beneath the filthy haze of smoke stretched a squalid network of mean streets, and clusters of chimneys poked their ugly black fingers up at the sky of yellowish grey, from which descended a drizzle that laid a slimy polish upon roofs and pavements. A little down-and-out industrial town, Mr Morpeth called it; Brewster agreed with the description. Even from the train one could perceive the ugly languor of poverty in the movements of figures about the streets.

The thought that, but for this chance meeting, he would have been condemned to three hours' solitude in such a place, sent a shudder down Brewster's spine. He could imagine what the station, or the hotels, would be like.

He was now positive that Morpeth was raving mad to purchase a theatre in such a town. Something called the Coliseum raised its leprous façade above the railway line: it carried a few tattered posters of old-fashioned films; its upper windows were black with grime, its woodwork had obviously had no acquaintance with the paint-brush for many years. Apparently, Coalford could not support one picture-house, let alone two.

Brewster turned a look of recrimination upon his companion, and was startled by the curious change which had come over the aspect of Mr Henry Morpeth. His thin, colourless face was twitching with excitement; smiles came and went about his nervously moving lips; his turquoise-blue eyes glittered with light.

'I used to live here, you know,' he babbled, 'years ago. I was living here when I wrote my play—the one Maureen Maguire acted in. It was a frightfully important thing for me. Of course, no one knew how important it was—except for Maureen and Caryll.' He gave a little laugh. 'How it would surprise—both of them! If they knew I'd bought the theatre.'

When they were out upon the sticky, mud-printed platform, and Brewster had sent a necessary wire or two, Morpeth turned to him eagerly.

'Do you mind walking? It is only a step or two, and we can share my umbrella.'

Henry Morpeth walked with the quick, short steps of a man with a definite object before him: holding his head down, hunching his shoulders, driving his spare body between the dull crowds of the pavements with such sure effect that presently Brewster was left behind him—plodding along, with coat-collar turned up, rain trickling from his hat-brim, and a murderous feeling in his heart. What a devilish hole! It actually made one feel poor oneself, he was reflecting, when he saw Morpeth beckoning him from the corner of a murky-looking alley which took them out of the main traffic stream into one of those unspeakably dreary backwaters wherein, usually, are situated stage-doors.

'I have the key,' muttered Henry Morpeth in his undertone of excitement. He fumbled with a latch, the door itself creaked open, and they passed into a darkness which drove chill to the very marrow of George Brewster's bones.

'Mind how you come,' said Morpeth's voice out of the darkness. 'You'll soon be used to it—your eyes, I mean. There *are* some windows, somewhere; I suppose they're covered up with dirt. Look out!—here's the door on to the stage; it's come partly off its hinges. Dear, dear, how tiresome! It's all right, I'm holding it up for you. Go straight ahead. Now you're on the stage itself.'

Gradually darkness was dissolving into twilight round George Brewster; he saw himself standing in the middle of a vast, empty space, with another space, blacker, on his left. And, almost simultaneously, he got the impression that of all places in the world there is none more evilly eerie than an empty, deserted theatre. A rat whisked across at an angle and vanished between the edges of some flats stacked in the scene-dock at the back of the stage. The boards he stood upon crackled with rottenness; things like immense, obscene cobwebs—he supposed they had once been scenery—hung down from above. And over all was the fearful, penetrating cold. It was a beast of a place. He loathed it.

'Look out for those trapdoors,' Henry Morpeth was saying in a voice louder and sharper than the one he had previously used. 'I should think the hinges are gone: you don't want to take an unexpected trip into the mezzanine, do you?'

'I don't want to take a trip anywhere,' snapped Brewster. 'I'm sorry, Morpeth—and it's no business of mine; but someone made the biggest mug in creation of you. The only thing this is fit for is burning. It's—it's——' He was going to add 'haunted', but was ashamed of the word. As though he had spoken it, Morpeth answered quietly:

'You feel it's ghostly, don't you? That's what they complained of, I believe; I mean the companies who came, afterwards, to play here. Of course, you're standing, as a matter of fact, on just about the place where the murder happened.'

George Brewster ached all over with the effort he made not to take a sideways leap from the spot where he was standing. Instead, he achieved a laugh, which went echoing horridly out into the empty auditorium.

'So there was a murder, was there? I must say I think your taste's a bit morbid.'

'In full view of the audience,' said the voice of Morpeth behind his shoulder. 'And nobody moved a muscle. You see, quite naturally, they thought it was part of the play.'

'Oh, hell!' said Brewster, feeling his nerves cracking up. 'I suppose you've brought me here to tell me about it. Can't we find a place a bit less—a bit more agreeable, for your story?'

'Just through there,' said Morpeth, pointing obligingly to a dark pit of a doorway, 'there's the dressing-room where they found

Peters—that was the ASM—I don't know if you're accustomed to these theatrical terms, but ASM stands for assistant stage-manager—bound and gagged after the murder took place. He died, incidentally, as well—of suffocation. I always think that was a mistake; I mean it wasn't intended. The person who committed the murder trussed Peters up closer than he intended—no one had anything against Peters. I don't doubt there'll be a chair in his dressing-room; we can go in there, if you like.'

'Thanks very much,' said Brewster, shortly. 'I think perhaps this will do after all.'

'Well, I'll go and get the chairs,' said Morpeth, calmly, and vanished into what resembled the mouth of the Black Hole of Calcutta, leaving Brewster alone upon the dim stage. He would have given all he possessed, at that moment, to turn round and walk straight out of the theatre. The few minutes which elapsed before Morpeth's return were an eternity filled with the most detestable and humiliating fears. Nor were these entirely banished by the return of his companion: for once again Brewster became aware of that underlying queerness that ran like an undercurrent of darkness beneath Morpeth's mild demeanour. Morpeth sat down and linked his hands about his knees.

'It takes rather an effort of the imagination,' he offered, peering at Brewster, 'to see Maureen Maguire on this stage, now?'

'She wouldn't like the rats,' mumbled Brewster, seeing out of the corner of his eye a particularly large, aggressive specimen.

'She didn't then,' said Morpeth, quickly. 'Caryll used to put them in her dressing-room, so as to scare her, while they were rehearsing.'

'Unpleasant fellow, evidently, this Caryll,' observed Brewster.

'Oh, very!' agreed Morpeth, casually. 'He was murdered, of course.'

'Look here,' said Brewster, suddenly 'although this allusive style of yours is very—what's it?—provocative, hadn't you better get down to brass tacks and tell me the whole tale, straight through?'

'It's an odd thing,' returned Morpeth, with his look of rather foolish surprise. 'That's a thing I've always had the greatest difficulty in doing. Other things snatch at my attention. I could never, for instance, write a novel; and perhaps that's why I couldn't write a decent play. However, I'll do my best.

'You see, Caryll bought my play. I'd written it, of course, for Maureen Maguire, because I'd seen her in some other show—a melodrama, I think it was—and I suppose I'd fallen for that little tragic way of hers: it reminded me rather of a wood-anemone that has been beaten down by rain. Excuse me, won't you? That sort of thing will strike you as old-fashioned, but I find the greatest difficulty in moving with the times.

'Caryll bought my play—I think he gave me five pounds for it. Not excessive; but as things turned out—I mean to say, when I found out what a rotten, lying, yellow cheat Caryll was I thought I was pretty lucky to have got a fiver out of him.' For some reason, the very coolness of the tone in which Morpeth affixed these opprobrious epithets to the name of Caryll sent a shiver down Brewster's back.

'Then they came down here to rehearse, with a little company of sorts; I say of sorts because you couldn't expect a troupe of Beerbohm Trees or Tempests for the money Caryll was paying. Maureen was his leading lady, and she got two pounds a week— except when he talked her out of it. Those were the times she was adoring him. There were other times she hated him; and always she had a terror of him that made one a little—well, sick to watch them together. Caryll had a gift for playing on her terror.'

'I suppose she could have found another manager,' put in Brewster, gruffly.

'She wasn't famous then, you know,' said Morpeth, mildly. 'And I know she was keeping somebody. The women, who were jealous of her, said it was a child; and the men swore it was her old mother. I never bothered about it much. You see, I loved Maureen; I would quite cheerfully have cut my own throat if it would have given her any pleasure—or saved her from Caryll. He was the kind of thing lady novelists describe, I believe, as a "hulking brute", and I—well, you see me. I don't think I ever topped the scale much above nine stone. Besides, if I'd interfered he would only have taken it out of Maureen, so I was as polite to him as I knew how, although he spent the greater part of rehearsals in telling me the play was— what's the modern word?—lousy. *Not* a pretty word; but Caryll's language was worse. It used to make me feel quite sick, sometimes, when Maureen was there, looking like a wood-an—looking like she always did: so sweet and gentle, and pitiful for me and for all of them, when Caryll knocked them about at rehearsals.

'Of course, it was a frightfully bad play. I should say the only reason for Caryll's buying it was that I was unknown, and therefore easy to pluck, and that it had a showy part for him. Though he loathed being killed in the second act. That shows you how much I knew about play-writing; I killed the hero in the second act. It was altered, of course; Caryll got stabbed and the audience thought he was dead, and then he turned up in a hospital bed at the beginning of Act Three—an extra bit I had to write in, as well as Caryll's part for the rest of the play.

'The supposed "murder", I must say, was absolutely transpontine; it took place in a blue light, and Caryll was supposed to be stabbed from behind by a man with a sort of hood over his face. The fellow who did this was Peters, the ASM, because the villain, who should have done it, had a quick change just then. You see how it was? Not a word was spoken, and the man wore a mask, so anyone who happened to be about the same height and build as the villain could rush on and do it; the business only took a few seconds; then the curtain came down. I rather fancied that bit, myself; thought it was neat.

'Of course, after rehearsals started I didn't think of anything very much accept Maureen. I suppose she was a good actress; I haven't the slightest idea. All I can tell you is that her slightest movement, a quiver of her lip, the droop of her little shoulders, simply drove all the blood away from my heart and I could have fainted. Rather exaggerated—what? I assure you that's how it was with me—and not only with me, but with one or two of the others as well.

'I suppose I was very young and green in those days, and Caryll saw it and got a lot of fun out of me.

'Someone said he was a good lover. Maureen didn't look like it. One day he'd be all over her, making love and mauling her in public until no one knew where to look; and the next day he'd call her every foul name you can think of, in front of the whole company—and twice he struck her.

'I dare say you think we were a poor lot to stand for that. I, as I've said, was about nine stone to Caryll's fifteen; and the rest were dependent upon him for their bread-and-butter. It's odd how that soaks the natural nobility out of men.

'Sometimes the air was so think with hate you could feel it shiver;

and Caryll would come down through the shivering air—great blond beast, six feet or more in height—smiling, and be filthily rude to Maureen in front of everyone; and then he'd turn round and grin at the company, as much as to say, "You see who's master of this theatre—and this woman!"

'You mustn't let me start on about Caryll!' screamed Morpeth, suddenly. 'It's past—that madness! It must never, never come back again!'

'Shut up!' bellowed Brewster, shaken out of his uncertain self-control by Morpeth's outburst, which went ringing round the emptiness like a shrieking ghost. Quite suddenly, Morpeth was still: deadly still, as though Brewster's words had stunned him. Then, once again, he gave his soft, infinitely strange laugh.

'We must be getting on,' said Morpeth, softly. 'Have you noticed how dark it's growing? It will soon be time for you to catch your train.

'Well, to cut a long story short—the play was somehow pushed and banged into some kind of shape which Caryll said would do for the public, and we were billed to produce on a Monday night; you know the way it's done in the provinces. Of course, I recognized by now what tripe it was, and my one consolation was that it was being done in a place like Coalford, where no one would ever hear about it—although Caryll, in one of his "big" moods, had blustered about getting down some of the London managers to see him in the new part. I don't suppose he knew any of the London managers, even by sight.

'On that day, of all days, Caryll chose to treat us all to a first-rate display of his diabolism. He called a morning rehearsal and had the whole crowd in pulp. It was the only occasion on which I—or, I believe, any of them—had seen Maureen go to pieces. She stopped suddenly, covered her face with her hands, and screamed out: "Don't! You mustn't! I absolutely can't do a thing if you treat me like this!"

'You can't imagine what the effect of Maureen's breakdown was upon the rest of the crowd. I didn't then—I don't now—know anything about play-producing, but even I knew from that moment that the play was done for. The whole lot of them became simply blethering idiots. Maureen rushed off the stage, and after a minute Caryll, black as ink, followed her.'

*

Morpeth's face was a white rectangle in the gloom; the sockets of his eyes seemed to Brewster to have developed into two dark chasms, like the eye-sockets of a skull; and his hands were twisting between his knees. In the silence there was a creak and a slither; Brewster could feel his heart thudding against his breast-bone.

'He thrashed her,' continued Morpeth, in a thin, distant voice. 'Let me say for Peters that he threw himself at the dressing-room door, but Caryll had locked it. Peters was not much bigger than I; it was brave of him.

'I'd bought a few flowers for Maureen, and when I came down to the theatre at night I took them to her dressing-room. I'd meant to have them handed, in the conventional way, across the footlights, but I thought if she had them first they might comfort her—give her a little courage. I had not meant to say anything else to her, but I suddenly found myself begging her to leave Caryll; to marry me. It was ridiculous, because I was only, then, earning a few shillings a week. But I forgot all that. She was wearing a thin kind of scarf across the shoulders of the evening gown she wore in the first act, and I knew why it was there. She shook her head very gently, and I remembered about the person—whoever it was—she had to keep. And she said, "Dear Henry. I promise you I will do my very best with your play tonight."

'I met Peters in the passage: as we passed each other he caught hold of my arm and whispered, "By God, I'll *murder* Caryll some day!" Odd, wasn't it? Of course, I never mentioned that to anybody. But I remember when I went into a room where several of the men were dressing, thinking that the same look was in each man's eyes. No one said much; there was a lot of drinking, among the few who could afford it. But there was the *murder* thought, as big and black as a thundercloud, behind the stage that night.

'All the seats were cheap, and the house was soon packed. I was too nervous, at the beginning, to go in front; I hung about the wings and the dressing-rooms, watching for Caryll. I was determined, if he did anything to Maureen then, that I'd go for him—whatever the effect was on the play.

'But he came down presently, beaming, considerably drunk, and clapped me on the back, as if I were his best friend. I could have done it then. . . .

'The first act went through all right, apparently. Coalford isn't critical. Caryll swaggered and posed and gave them what they considered value for their money. I simply couldn't watch Maureen.

'They came off stage together; I was standing just behind a flat, and two or three of the others were with me. We all heard him say to Maureen, "If you can't support me better than that in the next act, I'll give you hell!" Those were his exact words. We all heard them. And the black cloud—the murder thought—seemed to drop lower upon us all. We felt it; we saw it in each other's eyes. One of the men muttered to me—well, never mind what he said.

'You know now, of course, what happened? When at the end of the second act the curtain came down (to a good deal of applause) and the stage hands started to rush forward to change the set, Caryll didn't get up. Before they got to him they could see what had happened, from the stage-cloth.

'The property dagger with which the "murder" was always committed was found on Peters's dressing-bench. There was a door, centre-back, through which the murderer, whoever he was, had made his escape. There was never anyone by that door; the "hands" were down at the sides, waiting for their signal, which Peters was supposed to give them when he ran round. When he didn't appear they simply did what they were accustomed to doing. The "murderer" wore ordinary evening dress: anyone in evening dress could have done it, with Peter's hood, or bag, with the eyeholes cut in it, over his face.

'The whole cast had a complete alibi; no one was on the stage at that moment, except Caryll and, usually, Peters; the others were changing into day clothes, for the next act. The stage hands, and the SM himself, had the obvious alibi of their working suits. And, of course, there was pandemonium behind, as soon as it was found out; anyone could have slipped through the pass door, or even out into the street, because it was found out afterwards the stage doorkeeper had been indulging his usual weakness in the neighbouring pub.'

Brewster moved uneasily. The story left him with a sneaking apprehension of something moving in the shadows that might any moment launch itself upon his own defenceless shoulders.

Morpeth had risen, and was tiptoeing with an odd movement about the stage. His movements had something of the effect of a macabre dance, they had a kind of rhythm, he was waving his hands.

'The oddest thing,' he said, in his thin, light voice, 'was that the weapon was never found with which the crime was committed! They found out what it was—or what they thought it was— afterwards; a large chisel was found to be missing from the carpenter's bench—just through there. The wound was at the base of Caryll's skull—not in the shoulder, where Peters had always planted it at rehearsal. Of course, the murderer knew that the chisel, however sharp, wouldn't go through the cloth and the underclothing—unless, at any rate, it had been driven by a very big and heavy man. Now, how could a large thing, bloodstained, as the chisel must have been, be disposed of, hurriedly, as the murderer must have disposed of it? Every inch of the mezzanine was searched, to see if it had gone down one of the traps when they jerked the stage-cloth up. Nowhere. Odd, isn't it?'

'I've had enough of this,' said Brewster, suddenly. 'Thanks very much for your story—you can keep your theatre! I doubt if, as a movie-house, it will shake off the—shake off the——'

'Oh, wait just a moment!' said Morpeth, coming up to him and pawing him softly—an action which filled Brewster with an indescribable feeling of repulsion. 'Can't you see what a fascination the place has got for me? All these years it has never lost its fascination. I've only to look at this stage and I can see Maureen drifting across it—as she did at rehearsals. Look—can't you see? There she goes—there!—with her timid smile and that little droop of the shoulder——'

'Pull yourself together!' said Brewster abruptly, and shook the little man by the shoulder. 'If you take my advice you'll re-sell the place—or throw it away!'

With a high, eerie laugh, Morpeth threw off the detaining hand and again flitted across the stage.

'It was here, just here, where I am standing, that Caryll was murdered. Up here'—he moved a few paces upstage—'was the door, centre-back, through which the murderer escaped. Everyone was watching; the men on the curtain—down there, where the screen will hang—the screen on which Maureen will appear—were waiting for their signal from the stage manager, who had to count ten from the time when Caryll fell, and then ring down.

'The murderer came out through this door—here, like this. Straight opposite the scene dock.'

He flitted, still with his odd, dancing movements, up towards the stack of flats, which had been leaning, for heaven knows how many years, against the wall of the dock. The dust lay upon them, an inch deep of grey powder; the lower edges had been torn and nibbled away by the theatre rats.

Morpeth flung a glance across his shoulder at Brewster, before dropping on his knees. A blade of horrible certainty drove into Brewster's mind. There was a scuffle; a whole stream of rats darted out, and a spider with a body the size of a walnut came trundling down the rake of the stage. Only the lower part of Morpeth's legs were visible; an acute nausea seized upon Brewster as he imagined the depths into which Morpeth's body was exploring.

Now he was wriggling backwards. As he finally emerged cobwebs were clarted upon his shoulders and his hair, where they formed a hideous crown, hanging pendant to his eyebrows. In his hand he held something. . . .

'I thought,' said Morpeth, softly, insanely, 'it would still be there!'

The Man Who Dreamed Too Much

Quentin Reynolds

'I MAY have to murder a man,' Baron Von Genthner said very softly. I looked up, but he wasn't smiling. He was standing there, slim, straight, every inch the German aristocrat.

Since the war Von Genthner had spent most of his time with his music and his science. I could think of none less liable to harbour thoughts of murder. And our conversation had started so innocently, too.

'The American, Fulton Kramer, arrives in Berlin on Monday,' he had begun. 'Why not have a dinner party for him?'

I had laughed, 'Kramer is probably the richest man in America, Von Genthner. He is hardly likely to accept a dinner invitation from a foreign newspaper correspondent he doesn't know.'

'Yes, he'll accept.' Von Genthner lit a cigarette. 'In fact,' he added calmly, 'he has accepted already. He phoned me from Vienna this morning. This, really is *my* dinner party. I merely want you to hold it at your flat. By the way, here's the menu.'

He handed me a menu which made me gasp. 'Caviare, Consommé aux Nids d'Hirondelle, Filet de Sole Regence, Barquettes d'Ecre Suprême d'Agneau. . . . Von Genthner, I'm a newspaper man, not an oil magnate like Kramer. . . . Château Loudenne, Enkirschner Steffensberg Moselle, 1921, Perrier Jouet, 1921; Hine's Brandy, 1875 . . .'

'It is a good dinner, isn't it?' Von Genthner smiled. 'As a matter of fact, it's the same dinner that Sir Austen Chamberlain gave at Locarno a few months ago. The French Ambassador gave me a copy of the menu. He, incidentally, will be one of our guests. And,

by the way, the cost of the dinner does not matter. I will take care
of that. My friend,' he added slowly, 'if this dinner turns out as we
hope it will, no possible cost would be excessive. And here is our
guest list.'

He handed me a list of six men and I sat down weakly. In
addition to my name and Von Genthner's, there was Henri
Beaumont, the French Ambassador to Germany; Heinrich Hoben,
the munitions king, probably Germany's wealthiest man; Dr Gerhardt Schuler, the so-called wizard of the mind, undoubtedly the
world's greatest psychiatrist, the man who began where Freud and
Jung ended; and then there was Fulton Kramer.

'There's lots of dynamite mixed up here, Von Genthner,' I said.
'Whatever can the French Ambassador, Germany's largest maker of
munitions, America's wealthiest man, and a great psychiatrist have
in common?'

'They all knew Mordaunt Kramer well. Mordaunt Kramer was a
very great man, a very great friend of us all. He died just seven
years ago, seven years ago next Wednesday. Let us say that this
dinner is in memory of him. He, you know, was Fulton Kramer's
older brother. During the war Mordaunt Kramer served with the
French army. I won't go into details, but he saved the life of Henri
Beaumont at the risk of his own. Afterwards he and Beaumont were
inseparable, like two brothers. Heinrich Hoben? Hoben was educated in America. He and Mordaunt Kramer were college friends,
and later Mordaunt married his sister.'

'Was Mordaunt Kramer a friend of Gerhardt Schuler, too?'

'When Mordaunt died it was discovered he had left Schuler
twenty thousand pounds in his will,' Von Genthner said softly.

'They must have been friends. But, Von Genthner'—I looked at
him steadily—'there's something else here. I have a feeling that this
is a very important dinner.'

Von Genthner looked at me for a moment, and it was then that
he said, 'I may have to murder a man.'

'You may have to murder a man?' I stared at him.

He turned to me sharply. 'It is a dreadful thing to say, but apart
from Hoben you are the only man in Germany I can trust
completely. We are good friends. Now I put your friendship to a
test. For certain reasons I want to hold this dinner at your flat. I
have assured my friends who are to be our guests that you are the

most discreet man in Berlin. You and I have been through some interesting times, friend, have we not?'

I nodded. I had known Von Genthner for several years and no two men could be closer.

'Now leave all the details to me,' he went on. 'All you know is that you are giving a dinner for Fulton Kramer. Kramer is very much interested in psychoanalysis, and he is thinking of endowing a college of mental research here in Berlin. Naturally he wants to consult Gerhardt Schuler. That accounts for Schuler's presence at the dinner. The French Ambassador is a friend of Kramer's, and so are Hoben and myself. So forget all I have said except that. My servants will take charge that night if you don't mind. Not,' he added hastily, 'that I don't trust your excellent Martha, but she should have a night off now and then. And now, friend, auf wiedersehen.'

'Wiedersehen,' I mumbled; and he was gone, leaving me with a lot of jumbled thoughts.

Von Genthner dropped in on the afternoon of the dinner to make final arrangements. He was as much at home in a kitchen as he was in a laboratory. He could talk about a mushroom sauce to a cook just as he could talk about a Beethoven symphony to Toscanini. He could taste a wine and tell its origin as he could dissect the esoteric philosophy of a Schopenhauer.

'And now'—he rubbed his hands together in satisfaction—'I think everything is ready. Yes, it will be a dinner worthy of Mordaunt Kramer's memory.'

'How did he die?' I asked idly.

'That,' Von Genthner said slowly, 'is what we expect to find out tonight.'

'I remember his death vaguely. Didn't he fall or leap from his hotel window here in Berlin?'

'Yes . . . yes.' Von Genthner changed the subject quickly. 'Instead of cocktails we will have sherry. I have brought this one bottle. It will be enough. Our guests are all moderate drinkers. . . . I have told our guests that nothing which happens tonight shall go beyond the confines of your dining-room.'

'All right, I won't talk. After that dinner I probably won't be able to talk. By the way, we wear black ties, I suppose?'

Von Genthner threw up his hands in horror. 'Black ties, indeed! Here we have four of the world's most important men to dinner and you won't even dress for them. We wear white ties and tails, of course.'

Promptly at seven-thirty the bell rang, and one of Von Genthner's wooden-faced servants announced solemnly, 'The Baron Ludwig Von Genthner and Herr Fulton Kramer.'

Fulton Kramer looked exactly like his pictures, which was a bit of a surprise. Tall, broad-shouldered, clean-shaven, he was the motion-picture conception of an industrial magnate. He was a very big man, and when one shook hands with him and felt the straight gaze of his steady eye one realized that here was one out of the ordinary. Then he smiled and spoke and the impression was gone. He was merely a quiet, very soft-spoken gentleman.

'Nice of you to have this dinner,' he said.

Just then a servant appeared with a tray on which there was an enormous bowl of caviare embedded in a block of ice. And on the tray was that bottle of sherry and several glasses.

It was at this moment that Von Genthner's man announced sonorously 'His Excellency the French Ambassador.'

I had interviewed Beaumont a dozen times and he remembered me. An amazing diplomat, Beaumont, one of the most able in Europe. He was everything that a diplomat usually is not. Huge, with a mass of black hair that was constantly tumbling down over his forehead; his moustache was untidy and his large brown eyes were constantly twinkling. A great gourmet and raconteur, Monsieur Beaumont would talk—even to newspapermen—by the hour. But when he finished one realized that he had only been charming— not informative. He was much like Litvinoff, the Russian.

While he was greeting Von Genthner and Kramer, Herr Heinrich Hoben was announced. Hoben was a real mystery man. He had never been interviewed, never photographed. He was slim and spare, and his closely cropped head, his monocle, and the duelling scar on his cheek all combined to make him look the typical Prussian.

'It is nice to be among friends again,' he said rather strangely, and turning to me, 'Von Genthner says you are his best friend. That means that I am at your service.'

'You will serve me best by sampling this sherry.' I poured five glasses, and the servant who had been hovering about passed them round.

'But this is treason,' Beaumont exploded, 'giving a Frenchman sherry, a Spanish wine.'

'The French wines are too important to drink before dinner,' I told him. 'We need them to embellish my poor food.'

'And this,' Von Genthner said very softly, 'this is a very special sherry. Look at the label.'

Beaumont, Hoben, and Fulton Kramer looked at the bottle. Kramer drew a sharp breath. Suddenly they were all strangely quiet.

'It is the only wine he ever drank,' Kramer said softly. 'Manzanilla, 1875, a fine sherry, and how thoughtful of you, Von Genthner.'

'Just before he . . . he . . . shall I say died? Just before he died he gave me a case of it. I thought tonight we might drink a toast to him.'

We raised our glasses. Hoben's face was set in an immobile mask. The Ambassador straightened his huge frame and sadness replaced the laughter in his eyes. Kramer's hand shook and a few drops spilled over his glass.

'To my brother, whom we all loved in life and whose memory we revere in death,' Kramer's voice was softer than ever. 'Soon we may drink another toast to you, my brother. Soon we may drink to you and say, "Brother, you have been avenged."'

There was a moment of silence as we drank. There was something tremendous in the room now. I sensed it without knowing what it was.

Then, 'Herr Doktor Gerhardt Schuler,' the butler announced, and the spell, the spectre of something which had insinuated itself into the room, vanished, and again there were four cultured, smiling men greeting a distinguished guest. Von Genthner introduced Dr Schuler to us all.

Schuler was truly a great man. He had studied with Freud and then with Adler and Jung, and he had used their knowledge and experience as a springboard from which he jumped far out into the mighty expanse of the subconscious mind. He was rather short and plump and everything about him was tidy. Often I have been able to tell a man's character by two things—his hands and his eyes. Schuler had very grey and very steady eyes which almost met under thin eyebrows, but his hands were thin and soft and they were never quiet. It was as though they were the reflection of an extraordinarily active mind that just could not relax. The hands contradicted the eyes. He had a short pointed black beard, and his age, I imagined, was about fifty.

'So decent of you to come,' Kramer smiled. 'I am interested in your subject and have been thinking of endowing a college of mental research in Berlin. After all, you are the leading psychiatrist of our age. It seems ridiculous that Vienna should be the capital of mental research and not Berlin.'

'Some of my colleagues in Vienna might not agree,' Schuler smiled. Schuler had a lovely voice, a beautiful voice, if the voice of a man can be so appraised. It had a soothing quality. The most ridiculous thought occurred to me. What a great radio announcer this man would have made!

'You have done a marvellous thing, Doctor,' Kramer said. 'You have dragged the subconscious mind out of its hiding-place and into the open where we can see it. You are never afraid of anything you can see.'

'I have tried to banish fear,' Schuler nodded.

'In America we have always thought of psychoanalysis and psychiatry as a sort of witchcraft until you came along. But you made the subconscious mind a friendly little thing that we can understand,' Kramer told him.

The scientist seemed quite pleased. 'A friendly little thing, that is good, that is very good, Mr Kramer.'

Dinner was announced, and we trooped into the dining-room. There is a large crystal chandelier over my table and it twinkled a welcome, and then the light from it shone down whitely on a really distinguished-looking gathering.

Course followed course and we chatted of many things. Eventually the Ambassador turned to Hoben. 'A French journalist tells me an interesting thing, Hoben. He tells me that every typewriter factory in Germany is manufacturing machine-guns.'

'That is true,' Hoben said solemnly. 'I hear that a French journalist bought a German typewriter and that it fired eighty shots to the minute—all directed against the Rhineland.'

Von Genthner laughed. 'War . . . war . . . everyone talks of war. I think war is just an idle dream.'

Hoben broke in smoothly, 'Dreams are in the province of Dr Schuler. If war is a dream he should know about it.'

'War isn't a dream,' Schuler laughed. 'War is a nightmare.'

'Dreams are amazing things,' Von Genthner smiled. 'We used to think them the result of eating too much. Now people like you use them to cure all sorts of mental disturbances, don't you, Doctor?'

'Not to cure so much as to find out what is wrong,' Schuler smiled. 'A dream itself is not so important—it is only important in that it is a reflection of something hidden in the subconscious. That is important.'

He spoke slowly, in perfect but unfamiliar English which out of deference to Fulton Kramer we were all using. Slowly, caressingly, carefully, his beautiful voice flowed across the table seeming to fill every corner of the room. I felt a touch of tension which hadn't been there before. I felt somehow that everything that had gone before was merely part of a well-laid plan that was reaching its culmination. How had the conversation come round to this talk of dreams? It seemed a bit too pat to have been accidental.

I looked round the table. Had the lines about Kramer's jaw tightened a bit? Had Ambassador Beaumont's eyes lost their twinkle? Was Hoben leaning forward a bit further than he had been, and what was that expression in his eyes? They were all looking at Dr Schuler. If there was a feeling of tension in the room, certainly Dr Schuler and Von Genthner were free from it. Von Genthner was smiling gently and casually polishing his monocle.

Servants brought in dishes, removed them, brought in wine, took away empty bottles, and we ate and drank appreciatively—all but Dr Schuler, who hardly touched his food and who drank nothing at all. And his voice went on, a slight soft accent, adding something to it.

'To explain psychoanalysis and the interpretation of dreams,' he went on, 'let us use an analogy. Take this glass of wine in front of me. I read the label. I see that it is a claret, Loudenne. Still, that doesn't tell me an awful lot. Anyone can put a Château Loudenne label on a wine bottle. Now I taste the wine.' He sipped it slowly, then turned to me apologetically. 'I have a rather bad heart, and my physicians tell me that I should not drink at all; that is why I really cannot do justice to your wine. However, I taste it.

'Now I know a great deal about the wine. I can peer behind the label. I know that the wine has been bottled at the Château Loudenne, an old and beautiful château on the west side of the estuary of the Gironde some thirty-five miles north of Bordeaux at the juncture of the Haut and Bas Médoc. The wine itself is merely the reflection of the grapes which mothered it—just as a dream is the reflection of the hidden thoughts lying in the subconscious mind.'

'And this is what you call psychoanalysis,' Kramer interposed. 'Never before have I thought of psychoanalysing a bottle of wine.'

'Freud calls it psychoanalysis,' Gerhardt Schuler laughed. 'Adler calls it individual psychology. Jung calls it analytical psychology. Any term will do—it all means the same thing. Our science is that science which allows us an access to the subconscious mind.'

Now and then Von Genthner or Kramer threw in a question. Hoben still sat there leaning forward, immobile. The Ambassador was hunched forward, too, his eyes never leaving Schuler's face. The *corbeille de fruits* came and went and we sipped champagne, Perrier Jouet, 1921. As Dr Schuler spoke, I was suddenly conscious that except for his voice we were surrounded by utter silence. There wasn't a sound from the kitchen.

'But just what do dreams prove?' Von Genthner insisted—a bit rudely, I thought.

'What does the front of a house prove?' Schuler answered suavely. 'It doesn't actually tell you what is inside the house—but it gives a good indication. Freud always speaks of the dream façade, and I agree with him. He would be very much annoyed,' Schuler added dryly, 'to find me agreeing with him. He means that the dream is merely the façade of our mental house. Behind the dream is our subconscious mind. We must get behind that dream to see what it hides.'

'But how?' Kramer asked. 'How can a man even as gifted as you peer behind that dream, discovering fears and inhibitions, to see what is really troubling the mind, and how can you throw out those fears and those dark thoughts which apparently cause most dreams?'

'It is not always easy,' Schuler admitted. 'There are certain dreams which always indicate, for instance, a fear of the dark. Some early childhood experience about the dark has entered the subconscious mind of a man. He himself is hardly conscious of this fear. His dreams reveal it to us. Then I set to work to cure his subconscious mind of this fear.'

'But how?' Von Genthner asked.

Schuler shrugged his shoulders and brought the fingers of his thin hands together. 'There are many ways. I find hypnotism the best method. It may sound melodramatic, but I actually hypnotize a man out of this fear of the dark. By hypnosis, a very loose term, incidentally, I mean this. I put his conscious mind to sleep and then talk to his subconscious mind. I convince his subconscious mind that it has no need to fear the dark, and gradually the subconscious gets that thought across to the conscious mind. Then the patient is cured.'

'You wield a strange power, Doctor,' Hoben said, speaking for the first time. 'When you have a man hypnotized you can convince his subconscious mind of almost anything.'

Schuler hesitated. 'Yes . . . yes,' he said slowly. 'I suppose that is right. But, of course, I am only a doctor—a doctor of the mind— and my province is curing. A psychoanalyst really widens the scope of the conscious.'

'I had a dream the other night that was strangely exhilarating,' Von Genthner broke in, laughing. 'I who never dream dreamed this night that I was climbing, climbing up into the ether. There was nothing but air supporting me and yet I kept on going upwards, and the higher I climbed the greater was my feeling of exhilaration and happiness. What, for instance, does that dream mean, Schuler, if anything?'

'That's one of the most common dreams in my experience,' Schuler laughed. 'If the same dream occurs again and again, look out, Von Genthner. Your subconscious mind for some reason or other has a wild desire to leap out into space. So long as your conscious mind can control that hidden desire no harm will come, but if the dream comes back it means that your subconscious mind is getting the upper hand. Stay away, Von Genthner, from high places.'

There was a sharp tinkle of broken glass. Hoben was peering at the broken stem of his wine glass. There wasn't a trace of colour in his face. His eyes were as cold as the crystals on the chandelier above us. Now the room was charged with something electric. I looked at Monsieur Beaumont. He was leaning forward looking at Schuler, and at the moment the jovial face was gone and he reminded me of a huge spider that is about to leap at a fly. He wasn't the genial diplomat now. Fulton Kramer, too, was staring at Gerhardt Schuler, and his eyes showed that he was looking at something which his mind told him was loathsome. Only Von Genthner's expression remained unchanged. A small smile played round the corners of his mouth, but his eyes weren't smiling. Wordlessly he went on polishing his monocle on his napkin.

Gerhardt Schuler looked from one to another. Now he, too, realized that something was wrong. His thin soft hands fluttered nervously. 'But, gentlemen . . . gentlemen . . . why . . . why . . . are you looking at me so strangely?'

'You didn't tell my brother to stay away from high places.' Kramer's voice was hardly audible, but in it there was a note that showed the inherent strength of the man.

Hoben straightened up. He was every inch the Prussian officer now. 'We have learned enough, my friend.' The words dropped on the table metallically. 'We have a duty to perform. Come, Kramer, tell Gerhardt Schuler a story that he well knows already. Tell him of how your brother, our friend, met his death.'

'But, gentlemen,' Schuler laughed uncertainly, but his eyes remained steady. 'I do not . . .'

'Quiet, please,' Hoben's voice snapped. 'Go on, Kramer.'

'My brother, Mordaunt Kramer, died seven years ago tonight,' Kramer began. He took two faded letters from his pocket. 'I was in New York when he died, and on that day I received a letter from him. I had received another just a week previously. Here are the letters. I won't bother reading them all.'

The room was absolutely quiet. Not even the rumble of the street traffic seeped through to my dining-room. Kramer began very softly, but as he went on the tempo of his words quickened and his voice rose.

'Seven years ago my brother was in Berlin,' he went on. 'He had been working hard, very hard, and an inevitable reaction set in. He couldn't sleep, and when he did sleep his sleep was broken by dreams. He had occasional dizzy spells, but his physician told him that organically he was absolutely sound. Yet he was close to a nervous breakdown. He was advised to consult you, Dr Schuler, and he did.

'He told you of one recurring dream that bothered him. It was a dream in which he was climbing a mountain, and in his dream he reached the top, then soared out into the air climbing higher and higher. Sometimes it was from a roof top that he soared, sometimes from a balcony; but invariably there was this climbing upwards into the air above.

'You told him, and quite rightly, I'll admit, that this was merely the protest that his subconscious mind was making against the driving that he had been giving it of late. He had, let us say, what we laymen call a common case of nerves—the kind that a long rest will cure. But you did not recommend a long rest. You recommended psychoanalysis. Yes, it is here in the letter, Doctor. Mordaunt and I were very close, and he told me almost every detail of your treatment.

'You used hypnotism on my brother. Within a week he felt better. He was able to sleep, but only after you had soothed him, after you had, to use your own words, put his conscious mind to sleep. He became enthusiastic about your treatment. He tried to force money on you. Mordaunt was one of the world's wealthiest men, and he was generous, too. But you refused his money. You told him that it was satisfaction enough for you to make a convert of him, a convert to psychoanalysis.'

Schuler broke in and his lovely voice was pitched higher than it had been. 'Yes, I had forgotten it. I gave your brother one or two treatments. I felt very badly when he——'

'Quiet!' Hoben's voice was full of menace.

'Then one day,' Kramer went on, 'my brother suggested to you that he would like to give something to help mental research. He suggested that he leave you twenty thousand pounds in his will, and you very casually agreed. My brother wrote to me enclosing a codicil to his will, asking me to execute it. I submit, Dr Schuler, that by this time you had the subconscious mind of my brother thoroughly under your control. As you have explained to us, it is possible for the subconscious mind absolutely to dominate the conscious. I submit, Doctor Schuler, that you implanted into his subconsciousness the idea of leaving you twenty thousand pounds. Once you learned that he had done that you changed your treatment.

'You encouraged his subconscious mind in its mad desire to leap into space. Under hypnosis you fostered this desire, until it became almost uncontrollable. Shall I read just a paragraph or two from my brother's last letter?'

Kramer picked up the letter. '"This past week, after being on the verge of a complete cure," he read, "I have had a relapse. I wake up at night and find myself looking down into the street from my window. The street below seems to fascinate me. Dr Schuler tells me that this is but the last fight my subconscious mind is making for control. Within a week, he tells me, I shall be completely cured. I trust him completely, brother—he has a soothing voice, and when I listen to it I drop right off to sleep. Sometimes it seems to me that his voice continues in my sleep. I hear it faintly, but that I imagine is just a fancy. He began the last phase of my treatment today. He has told me to look out of my window just before I retire, to stare down into the street below. The prospect, I admit, frightens me a bit, but he says that the only way to overcome this fear of high places, this desire to jump and those occasional dizzy spells, is to fight against them. Tonight I will do as he says."'

Kramer stopped. I looked at Schuler. His face gleamed white under the brightness of the chandelier. He passed a thin hand across his brow and then stared at the moisture on it.

'That night he did as you told him to do,' Kramer went on. 'That night he leaned over the window-sill. Then? Then that thought you had implanted in his consciousness grew and grew like a fire in a wooden house. I can visualize him leaning over that window staring at the street below, trying desperately, bravely, to overcome this horrible thought which was paralysing his consciousness. Then you know what happened. He fell, and a moment later the world had lost a great man, a man who had not a single fault.'

'He had just one fault, Kramer,' Von Genthner said softly. 'He was a man who dreamed too much.'

'Will you continue, Von Genthner?' Kramer's voice trembled just a bit.

'Gerhardt Schuler,' Von Genthner said, and his voice might have been that of a schoolmaster, so devoid of emotion was it; yes, or the voice of a judge pronouncing sentence, 'we accuse you of the murder of Mordaunt Kramer.'

'You are mad . . . mad!' Schuler's hands went out, palms upstretched. 'This is ridiculous.'

'Murder is never ridiculous,' Hoben said in his clipped, accented voice. 'Sometimes it is sad, as in Mordaunt Kramer's case. Sometimes it is necessary, as in your case.'

Schuler's mouth worked under his dark tidy beard. His eyes widened, and for the first time fear showed through those two windows of the heart which we call the eyes.

'At one time or another during his lifetime,' Von Genthner continued, 'Mordaunt Kramer did something very tremendous for each one of us.' I was sitting there fascinated, seeing but not believing. The others had entirely forgotten my presence. 'Each one of us loved Mordaunt Kramer. We are four intelligent men, Dr Schuler. We felt that there was something out of the ordinary in Mordaunt Kramer's death. A hunch is the American expression, I believe. There was no tangible concrete fact to show us that Mordaunt Kramer's death was not a natural one. But we felt that Mordaunt's life did not explain his death—and we felt that his death was an entire contradiction of his life. A man who has built a railway over the Andes does not die by a fall from a window. A man who has won every possible honour in war does not die like a neurotic, feeble-minded fool.

'For seven years now we four have tried to find something which would explain his death. All we had were two letters from him, and the codicil to his will. Yet strangely we could not connect you with his death, for none of us knew much of psychoanalysis. Then Fulton Kramer went to Vienna. He talked to the leading men in your field, Dr Schuler. He showed them the letter which told of the treatment you had ordered. You never should have allowed Mordaunt to write that letter, Dr Schuler. It was your one slip.'

Von Genthner stopped and Kramer took up the story. 'When I showed the men in Vienna that letter they shook their heads in bewilderment,' he went on. '"Schuler must have slipped badly," they told me. "Why, he gave your brother the worst possible advice. The treatment in such cases is the very reverse of what Schuler ordered. A patient with a desire for leaping into space must be treated along the lines first used and with great success by Jung. He must be kept from high places, kept from temptation, until that desire is rooted out of the subconscious."

'That,' Kramer continued, 'gave us the story. We four discussed the matter. We came to the conclusion that you deliberately murdered my brother for that twenty thousand pounds. Why did you need that money and need it so quickly? You were wealthy, but your wealth was tied up in a Swedish match firm. One never thinks of a doctor as being a heavy investor, but *you* were, Dr Schuler. The firm was crumbling. If its credit could be maintained for a few months the crisis would be passed. That is why you murdered Mordaunt Kramer.'

'You can't prove any of this.' Schuler leaped to his feet and his face was pasty. 'This is nonsense. You can never prove it. Perhaps I made a mistake in my treatment of your brother. All doctors make mistakes. You can prove nothing.'

'You convicted yourself a few moments ago.' Hoben was talking now. 'Mordaunt's dream of leaping from high places was in essence the same as Von Genthner's imaginery dream of climbing into the ether. And the warning you gave Von Genthner would have saved Mordaunt Kramer.'

'You can prove nothing,' Gerhardt Schuler repeated more calmly.

'That is correct.' Monsieur Henri Beaumont spoke for the first time, but his voice was not the voice of the French Ambassador. It was the calm judicial voice of a prosecuting attorney. 'We have consulted the best lawyers in my country and in Germany. It would be quite impossible to convict you legally. Yet you are a murderer, Dr Schuler. You are a menace to society, and we have decided that you must die as any murderer dies. And it is most appropriate that you die tonight. It was seven years ago tonight that Mordaunt Kramer died.'

'We waste time,' Hoben broke in. 'Von Genthner, give the Doctor his orders.'

'You can't . . . you can't murder me in cold blood. My God! you are intelligent, cultured men.' His eyes searched frantically from one to another. 'You can't . . .'

'We have all seen men die,' Von Genthner said, and his voice was edged with contempt. 'We were all in the war, Dr Schuler.'

I sat there, and there was moisture on the palms of my hands. I sat there and felt as though a piece of ice was lying against my spine. I sat there and told myself, 'This is not real. It can't be. I am not watching four of the world's greatest men execute another man.' I told myself that and looked round the silent table.

Von Genthner wasn't the cultured soft-spoken Baron now. He was the German war ace; the cold, merciless man who had downed forty planes. The French Ambassador? Once again he was Colonel Henri Beaumont, leader of one of France's greatest regiments. He was the stern soldier to whom life was a game, the loss of which means death. Hoben? He was the Prussian soldier now. There was no pity on his face—on it was the look of disgust of one who peers at some crawling thing. Fulton Kramer? The man who had fought his way from nowhere to a great industrial position was showing nothing but a mask. His eyes were steady and cold. Now at this moment they weren't four cultured gentlemen. They were a court of summary judgement assembled to pass sentence on one who had broken the law.

Von Genthner reached into his waistcoat pocket. He drew forth a tiny white pill. He reached across the table and dropped it into the glass of champagne which stood in front of Gerhardt Schuler. The tiny white pill danced merrily in the bubbles and then slowly began to disintegrate. Schuler watched the glass as though it hypnotized him. 'What is that, Von Genthner? What is that?'

'Just a little pill, Doctor.' Von Genthner's voice was as calm as a soft breeze. 'Merely ten grains of veronal. That's only a sleeping potion, Doctor, as you know. Ten grains would scarcely hurt a child.'

Hoben drew forth a similar pill from his waistcoat pocket. He reached over, too, and dropped it into Schuler's glass. 'There's another one, Doctor,' he said.

'I have also one for you, Doctor Schuler.' Monsieur Beaumont dropped a third pill into the glass.

'And here is mine,' Fulton Kramer's soft voice spoke.

All of us watched the pills dissolve. Von Genthner filled his glass with champagne and passed the bottle to Hoben. First he, then Kramer and Beaumont filled their glasses.

'Forty grains . . . forty grains of veronal . . . Good God! Forty grains of veronal will kill a man.' I thought Schuler was going to break down completely.

'Yes,' Von Genthner said calmly, 'forty grains will kill a man— and a fall from the tenth-storey window of the Hotel Imperial will kill a man—and did. You will merely go to sleep, Doctor, but you will not awake. No one of us will have killed you, Doctor. We are unselfish, Doctor Schuler. Each of us wanted to avenge the murder of Mordaunt Kramer. But we are unselfish. Each of us was willing to allow the others to take a part in your execution.'

Schuler's eyes never left that wine glass. Now the pills had been completely dissolved. The bubbles had quieted and the wine looked like any other wine.

Von Genthner rose. The others followed. I found myself on my feet, too.

'Now, Doctor Schuler, will you join us in a toast?' Von Genthner's words cut across the table like knife thrusts into the stunned consciousness of Schuler. Schuler rose almost mechanically.

'If I refuse?' his beautiful voice was but a husky whisper now. He looked round at the grim faces which were peering at him.

'You will not refuse,' Von Genthner assured him. 'There is no help for you, Doctor. You are facing a firing squad, but a humane firing squad. We are alone, Doctor. The servants have left. There is no help for you, Doctor.'

'You will join us in a toast, Doctor, won't you?' Hoben's voice was as biting as the unexpected blast of an icy wind.

'You see, Doctor Schuler,' Monsieur Henri Beaumont said in a matter-of-fact tone, 'there is nothing else for you to do.'

Fulton Kramer raised his glass. 'To my brother,' he said simply. The others raised their glasses too, but they kept their eyes on Schuler. Mechanically, almost as if some force over which he had no control was actuating him, Schuler raised his glass until it touched his lips. Then he drank. He drank it in one horrible gulp. Then he reached for the back of his chair and he clung to it with one hand. The others finished and replaced their glasses on the table.

'Forty grains of veronal . . .' Schuler's face was not pretty to see. 'Forty grains,' he whispered. 'In ten minutes I will be . . .'

'In four minutes, Doctor Schuler,' Von Genthner broke in. 'In four minutes you will be dead. Veronal works very quickly, Doctor. Even now, I dare say, you can feel a slight constriction in your throat. Your throat is dry, Doctor. You can feel the muscles tightening. . . . Now, Doctor, the veronal has reached your heart. You can feel the muscles of the heart contracting, Doctor. They are gripping the heart with iron bands. You can feel them, Doctor. You can . . .'

Schuler's glass crashed to the table. He sobbed out a choked, 'Yes, yes, I can feel it. You had no right to do this.'

He raised a shaking hand to his collar and a fleck of foam appeared against the darkness of his beard. 'You are murderers, do you hear me? I killed Mordaunt Kramer. Yes, I killed him as you said I did. I killed him and I would kill you . . .' His voice was a hysterical scream now. 'I killed him . . . killed him . . . killed him . . .'

Suddenly a spasm crossed his face. Then he raised his head and his eyes grew big. They grew bigger and he too seemed to grow in stature. A hand went jerkily to his heart and then—then his head dropped quickly, and he slumped forward grotesquely, catching at the chair for a moment, only to slide to the floor.

Von Genthner crossed the room in three strides. Von Genthner bent over him. 'Dead,' he said solemnly. 'Dead. His heart was very bad, you know. Too bad, gentlemen. He was a great scientist.' Von Genthner turned to me. 'Call an ambulance, will you? We must have him brought to his home.'

'But . . . but the police,' I stammered.

'The police? What have they to do with this?' Von Genthner's face was innocent of guile.

'They will find . . .'

'They will find that he died of heart failure,' Von Genthner said quietly.

'An autopsy will show the veronal.' I was shaking a bit now.

'Veronal? Come now,' Von Genthner actually smiled. 'Those four pills we gave Dr Schuler were only sugar. Just ordinary sugar pills. We did not kill Dr Schuler. His subconscious mind killed him.'

I looked round in bewilderment. Hoben nodded. So did Beaumont, and Kramer said quietly, 'Has Von Genthner ever lied to you?'

Von Genthner laid a hand on my arm. 'It was a case of self-execution. We used this method at the suggestion of Dr Schuler himself, that is, at the suggestion of something we found in one of his books. I remember the quotation well, it goes:

The subconscious mind can be a powerful enemy. A thought can be placed in the conscious mind, and if that thought is powerful enough it will enter and dominate the subconscious. The conscious mind may try to reject that thought as being absurd, but sometimes the subconscious will prove too powerful and it will hold the thought. If the thought is powerful enough it can even control the heart and the other organs of the body. In some cases a thought can enter the subconsciousness and be so terrifying as to cause death.'

Von Genthner paused. 'Let us go into the other room . . . You see, my friend, we implanted a terrifying thought into the mind of Gerhardt Schuler. It took complete possession of him, and although his conscious mind tried to reject it, it could not. And his heart, not strong at best, succumbed to the suggestion of the subconscious. Now will you phone for an ambulance?'

I reached for the telephone. As I asked for the Berlin hospital I heard Fulton Kramer's voice say quietly, 'I shall sleep peacefully tonight for the first time in seven years.'

Inquest

Loel Yeo

MEMORY is an odd thing. I can always remember to perfection a mass of unimportant details. So many men stretched end on end would encircle the earth; the exact number is 23,549,115. Thirty and a quarter square yards equal one square rod, pole, or perch. These things and many more I never forget. Yet on the occasional days I can snatch to go up to London (and I being a country doctor they are rare enough), I never fail to leave my shopping list behind. It is only as the train pulls out of London that I remember the instruments I meant to buy.

I overtook the Stanton express as it was grumbling out of the station, and flung myself on to somebody's lap. My apologies were accepted. He was elderly and inconspicuous and neat, and I knew I had seen him before, but though I still knew rice, sago, and pepper to be the chief exports of North Borneo, I couldn't remember where we had met.

People who live the same sort of lives grow to look alike. Thirty years of the same office, the same suburb, the same daily papers, and they end with the same face. Thin and a little anaemic. Eyes the faded blue of much-washed laundry. In summer and winter always a raincoat and an evening paper.

It was a chilly, foggy evening, the typical raw January day which the inconsequence of the English climate always produces in the middle of October; the window-panes were steaming with the heat of the compartment, and I lay back recovering my breath, wondering where I had seen the man opposite me before. A high white collar held his chin erect. He sat upright on the edge of the seat.

Suddenly he coughed. It was more of a mannerism than a cough, you felt it did his throat no good at all. And I remembered that we had last met on the afternoon of the coroner's inquest two years ago at Langley Abbey.

As one noticed little things in the midst of great excitement during the occasional silences in the dining-room on that day, I remember watching the shadow of the elms stretch themselves across the lawn, hearing the cawing of the rooks, and in the room the creaking of the constable's boots and the dry little cough of the solicitor's clerk who gave his unimportant but necessary evidence clearly and concisely.

The only thing about Langley that suggests an Abbey is the stained-glass window of the bathroom, otherwise it is just one of those solid square Georgian houses. Its gardens and park are lovely. I was practically brought up there with the Neville boys, so I know the place backwards. When they were both killed in 1917 old Sir Guy Neville sold it as it stood to John Hentish.

It's funny how the character of a place changes with its owner. Under the Nevilles, Langley had been a friendly house. The park gates stood open and so did the doors and windows of the house itself, muslin curtains swinging gaily in the breeze. There were village fêtes in the park, and the Abbey was part of the life and conversation of all the villages round.

With John Hentish there came a change. Sir Guy was asked to inform the county that the future tenants disliked society, and hoped people would not give themselves the trouble of calling. The park gates were shut and stayed shut. The windows were tightly closed and the muslin curtains hung straight and lifeless behind them. The house developed a thin-lipped, austere look. The only people who gave themselves the trouble of calling were the postman and the tradesmen. And gradually Langley Abbey dropped out of the annals and conversation of the county.

As for me, the house that had been so much a part of my life having shut me out, for ten years as I drove over to Maddenly to prescribe for Miss Taunton's varicose veins or dose Master Willie Twinger, I averted my eyes from the park gates as one would passing a friendly dog whose temper had become changed and uncertain. And then one afternoon four years ago I found a

message in my consulting room asking me to go up to the Abbey at
once.

After that I went there regularly, at least three times a week.
Practically the whole house, I found, presumably through lack of
interest, had been left exactly as it was bought from the Nevilles.
The hall was large and ran the width of the house, that is French
windows opening on to the lawn faced the front door. The floor had
a higher polish than I remembered, and there were fewer lights.
The furniture was ugly but solid, mostly Victorian. Two long
tables, an oak chest, some stiff chairs, and a Burmese gong. There
were several pairs of antlers on the walls, some lithographs of the
early Christian martyrs, Saint Sebastien looking extrordinarily fit
and cheerful with about forty arrows through his body, a twenty-
pound trout Sir Guy had caught in Scotland, and one fairly good
tapestry.

Old Hentish had converted what had been Lady Neville's morning-room into a bedroom and bathroom. Off the bedroom, what we
had known as the drawing-room had been made into a very beautiful
library. Both rooms were large, with high ceilings, and had French
windows opening on to the lawn. He lived almost entirely in this
suite and seldom left it.

Hentish, though he had faith in me as a doctor, disliked me as he
consistently disliked everyone. He was, without exception, the most
unpleasant, disagreeable old swine I have ever met. Practically the
only pleasure I ever received in his company was derived from
jabbing the needle into his arm. He soon exhausted the supply of
London nurses, and finally I persuaded Miss Mavey from Maddenly
village to take the post, she having nursed an invalid mother for
fifteen years who could have given even old Hentish points for
unpleasantness. No man, of course, could live long in John Hentish's condition, for, besides heart-trouble, he had advanced cirrho-
sis of the liver, but because death frightened him he listened to me,
and so with electrical treatments, diet, and drugs, his general health
improved.

Some women are eerie. Miss Taunton has been bedridden for years,
yet she's one of those women whose cousin always knew the
murdered man's aunt. This time her sister-in-law's maid's niece had
married the son of the overseer of the Hentish Paper Mills in

Ontario. Like all women, Miss Taunton had a profound contempt for detailed accuracy, but fundamentally her facts are always correct. Hentish, apparently, during the first forty years of his life had spent seven separate fortunes; the figures are Miss Taunton's. He had been the most dissolute man in London, also in Buenos Aires, where the standard is higher and competition keener. He was hard, grasping, and avid for power; there wasn't a man in his paper mills or his gold mine that wouldn't be glad to see him boiled in oil. 'And that,' said Miss Taunton, impressively, 'I got more or less straight from the lips of his own overseer.'

Miss Taunton's attitude to God is rather that of a proud aunt; she sees all the motives so clearly and is often a jump ahead of the game. When John Hentish's health failed, her attitude was that of one whose advice had been taken, for she was a firm believer in the wages of sin. Her own varicose veins she knew had been sent to test her—take the well-known case of Job—she took them rather as a compliment than otherwise, applauded God's attempt at impartiality, and forgave him frequently.

I never knew whether old Hentish had any affection for his nephew or not. William was his heir and they quarrelled, of course—over money, among other things—but I think more than disapproval he enjoyed the sense of power it gave him to see his nephew flush as he threatened to stop his allowance, which was a generous one. William's specialities were women and horses. I suppose he was good-looking in a dark, sinister sort of way; he had inherited all his uncle's unpleasantness and developed it with some ideas of his own. He used to motor down to Langley occasionally for two or three days at a time.

So life drifted on placidly and uneventfully. Sometimes after I had seen old Hentish I used to wander down to the boathouse, for the lawn sloped down to a lake fringed with red willow, and I would sit there thinking out beautiful unappetizing diets for the old man. Then one afternoon my telephone rang. It was Miss Mavey.

'Dr Mellan? Oh, Dr Mellan, will you please come down at once. Mr Hentish is dead!'

John Hentish had died from an overdose of morphia taken in a glass of sal volatile. The inquest was held that same evening in the Abbey dining-room. Mr Duffy, the coroner, sat with Police-constable Perker at the table, the rest of the household at the end of the room. Mr Duffy blew his nose, and the Vapex on his handkerchief mingled with the smell of leather and pickles. He turned a watery eye on Croucher, the butler.

'Is everybody here?'

'Everyone with the exception of Mr William Hentish, sir. He has not yet returned home.'

'Thank you. Call Dr Mellan.'

My testimony did not take long. History of John Hentish's illness, cause of death, etc. Miss Mavey was called next, and under the impression that she was on trial for her life, opened with a magnificent defence, giving seven distinct alibis for the afternoon.

'You say,' the coroner asked her, 'that the morphia with which you sometimes had occasion to inject the deceased in order to relieve intense pain was kept on the top shelf of a medicine cupboard, clearly labelled "morphia"?'

'I do,' said Miss Mavey, looking like the Trial of Mary Dugan. 'Anyone else will say the same.'

'The cupboard has a glass door, I understand. The sal volatile and a glass were placed on a small table beneath the cupboard containing the morphia. Is that correct, Miss Mavey?'

Miss Mavey paled, knowing that all she said would be used in evidence against her.

'In a sense, yes.'

'In a sense?'

'A spoon was also kept on the table,' said Miss Mavey, determined to conceal nothing.

'This medicine, this sal volatile, did the deceased take it at regular hours?'

Miss Mavey turned this over. A trap?

'No, sir, only to relieve the pain if it came on sudden,' she said, guardedly.

'When Dr Mellan gave his opinion that death was not due to natural causes, but to an overdose of morphia, you looked in the bathroom. You found the phial, which when you went off duty was in the cupboard and had contained twenty grains of morphia, lying empty on the table beside the sal volatile. Is that correct?'

'Dr Mellan asked me to look when he saw that the morphia had been put in the glass of sal volatile. I touched nothing, I swear it before Almighty God.'

'Was Mr Hentish in the habit of helping himself to this sal volatile?'

'Yes, sir, if there was no one in the room to get it for him.'

'Miss Mavey, are you of the same opinion as Dr Mellan that the morphia could not have been taken accidentally?'

'No.'

'No! Then you think it could have been taken accidentally?'

'Yes. I mean yes I'm of the opinion that no it couldn't have been taken accidentally.'

'That is all. Thank you.'

Miss Mavey, still under the shadow of the scaffold, gave a shuddering sigh, and borrowing the coroner's Vapex, sank on to a chair, inhaling deeply.

Croucher, the butler, was questioned next.

'You say,' said the coroner, 'that on receipt of the telegram this morning, Mr Hentish showed signs of anger?'

'Distinctly, sir.'

'What then?'

'He asked if Mr William was in.'

'Was he?'

'No, sir, he had left in his car at 9.30.'

'What then?'

'He told me to go to hell, sir, and take his blasted nephew with me, sir, but before I went to get Troubridge and Hay on the telephone.'

'His solicitors?'

'Exactly, sir.'

'Then what?'

'He rang and gave me instructions for the car to meet the 1.45 train. His solicitors were sending down a member of the firm.'

'On arrival he was shown straight into the library, I understand?'

'Yes, sir.'

'What then?'

'After about fifteen minutes the library bell rang and Mr Hentish asked me to witness his signature to a new will.'

'After you had signed the will, anything else?'

'The usual instructions to go to hell, sir.'

'Then I understand the house was quiet until 4.30?'

'Yes, sir. The solicitor's gentleman left the library a few moments after I did. There were standing instructions never to disturb Mr Hentish until Miss Mavey woke him at 4.30. Today the bell pealed violently, and on my entering the library Miss Mavey informed me that Mr Hentish was dead. I remained in the room until the doctor's arrival.'

The solicitor's clerk was called.

'Your firm had instructions from Mr Hentish by telephone this morning, I understand, to draft out a new will?'

'Yes, sir.'

'You were shown into the library on your arrival. What happened?'

'I read Mr Hentish the new draft, which he approved with one alteration. He rang for the butler and we both witnessed the signature.'

'Did it strike you there was anything in Mr Hentish's manner to suggest he contemplated suicide?'

'Difficult to say, sir.'

'And after you had signed the will?'

'I remained with Mr Hentish ten minutes or so. He wished to discuss a matter of income tax. I then left the library and went and sat in the garden until train time, as is my custom.'

'You've been here before then? On the same errand?'

'Usually, sir.'

'Mr Hentish was in the habit of changing his will?'

'Yes, sir.'

'Often?'

'Seven times in the last ten years, sir.'

There was a silence. The butler was called again.

'I find a memorandum on Mr Hentish's desk, Twiller and Dwight, Thursday at 12. Can you explain this?'

'His tailors, sir. He told me to telephone and have a fitter sent down tomorrow at twelve.'

'When did he give this order?'

'At breakfast, sir.'

'Then as late as the breakfast hour he was obviously not contemplating suicide. Was he in a bad or good mood?'

'Mr Hentish was never exactly sunny-tempered, sir, but he seemed average.'

'It was only after he received the telegram that his mood changed for the worse?'

'Yes, sir.'

'Mr William came down from London last night, you say?'

'Yes, sir.'

'Did he appear on good terms with his uncle?'

'He seemed slightly nervous at dinner, if I may say so, but trying to be pleasant, I thought, sir.'

'You say he hasn't been in all day?'

'Oh yes, sir. He returned this afternoon but went out again.'

'This afternoon! At what time?'

'Well, sir, I noticed his car in the drive when I passed through the hall to witness the signature, sir. That would be about 2.30, and it was still there when Miss Mavey rang, but when I opened the front door to the doctor about fifteen minutes later it had gone.'

In the silence the smell of pickles became sharper. All our chairs creaked. The same idea had suddenly occurred to everybody.

'Did Mr William know of the arrival of the telegram?'

'No, sir, he had already left when it came.'

There was another silence.

'Then he didn't know that Mr Hentish intended changing his will or that Mr—Mr—that his solicitor was sending down a representative?'

'No, sir.'

People are funny; they can see a man every day for twenty years, know his face, mannerisms, idiosyncrasies, but they've only to hear that his wife has left him, that he's shot his mother, and they'll stand for hours waiting for a glimpse of him.

Practically all of us at the inquest had seen Mr William Hentish frequently during the last two years, some longer; and none of us had ever been particularly elated at the sight, yet when the front door banged as Croucher stopped speaking, and footsteps echoed on the polished floor of the hall, all the eyes in the room turned and became fixed on the handle of the mahogany door. There were people in that room to my certain knowledge, notably the butler and myself, whose day ordinarily could be made simply by not seeing Mr William Hentish, yet as his footsteps echoed nearer, the drone of a solitary bluebottle in the room seemed like the roar of an aeroplane in the silence. Our chairs creaked as each of us leant forward and became still.

The footsteps stopped, the handle turned, and our chairs creaked sharply once again.

I don't know exactly what change we all expected to see in William Hentish, but I remember a feeling of vague disappointment as he stood in the doorway looking just the same as when I had last seen him. When he was told of his uncle's death, and the manner of it, he seemed surprised.

I've often wondered why magistrates and coroners ask the questions they do. Mr Duffy knew William Hentish as well as I did, he'd been splashed often enough with mud from his car in the winter in our narrow village street, yet the next fifteen minutes was entirely taken up with proving his identity.

The questions seemed to go on endlessly. William Hentish wore his customary look of not caring much for the smell of those immediately about him, but he gave his answers quietly and without emotion. He said that he had returned soon after lunch, gone straight through the hall on to the lawn to the boathouse. He sat there until the stable clock struck 4.30, then returned to the house, intending to go in and see his uncle, who, he knew, would be awake by then. He didn't go in because when he reached the hall the library door was ajar.

Police-constable Perker, the official recorder at the inquest, was taking down notes in longhand. A hollow moan was his signal that the pace was too much for him and the questions would cease until he caught up. Presently the coroner continued:

'Through the open door you say you heard Miss Mavey telephone Dr Mellan? But why should this stop you from seeing your uncle?'

'I thought he had probably had another attack and wouldn't want to see me just then.'

'I understand you were not here when the telegram arrived.'

'Telegram?'

The coroner turned to Perker. 'Constable, please read out the telegram.'

Police-constable Perker first got his notes up to date, then there was a roll of drums as he cleared his throat.

'Telegram to John Hentish, Langley Abbey, Langley, Norfolk. Subject secretly married to Miriel Demar yesterday two p.m. Duke Street register office. Awaiting instructions. Signed Ross.'

All our eyes were on William Hentish. I think be became a little more rigid and a pulse throbbed in his temple. The cruet-stand on the table rattled like an express train as Constable Perker settled down to his notes again.

'Is this information correct, Mr Hentish?'

'Yes.'

'You were not aware that your uncle had your movements watched.'

'No.'

'You were married secretly, I presume, because you felt Miss Demar would not have been your uncle's choice of a wife for you?'

William Hentish flushed. 'My uncle was a difficult man. He disapproved of whatever he hadn't arranged himself. My wife was a chorus girl. In time he would have come round, he always did.'

'And in the meantime?'

'He would have forbidden me the house for a month or two, I suppose.'

'And cut you off in his will?'

'Probably.'

'Supposing he had died before reinstating you in the will?'

William Hentish smiled.

'That is a remote contingency now.'

There was an angry moan from Constable Perker, who spelt by ear and preferred words that he had heard before.

'You haven't seen this gentleman before, then?'

Mr Duffy pointed out the solicitor's clerk, who coughed discreetly. William Hentish looked at him, then turned back to the coroner.

'Not consciously. Who is he?'

'He was sent down on your uncle's instructions from Troubridge and Hay with the draft of a new will.'

William Hentish turned quickly to the clerk.

'Did my uncle sign it?'

'Yes, sir.'

'May I ask the contents of the new will, the existing one?'

The clerk managed to clear his throat in the form of a question to the coroner, who nodded back an answer.

'Mr Hentish left his entire fortune to cancer research.'

'And the former will? The one he revoked?' the coroner asked.

'Everything to his nephew, William Hentish.'

While the clerk was speaking William Hentish sat silent, except that a pulse hammered again in his temple. By chance he caught the cook's eye. I saw him start. She was so obviously a woman who hadn't murdered her uncle looking at a man who had murdered him. And I think it was only then that he realized the danger of the case building up against him.

He had known his uncle would disapprove of a marriage which could probably not remain secret long. He had known his uncle's precarious state of health, had often prepared John Hentish's sal volatile for him, and knew about the morphia. He had only to walk into the library from the garden. He would know from experience that his uncle's rage at being disturbed in the middle of the afternoon would be enough to bring on an attack; and as he had often done before, he would get old Hentish some sal volatile from the bathroom, this time with a generous helping of morphia. Perhaps he had stood with curiosity watching his uncle gulp it down, had seen the purple settle under the eyes, then picking up his book, had walked quietly back to the boathouse. Perhaps he had even sat there reading until the stable clock chimed.

The coroner spoke.

'You say, Mr Hentish, that you didn't leave the garden until you heard the clock strike?'

Until then William Hentish had answered the questions put to him abruptly and with an appearance of indifference. Now his answers became more hesitant, and he paused before he spoke. He was already on the defensive. Our chairs creaked as we leant forward for his answer.

'No.'

'You didn't go near the library the whole afternoon?'

'No.'

'But you could have. Without being observed. Isn't that so, Mr Hentish?'

'Yes, I suppose so. But I repeat that I didn't.'

The cook's sniff re-echoed round the room, which had become nearly dark. Our faces were now only a blurred outline, and a cold breeze rustled Constable Perker's notes. The stable clock clanged eight.

'Then we have only your word for it that you sat in the boathouse all afternoon, Mr Hentish?'

'I'm afraid so.'

There was a silence. Suddenly the solicitor's clerk cleared his throat and spoke.

'It is quite true what Mr Hentish says with regard to his movements. I can substantiate that. Directly I left Mr Hentish I went and sat under the cedar tree whilst waiting my train time. I noticed young Mr Hentish sitting in the boathouse smoking. I don't think he saw me, but his statement is correct. He never left there until the stable clock struck.'

Human nature is weird. Instead of a deep sense of thankfulness that a fellow-creature's hands were not stained with the blood of another fellow-creature, I think that everyone in that room, with perhaps the exception of the coroner, who saw a chance of getting home to a hot mustard bath after all, felt aggrieved that William Hentish's hands were not stained with blood. Probably it was because anyone with an eye for drama could see that William Hentish was perfect for the role of villain, an aggressive manner, tall, with a black moustache and large white teeth. His hands *should* have been stained with his uncle's blood, he looked better that way, it suited him. Speaking for myself, preferring, as I do, like the rest of mankind, to believe the worst of my fellow-men, I felt that if he had not murdered his uncle, it was simply because he didn't happen to think of it.

After we had recovered from our natural disappointment, Croucher lit the gas brackets, and the questions, innumerable and interminable, began again. The clerk could add nothing, he could only say that he had seen Mr Hentish sitting as he had said in the boathouse the whole afternoon. The butler was called again, so were Miss Mavey, still at bay, and I. The question of the morphia arose.

'Might not Mr Hentish's insistence,' Mr Duffy asked the room in general, 'on the presence of morphia easily accessible, be attributed, apart from its properties in the alleviation of pain, to his possible contemplation of self-destruction?'

Constable Perker put down his pencil.

'That's coming it too hot for me, sir. Can I put it in my own words? You mean, did he pop himself off, sir?'

The questions and answers continued, but the evidence of a completely disinterested witness was too overwhelming, and on a statement from Miss Mavey that the old man had often spoken wholeheartedly in favour of self-slaughter (actually, I think, he was advocating it for her and not for himself), the coroner, as the stable clock clanged nine, brought in a verdict of suicide while of an unsound mind.

I didn't see whether William Hentish spoke to the little clerk in the dining-room or not, but he walked, frowning, across the hall as if it were empty, through the huddled group of servants, past the rest of us without a sign or word; the front door slammed, his motor roared and whined, and he was gone.

The presence of death does strange things to a place. As we stood in a group near the front door, making arrangements for the following day, the hall seemed lifeless and cold, our footsteps and voices had a hollow sound; somehow the windows reminded me of staring, dead black eyes, for the curtains had not been drawn. The gas jet droned and made the shadows of the stag's head and horns flicker and leap jerkily across the ceiling. A steady draught from an open door edged behind the tapestry, bellying it out till a naked old satyr leaned amorously towards Miss Mavey. She stood gazing after William Hentish.

'Think of losing a fortune, all that money wasted on charity!'

She sighed and sneezed. The solicitor's clerk put down his satchel and helped her on with her coat.

'It won't be wasted,' he said, gently.

A car drew up to the door, the coroner looked at his watch and turned to the clerk. 'That will be the car to take you to the station, I think. Thank you for your evidence. We shall need you again, I'm afraid. I'll communicate with you in a day or so.'

The clerk picked up his satchel and coat and hat.

'I shall be at your convenience, sir. Goodnight, gentlemen.'

The screech of the engine's whistle jerked me awake. I must have dozed for about two hours, because the train was already rattling over the points approaching Cranham Junction. My back was numb from lying so long in one position, huddled in my overcoat. I stretched myself. The clerk was still opposite, sitting stiffly erect, his worn gloves neatly buttoned over his wrists, his satchel by his side. I leant forward.

'You don't remember me?'

'Indeed, yes, sir. It is Dr Mellan. I had the pleasure at the inquest at Langley Abbey.' He coughed. 'The Abbey is still for sale, I understand.'

'Yes. Quite deserted. I often wander over there; I've known the place all my life, you know.'

I yawned.

'So the Hentish fortune went to charity after all. I wonder young William didn't contest the will. He would have had a case—uncertain temper of the old man, suicide while of unsound mind, etc.'

'I suppose he was afraid he might be reaccused of murder, sir. There was only my word for it that he didn't leave the boathouse. My word between him and a certain accusation of murder with strong motives for it.'

'He's gone abroad, they say.'

'To South America, sir. His mother left him a piece of property in the Argentine. He is doing well, I understand, sir. Mr Troubridge, head of my firm, sir, says it has been the making of him.'

'He'd have only gambled the money away if he'd had it. He promised to be as hard and selfish as his uncle was. It's funny—though he altered his will so often, I always thought old Hentish meant his nephew to have the money in the end. I thought he just enjoyed frightening William by disinheriting him.'

'A sense of power, sir?'

'Yes, the idea of doing good always seemed to sicken him. Odd, he loathed humanity, yet he will be remembered as one of its great benefactors. All that money to cancer research . . .'

I leant forward.

'It's curious,' I said, 'that no one has ever noticed that you can't see the boathouse from the cedar tree. The willows screen it from view. I've often wondered if you planned it or whether it was on an impulse.'

The lights flickered as the train rattled through a tunnel. The little clerk coughed.

'Purely impulse, sir. In a small way I am a student of literature, and it has always struck me as curious that it is generally considered the unhappy ending if charity gets the money instead of the dissolute young heir. An alternative to be averted at all costs. The book I am reading now, sir, deals with a missing will. The hero is at the moment lying handcuffed and gagged on a deserted wharf.'

'And the tide is rising?'

'Swiftly, sir. He has three hours till midnight, in which to find a certain paper, otherwise his aunt's fortune reverts to charity.'

'And he finds it in time?'

'Yes, sir.'

'You'd have ended it differently?'

'Yes, sir.'

There was a silence.

'I've always wanted to know when the idea occurred to you,' I said.

He coughed.

'Mr Hentish's days were obviously numbered, sir. When he was signing the will I thought what a fine thing it would be if he should die before a change of heart. Otherwise, I knew I should soon be down at the Abbey to alter the will again in young Mr Hentish's favour, and I knew him too well to hope that anyone but himself and the bookmakers would benefit by the money. Too like his uncle, sir.'

'I suppose old Hentish started talking about William and got into a rage at having been deceived over the wedding. That would bring on one of his attacks.'

'Yes, sir. His face got purple and his lips went white. I stood watching him, hoping it might be fatal. He told me to go and pour him out a glass of medicine from the bottle on the table in the bathroom. The directions were on the bottle, he said. I'm a little short-sighted, sir; it took me a little while to get my bearings. When I got my reading glasses on the first thing that caught my eye was the phial labelled morphia, and while he was yelling at me from the library I opened the cupboard door, took out the morphia, and poured it into the glass of medicine. He took the glass from me. "You damn fool," he said, and drank it down.'

'Swallowed it too quickly to suspect anything, I suppose.'

'He just drew a deep breath, closed his eyes, and leaned back in the chair. I went into the bathroom and wiped my fingerprints off everything, which I understand is the correct procedure in murder.

Then I returned to the library, collected my papers and replaced them in my brief case. Mr Hentish sat perfectly still. I don't know whether he was breathing or not. When everything was in order I went out into the hall, closing the library door quietly behind me. I rang the bell for Mr Croucher, and told him I should remain in the garden till my train time. "Is the old screw quiet?" he asked me, and I said he was.'

'Did it occur to you that William Hentish might be accused?'

'No, sir; the fact that the will was not in his favour seemed to preclude that. I didn't know he was unaware of my presence at the Abbey, or the reason for it.'

'I suppose you saw him across the lawn to the boathouse?'

'No, sir, I didn't. I must have been dozing at the time. I took a chance on corroborating his story. It was the least I could do, I thought, sir.'

'Do you never feel a twinge of remorse about it?'

He looked surprised.

'Remorse! The money went to cancer research, sir. Have you read their last report? They've made great strides forward. Remorse! Oh no, sir. I've too great a regard for human life for that.'

The train quivered as the brakes checked the engine's speed, and the clerk peered out of the window. 'This will be my station, I think.' He gathered up the evening paper and his brief case. As the train groaned to a standstill a porter flung the door open and the fog bellied into the carriage.

'Cranham Junction. All change for Kedam, Stukely, Rye, and Wyming. All change,' he chanted. 'Any baggage, sir?'

'No thank you.' He turned to me. 'I've enjoyed our conversation very much, sir. I wish you good night.'

There is no silence more complete than the silence which follows the cessation of machinery. It intensifies all other sounds, the hiss of escaping steam, the clank and rattle of milk cans and the muffled chant of the porter. 'All ch-aa-nn-ge.' Suddenly the engine throbs, there is a jerk and a scraping as the wheels turn. Green lights, red lights, porters, old women, solicitors' clerks, loom large in the mist for a second through the moisture on the window-panes; the scraping of the wheels becomes more rhythmic, takes on a deeper whine; and the train rolls you on beyond them all.

VI

THE MASTER

On the whole, when anthologizing the Sherlock Holmes stories of *Arthur Conan Doyle* (1859–1930) two courses are open to the anthologist: either print the best, or the least known. 'The best', it is frequently argued, are those written prior to Doyle's act of revenge upon his Frankenstein's monster: his hurling of Holmes over the Reichenbach Falls locked in the arms of his most troublesome adversary. There is a body of opinion which swears the Great Detective was by no means as great after he returned, though not all Holmes enthusiasts subscribe to it. The latter course, printing the least known, is rarely taken since, clearly, the reason the stories are little known is because they are less good than 'the best'. This too is a moot point. Such stories as 'The Red-Headed League', 'The Speckled Band', or 'Silver Blaze' are, of course, superlative examples of Holmes at his best—no, *Doyle* at his best; let us not fall into the unfair whimsy indulged in by so many Holmes fanatics that Doyle was a mere 'literary agent' and not the great and skilful story-teller he so patently was. In any case, the later adventures have their music too. 'Charles Augustus Milverton' is a fascinating story for a number of reasons: because it shows Holmes had humanity; because there is one horrible detail (the murderer's first act after the victim falls to the floor) that reveals Doyle in a tough and unsqueamish light; and because the eponymous villain is based on a real person, the notorious Victorian blackmailer Charles Augustus Howell (already dead when Doyle wrote the story, hence his use of the identifying given names). Amongst others, Howell blackmailed Swinburne's parents (there were some ugly letters the young poet had written describing in graphic detail flogging orgies at Eton), and the Headmaster of Harrow, the egregious Dr Vaughan (rather stupidly, Vaughan had written explicit notes concerning his relations with certain of his younger charges, or 'bitches' as he preferred to call them). Howell is said to have ended up in a Chelsea gutter with his throat cut and a half-sovereign wedged between his teeth— the traditional punishment meted out to a slanderer. The plot of 'The Creeping Man', too, had a more or less contemporary basis: the sudden interest, in the early 1920s, in the use of extracts of animal glands as a kind of pick-me-up—clinics specializing in this singular treatment proliferated in Switzerland, to no good effect as far as one can tell. Many ardent Sherlockians dismiss 'The Lion's Mane', recounted by Holmes himself, as a fake—written by Lestrade, say, or Mrs Watson, or even perhaps Professor Moriarty (after all, if Holmes survived the Reichenbach Falls, why not he?). The less easily led prefer to see it as an interesting experiment by Doyle that largely succeeds.

Mgr. *Ronald Knox* (1888–1957) was a younger brother of the humorist E. V. Knox ('Evoe', editor of *Punch*, 1932–49), and a passionate advocate of the detective story, creating in the 1920s a Decalogue for writers in the genre that still has some relevance today (no 'poisons unknown to science', no identical twins, no unidentified clues, and so on), and which was then taken up, suitably refined, as the rules of the Detection Club. Ironically, some of Knox's own novels stray from those same principles. Knox's path to religious faith bears some resemblance to that of the writer R. H. Benson. Benson, son of the Archbishop of Canterbury, was ordained into the Church of England then turned to Rome and became secretary to Pius X. Knox, son of the Bishop of Manchester, followed much the same route: ordained into the established Church in 1911, converted to Catholicism and re-ordained in 1919. He was a prolific essayist, an artful parodist, and wrote six undistinguished detective novels. His translation of the Vulgate into modern English in three volumes was favourably received. His fame, however, rests on his championship (at times refreshingly tongue-in-cheek) of Sherlock Holmes; he virtually created Sherlockian scholarship and his 1912 'Studies in the Literature of Sherlock Holmes' (collected in 1928) are still amongst the discipline's most readable. As an exercise in pastiche, 'The Adventure of the First Class Carriage' is highly entertaining and clever; stylistically, it is very nearly faultless.

The Adventure of
Charles Augustus Milverton

Arthur Conan Doyle

IT is years since the incidents of which I speak took place, and yet it is with diffidence that I allude to them. For a long time, even with the utmost discretion and reticence, it would have been impossible to make the facts public; but now the principal person concerned is beyond the reach of human law, and with due suppression the story may be told in such fashion as to injure no one. It records an absolutely unique experience in the career both of Mr Sherlock Holmes and of myself. The reader will excuse me if I conceal the date or any other fact by which he might trace the actual occurrence.

We had been out for one of our evening rambles, Holmes and I, and had returned about six o'clock on a cold, frosty winter's evening. As Holmes turned up the lamp the light fell upon a card on the table. He glanced at it, and then, with an ejaculation of disgust, threw it on the floor. I picked it up and read:

CHARLES AUGUSTUS MILVERTON,
APPLEDORE TOWERS,

AGENT.   HAMPSTEAD.

'Who is he?' I asked.

'The worst man in London,' Holmes answered, as he sat down and stretched his legs before the fire. 'Is anything on the back of the card?'

I turned it over.

'Will call at 6.30—C. A. M.,' I read.

'Hum! He's about due. Do you feel a creeping, shrinking sensation, Watson, when you stand before the serpents in the Zoo and see the slithery, gliding, venomous creatures, with their deadly eyes and wicked, flattened faces? Well, that's how Milverton impresses me. I've had to do with fifty murderers in my career, but the worst of them never gave me the repulsion which I have for this fellow. And yet I can't get out of doing business with him—indeed, he is here at my invitation.'

'But who is he?'

'I'll tell you, Watson. He is the king of all the blackmailers. Heaven help the man, and still more the woman, whose secret and reputation come into the power of Milverton. With a smiling face and a heart of marble he will squeeze and squeeze until he has drained them dry. The fellow is a genius in his way, and would have made his mark in some more savoury trade. His method is as follows: He allows it to be known that he is prepared to pay very high sums for letters which compromise people of wealth or position. He receives these wares not only from treacherous valets or maids, but frequently from genteel ruffians who have gained the confidence and affection of trusting women. He deals with no niggard hand. I happen to know that he paid seven hundred pounds to a footman for a note two lines in length, and that the ruin of a noble family was the result. Everything which is in the market goes to Milverton, and there are hundreds in this great city who turn white at his name. No one knows where his grip may fall, for he is far too rich and far too cunning to work from hand to mouth. He will hold a card back for years in order to play it at the moment when the stake is best worth winning. I have said that he is the worst man in London, and I would ask you how could one compare the ruffian who in hot blood bludgeons his mate with this man, who methodically and at his leisure tortures the soul and wrings the nerves in order to add to his already swollen money-bags?'

I had seldom heard my friend speak with such intensity of feeling.

'But surely,' said I, 'the fellow must be within the grasp of the law?'

'Technically, no doubt, but practically not. What would it profit a woman, for example, to get him a few months' imprisonment if her own ruin must immediately follow? His victims dare not hit back. If ever he blackmailed an innocent person, then, indeed, we should have him; but he is as cunning as the Evil One. No, no: we must find other ways to fight him.'

'And why is he here?'

'Because an illustrious client has placed her piteous case in my hands. It is the Lady Eva Brackwell, the most beautiful débutante of last season. She is to be married in a fortnight to the Earl of Dovercourt. This fiend has several imprudent letters—imprudent, Watson, nothing worse—which were written to an impecunious young squire in the country. They would suffice to break off the match. Milverton will send the letters to the Earl unless a large sum of money is paid him. I have been commissioned to meet him, and—to make the best terms I can.'

At that instant there was a clatter and a rattle in the street below. Looking down I saw a stately carriage and pair, the brilliant lamps gleaming on the glossy haunches of the noble chestnuts. A footman opened the door, and a small, stout man in a shaggy astrachan overcoat descended. A minute later he was in the room.

Charles Augustus Milverton was a man of fifty, with a large, intellectual head, a round, plump, hairless face, a perpetual frozen smile, and two keen grey eyes, which gleamed brightly from behind broad, golden-rimmed glasses. There was something of Mr Pick-wick's benevolence in his appearance, marred only by the insincerity of the fixed smile and by the hard glitter of those restless and penetrating eyes. His voice was as smooth and suave as his countenance, as he advanced with a plump little hand extended, murmuring his regret for having missed us at his first visit. Holmes disregarded the outstretched hand and looked at him with a face of granite. Milverton's smile broadened; he shrugged his shoulders, removed his overcoat, folded it with great deliberation over the back of a chair, and then took a seat.

'This gentleman?' said he, with a wave in my direction. 'Is it discreet? Is it right?'

'Dr Watson is my friend and partner.'

'Very good, Mr Holmes. It is only in your client's interests that I protested. The matter is so very delicate——'

'Dr Watson has already heard of it.'

'Then we can proceed to business. You say that you are acting for Lady Eva. Has she empowered you to accept my terms?'

'What are your terms?'

'Seven thousand pounds.'

'And the alternative?'

'My dear sir, it is painful to me to discuss it; but if the money is not paid on the 14th there certainly will be no marriage on the 18th.' His insufferable smile was more complacent than ever.

Holmes thought for a little.

'You appear to me,' he said, at last, 'to be taking matters too much for granted. I am, of course, familiar with the contents of these letters. My client will certainly do what I may advise. I shall counsel her to tell her future husband the whole story and to trust to his generosity.'

Milverton chuckled.

'You evidently do not know the Earl,' said he.

From the baffled look upon Holmes's face I could clearly see that he did.

'What harm is there in the letters?' he asked.

'They are sprightly—very sprightly,' Milverton answered. 'The lady was a charming correspondent. But I can assure you that the Earl of Dovercourt would fail to appreciate them. However, since you think otherwise, we will let it rest at that. It is purely a matter of business. If you think that it is in the best interests of your client that these letters should be placed in the hands of the Earl, then you would indeed be foolish to pay so large a sum of money to regain them.' He rose and seized his astrachan coat.

Holmes was grey with anger and mortification.

'Wait a little,' he said. 'You go too fast. We would certainly make every effort to avoid scandal in so delicate a matter.'

Milverton relapsed into his chair.

'I was sure that you would see it in that light,' he purred.

'At the same time,' Holmes continued, 'Lady Eva is not a wealthy woman. I assure you that two thousand pounds would be a drain upon her resources, and that the sum you name is utterly beyond her power. I beg, therefore, that you will moderate your demands, and that you will return the letters at the price I indicate, which is, I assure you, the highest that you can get.'

Milverton's smile broadened and his eyes twinkled humorously.

'I am aware that what you say is true about the lady's resources,' said he. 'At the same time, you must admit that the occasion of a lady's marriage is a very suitable time for her friends and relatives to make some little effort upon her behalf. They may hesitate as to an acceptable wedding present. Let me assure them that this little bundle of letters would give more joy than all the candelabra and butter-dishes in London.'

'It is impossible,' said Holmes.

'Dear me, dear me, how unfortunate!' cried Milverton, taking out a bulky pocket-book. 'I cannot help thinking that ladies are ill-advised in not making an effort. Look at this!' He held up a little note with a coat-of-arms upon the envelope. 'That belongs to— well, perhaps, it is hardly fair to tell the name until tomorrow morning. But at that time it will be in the hands of the lady's husband. And all because she will not find a beggarly sum which she could get in an hour by turning her diamonds into paste. It *is* such a pity. Now, you remember the sudden end of the engagement between the Honourable Miss Miles and Colonel Dorking? Only two days before the wedding there was a paragraph in the *Morning Post* to say that it was all off. And why? It is almost incredible, but the absurd sum of twelve hundred pounds would have settled the whole question. Is it not pitiful? And here I find you, a man of sense, boggling about terms when your client's future and honour are at stake. You surprise me, Mr Holmes.'

'What I say is true,' Holmes answered. 'The money cannot be found. Surely it is better for you to take the substantial sum which I offer than to ruin this woman's career, which can profit you in no way?'

'There you make a mistake, Mr Holmes. An exposure would profit me indirectly to a considerable extent. I have eight or ten similar cases maturing. If it was circulated among them that I had made a severe example of the Lady Eva I should find all of them much more open to reason. You see my point?'

Holmes sprang from his chair.

'Get behind him, Watson! Don't let him out! Now, sir, let us see the contents of that notebook.'

Milverton had glided as quick as a rat to the side of the room, and stood with his back against the wall.

'Mr Holmes, Mr Holmes,' he said, turning the front of his coat and exhibiting the butt of a large revolver, which projected from the inside pocket. 'I have been expecting you to do something original. This has been done so often, and what good has ever come from it? I assure you that I am armed to the teeth, and I am perfectly prepared to use my weapons, knowing that the law will support me. Besides, your supposition that I would bring the letters here in a notebook is entirely mistaken. I would do nothing so foolish. And now, gentlemen, I have one or two little interviews this evening, and it is a long drive to Hampstead.' He stepped forward, took up his coat, laid his hand on his revolver, and turned to the door. I picked up a chair, but Holmes shook his head and I laid it down again. With a bow, a smile, and a twinkle Milverton was out of the room, and a few moments after we heard the slam of the carriage door and the rattle of the wheels as he drove away.

Holmes sat motionless by the fire, his hands buried deep in his trouser pockets, his chin sunk upon his breast, his eyes fixed upon the glowing embers. For half an hour he was silent and still. Then, with the gesture of a man who has taken his decision, he sprang to his feet and passed into his bedroom. A little later a rakish young workman with a goatee beard and a swagger lit his clay pipe at the lamp before descending into the street. 'I'll be back some time, Watson,' said he, and vanished into the night. I understood that he had opened his campaign against Charles Augustus Milverton; but I little dreamed the strange shape which that campaign was destined to take.

For some days Holmes came and went at all hours in this attire, but beyond a remark that his time was spent at Hampstead, and that it was not wasted, I knew nothing of what he was doing. At last, however, on a wild, tempestuous evening, when the wind screamed and rattled against the windows, he returned from his last expedition, and having removed his disguise he sat before the fire and laughed heartily in his silent inward fashion.

'You would not call me a marrying man, Watson?'

'No, indeed!'

'You'll be interested to hear that I am engaged.'

'My dear fellow! I congrat——'

'To Milverton's housemaid.'

'Good heavens, Holmes!'

'I wanted information, Watson.'

'Surely you have gone too far?'

'It was a most necessary step. I am a plumber with a rising

business, Escott by name. I have walked out with her each evening, and I have talked with her. Good heavens, those talks! However, I have got all I wanted. I know Milverton's house as I know the palm of my hand.'

'But the girl, Holmes?'

He shrugged his shoulders.

'You can't help it, my dear Watson. You must play your cards as best you can when such a stake is on the table. However, I rejoice to say that I have a hated rival who will certainly cut me out the instant that my back is turned. What a splendid night it is!'

'You like this weather?'

'It suits my purpose. Watson, I mean to burgle Milverton's house tonight.'

I had a catching of the breath, and my skin went cold at the words, which were slowly uttered in a tone of concentrated resolution. As a flash of lightning in the night shows up in an instant every detail of a wide landscape, so at one glance I seemed to see every possible result of such an action—the detection, the capture, the honoured career ending in irreparable failure and disgrace, my friend himself lying at the mercy of the odious Milverton.

'For Heaven's sake, Holmes, think what you are doing,' I cried.

'My dear fellow, I have given it every consideration. I am never precipitate in my actions, nor would I adopt so energetic and indeed so dangerous a course if any other were possible. Let us look at the matter clearly and fairly. I suppose that you will admit that the action is morally justifiable, though technically criminal. To burgle his house is no more than to forcibly take his pocket-book—an action in which you were prepared to aid me.'

I turned it over in my mind.

'Yes,' I said; 'it is morally justifiable so long as our object is to take no articles save those which are used for an illegal purpose.'

'Exactly. Since it is morally justifiable I have only to consider the question of personal risk. Surely a gentleman should not lay much stress upon this when a lady is in most desperate need of his help?'

'You will be in such a false position.'

'Well, that is part of the risk. There is no other possible way of regaining these letters. The unfortunate lady has not the money, and there are none of her people in whom she could confide. Tomorrow is the last day of grace, and unless we can get the letters tonight this villain will be as good as his word and will bring about her ruin. I must, therefore, abandon my client to her fate or I must play this last card. Between ourselves, Watson, it's a sporting duel between this fellow Milverton and me. He had, as you saw, the best of the first exchanges; but my self-respect and my reputation are concerned to fight it to a finish.'

'Well, I don't like it; but I suppose it must be,' said I. 'When do we start?'

'You are not coming.'

'Then you are not going,' said I. 'I give you my word of honour—and I never broke it in my life—that I will take a cab straight to the police station and give you away unless you let me share this adventure with you.'

'You can't help me.'

'How do you know that? You can't tell what may happen. Anyway, my resolution is taken. Other people beside you have self-respect and even reputations.'

Holmes had looked annoyed, but his brow cleared, and he clapped me on the shoulder.

'Well, well, my dear fellow, be it so. We have shared the same room for some years, and it would be amusing if we ended by sharing the same cell. You know, Watson, I don't mind confessing to you that I have always had an idea that I would have made a highly efficient criminal. This is the chance of my lifetime in that direction. See here!' He took a neat little leather case out of a drawer, and opening it he exhibited a number of shining instruments. 'This is a first-class, up-to-date burgling kit, with nickel-plated jemmy, diamond-tipped glass-cutter, adaptable keys, and every modern improvement which the march of civilization demands. Here, too, is my dark lantern. Everything is in order. Have you a pair of silent shoes?'

'I have rubber-soled tennis shoes.'

'Excellent. And a mask?'

'I can make a couple out of black silk.'

'I can see that you have a strong natural turn for this sort of thing. Very good; do you make the masks. We shall have some cold supper before we start. It is now nine-thirty. At eleven we shall drive as far as Church Row. It is a quarter of an hour's walk from there to Appledore Towers. We shall be at work before midnight. Milverton is a heavy sleeper and retires punctually at ten-thirty. With any luck we should be back here by two, with the Lady Eva's letters in my pocket.'

Holmes and I put on our dress-clothes, so that we might appear to be two theatre-goers homeward bound. In Oxford Street we picked up a hansom and drove to an address in Hampstead. Here we paid off our cab, and with our greatcoats buttoned up, for it was bitterly cold and the wind seemed to blow through us, we walked along the edge of the Heath.

'It's a business that needs delicate treatment,' said Holmes. 'These documents are contained in a safe in the fellow's study, and the study is the ante-room of his bedchamber. On the other hand, like all these stout, little men who do themselves well, he is a plethoric sleeper. Agatha—that's my fiancée—says it is a joke in the servants' hall that it's impossible to wake the master. He has a secretary who is devoted to his interests and never budges from the study all day. That's why we are going at night. Then he has a beast of a dog which roams the garden. I met Agatha late the last two evenings, and she locks the brute up so as to give me a clear run. This is the house, this big one in its own grounds. Through the gate—now to the right among the laurels. We might put on our masks here, I think. You see, there is not a glimmer of light in any of the windows, and everything is working splendidly.'

With our black silk face-coverings, which turned us into two of the most truculent figures in London, we stole up to the silent, gloomy house. A sort of tiled veranda extended along one side of it, lined by several windows and two doors.

'That's his bedroom,' Holmes whispered. 'This door opens straight into the study. It would suit us best, but it is bolted as well as locked, and we should make too much noise getting in. Come round here. There's a greenhouse which opens into the drawing-room.'

The place was locked, but Holmes removed a circle of glass and turned the key from the inside. An instant afterwards he had closed the door behind us, and we had become felons in the eyes of the law. The thick, warm air of the conservatory and the rich, choking fragrance of exotic plants took us by the throat. He seized my hand in the darkness and led me swiftly past banks of shrubs which brushed against our faces. Holmes had remarkable powers, carefully cultivated, of seeing in the dark. Still holding my hand in one of his he opened a door, and I was vaguely conscious that we had entered a large room in which a cigar had been smoked not long before. He felt his way among the furniture, opened another door, and closed it behind us. Putting out my hand I felt several coats hanging from the wall, and I understood that I was in a passage. We passed along it, and Holmes very gently opened a door upon the right-hand side. Something rushed out at us and my heart sprang into my mouth, but I could have laughed when I realized that it was the cat. A fire was burning in this new room, and again the air was heavy with tobacco smoke. Holmes entered on tiptoe, waited for me to follow, and then very gently closed the door. We were in Milverton's study, and a *portière* at the further side showed the entrance to his bedroom.

It was a good fire, and the room was illuminated by it. Near the door I saw the gleam of an electric switch, but it was unnecessary, even if it had been safe, to turn it on. At one side of the fireplace was a heavy curtain, which covered the bay window we had seen from outside. On the other side was the door which communicated with the veranda. A desk stood in the centre, with a turning chair of shining red leather. Opposite was a large bookcase, with a marble bust of Athene on the top. In the corner between the bookcase and the wall there stood a tall green safe, the firelight flashing back from the polished brass knobs upon its face. Holmes stole across and looked at it. Then he crept to the door of the bedroom, and stood with slanting head listening intently. No sound came from within. Meanwhile it had struck me that it would be wise to secure our retreat through the outer door, so I examined it. To my amazement it was neither locked nor bolted! I touched Holmes on the arm, and he turned his masked face in that direction. I saw him start, and he was evidently as surprised as I.

'I don't like it,' he whispered, putting his lips to my very ear. 'I can't quite make it out. Anyhow, we have no time to lose.'

'Can I do anything?'

'Yes; stand by the door. If you hear anyone come, bolt it on the inside, and we can get away as we came. If they come the other way, we can get through the door if our job is done, or hide behind these window curtains if it is not. Do you understand?'

I nodded and stood by the door. My first feeling of fear had passed away, and I thrilled now with a keener zest than I had ever enjoyed when we were the defenders of the law instead of its defiers. The high object of our mission, the consciousness that it was unselfish and chivalrous, the villainous character of our opponent, all added to the sporting interest of the adventure. Far from feeling guilty, I rejoiced and exulted in our dangers. With a glow of admiration I watched Holmes unrolling his case of instruments and choosing his tool with the calm, scientific accuracy of a surgeon who performs a delicate operation. I knew that the opening of safes was a particular hobby with him, and I understood the joy which it gave him to be confronted with this green and gold monster, the dragon which held in its maw the reputations of many fair ladies. Turning up the cuffs of his dress-coat—he had placed his overcoat on a chair—Holmes laid out two drills, a jemmy, and several skeleton keys. I stood at the centre door with my eyes glancing at each of the others, ready for any emergency: though, indeed, my plans were somewhat vague as to what I should do if we were interrupted. For half an hour Holmes worked with concentrated energy, laying down one tool, picking up another, handling each with the strength and delicacy of the trained mechanic. Finally, I heard a click, the broad green door swung open, and inside I had a glimpse of a number of paper packets, each tied, sealed, and inscribed. Holmes picked one out, but it was hard to read by the flickering fire, and he drew out his little dark lantern, for it was too dangerous, with Milverton in the next room, to switch on the electric light. Suddenly I saw him halt, listen intently, and then in an instant he had swung the door of the safe to, picked up his coat, stuffed his tools into the pockets, and darted behind the window curtain, motioning me to do the same.

It was only when I had joined him there that I heard what had alarmed his quicker senses. There was a noise somewhere within the house. A door slammed in the distance. Then a confused, dull murmur broke itself into the measured thud of heavy footsteps rapidly approaching. They were in the passage outside the room. They paused at the door. The door opened. There was a sharp snick as the electric light was turned on. The door closed once more, and the pungent reek of a strong cigar was borne to our nostrils. Then the footsteps continued backwards and forwards, backwards and forwards, within a few yards of us. Finally, there was a creak from a chair, and the footsteps ceased. Then a key clicked in a lock and I heard the rustle of papers.

So far I had not dared to look out, but now I gently parted the division of the curtains in front of me and peeped through. From the pressure of Holmes's shoulder against mine I knew that he was sharing my observations. Right in front of us, and almost within our reach, was the broad, rounded back of Milverton. It was evident that we had entirely miscalculated his movements, that he had never been to his bedroom, but that he had been sitting up in some smoking or billiard room in the further wing of the house, the windows of which we had not seen. His broad, grizzled head, with its shining patch of baldness, was in the immediate foreground of our vision. He was leaning far back in the red leather chair, his legs outstretched, a long black cigar projecting at an angle from his mouth. He wore a semi-military smoking jacket, claret-coloured, with a black velvet collar. In his hand he held a long legal document, which he was reading in an indolent fashion, blowing rings of tobacco smoke from his lips as he did so. There was no promise of a speedy departure in his composed bearing and his comfortable attitude.

I felt Holmes's hand steal into mine and give me a reassuring shake, as if to say that the situation was within his powers and that he was easy in his mind. I was not sure whether he had seen what was only too obvious from my position, that the door of the safe was imperfectly closed, and that Milverton might at any moment observe it. In my own mind I had determined that if I were sure, from the rigidity of his gaze, that it had caught his eye, I would at once spring out, throw my greatcoat over his head, pinion him, and leave the rest to Holmes. But Milverton never looked up. He was languidly interested by the papers in his hand, and page after page was turned as he followed the argument of the lawyer. At least, I thought, when he has finished the document and the cigar he will go to his room; but before he had reached the end of either there came a remarkable development which turned our thoughts into quite another channel.

Several times I had observed that Milverton looked at his watch, and once he had risen and sat down again, with a gesture of impatience. The idea, however, that he might have an appointment at so strange an hour never occurred to me until a faint sound reached my ears from the veranda outside. Milverton dropped his papers and sat rigid in his chair. The sound was repeated, and then there came a gentle tap at the door. Milverton rose and opened it.

'Well,' said he, curtly, 'you are nearly half an hour late.'

So this was the explanation of the unlocked door and of the nocturnal vigil of Milverton. There was the gentle rustle of a woman's dress. I had closed the slit between the curtains as Milverton's face had turned in our direction, but now I ventured very carefully to open it once more. He had resumed his seat, the cigar still projecting at an insolent angle from the corner of his mouth. In front of him, in the full glare of the electric light, there stood a tall, slim, dark woman, a veil over her face, a mantle drawn round her chin. Her breath came quick and fast, and every inch of the lithe figure was quivering with strong emotion.

'Well,' said Milverton, 'you've made me lose a good night's rest, my dear. I hope you'll prove worth it. You couldn't come any other time—eh?'

The woman shook her head.

'Well, if you couldn't you couldn't. If the Countess is a hard mistress you have your chance to get level with her now. Bless the girl, what are you shivering about? That's right! Pull yourself together! Now, let us get down to business.' He took a note from the drawer of his desk. 'You say that you have five letters which compromise the Countess d'Albert. You want to sell them. I want to buy them. So far so good. It only remains to fix a price. I should want to inspect the letters, of course. If they are really good specimens—— Great heavens, is it you?'

The woman without a word had raised her veil and dropped the mantle from her chin. It was dark, handsome, clear-cut face which confronted Milverton, a face with a curved nose, strong, dark eyebrows shading hard, glittering eyes, and a straight, thin-lipped mouth set in a dangerous smile.

'It is I,' she said; 'the woman whose life you have ruined.'

Milverton laughed, but fear vibrated in his voice. 'You were so very obstinate,' said he. 'Why did you drive me to such extremities? I assure you I wouldn't hurt a fly of my own accord, but every man has his business, and what was I to do? I put the price well within your means. You would not pay.'

'So you sent the letters to my husband, and he—the noblest

gentleman that ever lived, a man whose boots I was never worthy to lace—he broke his gallant heart and died. You remember that last night when I came through that door I begged and prayed you for mercy, and you laughed in my face as you are trying to laugh now, only your coward heart cannot keep your lips from twitching? Yes, you never thought to see me here again, but it was that night which taught me how I could meet you face to face, and alone. Well, Charles Milverton, what have you to say?'

'Don't imagine that you can bully me,' said he, rising to his feet. 'I have only to raise my voice, and I could call my servants and have you arrested. But I will make allowance for your natural anger. Leave the room at once as you came, and I will say no more.'

The woman stood with her hand buried in her bosom, and the same deadly smile on her thin lips.

'You will ruin no more lives as you ruined mine. You will wring no more hearts as you wrung mine. I will free the world of a poisonous thing. Take that, you hound, and that!—and that!—and that!—and that!'

She had drawn a little, gleaming revolver, and emptied barrel after barrel into Milverton's body, the muzzle within two feet of his shirt front. He shrank away and then fell forward upon the table, coughing furiously and clawing among the papers. Then he staggered to his feet, received another shot, and rolled upon the floor. 'You've done me,' he cried, and lay still. The woman looked at him intently and ground her heel into his upturned face. She looked again, but there was no sound or movement. I heard a sharp rustle, the night air blew into the heated room, and the avenger was gone.

No interference upon our part could have saved the man from his fate; but as the woman poured bullet after bullet into Milverton's shrinking body I was about to spring out, when I felt Holmes's cold, strong grasp upon my wrist. I understood the whole argument of that firm, restraining grip—that it was no affair of ours; that justice had overtaken a villain; that we had our own duties and our own objects which were not to be lost sight of. But hardly had the woman rushed from the room when Holmes, with swift, silent steps, was over at the other door. He turned the key in the lock. At the same instant we heard voices in the house and the sound of hurrying feet. The revolver shots had roused the household. With perfect coolness Holmes slipped across to the safe, filled his two arms with bundles of letters, and poured them all into the fire. Again and again he did it, until the safe was empty. Someone turned the handle and beat upon the outside of the door. Holmes looked swiftly round. The letter which had been the messenger of death for Milverton lay all mottled with his blood, upon the table. Holmes tossed it in among the blazing papers. Then he drew the key from the outer door, passed through after me, and locked it on the outside. 'This way, Watson,' said he; 'we can scale the garden wall in this direction.'

I could not have believed that an alarm could have spread so swiftly. Looking back, the huge house was one blaze of light. The front door was open, and figures were rushing down the drive. The whole garden was alive with people, and one fellow raised a view-halloa as we emerged from the veranda and followed hard at our heels. Holmes seemed to know the ground perfectly, and he threaded his way swiftly among a plantation of small trees, I close at his heels, and our foremost pursuer panting behind us. It was a six-foot wall which barred our path, but he sprang to the top and over. As I did the same I felt the hand of the man behind me grab at my ankle; but I kicked myself free and scrambled over a glass-strewn coping. I fell upon my face among some bushes; but Holmes had me on my feet in an instant, and together we dashed away across the huge expanse of Hampstead Heath. We had run two miles, I suppose, before Holmes at last halted and listened intently. All was absolute silence behind us. We had shaken off our pursuers and were safe.

We had breakfasted and were smoking our morning pipe on the day after the remarkable experience which I have recorded when Mr Lestrade, of Scotland Yard, very solemn and impressive, was ushered into our modest sitting-room.

'Good morning, Mr Holmes,' said he; 'good morning. May I ask if you are very busy just now?'

'Not too busy to listen to you.'

'I thought that, perhaps, if you had nothing particular on hand, you might care to assist us in a most remarkable case which occurred only last night at Hampstead.'

'Dear me!' said Holmes. 'What was that?'

'A murder—a most dramatic and remarkable murder. I know

how keen you are upon these things, and I would take it as a great
favour if you would step down to Appledore Towers and give us
the benefit of your advice. It is no ordinary crime. We have had our
eyes upon this Mr Milverton for some time, and, between ourselves,
he was a bit of a villain. He is known to have held papers which he
used for blackmailing purposes. These papers have all been burned
by the murderers. No article of value was taken, as it is probable
that the criminals were men of good position, whose sole object was
to prevent social exposure.'

'Criminals!' said Holmes. 'Plural!'

'Yes, there were two of them. They were, as nearly as possible,
captured red-handed. We have their footmarks, we have their
description; it's ten to one that we trace them. The first fellow was
a bit too active, but the second was caught by the under-gardener
and only got away after a struggle. He was a middle-sized, strongly
built man—square jaw, thick neck, moustache, a mask over his
eyes.'

'That's rather vague,' said Sherlock Holmes. 'Why, it might be a
description of Watson!'

'It's true,' said the inspector, with much amusement. 'It might be
a description of Watson.'

'Well, I am afraid I can't help you, Lestrade,' said Holmes. 'The
fact is that I knew this fellow Milverton, that I considered him one
of the most dangerous men in London, and that I think there are
certain crimes which the law cannot touch, and which therefore, to
some extent, justify private revenge. No, it's no use arguing. I have
made up my mind. My sympathies are with the criminals rather
than with the victim, and I will not handle this case.'

Holmes had not said one word to me about the tragedy which we
had witnessed, but I observed all the morning that he was in his
most thoughtful mood, and he gave me the impression, from his
vacant eyes and his abstracted manner, of a man who is striving to
recall something to his memory. We were in the middle of our
lunch when he suddenly sprang to his feet. 'By Jove, Watson; I've
got it!' he cried. 'Take your hat! Come with me!' He hurried at his
top speed down Baker Street and along Oxford Street, until we had
almost reached Regent Circus. Here on the left hand there stands a
shop window filled with photographs of the celebrities and beauties

of the day. Holmes's eyes fixed themselves upon one of them, and following his gaze I saw the picture of a regal and stately lady in Court dress, with a high diamond tiara upon her noble head. I looked at that delicately curved nose, at the marked eyebrows, at the straight mouth, and the strong little chin beneath it. Then I caught my breath as I read the time-honoured title of the great nobleman and statesman whose wife she had been. My eyes met those of Holmes, and he put his finger to his lips as we turned away from the window.

The Adventure of the Creeping Man

Arthur Conan Doyle

M R SHERLOCK HOLMES was always of opinion that I should publish the singular facts connected with Professor Presbury, if only to dispel once for all the ugly rumours which some twenty years ago agitated the University and were echoed in the learned societies of London. There were, however, certain obstacles in the way, and the true history of this curious case remained entombed in the tin box which contains so many records of my friend's adventures. Now we have at last obtained permission to ventilate the facts which formed one of the very last cases handled by Holmes before his retirement from practice. Even now a certain reticence and discretion have to be observed in laying the matter before the public.

It was one Sunday evening early in September of the year 1902 that I received one of Holmes's laconic messages: 'Come at once if convenient—if inconvenient come all the same.—S. H.' The relations between us in those latter days were peculiar. He was a man of habits, narrow and concentrated habits, and I had become one of them. As an institution I was like the violin, the shag tobacco, the old black pipe, the index books, and others perhaps less excusable. When it was a case of active work and a comrade was needed upon whose nerve he could place some reliance, my role was obvious. But apart from this I had uses. I was a whetstone for his mind. I stimulated him. He liked to think aloud in my presence. His remarks could hardly be said to be made to me—many of them would have been as appropriately addressed to his bedstead—but none the less, having formed the habit, it had become in some way helpful that I should register and interject. If I irritated him by a certain methodical slowness in my mentality, that irritation served only to make his own flame-like intuitions and impressions flash up the more vividly and swiftly. Such was my humble role in our alliance.

When I arrived at Baker Street I found him huddled up in his armchair with up-drawn knees, his pipe in his mouth and his brow furrowed with thought. It was clear that he was in the throes of some vexatious problem. With a wave of his hand he indicated my old armchair, but otherwise for half an hour he gave no sign that he was aware of my presence. Then with a start he seemed to come from his reverie, and, with his usual whimsical smile, he greeted me back to what had once been my home.

'You will excuse a certain abstraction of mind, my dear Watson,' said he. 'Some curious facts have been submitted to me within the last twenty-four hours, and they in turn have given rise to some speculations of a more general character. I have serious thoughts of writing a small monograph upon the uses of dogs in the work of the detective.'

'But surely, Holmes, this has been explored,' said I. 'Blood-hounds—sleuth-hounds——'

'No, no, Watson; that side of the matter is, of course, obvious. But there is another which is far more subtle. You may recollect that in the case which you, in your sensational way, coupled with the Copper Beeches, I was able, by watching the mind of the child, to form a deduction as to the criminal habits of the very smug and respectable father.'

'Yes, I remember it well.'

'My line of thoughts about dogs is analogous. A dog reflects the family life. Whoever saw a frisky dog in a gloomy family, or a sad dog in a happy one? Snarling people have snarling dogs, dangerous people have dangerous ones. And their passing moods may reflect the passing moods of others.'

I shook my head. 'Surely, Holmes, this is a little far-fetched,' said I.

He had refilled his pipe and resumed his seat, taking no notice of my comment.

'The practical application of what I have said is very close to the problem which I am investigating. It is a tangled skein, you understand, and I am looking for a loose end. One possible loose end lies in the question: Why does Professor Presbury's faithful wolfhound, Roy, endeavour to bite him?'

I sank back in my chair in some disappointment. Was it for so trivial a question as this that I had been summoned from my work? Holmes glanced across at me.

'The same old Watson!' said he. 'You never learn that the gravest issues may depend upon the smallest things. But is it not on the face of it strange that a staid, elderly philosopher—you've heard of Presbury, of course, the famous Camford physiologist?—that such a man, whose friend has been his devoted wolfhound, should now have been twice attacked by his own dog? What do you make of it?'

'The dog is ill.'

'Well, that has to be considered. But he attacks no one else, nor does he apparently molest his master, save on very special occasions. Curious, Watson—very curious. But young Mr Bennett is before his time, if that is his ring. I had hoped to have a longer chat with you before he came.'

There was a quick step on the stairs, a sharp tap at the door, and a moment later the new client presented himself. He was a tall, handsome youth about thirty, well dressed and elegant, but with something in his bearing which suggested the shyness of the student rather than the self-possession of the man of the world. He shook hands with Holmes, and then looked with some surprise at me.

'This matter is very delicate, Mr Holmes,' he said. 'Consider the relation in which I stand to Professor Presbury, both privately and publicly. I really can hardly justify myself if I speak before any third person.'

'Have no fear, Mr Bennett. Dr Watson is the very soul of discretion, and I can assure you that this is a matter in which I am very likely to need an assistant.'

'As you like, Mr Holmes. You will, I am sure, understand my having some reserves in the matter.'

'You will appreciate it, Watson, when I tell you that this gentleman, Mr Trevor Bennett, is professional assistant to the great scientist, lives under his roof, and is engaged to his only daughter. Certainly we must agree that the Professor has every claim upon his loyalty and devotion. But it may best be shown by taking the necessary steps to clear up this strange mystery.'

'I hope so, Mr Holmes. That is my one object. Does Dr Watson know the situation?'

'I have not had time to explain it.'

'Then perhaps I had better go over the ground again before explaining some fresh developments.'

'I will do so myself,' said Holmes, 'in order to show that I have the events in their due order. The Professor, Watson, is a man of European reputation. His life has been academic. There has never been a breath of scandal. He is a widower with one daughter, Edith. He is, I gather, a man of very virile and positive, one might almost say combative, character. So the matter stood until a very few months ago.

'Then the current of his life was broken. He is sixty-one years of age, but he became engaged to the daughter of Professor Morphy, his colleague in the chair of Comparative Anatomy. It was not, as I understand, the reasoned courting of an elderly man, but rather the passionate frenzy of youth, for no one could have shown himself a more devoted lover. The lady, Alice Morphy, was a very perfect girl both in mind and body, so that there was every excuse for the Professor's infatuation. None the less, it did not meet with full approval in his own family.'

'We thought it rather excessive,' said our visitor.

'Exactly. Excessive and a little violent and unnatural. Professor Presbury was rich, however, and there was no objection upon the part of the father. The daughter, however, had other views, and there were already several candidates for her hand, who, if they were less eligible from a wordly point of view, were at least more of an age. The girl seemed to like the Professor in spite of his eccentricities. It was only age which stood in the way.

'About this time a little mystery suddenly clouded the normal routine of the Professor's life. He did what he had never done before. He left home and gave no indication where he was going. He was away a fortnight, and returned looking rather travel-worn. He made no allusion to where he had been, although he was usually the frankest of men. It chanced, however, that our client here, Mr Bennett, received a letter from a fellow-student in Prague, who said that he was glad to have seen Professor Presbury there, although he had not been able to talk to him. Only in this way did his own household learn where he had been.

'Now comes the point. From that time onwards a curious change came over the Professor. He became furtive and sly. Those around him had always the feeling that he was not the man that they had known, but that he was under some shadow which had darkened his higher qualities. His intellect was not affected. His lectures were as brilliant as ever. But always there was something new, something sinister and unexpected. His daughter, who was devoted to him, tried again and again to resume the old relations and to penetrate this mask which her father seemed to have put on. You, sir, as I understand, did the same—but all was in vain. And now, Mr Bennett, tell in your own words the incident of the letters.'

'You must understand, Dr Watson, that the Professor had no secrets from me. If I were his son or his younger brother, I could not have more completely enjoyed his confidence. As his secretary I handled every paper which came to him, and I opened and subdivided his letters. Shortly after his return all this was changed. He told me that certain letters might come to him from London which would be marked by a cross under the stamp. These were to be set aside for his own eyes only. I may say that several of these did pass through my hands, that they had the EC mark, and were in an illiterate handwriting. If he answered them at all the answers did not pass through my hands nor into the letter-basket in which our correspondence was collected.'

'And the box,' said Holmes.

'Ah, yes, the box. The Professor brought back a little wooden box from his travels. It was the one thing which suggested a Continental tour, for it was one of those quaint carved things which one associates with Germany. This he placed in his instrument cupboard. One day, in looking for a canula, I took up the box. To my surprise he was very angry, and reproved me in words which were quite savage for my curiosity. It was the first time such a thing had happened and I was deeply hurt. I endeavoured to explain that it was a mere accident that I had touched the box, but all the evening I was conscious that he looked at me harshly and that the incident was rankling in his mind.' Mr Bennett drew a little diary book from his pocket. 'That was on the 2nd of July,' said he.

'You are certainly an admirable witness,' said Holmes. 'I may need some of these dates which you have noted.'

'I learned method among other things from my great teacher. From the time that I observed abnormality in his behaviour I felt that it was my duty to study his case. Thus I have it here that it was on that very day, July 2nd, that Roy attacked the Professor as he came from his study into the hall. Again on July 11th there was a scene of the same sort, and then I have a note of yet another upon July 20th. After that we had to banish Roy to the stables. He was a dear, affectionate animal—but I fear I weary you.'

Mr Bennett spoke in a tone of reproach, for it was very clear that Holmes was not listening. His face was rigid and his eyes gazed abstractedly at the ceiling. With an effort he recovered himself.

'Singular! Most singular!' he murmured. 'These details were new to me, Mr Bennett. I think we have now fairly gone over the old ground, have we not? But you spoke of some fresh development.'

The pleasant, open face of our visitor clouded over, shadowed by some grim remembrance. 'What I speak of occurred the night before last,' said he. 'I was lying awake about two in the morning, when I was aware of a dull muffled sound coming from the passage. I opened my door and peeped out. I should explain that the Professor sleeps at the end of the passage——'

'The date being——?' asked Holmes.

Our visitor was clearly annoyed at so irrelevant an interruption.

'I have said, sir, that it was the night before last—that is, September 4th.'

Holmes nodded and smiled.

'Pray continue,' said he.

'He sleeps at the end of the passage, and would have to pass my door in order to reach the staircase. It was a really terrifying experience, Mr Holmes. I think that I am as strong-nerved as my neighbours, but I was shaken by what I saw. The passage was dark save that one window half-way along it threw a patch of light. I could see that something was coming along the passage, something dark and crouching. Then suddenly it emerged into the light, and I saw that it was he. He was crawling, Mr Holmes—crawling! He was not quite on his hands and knees. I should rather say on his hands and feet, with his face sunk between his hands. Yet he seemed to move with ease. I was so paralysed by the sight that it was not until he had reached my door that I was able to step forward and ask if I could assist him. His answer was extraordinary. He sprang up, spat out some atrocious word at me, and hurried on past me and down the staircase. I waited about for an hour, but he did not come back. It must have been daylight before he regained his room.'

'Well, Watson, what make you of that?' asked Holmes, with the air of the pathologist who presents a rare specimen.

'Lumbago, possibly. I have known a severe attack make a man walk in just such a way, and nothing would be more trying to the temper.'

'Good, Watson! You always keep us flat-footed on the ground. But we can hardly accept lumbago, since he was able to stand erect in a moment.'

'He was never better in health,' said Bennett. 'In fact, he is stronger than I have known him for years. But there are the facts, Mr Holmes. It is not a case in which we can consult the police, and yet we are utterly at our wits' end as to what to do, and we feel in some strange way that we are drifting towards disaster. Edith— Miss Presbury—feels as I do, that we cannot wait passively any longer.'

'It is certainly a very curious and suggestive case. What do you think, Watson?'

'Speaking as a medical man,' said I, 'it appears to be a case for an alienist. The old gentleman's cerebral processes were disturbed by the love affair. He made a journey abroad in the hope of breaking himself of the passion. His letters and the box may be connected with some other private transaction—a loan, perhaps, or share certificates, which are in the box.'

'And the wolfhound no doubt disapproved of the financial bargain. No, no, Watson, there is more in it than this. Now, I can only suggest——'

What Sherlock Holmes was about to suggest will never be known, for at this moment the door opened and a young lady was shown into the room. As she appeared Mr Bennett sprang up with a cry and ran forward with his hands out to meet those which she had herself outstretched.

'Edith, dear! Nothing the matter, I hope?'

'I felt I must follow you. Oh, Jack, I have been so dreadfully frightened! It is awful to be there alone.'

'Mr Holmes, this is the young lady I spoke of. This is my fiancée.'

'We were gradually coming to that conclusion, were we not, Watson?' Holmes answered, with a smile. 'I take it, Miss Presbury, that there is some fresh development in the case, and that you thought we should know?'

Our new visitor, a bright, handsome girl of a conventional English type, smiled back at Holmes as she seated herself beside Mr Bennett.

'When I found Mr Bennett had left his hotel I thought I should probably find him here. Of course, he had told me that he would consult you. But, oh, Mr Holmes, can you do nothing for my poor father?'

'I have hopes, Miss Presbury, but the case is still obscure. Perhaps what you have to say may throw some fresh light upon it.'

'It was last night, Mr Holmes. He had been very strange all day. I am sure that there are times when he has no recollection of what he does. He lives as in a strange dream. Yesterday was such a day. It was not my father with whom I lived. His outward shell was there, but it was not really he.'

'Tell me what happened.'

'I was awakened in the night by the dog barking most furiously. Poor Roy, he is chained now near the stable. I may say that I always sleep with my door locked; for, as Jack—as Mr Bennett—will tell you, we all have a feeling of impending danger. My room is on the second floor. It happened that the blind was up in my window, and there was bright moonlight outside. As I lay with my eyes fixed upon the square of light, listening to the frenzied barkings of the dog, I was amazed to see my father's face looking in at me. Mr Holmes, I nearly died of surprise and horror. There it was pressed against the window-pane, and one hand seemed to be raised as if to push up the window. If that window had opened, I think I should have gone mad. It was no delusion, Mr Holmes. Don't deceive yourself by thinking so. I dare say it was twenty seconds or so that I lay paralysed and watched the face. Then it vanished, but I could not—I could not spring out of bed and look out after it. I lay cold and shivering till morning. At breakfast he was sharp and fierce in manner, and made no allusion to the adventure of the night. Neither did I, but I gave an excuse for coming to town—and here I am.'

Holmes looked thoroughly surprised at Miss Presbury's narrative.

'My dear young lady, you say that your room is on the second floor. Is there a long ladder in the garden?'

'No, Mr Holmes; that is the amazing part of it. There is no possible way of reaching the window—and yet he was there.'

'The date being September 4th,' said Holmes. 'That certainly complicates matters.'

It was the young lady's turn to look surprised. 'This is the second time that you have alluded to the date, Mr Holmes,' said Bennett. 'Is it possible that it has any bearing upon the case?'

'It is possible—very possible—and yet I have not my full material at present.'

'Possibly you are thinking of the connection between insanity and phases of the moon?'

'No, I assure you. It was quite a different line of thought. Possibly you can leave your notebook with me and I will check the dates. Now I think, Watson, that our line of action is perfectly clear. This young lady has informed us—and I have the greatest confidence in her intuition—that her father remembers little or nothing which occurs upon certain dates. We will therefore call upon him as if he had given us an appointment upon such a date. He will put it down to his own lack of memory. Thus we will open our campaign by having a good close view of him.'

'That is excellent,' said Mr Bennett. 'I warn you, however, that the Professor is irascible and violent at times.'

Holmes smiled. 'There are reasons why we should come at once —very cogent reasons if my theories hold good. Tomorrow, Mr Bennett, will certainly see us in Camford. There is, if I remember right, an inn called the Chequers where the port used to be above mediocrity, and the linen was above reproach. I think, Watson, that our lot for the next few days might lie in less pleasant places.'

Monday morning found us on our way to the famous University town—an easy effort on the part of Holmes, who had no roots to pull up, but one which involved frantic planning and hurrying on my part, as my practice was by this time not inconsiderable. Holmes made no allusion to the case until after we had deposited our suitcases at the ancient hostel of which he had spoken.

'I think, Watson, that we can catch the Professor just before lunch. He lectures at eleven, and should have an interval at home.'

'What possible excuse have we for calling?'

Holmes glanced at his notebook.

'There was a period of excitement upon August 26th. We will assume that he is a little hazy as to what he does at such times. If we insist that we are there by appointment I think he will hardly venture to contradict us. Have you the effrontery necessary to put it through?'

'We can but try.'

'Excellent, Watson! Compound of the Busy Bee and Excelsior. We can but try—the motto of the firm. A friendly native will surely guide us.'

Such a one on the back of a smart hansom swept us past a row of ancient colleges, and finally turning into a tree-lined drive pulled up at the door of a charming house, girt round with lawns and covered with purple wistaria. Professor Presbury was certainly surrounded with every sign not only of comfort but of luxury. Even as we pulled up a grizzled head appeared at the front window, and we were aware of a pair of keen eyes from under shaggy brows which surveyed us through large horn glasses. A moment later we were actually in his sanctum, and the mysterious scientist, whose vagaries had brought us from London, was standing before us. There was certainly no sign of eccentricity either in his manner or appearance, for he was a portly, large-featured man, grave, tall, and frock-coated, with the dignity of bearing which a lecturer needs. His eyes were his most remarkable feature, keen, observant, and clever to the verge of cunning.

He looked at our cards. 'Pray sit down, gentlemen. What can I do for you?'

Mr Holmes smiled amiably.

'It was the question which I was about to put to you, Professor.'

'To me, sir!'

'Possibly there is some mistake. I heard through a second person that Professor Presbury of Camford had need of my services.'

'Oh, indeed!' It seemed to me that there was a malicious sparkle in the intense grey eyes. 'You heard that, did you? May I ask the name of your informant?'

'I am sorry, Professor, but the matter was rather confidential. If I

Arthur Conan Doyle

have made a mistake there is no harm done. I can only express my
regret.'

'Not at all. I should wish to go further into this matter. It interests
me. Have you any scrap of writing, any letter or telegram, to bear
out your assertion?'

'No, I have not.'

'I presume that you do not go so far as to assert that I summoned
you?'

'I would rather answer no questions,' said Holmes.

'No, I dare say not,' said the Professor, with asperity. 'However,
that particular one can be answered very easily without your aid.'

He walked across the room to the bell. Our London friend, Mr
Bennett, answered the call.

'Come in, Mr Bennett. These two gentlemen have come from
London under the impression that they have been summoned. You
handle all my correspondence. Have you a note of anything going
to a person named Holmes?'

'No, sir,' Bennett answered, with a flush.

'That is conclusive,' said the Professor, glaring angrily at my companion. 'Now, sir'—he leaned forward with his two hands upon the
table—'it seems to me that your position is a very questionable one.'

Holmes shrugged his shoulders.

'I can only repeat that I am sorry that we have made a needless
intrusion.'

'Hardly enough, Mr Holmes!' the old man cried, in a high
screaming voice, with extraordinary malignancy upon his face. He
got between us and the door as he spoke, and he shook his two
hands at us with furious passion. 'You can hardly get out of it so
easily as that.' His face was convulsed and he grinned and gibbered
at us in his senseless rage. I am convinced that we should have had
to fight our way out of the room if Mr Bennett had not intervened.

'My dear Professor,' he cried, 'consider your position! Consider
the scandal at the University! Mr Holmes is a well-known man.
You cannot possibly treat him with such discourtesy.'

Sulkily our host—if I may call him so—cleared the path to the
door. We were glad to find ourselves outside the house, and in the
quiet of the tree-lined drive. Holmes seemed greatly amused by the
episode.

'Our learned friend's nerves are somewhat out of order,' said he. 'Perhaps our intrusion was a little crude, and yet we have gained that personal contact which I desired. But, dear me, Watson, he is surely at our heels. The villain still pursues us.'

There were the sounds of running feet behind, but it was, to my relief, not the formidable Professor but his assistant who appeared round the curve of the drive. He came panting up to us.

'I am so sorry, Mr Holmes. I wished to apologize.'

'My dear sir, there is no need. It is all in the way of professional experience.'

'I have never seen him in a more dangerous mood. But he grows more sinister. You can understand now why his daughter and I are alarmed. And yet his mind is perfectly clear.'

'Too clear!' said Holmes. 'That was my miscalculation. It is evident that his memory is much more reliable than I had thought. By the way, can we, before we go, see the window of Miss Presbury's room?'

Mr Bennett pushed his way through some shrubs and we had a view of the side of the house.

'It is there. The second on the left.'

'Dear me, it seems hardly accessible. And yet you will observe that there is a creeper below and a water pipe above which give some foothold.'

'I could not climb it myself,' said Mr Bennett.

'Very likely. It would certainly be a dangerous exploit for any normal man.'

'There was one other thing I wished to tell you, Mr Holmes. I have the address of the man in London to whom the Professor writes. He seems to have written this morning and I got it from his blotting paper. It is an ignoble position for a trusted secretary, but what else can I do?'

Holmes glanced at the paper and put it into his pocket.

'Dorak—a curious name. Slavonic, I imagine. Well, it is an important link in the chain. We return to London this afternoon, Mr Bennett. I see no good purpose to be served by our remaining. We cannot arrest the Professor because he has done no crime, nor can we place him under constraint, for he cannot be proved to be mad. No action is as yet possible.'

'Then what on earth are we to do?'

'A little patience, Mr Bennett. Things will soon develop. Unless I am mistaken next Tuesday may mark a crisis. Certainly we shall be in Camford on that day. Meanwhile, the general position is undeniably unpleasant, and if Miss Presbury can prolong her visit——'

'That is easy.'

'Then let her stay till we can assure her that all danger is past. Meanwhile let him have his way and do not cross him. So long as he is in a good humour all is well.'

'There he is!' said Bennett, in a startled whisper. Looking between the branches we saw the tall, erect figure emerge from the hall door and look around him. He stood leaning forward, his hands swinging straight before him, his head turning from side to side. The secretary with a last wave slipped off among the trees, and we saw him presently rejoin his employer, the two entering the house together in what seemed to be animated and even excited conversation.

'I expect the old gentleman has been putting two and two together,' said Holmes, as we walked hotel-wards. 'He struck me as having a particularly clear and logical brain, from the little I saw of him. Explosive, no doubt, but then from his point of view he has something to explode about if detectives are put on his track and he suspects his own household of doing it. I rather fancy that friend Bennett is in for an uncomfortable time.'

Holmes stopped at a post office and sent off a telegram on our way. The answer reached us in the evening, and he tossed it across to me. 'Have visited the Commercial Road and seen Dorak. Suave person, Bohemian, elderly. Keeps large general store—Mercer.'

'Mercer is since your time,' said Holmes. 'He is my general utility man who looks up routine business. It was important to know something of the man with whom our Professor was so secretly corresponding. His nationality connects up with the Prague visit.'

'Thank goodness that something connects with something,' said I. 'At present we seem to be faced by a long series of inexplicable incidents with no bearing upon each other. For example, what possible connection can there be between an angry wolfhound and a visit to Bohemia, or either of them with a man crawling down a passage at night? As to your dates, that is the biggest mystification of all.'

Holmes smiled and rubbed his hands. We were, I may say, seated in the old sitting-room of the ancient hotel, with a bottle of the famous vintage of which Holmes had spoken on the table between us.

'Well, now, let us take the dates first,' said he, his fingertips together and his manner as if he were addressing a class. 'This excellent young man's diary shows that there was trouble upon July 2nd, and from then onwards it seems to have been at nine-day intervals, with, so far as I remember, only one exception. Thus the last outbreak upon Friday was on September 3rd, which also falls into the series, as did August 26th, which preceded it. The thing is beyond coincidence.'

I was forced to agree.

'Let us, then, form the provisional theory that every nine days the Professor takes some strong drug which has a passing but highly poisonous effect. His naturally violent nature is intensified by it. He learned to take this drug while he was in Prague, and is now supplied with it by a Bohemian intermediary in London. This all hangs together, Watson!'

'But the dog, the face at the window, the creeping man in the passage?'

'Well, well, we have made a beginning. I should not expect any fresh developments until next Tuesday. In the meantime we can only keep in touch with friend Bennett and enjoy the amenities of this charming town.'

In the morning Mr Bennett slipped round to bring us the latest report. As Holmes had imagined, times had not been easy with him. Without exactly accusing him of being responsible for our presence, the Professor had been very rough and rude in his speech, and evidently felt some strong grievance. This morning he was quite himself again, however, and had delivered his usual brilliant lecture to a crowded class. 'Apart from his queer fits,' said Bennett, 'he has actually more energy and vitality than I can ever remember, nor was his brain ever clearer. But it's not he—it's never the man whom we have known.'

'I don't think you have anything to fear now for a week at least,' Holmes answered. 'I am a busy man, and Dr Watson has his patients to attend to. Let us agree that we meet here at this hour next Tuesday, and I shall be surprised if before we leave you again we are not able to explain, even if we cannot perhaps put an end to, your troubles. Meanwhile, keep us posted in what occurs.'

I saw nothing of my friend for the next few days, but on the following Monday evening I had a short note asking me to meet him next day at the train. From what he told me as we travelled up to Camford all was well, the peace of the Professor's house had been unruffled, and his own conduct perfectly normal. This also was the report which was given us by Mr Bennett himself when he called upon us that evening at our old quarters in the Chequers. 'He heard from his London correspondent today. There was a letter and there was a small packet, each with the cross under the stamp which warned me not to touch them. There has been nothing else.'

'That may prove quite enough,' said Holmes, grimly. 'Now, Mr Bennett, we shall, I think, come to some conclusion tonight. If my deductions are correct we should have an opportunity of bringing matters to a head. In order to do so it is necessary to hold the Professor under observation. I would suggest, therefore, that you remain awake and on the look-out. Should you hear him pass your door do not interrupt him, but follow him as discreetly as you can. Dr Watson and I will not be far off. By the way, where is the key of that little box of which you spoke?'

'Upon his watch-chain.'

'I fancy our researches must lie in that direction. At the worst the lock should not be very formidable. Have you any other able-bodied man on the premises?'

'There is the coachman, Macphail.'

'Where does he sleep?'

'Over the stables.'

'We might possibly want him. Well, we can do no more until we see how things develop. Goodbye—but I expect that we shall see you before morning.'

It was nearly midnight before we took our station among some bushes immediately opposite the hall door of the Professor. It was a fine night, but chilly, and we were glad of our warm overcoats. There was a breeze and clouds were scudding across the sky, obscuring from time to time the half-moon. It would have been a dismal vigil were it not for the expectation and excitement which carried us along, and the assurance of my comrade that we had probably reached the end of the strange sequence of events which had engaged our attention.

'If the cycle of nine days holds good then we shall have the Professor at his worst tonight,' said Holmes. 'The fact that these strange symptoms began after his visit to Prague, that he is in secret correspondence with a Bohemian dealer in London, who presumably represents someone in Prague, and that he received a packet from him this very day, all point in one direction. What he takes and why he takes it are still beyond our ken, but that it emanates in some way from Prague is clear enough. He takes it under definite directions which regulate this ninth day system, which was the first point which attracted my attention. But his symptoms are most remarkable. Did you observe his knuckles?'

I had to confess that I did not.

'Thick and horny in a way which is quite new in my experience. Always look at the hands first, Watson. Then cuffs, trouser-knees, and boots. Very curious knuckles which can only be explained by the mode of progression observed by——' Holmes paused, and suddenly clapped his hand to his forehead. 'Oh, Watson, Watson, what a fool I have been! It seems incredible, and yet it must be true. All points in one direction. How could I miss seeing the connection of ideas? Those knuckles—how could I have passed those knuckles? And the dog! And the ivy! It's surely time that I disappeared into that little farm of my dreams. Look out, Watson! Here he is! We shall have the chance of seeing for ourselves.'

The hall door had slowly opened, and against the lamp-lit background we saw the tall figure of Professor Presbury. He was clad in his dressing-gown. As he stood outlined in the doorway he was erect but leaning forward with dangling arms, as when we saw him last.

Now he stepped forward into the drive, and an extraordinary change came over him. He sank down into a crouching position, and moved along upon his hands and feet, skipping every now and then as if he were overflowing with energy and vitality. He moved along the face of the house and then round the corner. As he disappeared Bennett slipped through the hall door and softly followed him.

'Come, Watson, come!' cried Holmes, and we stole as softly as we could through the bushes until we had gained a spot whence we could see the other side of the house, which was bathed in the light of the half-moon. The Professor was clearly visible crouching at the foot of the ivy-covered wall. As we watched him he suddenly began with incredible agility to ascend it. From branch to branch he sprang, sure of foot and firm of grasp, climbing apparently in mere joy at his own powers, with no definite object in view. With his dressing-gown flapping on each side of him he looked like some huge bat glued against the side of his own house, a great square dark patch upon the moonlit wall. Presently he tired of this amusement, and, dropping from branch to branch, he squatted down into the old attitude and moved towards the stables, creeping along in the same strange way as before. The wolfhound was out now, barking furiously, and more excited than ever when it actually caught sight of its master. It was straining on its chain, and quivering with eagerness and rage. The Professor squatted down very deliberately just out of reach of the hound, and began to provoke it in every possible way. He took handfuls of pebbles from the drive and threw them in the dog's face, prodded him with a stick which he had picked up, flicked his hands about only a few inches from the gaping mouth, and endeavoured in every way to increase the animal's fury, which was already beyond all control. In all our adventures I do not know that I have ever seen a more strange sight than this impassive and still dignified figure crouching frog-like upon the ground and goading to a wilder exhibition of passion the maddened hound, which ramped and raged in front of him, by all manner of ingenious and calculated cruelty.

And then in a moment it happened! It was not the chain that broke, but it was the collar that slipped, for it had been made for a thick-necked Newfoundland. We heard the rattle of falling metal, and the next instant dog and man were rolling on the ground together, the one roaring in rage, the other screaming in a strange shrill falsetto of terror. It was a very narrow thing for the Professor's life. The savage creature had him fairly by the throat, its fangs had bitten deep, and he was senseless before we could reach them and drag the two apart. It might have been a dangerous task for us, but

Bennett's voice and pressure brought the great wolfhound instantly to reason. The uproar had brought the sleepy and astonished coachman from his room above the stables. 'I'm not surprised,' said he, shaking his head. 'I've seen him at it before. I knew the dog would get him sooner or later.'

The hound was secured, and together we carried the Professor up to his room, where Bennett, who had a medical degree, helped me to dress his torn throat. The sharp teeth had passed dangerously near the carotid artery, and the haemorrhage was serious. In half an hour the danger was past, I had given the patient an injection of morphia, and he had sunk into deep sleep. Then, and only then, were we able to look at each other and to take stock of the situation.

'I think a first-class surgeon should see him,' said I.

'For God's sake, no!' cried Bennett. 'At present the scandal is confined to our own household. It is safe with us. If it gets beyond these walls it will never stop. Consider his position at the University, his European reputation, the feelings of his daughter.'

'Quite so,' said Holmes. 'I think it may be quite possible to keep the matter to ourselves, and also to prevent its recurrence now that we have a free hand. The key from the watch-chain, Mr Bennett. Macphail will guard the patient and let us know if there is any change. Let us see what we can find in the Professor's mysterious box.'

There was not much, but there was enough—an empty phial, another nearly full, a hypodermic syringe, several letters in a crabbed, foreign hand. The marks on the envelopes showed that they were those which had disturbed the routine of the secretary, and each was dated from the Commercial Road and signed 'A. Dorak'. They were mere invoices to say that a fresh bottle was being sent to Professor Presbury, or receipts to acknowledge money. There was one other envelope, however, in a more educated hand and bearing the Austrian stamp with the postmark of Prague. 'Here we have our material!' cried Holmes, as he tore out the enclosure.

Honoured Colleague, *it ran*. Since your esteemed visit I have thought much of your case, and though in your circumstances there are some special reasons for the treatment, I would none the less enjoin caution, as my results have shown that it is not without danger of a kind.

It is possible that the Serum of Anthropoid would have been better. I have, as I explained to you, used black-faced Langur because a specimen was accessible. Langur is, of course, a crawler and climber, while Anthropoid walks erect, and is in all ways nearer.

I beg you to take every possible precaution that there be no premature revelation of the process. I have one other client in England, and Dorak is my agent for both.

Weekly reports will oblige.

Yours with high esteem,

H. LOWENSTEIN

Lowenstein! The name brought back to me the memory of some snippet from a newspaper which spoke of an obscure scientist who was striving in some unknown way for the secret of rejuvenescence and the elixir of life. Lowenstein of Prague! Lowenstein with the wondrous strength-giving serum, tabooed by the profession because he refused to reveal its source. In a few words I said what I remembered. Bennett had taken a manual of Zoology from the shelves. '"Langur,"' he read, '"the great black-faced monkey of the Himalayan slopes, biggest and most human of climbing monkeys." Many details are added. Well, thanks to you, Mr Holmes, it is very clear that we have traced the evil to its source.'

'The real source,' said Holmes, 'lies, of course, in that untimely love affair which gave our impetuous Professor the idea that he could only gain his wish by turning himself into a younger man. When one tries to rise above Nature one is liable to fall below it. The highest type of man may revert to the animal if he leaves the straight road of destiny.' He sat musing for a little with the phial in his hand, looking at the clear liquid within. 'When I have written to this man and told him that I hold him criminally responsible for the poisons which he circulates, we will have no more trouble. But it may recur. Others may find a better way. There is danger there—a very real danger to humanity. Consider, Watson, that the material, the sensual, the worldly would all prolong their worthless lives. The spiritual would not avoid the call to something higher. It would be the survival of the least fit. What sort of cesspool may not our poor world become?' Suddenly the dreamer disappeared, and Holmes, the man of action, sprang from his chair. 'I think there is nothing more to be said, Mr Bennett. The various incidents will now fit themselves easily into the general scheme. The dog, of course, was aware of the change far more quickly than you. His smell would ensure that. It was the monkey, not the Professor, whom Roy attacked, just as it was the monkey who teased Roy. Climbing was a joy to the creature, and it was a mere chance, I take it, that the pastime brought him to the young lady's window. There is an early train to town, Watson, but I think we shall just have time for a cup of tea at the Chequers before we catch it.'

The Adventure of the Lion's Mane

Arthur Conan Doyle

It is a most singular thing that a problem which was certainly as abstruse and unusual as any which I have faced in my long professional career should have come to me after my retirement; and be brought, as it were, to my very door. It occurred after my withdrawal to my little Sussex home, when I had given myself up entirely to that soothing life of Nature for which I had so often yearned during the long years spent amid the gloom of London. At this period of my life the good Watson had passed almost beyond my ken. An occasional weekend visit was the most that I ever saw of him. Thus I must act as my own chronicler. Ah! had he but been with me, how much he might have made of so wonderful a happening, and of my eventual triumph against every difficulty! As it is, however, I must needs tell my tale in my own plain way, showing by my words each step upon the difficult road which lay before me as I searched for the mystery of the Lion's Mane.

My villa is situated upon the southern slope of the Downs, commanding a great view of the Channel. At this point the coastline is entirely of chalk cliffs, which can only be descended by a single, long, tortuous path, which is steep and slippery. At the bottom of the path lie a hundred yards of pebbles and shingle, even when the tide is at full. Here and there, however, there are curves and hollows, which make splendid swimming pools filled afresh with each flow. This admirable beach extends for some miles in each direction, save only at one point where the little cove and village of Fulworth break the line.

My house is lonely. I, my old housekeeper, and my bees have the

estate all to ourselves. Half a mile off, however, is Harold Stackhurst's well-known coaching establishment, The Gables, quite a
large place, which contains some score of young fellows preparing
for various professions, with a staff of several masters. Stackhurst
himself was a well-known rowing Blue in his day, and an excellent
all-round scholar. He and I were always friendly from the day I
came to the coast, and he was the one man who was on such terms
with me that we could drop in on each other in the evenings without
an invitation.

Towards the end of July, 1907, there was a severe gale, the wind
blowing up Channel, heaping the seas to the base of the cliffs, and
leaving a lagoon at the turn of the tide. On the morning of which I
speak the wind had abated, and all Nature was newly washed and
fresh. It was impossible to work upon so delightful a day, and I
strolled out before breakfast to enjoy the exquisite air. I walked
along the cliff path which led to the steep descent to the beach. As
I walked I heard a shout behind me, and there was Harold
Stackhurst waving his hand in cheery greeting.

'What a morning, Mr Holmes! I thought I should see you out.'

'Going for a swim, I see.'

'At your old tricks again,' he laughed, patting his bulging pocket.
'Yes. McPherson started early, and I expect I may find him there.'

Fitzroy McPherson was the science master, a fine upstanding
young fellow whose life had been crippled by heart trouble following rheumatic fever. He was a natural athlete, however, and excelled
in every game which did not throw too great a strain upon him.
Summer and winter he went for his swim, and, as I am a swimmer
myself, I have often joined him.

At this moment we saw the man himself. His head showed above
the edge of the cliff where the path ends. Then his whole figure
appeared at the top, staggering like a drunken man. The next instant
he threw up his hands and, with a terrible cry, fell upon his face.
Stackhurst and I rushed forward—it may have been fifty yards—
and turned him on his back. He was obviously dying. Those glazed
sunken eyes and dreadful livid cheeks could mean nothing else. One
glimmer of life came into his face for an instant, and he uttered two
or three words with an eager air of warning. They were slurred and
indistinct, but to my ear the last of them, which burst in a shriek
from his lips, were 'the lion's mane'. It was utterly irrelevant and

unintelligible, and yet I could twist the sound into no other sense. Then he half raised himself from the ground, threw his arms into the air, and fell forward on his side. He was dead.

My companion was paralysed by the sudden horror of it, but I, as may well be imagined, had every sense on the alert. And I had need, for it was speedily evident that we were in the presence of an extraordinary case. The man was dressed only in his Burberry overcoat, his trousers, and an unlaced pair of canvas shoes. As he fell over, his Burberry, which had been simply thrown round his shoulders, slipped off, exposing his trunk. We stared at it in amazement. His back was covered with dark red lines as though he had been terribly flogged by a thin wire scourge. The instrument with which this punishment had been inflicted was clearly flexible, for the long, angry weals curved round his shoulders and ribs. There was blood dripping down his chin, for he had bitten through his lower lip in the paroxysm of his agony. His drawn and distorted face told how terrible that agony had been.

I was kneeling and Stackhurst standing by the body when a shadow fell across us, and we found that Ian Murdoch was by our side. Murdoch was the mathematical coach at the establishment, a tall, dark, thin man, so taciturn and aloof that none can be said to have been his friend. He seemed to live in some high, abstract region of surds and conic sections with little to connect him with ordinary life. He was looked upon as an oddity by the students, and would have been their butt, but there was some strange outlandish blood in the man, which showed itself not only in his coal-black eyes and swarthy face, but also in occasional outbreaks of temper, which could only be described as ferocious. On one occasion, being plagued by a little dog belonging to McPherson, he had caught the creature up and hurled it through the plate-glass window, an action for which Stackhurst would certainly have given him his dismissal had he not been a very valuable teacher. Such was the strange, complex man who now appeared beside us. He seemed to be honestly shocked at the sight before him, though the incident of the dog may show that there was no great sympathy between the dead man and himself.

'Poor fellow! Poor fellow! What can I do? How can I help?'

'Were you with him? Can you tell us what has happened?'

'No, no. I was late this morning. I was not on the beach at all. I have come straight from The Gables. What can I do?'

'You can hurry to the police station at Fulworth. Report the matter at once.'

Without a word he made off at top speed, and I proceeded to take the matter in hand, while Stackhurst, dazed at this tragedy, remained by the body. My first task naturally was to note who was on the beach. From the top of the path I could see the whole sweep of it, and it was absolutely deserted, save that two or three dark figures could be seen far away moving towards the village of Fulworth. Having satisfied myself upon this point, I walked slowly down the path. There was clay or soft marl mixed with the chalk, and every here and there I saw the same footstep, both ascending and descending. No one else had gone down to the beach by this track that morning. At one place I observed the print of an open hand with the fingers towards the incline. This could only mean that poor McPherson had fallen as he ascended. There were rounded depressions, too, which suggested that he had come down upon his knees more than once. At the bottom of the path was the considerable lagoon left by the retreating tide. At the side of it McPherson had undressed, for there lay his towel on a rock. It was folded and dry, so that it would seem that after all he had never entered the water. Once or twice as I hunted round amid the hard shingle I came on little patches of sand where the print of his canvas shoe, and also of his naked foot, could be seen. The latter fact proved that he had made all ready to bathe, though the towel indicated that he had not actually done so.

And here was the problem clearly defined—as strange a one as had ever confronted me. The man had not been on the beach more than a quarter of an hour at the most. Stackhurst had followed him from The Gables, so there could be no doubt about that. He had gone to bathe and had stripped, as the naked footsteps showed. Then he had suddenly huddled on his clothes again—they were all dishevelled and unfastened—and he had returned without bathing, or at any rate without drying himself. And the reason for his change of purpose had been that he had been scourged in some savage, inhuman fashion, tortured until he bit his lip through in his agony, and was left with only strength enough to crawl away and to die.

Who had done this barbarous deed? There were, it is true, small grottoes and caves in the base of the cliffs, but the low sun shone directly into them, and there was no place for concealment. Then, again, there were those distant figures on the beach. They seemed too far away to have been connected with the crime, and the broad lagoon in which McPherson had intended to bathe lay between him and them, lapping up to the rocks. On the sea two or three fishing boats were at no great distance. Their occupants might be examined at our leisure. There were several roads for enquiry, but none which led to any very obvious goal.

When I at last returned to the body I found that a little group of wandering folk had gathered round it. Stackhurst was, of course, still there, and Ian Murdoch had just arrived with Anderson, the village constable, a big, ginger-moustached man of the slow, solid Sussex breed—a breed which covers much good sense under a heavy, silent exterior. He listened to everything, took note of all we said, and finally drew me aside.

'I'd be glad of your advice, Mr Holmes. This is a big thing for me to handle, and I'll hear of it from Lewes if I go wrong.'

I advised him to send for his immediate superior, and for a doctor; also to allow nothing to be moved, and as few fresh footmarks as possible to be made, until they came. In the meantime I searched the dead man's pockets. There were his handkerchief, a large knife, and a small folding card-case. From this projected a slip of paper, which I unfolded and handed to the constable. There was written on it in a scrawling, feminine hand: 'I will be there, you may be sure. Maudie.' It read like a love affair, an assignation, though when and where were a blank. The constable replaced it in the card-case and returned it with the other things to the pockets of the Burberry. Then, as nothing more suggested itself, I walked back to my house for breakfast, having first arranged that the base of the cliffs should be thoroughly searched.

Stackhurst was round in an hour or two to tell me that the body had been removed to The Gables, where the inquest would be held. He brought with him some serious and definite news. As I expected, nothing had been found in the small caves below the cliff, but he had examined the papers in McPherson's desk, and there were several which showed an intimate correspondence with a certain

Miss Maud Bellamy, of Fulworth. We had then established the identity of the writer of the note.

'The police have the letters,' he explained. 'I could not bring them. But there is no doubt that it was a serious love affair. I see no reason, however, to connect it with that horrible happening, save, indeed, that the lady had made an appointment with him.'

'But hardly at a bathing-pool which all of you were in the habit of using,' I remarked.

'It is mere chance,' said he, 'that several of the students were not with McPherson.'

'*Was* it mere chance?'

Stackhurst knit his brows in thought.

'Ian Murdoch held them back,' said he; 'he would insist upon some algebraic demonstration before breakfast. Poor chap, he is dreadfully cut up about it all.'

'And yet I gather that they were not friends.'

'At one time they were not. But for a year or more Murdoch has been as near to McPherson as he ever could be to anyone. He is not of a very sympathetic disposition by nature.'

'So I understand. I seem to remember your telling me once about a quarrel over the ill-usage of a dog.'

'That blew over all right.'

'But left some vindictive feeling, perhaps.'

'No, no; I am sure they were real friends.'

'Well, then, we must explore the matter of the girl. Do you know her?'

'Everyone knows her. She is the beauty of the neighbourhood— a real beauty, Holmes, who would draw attention everywhere. I knew that McPherson was attracted by her, but I had no notion that it had gone so far as these letters would seem to indicate.'

'But who is she?'

'She is the daughter of old Tom Bellamy, who owns all the boats and bathing-cots at Fulworth. He was a fisherman to start with, but is now a man of some substance. He and his son William run the business.'

'Shall we walk into Fulworth and see them?'

'On what pretext?'

'Oh, we can easily find a pretext. After all, this poor man did not ill-use himself in this outrageous way. Some human hand was on the handle of that scourge, if indeed it was a scourge which inflicted the injuries. His circle of acquaintance in this lonely place was surely limited. Let us follow it up in every direction and we can hardly fail to come upon the motive, which in turn should lead us to the criminal.'

It would have been a pleasant walk across the thyme-scented Downs had our minds not been poisoned by the tragedy we had witnessed. The village of Fulworth lies in a hollow curving in a semicircle round the bay. Behind the old-fashioned hamlet several modern houses have been built upon the rising ground. It was to one of these that Stackhurst guided me.

'That's The Haven, as Bellamy called it. The one with the corner tower and slate roof. Not bad for a man who started with nothing but—— By Jove, look at that!'

The garden gate of The Haven had opened and a man had emerged. There was no mistaking that tall, angular, straggling figure. It was Ian Murdoch, the mathematician. A moment later we confronted him upon the road.

'Hullo!' said Stackhurst. The man nodded, gave us a sideways glance from his curious dark eyes, and would have passed us, but his principal pulled him up.

'What were you doing there?' he asked.

Murdoch's face flushed with anger. 'I am your subordinate, sir, under your roof. I am not aware that I owe you any account of my private actions.'

Stackhurst's nerves were near the surface after all he had endured. Otherwise perhaps he would have waited. Now he lost his temper completely.

'In the circumstances your answer is pure impertinence, Mr Murdoch.'

'Your own question might perhaps come under the same heading.'

'This is not the first time that I have had to overlook your insubordinate ways. It will certainly be the last. You will kindly make fresh arrangements for your future as speedily as you can.'

'I had intended to do so. I have lost today the only person who made The Gables habitable.'

He strode off upon his way, while Stackhurst, with angry eyes, stood glaring after him. 'Is he not an impossible, intolerable man?' he cried.

The one thing that impressed itself forcibly upon my mind was that Mr Ian Murdoch was taking the first chance to open a path of escape from the scene of the crime. Suspicion, vague and nebulous, was now beginning to take outline in my mind. Perhaps the visit to the Bellamys might throw some further light upon the matter. Stackhurst pulled himself together and we went forward to the house.

Mr Bellamy proved to be a middle-aged man with a flaming red beard. He seemed to be in a very angry mood, and his face was soon as florid as his hair.

'No, sir, I do not desire any particulars. My son here'—indicating a powerful young man, with a heavy, sullen face, in the corner of the sitting-room—'is of one mind with me that Mr McPherson's attentions to Maud were insulting. Yes, sir, the word "marriage" was never mentioned, and yet there were letters and meetings, and a great deal more of which neither of us could approve. She has no mother, and we are her only guardians. We are determined——'

But the words were taken from his mouth by the appearance of the lady herself. There was no gainsaying that she would have graced any assembly in the world. Who could have imagined that so rare a flower would grow from such a root and in such an atmosphere? Women have seldom been an attraction to me, for my brain has always governed my heart, but I could not look upon her perfect clear-cut face, with all the soft freshness of the Downlands in her delicate colouring, without realizing that no young man would cross her path unscathed. Such was the girl who had pushed open the door and stood now, wide-eyed and intense, in front of Harold Stackhurst.

'I know already that Fitzroy is dead,' she said. 'Do not be afraid to tell me the particulars.'

'This other gentleman of yours let us know the news,' explained the father.

'There is no reason why my sister should be brought into the matter,' growled the younger man.

The sister turned a sharp, fierce look upon him. 'This is my business, William. Kindly leave me to manage it in my own way. By all accounts there has been a crime committed. If I can help to show who did it, it is the least I can do for him who is gone.'

She listened to a short account from my companion, with a composed concentration which showed me that she possessed strong character as well as great beauty. Maud Bellamy will always remain in my memory as a most complete and remarkable woman. It seems that she already knew me by sight, for she turned to me at the end.

'Bring them to justice, Mr Holmes. You have my sympathy and my help, whoever they may be.' It seemed to me that she glanced defiantly at her father and brother as she spoke.

'Thank you,' said I. 'I value a woman's instinct in such matters. You use the word "they". You think that more than one was concerned?'

'I knew Mr McPherson well enough to be aware that he was a brave and a strong man. No single person could ever have inflicted such an outrage upon him.'

'Might I have one word with you alone?'

'I tell you, Maud, not to mix yourself up in the matter,' cried her father, angrily.

She looked at me helplessly. 'What can I do?'

'The whole world will know the facts presently, so there can be no harm if I discuss them here,' said I. 'I should have preferred privacy, but if your father will not allow it, he must share the deliberations.' Then I spoke of the note which had been found in the dead man's pocket. 'It is sure to be produced at the inquest. May I ask you to throw any light upon it that you can?'

'I see no reason for mystery,' she answered. 'We were engaged to be married, and we only kept it secret because Fitzroy's uncle, who is very old and said to be dying, might have disinherited him if he had married against his wish. There was no other reason.'

'You could have told us,' growled Mr Bellamy.

'So I would, father, if you had ever shown sympathy.'

'I object to my girl picking up with men outside her own station.'

'It was your prejudice against him which prevented us from telling you. As to this appointment'—she fumbled in her dress and produced a crumpled note—'it was in answer to this.'

'Dearest,' ran the message: 'The old place on the beach just after sunset on Tuesday. It is the only time I can get away.—F. M.'

'Tuesday was today, and I had meant to meet him tonight.'

I turned over the paper. 'This never came by post. How did you get it?'

'I would rather not anwer that question. It has really nothing to do with the matter which you are investigating. But anything which bears upon that I will most freely answer.'

She was as good as her word, but there was nothing which was helpful in our investigation. She had no reason to think that her fiancé had any hidden enemy, but she admitted that she had had several warm admirers.

'May I ask if Mr Ian Murdoch was one of them?'

She blushed and seemed confused.

'There was a time when I thought he was. But that was all changed when he understood the relations between Fitzroy and myself.'

Again the shadow round this strange man seemed to me to be taking more definite shape. His record must be examined. His rooms must be privately searched. Stackhurst was a willing collaborator, for in his mind also suspicions were forming. We returned from our visit to The Haven with the hope that one free end of this tangled skein was already in our hands.

A week passed. The inquest had thrown no light upon the matter, and had been adjourned for further evidence. Stackhurst had made discreet enquiry about his subordinate, and there had been a superficial search of his room, but without result. Personally, I had gone over the whole ground again both physically and mentally, but with no new conclusions. In all my chronicles the reader will find no case which brought me so completely to the limit of my powers. Even my imagination could conceive no solution to the mystery. And then there came the incident of the dog.

It was my old housekeeper who heard of it first by that strange wireless by which such people collect the news of the countryside.

'Sad story this, sir, about Mr McPherson's dog,' said she one evening.

I do not encourage such conversations, but the words arrested my attention.

'What of Mr McPherson's dog?'

'Dead, sir. Died of grief for its master.'

'Who told you this?'

'Why, sir, everyone is talking of it. It took on terrible, and has eaten nothing for a week. Then today two of the young gentlemen from The Gables found it dead—down on the beach, sir, at the very place where its master met his end.'

'At the very place.' The words stood out clear in my memory. Some dim perception that the matter was vital rose in my mind. That the dog should die was after the beautiful, faithful nature of dogs. But 'in the very place'! Why should this lonely beach be fatal to it? Was it possible that it, also, had been sacrificed to some revenge feud? Was it possible——? Yes, the perception was dim, but already something was building up in my mind. In a few minutes I was on my way to The Gables, where I found Stackhurst in his study. At my request he sent for Sudbury and Blount, the two students who had found the dog.

'Yes, it lay on the very edge of the pool,' said one of them. 'It must have followed the trail of its dead master.'

I saw the faithful little creature, an Airedale terrier, laid out upon the mat in the hall. The body was stiff and rigid, the eyes projecting, and the limbs contorted. There was agony in every line of it.

From The Gables I walked down to the bathing-pool. The sun had sunk and the shadow of the great cliff lay black across the water, which glimmered dully like a sheet of lead. The place was deserted and there was no sign of life save for two sea-birds circling and screaming overhead. In the fading light I could dimly make out the little dog's spoor upon the sand round the very rock on which his master's towel had been laid. For a long time I stood in deep meditation while the shadows grew darker around me. My mind was filled with racing thoughts. You have known what it was to be in a nightmare in which you feel that there is some all-important thing for which you search and which you know is there, though it remains for ever just beyond your reach. That was how I felt that evening as I stood alone by that place of death. Then at last I turned and walked slowly homewards.

I had just reached the top of the path when it came to me. Like a flash, I remembered the thing for which I had so eagerly and vainly grasped. You will know, or Watson has written in vain, that I hold a vast store of out-of-the-way knowledge, without scientific system, but very available for the needs of my work. My mind is like a crowded box-room with packets of all sorts stowed away therein—

so many that I may well have but a vague perception of what was there. I had known that there was something which might bear upon this matter. It was still vague, but at least I knew how I could make it clear. It was monstrous, incredible, and yet it was always a possibility. I would test it to the full.

There is a great garret in my little house which is stuffed with books. It was into this that I plunged and rummaged for an hour. At the end of that time I emerged with a little chocolate and silver volume. Eagerly I turned up the chapter of which I had a dim remembrance. Yes, it was indeed a far-fetched and unlikely proposition, and yet I could not be at rest until I had made sure if it might, indeed, be so. It was late when I retired, with my mind eagerly awaiting the work of the morrow.

But that work met with an annoying interruption. I had hardly swallowed my early cup of tea and was starting for the beach when I had a call from Inspector Bardle of the Sussex Constabulary—a steady, solid, bovine man with thoughtful eyes, which looked at me now with a very troubled expression.

'I know your immense experience, sir,' said he. 'This is quite unofficial, of course, and need go no further. But I am fairly up against it in this McPherson case. The question is, shall I make an arrest, or shall I not?'

'Meaning Mr Ian Murdoch?'

'Yes, sir. There is really no one else when you come to think of it. That's the advantage of this solitude. We narrow it down to a very small compass. If he did not do it, then who did?'

'What have you against him?'

He had gleaned along the same furrows as I had. There was Murdoch's character and the mystery which seemed to hang round the man. His furious bursts of temper, as shown in the incident of the dog. The fact that he had quarrelled with McPherson in the past, and that there was some reason to think that he might have resented his attentions to Miss Bellamy. He had all my points, but no fresh ones, save that Murdoch seemed to be making every preparation for departure.

'What would my position be if I let him slip away with all this evidence against him?' The burly phlegmatic man was sorely troubled in his mind.

*

'Consider,' I said, 'all the essential gaps in your case. On the morning of the crime he can surely prove an alibi. He had been with his scholars till the last moment, and within a few minutes of McPherson's appearance he came upon us from behind. Then bear in mind the absolute impossibility that he could single-handed have inflicted this outrage upon a man quite as strong as himself. Finally, there is this question of the instrument with which these injuries were inflicted.'

'What could it be but a scourge or flexible whip of some sort?'

'Have you examined the marks?' I asked.

'I have seen them. So has the doctor.'

'But I have examined them very carefully with a lens. They have peculiarities.'

'What are they, Mr Holmes?'

I stepped to my bureau and brought out an enlarged photograph. 'This is my method in such cases,' I explained.

'You certainly do things thoroughly, Mr Holmes.'

'I should hardly be what I am if I did not. Now let us consider this weal which extends round the right shoulder. Do you observe nothing remarkable?'

'I can't say I do.'

'Surely it is evident that it is unequal in its intensity. There is a dot of extravasated blood here, and another there. There are similar indications in this other weal down here. What can that mean?'

'I have no idea. Have you?'

'Perhaps I have. Perhaps I haven't. I may be able to say more soon. Anything which will define what made that mark will bring us a long way towards the criminal.'

'It is, of course, an absurd idea,' said the policeman, 'but if a red-hot net of wire had been laid across the back, then these better-marked points would represent where the meshes crossed each other.'

'A most ingenious comparison. Or shall we say a very stiff cat-o'-nine-tails with small hard knots upon it?'

'By Jove, Mr Holmes, I think you have hit it.'

'Or there may be some very different cause, Mr Bardle. But your case is far too weak for an arrest. Besides we have those last words—"Lion's Mane".'

'I have wondered whether Ian——'

'Yes, I have considered that. If the second word had borne any resemblance to Murdoch—but it did not. He gave it almost in a shriek. I am sure that it was "Mane".'

'Have you no alternative, Mr Holmes?'

'Perhaps I have. But I do not care to discuss it until there is something more solid to discuss.'

'And when will that be?'

'In an hour—possibly less.'

The Inspector rubbed his chin and looked at me with dubious eyes.

'I wish I could see what was in your mind, Mr Holmes. Perhaps it's those fishing-boats.'

'No, no; they were too far out.'

'Well, then, is it Bellamy and that big son of his? They were not too sweet upon Mr McPherson. Could they have done him a mischief?'

'No, no; you won't draw me until I am ready,' said I with a smile. 'Now, Inspector, we each have our own work to do. Perhaps if you were to meet me here at midday——?'

So far we had got when there came the tremendous interruption which was the beginning of the end.

My outer door was flung open, there were blundering footsteps in the passage, and Ian Murdoch staggered into the room, pallid, dishevelled, his clothes in wild disorder, clawing with his bony hands at the furniture to hold himself erect. 'Brandy! Brandy!' he gasped, and fell groaning upon the sofa.

He was not alone. Behind him came Stackhurst, hatless and panting, almost as *distrait* as his companion.

'Yes, yes, brandy!' he cried. 'The man is at his last gasp. It was all I could do to bring him here. He fainted twice upon the way.'

Half a tumbler of the raw spirit brought about a wondrous change. He pushed himself up on one arm and swung his coat from off his shoulders. 'For God's sake! oil, opium, morphia!' he cried. 'Anything to ease this infernal agony!'

The Inspector and I cried out at the sight. There, criss-crossed upon the man's naked shoulder, was the same strange reticulated pattern of red inflamed lines which had been the death-mark of Fitzroy McPherson.

The pain was evidently terrible and was more than local, for the sufferer's breathing would stop for a time, his face would turn black, and then with loud gasps he would clap his hand to his heart, while his brow dropped beads of sweat. At any moment he might die. More and more brandy was poured down his throat, each fresh dose bringing him back to life. Pads of cotton wool soaked in salad-oil seemed to take the agony from the strange wounds. At last his head fell heavily upon the cushion. Exhausted Nature had taken refuge in its last storehouse of vitality. It was half a sleep and half a faint, but at least it was ease from pain.

To question him had been impossible, but the moment we were assured of his condition Stackhurst turned upon me.

'My God!' he cried, 'what is it, Holmes? What is it?'

'Where did you find him?'

'Down on the beach. Exactly where poor McPherson met his end. If this man's heart had been weak as McPherson's was he would not be here now. More than once I thought he was gone as I brought him up. It was too far to The Gables, so I made for you.'

'Did you see him on the beach?'

'I was walking on the cliff when I heard his cry. He was at the edge of the water, reeling about like a drunken man. I ran down, threw some clothes over him, and brought him up. For Heaven's sake, Holmes, use all the powers you have and spare no pains to lift the curse from this place, for life is becoming unendurable. Can you, with all your world-wide reputation, do nothing for us?'

'I think I can, Stackhurst. Come with me now! And you, Inspector, come along! We will see if we cannot deliver this murderer into your hands.'

Leaving the unconscious man in the charge of my housekeeper, we all three went down to the deadly lagoon. On the shingle there was piled a little heap of towels and clothes, left by the stricken man. Slowly I walked round the edge of the water, my comrades in Indian file behind me. Most of the pool was quite shallow, but under the cliff where the beach was hollowed out it was four or five feet deep. It was to this part that a swimmer would naturally go, for it formed a beautiful pellucid green pool as clear as crystal. A line of rocks lay above it at the base of the cliff, and along this I led the way, peering eagerly into the depths beneath me. I had reached the deepest and stillest pool when my eyes caught that for which they were searching, and I burst into a shout of triumph.

'Cyanea!' I cried. 'Cyanea! Behold the Lion's Mane!'

The strange object at which I pointed did indeed look like a tangled mass torn from the mane of a lion. It lay upon a rocky shelf some three feet under the water, a curious waving, vibrating, hairy creature with streaks of silver among its yellow tresses. It pulsated with a slow, heavy dilation and contraction.

'It has done mischief enough. Its day is over!' I cried. 'Help me, Stackhurst! Let us end the murderer for ever.'

There was a big boulder just above the ledge, and we pushed it until it fell with a tremendous splash into the water. When the ripples had cleared we saw that it had settled upon the ledge below. One flapping edge of yellow membrane showed that our victim was beneath it. A thick oily scum oozed out from below the stone and stained the water round, rising slowly to the surface.

'Well, this gets me!' cried the Inspector. 'What was it, Mr Holmes? I'm born and bred in these parts, but I never saw such a thing. It don't belong to Sussex.'

'Just as well for Sussex,' I remarked. 'It may have been the south-west gale that brought it up. Come back to my house, both of you, and I will give you the terrible experience of one who has good reason to remember his own meeting with the same peril of the seas.'

When we reached my study, we found that Murdoch was so far recovered that he could sit up. He was dazed in mind, and every now and then was shaken by a paroxysm of pain. In broken words he explained that he had no notion what had occurred to him, save that terrific pangs had suddenly shot through him, and that it had taken all his fortitude to reach the bank.

'Here is a book,' I said, taking up the little volume, 'which first brought light into what might have been for ever dark. It is *Out of Doors*, by the famous observer J. G. Wood. Wood himself very nearly perished from contact with this vile creature, so he wrote with a very full knowledge. *Cyanea Capillata* is the miscreant's full name, and he can be as dangerous to life as, and far more painful than, the bite of the cobra. Let me briefly give this extract.

'"If the bather should see a loose roundish mass of tawny membranes and fibres, something like very large handfuls of lion's mane and silver paper, let him beware, for this is the fearful stinger,

Cyanea Capillata." Could our sinister acquaintance be more clearly described?

'He goes on to tell his own encounter with one when swimming off the coast of Kent. He found that the creature radiated almost invisible filaments to the distance of fifty feet, and that anyone within that circumference from the deadly centre was in danger of death. Even at a distance the effect upon Wood was almost fatal. "The multitudinous threads caused light scarlet lines upon the skin which on closer examination resolved into minute dots or pustules, each dot charged as it were with a red-hot needle making its way through the nerves."

'The local pain was, as he explains, the least part of the exquisite torment. "Pangs shot through the chest, causing me to fall as if struck by a bullet. The pulsation would cease, and then the heart would give six or seven leaps as if it would force its way through the chest."

'It nearly killed him, although he had only been exposed to it in the disturbed ocean and not in the narrow calm waters of a bathing-pool. He says that he could hardly recognize himself afterwards, so white, wrinkled, and shrivelled was his face. He gulped down brandy, a whole bottleful, and it seems to have saved his life. There is the book, Inspector. I leave it with you, and you cannot doubt that it contains a full explanation of the tragedy of poor McPherson.'

'And incidentally exonerates me,' remarked Ian Murdoch with a wry smile. 'I do not blame you, Inspector, nor you, Mr Holmes, for your suspicions were natural. I feel that on the very eve of my arrest I have only cleared myself by sharing the fate of my poor friend.'

'No, Mr Murdoch. I was already upon the track, and had I been out as early as I intended I might well have saved you from this terrific experience.'

'But how did you know, Mr Holmes?'

'I am an omnivorous reader with a strangely retentive memory for trifles. That phrase "Lion's Mane" haunted my mind. I knew that I had seen it somewhere in an unexpected context. You have seen that it does describe the creature. I have no doubt that it was floating on the water when McPherson saw it, and that this phrase was the only one by which he could convey to us a warning as to the creature which had been his death.'

'Then I, at least, am cleared,' said Murdoch, rising slowly to his feet. 'There are one or two words of explanation which I should give, for I know the direction in which your enquiries have run. It is true that I loved this lady, but from the day when she chose my friend McPherson my one desire was to help her to happiness. I was well content to stand aside and act as their go-between. Often I carried their messages, and it was because I was in their confidence and because she was so dear to me that I hastened to tell her of my friend's death, lest someone should forestall me in a more sudden and heartless manner. She would not tell you, sir, of our relations lest you should disapprove and I might suffer. But with your leave I must try to get back to The Gables, for my bed will be very welcome.'

Stackhurst held out his hand. 'Our nerves have all been at concert-pitch,' said he. 'Forgive what is past, Murdoch. We shall understand each other better in the future.' They passed out together with their arms linked in friendly fashion. The Inspector remained, staring at me in silence with his ox-like eyes.

'Well, you've done it!' he cried at last. 'I had read of you, but I never believed it. It's wonderful!'

I was forced to shake my head. To accept such praise was to lower one's own standards.

'I was slow at the outset—culpably slow. Had the body been found in the water I could hardly have missed it. It was the towel which misled me. The poor fellow had never thought to dry himself, and so I in turn was led to believe that he had never been in the water. Why, then, should the attack of any water creature suggest itself to me? That was where I went astray. Well, well, Inspector, I have often ventured to chaff you gentlemen of the police force, but *Cyanea Capillata* very nearly avenged Scotland Yard.'

The Adventure of the First Class Carriage

Ronald Knox

THE general encouragement extended to my efforts by the public is my excuse, if excuse were needed, for continuing to act as chronicler of my friend Sherlock Holmes. But even if I confine myself to those cases in which I have had the honour of being personally associated with him, I find it difficult to make a selection among the large amount of matter at my disposal.

As I turn over my records, I find that some of them deal with events of national or even international importance; but the time has not yet come when it would be safe to disclose (for instance) the true facts about the recent change of government in Paraguay. Others (like the case of the Missing Omnibus) would do more to gratify the modern craving for sensation; but I am well aware that my friend himself is the first to deplore it when I indulge what is, in his own view, a weakness.

My preference is for recording incidents whose bizarre features gave special opportunity for the exercise of that analytical talent which he possessed in such a marked degree. Of these, the case of the Tattooed Nurseryman and that of the Luminous Cigar-Box naturally suggest themselves to the mind. But perhaps my friend's gifts were even more signally displayed when he had occasion to investigate the disappearance of Mr Nathaniel Swithinbank, which provoked so much speculation in the early days of September, five years back.

Mr Sherlock Holmes was, of all men, the least influenced by

what are called class distinctions. To him the rank was but the guinea stamp; a client was a client. And it did not surprise me, one evening when I was sitting over the familiar fire in Baker Street— the days were sunny but the evenings were already falling chill—to be told that he was expecting a visit from a domestic servant, a woman who 'did' for a well-to-do, childless couple in the southern Midlands. 'My last visit,' he explained, 'was from a countess. Her mind was uninteresting, and she had no great regard for the truth; the problem she brought was quite elementary. I fancy Mrs John Hennessy will have something more important to communicate.'

'You have met her already, then?'

'No, I have not had the privilege. But anyone who is in the habit of receiving letters from strangers will tell you the same—hand-writing is often a better form of introduction than hand-shaking. You will find Mrs Hennessy's letter on the mantelpiece; and if you care to look at her j's and her w's, in particular, I think you will agree that it is no ordinary woman we have to deal with. Dear me, there is the bell ringing already; in a moment or two, if I mistake not, we shall know what Mrs Hennessy, of the Cottage, Guisebor-ough St Martin, wants of Sherlock Holmes.'

There was nothing in the appearance of the old dame who was shown up, a few minutes later, by the faithful Mrs Hudson, to justify Holmes's estimate. To the outward view she was a typical representative of her class; from the bugles on her bonnet to her elastic-sided boots everything suggested the old-fashioned caretaker such as you may see polishing the front doorsteps of a hundred office buildings any spring morning in the city of London. Her voice, when she spoke, was articulated with unnecessary care, as that of the respectable working-class woman is apt to be. But there was something precise and business-like about the statement of her case which made you feel that this was a mind which could easily have profited by greater educational advantages.

'I have read of you, Mr Holmes,' she began, 'and when things began to go wrong up at the Hall it wasn't long before I thought to myself, If there's one man in England who will be able to see light here, it's Mr Sherlock Holmes. My husband was in good employ-ment, till lately, on the railway at Chester; but the time came when the rheumatism got hold of him, and after that nothing seemed to go well with us until he had thrown up his job, and we went to live in a country village not far from Banbury, looking out for any odd work that might come our way.

'We had only been living there a week when a Mr Swithinbank and his wife took the old Hall, that had long been standing empty. They were newcomers to the district, and their needs were not great, having neither chick nor child to fend for; so they engaged me and Mr Hennessy to come and live in the lodge, close by the house, and do all the work of it for them. The pay was good and the duties light, so we were glad enough to get the billet.'

'One moment!' said Holmes. 'Did they advertise, or were you indebted to some private recommendation for the appointment?'

'They came at short notice, Mr Holmes, and were directed to us for temporary help. But they soon saw that our ways suited them, and they kept us on. They were people who kept very much to themselves, and perhaps they did not want a set of maids who would have followers, and spread gossip in the village.'

'That is suggestive. You state your case with admirable clearness. Pray proceed.'

'All this was no longer ago than last July. Since then they have once been away in London, but for the most part they have lived at Guiseborough, seeing very little of the folk round about. Parson called, but he is not a man to put his nose in where he is not wanted, and I think they must have made it clear they would sooner have his room than his company. So there was more guessing than gossiping about them in the countryside. But, sir, you can't be in domestic employment without finding out a good deal about how the land lies; and it wasn't long before my husband and I were certain of two things. One was that Mr and Mrs Swithinbank were deep in debt. And the other was that they got on badly together.'

'Debts have a way of reflecting themselves in a man's correspondence,' said Holmes, 'and whoever has the clearing of his wastepaper basket will necessarily be conscious of them. But the relations between man and wife? Surely they must have gone very wrong indeed before there is quarrelling in public.'

'That's as may be, Mr Holmes, but quarrel in public they did. Why, it was only last week I came in with the blancmange, and he was saying, *The fact is, no one would be better pleased than you to see me in my coffin*. To be sure, he held his tongue after that, and looked a bit confused; and she tried to put a brave face on it. But I've lived long enough, Mr Holmes, to know when a woman's been crying. Then last Monday, when I'd been in drawing the curtains, he burst out just before I'd closed the door behind me, *The world isn't big enough for both of us.* That was all I heard, and right glad I'd have been to hear less. But I've not come round here just to repeat servants'-hall gossip.

'Today, when I was cleaning out the waste-paper basket, I came across a scrap of a letter that tells the same story, in his own handwriting. Cast your eye over that, Mr Holmes, and tell me whether a Christian woman has the right to sit by and do nothing about it.'

She had dived her hand into a capacious reticule and brought out, with a triumphant flourish, her documentary evidence. Holmes knitted his brow over it, and then passed it on to me. It ran: 'Being of sound mind, whatever the numskulls on the jury may say of it.'

'Can you identify the writing?' my friend said.

'It was my master's,' replied Mrs Hennessy. 'I know it well enough; the bank, I am sure, will tell you the same.'

'Mrs Hennessy, let us make no bones about it. Curiosity is a well-marked instinct of the human species. Your eye having lighted on this document, no doubt inadvertently, I will wager you took a look round the basket for any other fragments it might contain.'

'That I did, sir; my husband and I went through it carefully together, for who knew but the life of a fellow-creature might depend on it? But only one other piece could we find written by the same hand, and on the same notepaper. Here it is.' And she smoothed out on her knee a second fragment, to all appearances part of the same sheet, yet strangely different in its tenor. It seemed to have been torn away from the middle of a sentence; nothing survived but the words 'in the reeds by the lake, taking a bearing at the point where the old tower hides both the middle first-floor windows'.

'Come,' I said, 'this at least gives us something to go upon. Mrs Hennessy will surely be able to tell us whether there are any landmarks in Guiseborough answering to this description.'

'Indeed there are, sir; the directions are plain as a pikestaff. There is an old ruined building which juts out upon the little lake at the bottom of the garden, and it would be easy enough to hit on the place mentioned. I daresay you gentlemen are wondering why we haven't been down to the lakeside ourselves to see what we could find there. Well, the plain fact is, we were scared. My master is a quiet-spoken man enough at ordinary times, but there's a wild look in his eye when he's roused, and I for one should be sorry to cross him. So I thought I'd come to you, Mr Holmes, and put the whole thing in your hands.'

'I shall be interested to look into your little difficulty. To speak frankly, Mrs Hennessy, the story you have told me runs on such familiar lines that I should have been tempted to dismiss the whole case from my mind. Dr Watson here will tell you that I am a busy man, and the affairs of the Bank of Mauritius urgently require my presence in London. But this last detail about the reeds by the lakeside is piquant, decidedly piquant, and the whole matter shall be gone into. The only difficulty is a practical one. How are we to explain my presence at Guiseborough without betraying to your employers the fact that you and your husband have been intruding on their family affairs?'

'I have thought of that, sir,' replied the old dame, 'and I think we can find a way out. I slipped away today easily enough because my mistress is going abroad to visit her aunt, near Dieppe, and Mr Swithinbank has come up to Town with her to see her off. I must go back by the evening train, and had half thought of asking you to accompany me. But no, he would get to hear of it if a stranger visited the place in his absence. It would be better if you came down by the quarter-past ten train tomorrow, and passed yourself off for a stranger who was coming to look at the house. They have taken it on a short lease, and plenty of folks come to see it without troubling to obtain an order-to-view.'

'Will your employer be back so early?'

'That is the very train he means to take; and to speak truth, sir, I should be the better for knowing that he was being watched. This wicked talk of making away with himself is enough to make anyone anxious about him. You cannot mistake him, Mr Holmes,' she went on; 'what chiefly marks him out is a scar on the left-hand side of his chin, where a dog bit him when he was a youngster.'

'Excellent, Mrs Hennessy; you have thought of everything. Tomorrow, then, on the quarter-past ten for Banbury without fail. You will oblige me by ordering the station fly to be in readiness. Country walks may be good for health, but time is more precious. I will drive straight to your cottage, and you or your husband shall escort me on my visit to this desirable country residence and its mysterious tenant.' With a wave of his hand, he cut short her protestations of gratitude.

'Well, Watson, what did you make of her?' asked my companion when the door had closed on our visitor.

'She seemed typical of that noble army of women whose hard scrubbing makes life easy for the leisured classes. I could not see her well because she sat between us and the window, and her veil was lowered over her eyes. But her manner was enough to convince me that she was telling us the truth, and that she is sincere in her anxiety to avert what may be an appalling tragedy. As to its nature, I confess I am in the dark. Like yourself, I was particularly struck by the reference to the reeds by the lakeside. What can it mean? An assignation?'

'Hardly, my dear Watson. At this time of the year a man runs enough risk of cold without standing about in a reed-bed. A hiding-place, more probably, but for what? And why should a man take the trouble to hide something, and then obligingly litter his waste-paper basket with clues to its whereabouts? No, these are deep waters, Watson, and we must have more data before we begin to theorize. You will come with me?'

'Certainly, if I may. Shall I bring my revolver?'

'I do not apprehend any danger, but perhaps it is as well to be on the safe side. Mr Swithinbank seems to strike his neighbours as a formidable person. And now, if you will be good enough to hand me the more peaceful instrument which hangs beside you, I will try out that air of Scarlatti's, and leave the affairs of Guiseborough St Martin to look after themselves.'

I often had occasion to deprecate Sherlock Holmes's habit of catching trains with just half a minute to spare. But on the morning after our interview with Mrs Hennessy we arrived at Paddington station no later than ten o'clock—to find a stranger, with a pronounced scar on the left side of his chin, gazing out at us languidly from the window of a first-class carriage.

'Do you mean to travel with him?' I asked, when we were out of earshot.

'Scarcely feasible, I think. If he is the man I take him for, he has secured solitude all the way to Banbury by the simple process of

slipping half a crown into the guard's hand.' And, sure enough, a
few minutes later we saw that functionary shepherd a fussy-looking
gentleman, who had been vigorously assaulting the locked door, to
a compartment further on. For ourselves, we took up our post in
the carriage next but one behind Mr Swithinbank. This, like the
other first-class compartments, was duly locked when we had
entered it; behind us the less fortunate passengers accommodated
themselves in seconds.

'The case is not without its interest,' observed Holmes, laying
down his paper as we steamed through Burnham Beeches. 'It
presents features which recall the affairs of James Phillimore, whose
disappearance (though your loyalty may tempt you to forget it) we
investigated without success. But this Swithinbank mystery, if I
mistake not, cuts even deeper. Why, for example, is the man so
anxious to parade his intention of suicide, or fictitious suicide, in
the presence of his domestic staff? It can hardly fail to strike you
that he chose the moment when the good Mrs Hennessy was just
entering the room, or just leaving it, to make those remarkable
confidences to his wife. Not content with that, he must leave
evidence of his intentions lying about in the waste-paper basket.
And yet this involved the risk of having his plans foiled by good-
natured interference. Time enough for his disappearance to become
public when it became effective! And why, in the name of fortune,
does he hide something only to tell us where he has hidden it?'

Amid a maze of railway tracks, we came to a standstill at Reading.
Holmes craned his neck out of the window, but reported that all
the doors had been left locked. We were not destined to learn
anything about our elusive travelling-companion until, just as we
were passing the pretty hamlet of Tilehurst, a little shower of paper
fragments fluttered past the window on the right-hand side of the
compartment, and two of them actually sailed in through the space
we had dedicated to ventilation on that bright morning of autumn.
It may easily be guessed with what avidity we pounced on them.

The messages were in the same handwriting with which Mrs
Hennessy's find had made us familiar; they ran, respectively, 'Mean
to make an end of it all' and 'This is the only way out.' Holmes sat
over them with knitted brows, till I fairly danced with impatience.

'Should we not pull the communication-cord?' I asked.

'Hardly,' answered my companion, 'unless five-pound notes are more plentiful with you than they used to be. I will even anticipate your next suggestion, which is that we should look out of the windows on either side of the carriage. Either we have a lunatic two doors off, in which case there is no use in trying to foresee his next move, or he intends suicide, in which case he will not be deterred by the presence of spectators, or he is a man with a scheming brain who is sending us these messages in order to make us behave in a particular way. Quite possibly, he wants to make us lean out of the window, which seems to me an excellent reason for not leaning out of the windows. At Oxford we shall be able to read the guard a lesson on the danger of locking passengers in.'

So indeed it proved; for when the train stopped at Oxford there was no passenger to be found in Mr Swithinbank's carriage. His overcoat remained, and his wide-awake hat; his portmanteau was duly identified in the guard's van. The door on the right-hand side of the compartment, away from the platform, had swung open; nor did Holmes's lens bring to light any details about the way in which the elusive passenger had made his exit.

It was an impatient horse and an injured cabman that awaited us at Banbury, when we drove through golden woodlands to the little village of Guiseborough St Martin, nestling under the shadow of Edge Hill. Mrs Hennessy met us at the door of her cottage, dropping an old-fashioned curtsy; and it may easily be imagined what wringing of hands, what wiping of eyes with her apron, greeted the announcement of her master's disappearance. Mr Hennessy, it seemed, had gone off to a neighbouring farm upon some errand, and it was the old dame herself who escorted us up to the Hall.

'There's a gentleman there already, Mr Holmes,' she informed us. 'Arrived early this morning and would take no denial; and not a word to say what business he came on.'

'That is unfortunate,' said Holmes. 'I particularly wanted a free field to make some investigations. Let us hope that he will be good enough to clear off when he is told that there is no chance of an interview with Mr Swithinbank.'

Guiseborough Hall stands in its own grounds a little way outside the village, the residence of a squire unmistakably, but with no airs of baronial grandeur. The old, rough walls have been refaced with pointed stone, the mullioned windows exchanged for a generous expanse of plate-glass, to suit a more recent taste, and a portico has been thrown out from the front door to welcome the traveller with its shelter. The garden descends at a precipitous slope from the main terrace, and a little lake fringes it at the bottom, dominated by a ruined eminence that serves the modern owner for a gazebo.

Within the house, furniture was of the scantiest, the Swithinbanks having evidently rented it with what fittings it had, and introduced little of their own. As Mrs Hennessy ushered us into the drawing-room, we were not a little surprised to be greeted by the wiry figure and melancholy features of our old rival, Inspector Lestrade.

'I knew you were quick off the mark, Mr Holmes,' he said, 'but it beats me how you ever heard of Mr Swithinbank's little goings-on; let alone that I didn't think you took much stock in cases of common fraud like this.'

'Common fraud?' repeated my companion. 'Why, what has he been up to?'

'Drawing cheques, and big ones, Mr Holmes, when he knew that his bank wouldn't honour them; only little things of that sort. But if you're on his track I don't suppose he's far off, and I'll be grateful for any help you can give me to lay my hands on him.'

'My dear Lestrade, if you follow out your usual systematic methods, you will have to patrol the Great Western line all the way from Reading to Oxford. I trust you have brought a drag-net with you, for the line crossed the river no less than four times in the course of the journey.' And he regaled the astonished inspector with a brief summary of our investigations.

Our informatiorn worked like a charm on the little detective. He was off in a moment to find the nearest telegraph office and put himself in touch with Scotland Yard, with the Great Western Railway authorities, with the Thames Conservancy. He promised, however, a speedy return, and I fancy Holmes cursed himself for not having dismissed the jarvey who had brought us from the station, an undeserved windfall for our rival.

'Now, Watson!' he cried, as the sound of the wheels faded away into the distance.

'Our way lies to the lakeside, I presume.'

'How often am I to remind you that the place where the criminal tells you to look is the place not to look? No, the clue to the mystery lies, somehow, in the house, and we must hurry up if we are to find it.'

Quick as a thought, he began turning out shelves, cupboards, escritoires, while I, at his direction, went through the various rooms of the house to ascertain whether all was in order, and whether anything suggested the anticipation of a hasty flight. By the time I returned to him, having found nothing amiss, he was seated in the most comfortable of the drawing-room armchairs, reading a book he had picked out of the shelves—it dealt, if I remember right, with the aborigines of Borneo.

'The mystery, Holmes!' I cried.

'I have solved it. If you will look on the bureau yonder, you will find the household books which Mrs Swithinbank has obligingly left behind. Extraordinary how these people always make some elementary mistake. You are a man of the world, Watson; take a look at them and tell me what strikes you as curious.'

It was not long before the salient feature occurred to me. 'Why, Holmes,' I exclaimed, 'there is no record of the Hennessys being paid any wages at all!'

'Bravo, Watson! And if you will go into the figures a little more closely, you will find that the Hennessys apparently lived on air. So now the whole facts of the story are plain to you.'

'I confess,' I replied, somewhat crestfallen, 'that the whole case is as dark to me as ever.'

'Why, then, take a look at that newspaper I have left on the occasional table; I have marked the important paragraph in blue pencil.'

It was a copy of an Australian paper, issued some weeks previously. The paragraph to which Holmes had drawn my attention ran thus:

ROMANCE OF RICH MAN'S WILL

The recent lamented death of Mr John Macready, the well-known sheepfarming magnate, has had an unexpected sequel in the circumstance that the dead man, apparently, left no will. His son, Mr Alexander Macready, left for England some years back, owing to a misunderstanding with his father—it was said—because he announced his intention of marrying a lady from the stage. The young man has completely disappeared, and energetic steps are being taken by the lawyers to trace his whereabouts. It is estimated that the fortunate heirs, whoever they be, will be the richer by not far short of a hundred thousand pounds sterling.

Horse-hoofs echoed under the archway, and in another minute Lestrade was again of our party. Seldom have I seen the little detective looking so baffled and ill at ease. 'They'll have the laugh of me at the Yard over this,' he said. 'We had word that Swithinbank was in London, but I made sure it was only a feint, and I came racing up here by the early train, instead of catching the quarter-past ten and my man in it. He's a slippery devil, and he may be half-way to the Continent by this time.'

'Don't be down-hearted about it, Lestrade. Come and interview Mr and Mrs Hennessy, at the lodge; we may get news of your man down there.'

A coarse-looking fellow in a bushy red beard sat sharing his tea with our friend of the evening before. His greasy waistcoat and corduroy trousers proclaimed him a manual worker. He rose to meet us with something of a defiant air; his wife was all affability.

'Have you heard any news of the poor gentleman?' she asked.

'We may have some before long,' answered Holmes. 'Lestrade, you might arrest John Hennessy for stealing that porter's cap you see on the dresser, the property of the Great Western Railway Company. Or, if you prefer an alternative charge, you might arrest him as Alexander Macready, alias Nathaniel Swithinbank.' And while we stood there literally thunderstruck, he tore off the red beard from a chin marked with a scar on the left-hand side.

'The case was difficult,' he said to me afterwards, 'only because we had no clue to the motive. Swithinbank's debts would almost have swallowed up Macready's legacy; it was necessary for the couple to disappear, and take up the claim under a fresh alias. This meant a duplication of personalities, but it was not really difficult. She had been an actress; he had really been a railway porter in his hard-up days. When he got out at Reading, and passed along the six-foot way to take his place in a third-class carriage, nobody marked the circumstance, because on the way from London he had changed into a porter's clothes; he had the cap, no doubt, in his pocket. On the sill of the door he left open, he had made a little pile of suicide-messages, hoping that when it swung open these would be shaken out and flutter into the carriages behind.'

'But why the visit to London? And, above all, why the visit to Baker Street?'

'That is the most amusing part of the story; we should have seen through it at once. He wanted Nathaniel Swithinbank to disappear finally, beyond all hope of tracing him. And who would hope to trace him, when Mr Sherlock Holmes, who was travelling only two carriages behind, had given up the attempt? Their only fear was that I should find the case uninteresting; hence the random reference to a hiding-place among the reeds, which so intrigued you. Come to think of it, they nearly had Inspector Lestrade in the same train as well. I hear he has won golden opinions with his superiors by cornering his man so neatly. *Sic vos non vobis*, as Virgil said of the bees; only they tell us nowadays the lines are not by Virgil.'

Sources

The stories in this collection originally appeared in the *Strand Magazine* as follows:

October 1903: W. Somerset Maugham, 'A Point of Law' (*Seventeen Lost Stories*, ed. Craig V. Showalter, 1969)

April 1904: Arthur Conan Doyle, 'The Adventure of Charles Augustus Milverton (*The Return of Sherlock Holmes*, 1905)

December 1919: Sapper, 'The Idol's Eye' (*The Finger of Fate*, 1930)

February 1923: Aldous Huxley, 'A Deal in Old Masters'

March 1923: Arthur Conan Doyle, 'The Adventure of the Creeping Man' (*The Casebook of Sherlock Holmes*, 1927)

September 1923: Seamark, 'The Perfect Crime'

November 1925: W. W. Jacobs, 'The Interruption' (*Sea Whispers*, 1926)

December 1926: Arthur Conan Doyle, 'The Adventure of the Lion's Mane' (*The Casebook of Sherlock Holmes*, 1927)

July 1930: H. Warner Allen, 'Tokay of the Comet Year'

December 1930: Edgar Wallace, 'The Chobham Affair' (*The Woman from the East*, 1934)

April 1932: Loel Yeo, 'Inquest' (*Great Short Stories of Detection, Mystery and Horror: 3rd Series*, ed. Dorothy L. Sayers, 1934)

September 1933: A. J. Alan, 'Private Water'

March 1934: Hylton Cleaver, 'By Kind Permission of the Murdered Man'

June 1934: Marguerite Steen, 'In View of the Audience'

August 1936: G. K. Chesterton, 'The Vampire of the Village' (*The Vampire of the Village*, privately printed, 1947)

September 1936: Quentin Reynolds, 'The Man Who Dreamed Too Much'

February 1938: Agatha Christie, 'The Dream' (*The Adventure of the Christmas Pudding*, 1960)

September 1938: Augustus Muir, 'The Intruder'

November 1938: E. C. Bentley, 'The Ministering Angel' (*To the Queen's Taste*, ed. Ellery Queen, 1949)

January 1939: Will Scott, 'Not Guilty'

August 1940: A. E. W. Mason, 'The Ginger King' (*Great Stories of Detection*, ed. R. C. Bull, 1960)

August 1941: Richard Keverne, 'Cast-Iron Alibi'

December 1941: D. L. Murray, 'A Gift from the Nabob'

February 1947: Ronald Knox, 'The Adventure of the First Class Carriage' (*The Sherlock Holmes Scrapbook*, ed. Peter Haining, 1973)

November 1948: J. Maclaren-Ross, 'The Episcopal Seal'

Acknowledgements

The editor and publishers gratefully acknowledge permission to reproduce copyright material in this book.

E. C. Bentley, 'The Ministering Angel'. Copyright E. C. Bentley 1938. Reproduced by permission of Curtis Brown, London, on behalf of the Estate of E. C. Bentley.

G. K. Chesterton, 'The Vampire of the Village'. Used by permission of A. P. Watt Ltd. on behalf of The Royal Literary Fund.

Agatha Christie, 'The Dream', reprinted in the UK and Commonwealth in *The Adventure of the Christmas Pudding*, copyright © 1960 Agatha Christie Limited, and reprinted in the United States in *The Regatta Mystery & Other Stories*, copyright 1932, 1934, 1935, 1936, 1937, 1939 Agatha Christie Mallowan. Copyright © renewed 1959, 1961, 1962, 1963, 1964, 1967 by Agatha Christie Mallowan. Used by permission of Aitken & Stone Ltd.

Hylton Cleaver, 'By Kind Permission of the Murdered Man'. Copyright 1934 Hylton Cleaver.

Aldous Huxley, 'A Deal in Old Masters'. Used by permission of Mrs Laura Huxley, and The Hogarth Press as British publishers; published in the USA by Harper & Row Publishers.

W. W. Jacobs, 'The Interruption'. Used by permission of The Society of Authors as the literary representative of the estate of W. W. Jacobs.

Richard Keverne, 'Cast-Iron Alibi'. Copyright 1941 Richard Keverne.

Ronald Knox, 'The Adventure of the First Class Carriage'. Used by permission of A. P. Watt Ltd. on behalf of the Earl of Oxford and Asquith.